Foundations of
ISLAM

Benjamin Walker

FOUNDATIONS OF
ISLAM

The Making of a World Faith

PETER OWEN
LONDON AND CHESTER SPRINGS

PETER OWEN PUBLISHERS
73 Kenway Road London SW5 0RE
Peter Owen books are distributed in the USA by
Dufour Editions Inc. Chester Springs PA 19425-0007

First published in Great Britain 1998
© Benjamin Walker 1998

ISBN 0 7206 1038 9

A catalogue record for this book is available from the British Library

Printed in Great Britain by Redwood Books of Trowbridge, Wiltshire

CONTENTS

LIST OF ILLUSTRATIONS

PREFACE

The principal object of the present work is to give an account of the many contributions made to the religion of Islam by non-Muslim peoples, and it may claim to be original in the sense that it deals exclusively and comprehensively with this debt.

These foreign influences can be traced to a period long before the birth of Muhammad. The early contacts the pagan Arabs had with the peoples of the ancient world, from the Egyptians and Babylonians to the Greeks and Romans, helped in laying down the first course of the foundations of Islam. The close association of the Prophet with the Jews and Christians of Arabia, and later of the Muslims with the various nations they encountered in the course of their conquests, provided the inspiration for many features of Islam as it evolved over the centuries.

Like any other author writing today on the subject of the present survey, I have had to fall back for many of my facts on the work of eminent scholars and specialists in their respective fields. These include Ignaz Goldziher, W. Montgomery Watt, H. A. R. Gibb, Alfred Guillaume, Richard Bell, Tor Andrae, R. A. Nicholson, Maxime Rodinson, Syed Ameer Ali and others, all of whom are listed in the Bibliography and more specifically acknowledged in the text.

For the transliteration of Arabic words I have observed the practice, adopted by many authorities writing for a general readership, of dropping the use of diacritical marks and simplifying the spelling of Arabic names.

Readers unfamiliar with a term should refer to the Index to locate the page where the term is explained. All dates are AD unless otherwise stated. Also, unless otherwise indicated, all foreign words in brackets are Arabic or of Arabic derivation.

All figures in brackets in the form (3:35) refer to a chapter and verse of the Koran. As the verse numberings of the Koran are not uniformly given in all texts, readers unable to find a Koranic reference in their copies should look up a verse or two before or after the verse cited.

1
ANCIENT CONTACTS

Large parts of the Arabian peninsula are sandy wastes and were spoken of in the classical writings as Arabia Deserta. This includes an extensive empty region in the south (the Rub al-Khali), another in the north (the Nefud), and another still further north (the Syrian Desert). But the country has many areas of fertile territory, and from an early period it had flourishing trading centres which grew into prosperous towns.

Although geographically Arabia is the land mass lying between the Syrian desert and the Indian Ocean, historically the area of Arab occupation includes not only the peninsula of Arabia but parts of Syria, Palestine and Mesopotamia as well.

The regions where the Arabs dwelt were criss-crossed by international trade routes, and over the centuries they remained in continuous contact with the neighbouring countries of the Middle East. Arabian culture evolved in a region where civilizations of an advanced type had met and mingled from remote times, and was thus subject to a ceaseless process of change and development.

Many Arab tribes helped to maintain the profitable commercial links across the desert, and their neutrality or alliance was useful to foreign traders, because of their knowledge of wells and safe routes. They furnished the means of transport, such as camels and guides, as well as armed guards for the convoys, to provide protection against marauding nomads who attacked caravans for plunder and slaves.

Outside contacts were further strengthened with the establishment of foreign garrisons to protect the outlying trading posts, and sometimes even by colonization. This often brought rival nations into conflict in which the Arab tribes in turn became involved. Trade agents and missionaries of various faiths also entered the country.

The Arabs, both nomad and settled, are mentioned intermittently in the hieroglyphic records of the ancient Egyptians, the cuneiform annals of Mesopotamia and the epigraphic inscriptions of the Achaemenian Persians, as well as in the chronicles of the Jews, Greeks and Romans. Syriac and Byzantine writings furnish more information about them. However, Arab writers of the Muslim period were generally reluctant to give credit to the civilizations that preceded Islam (see Section 13.12), so the information from Arabic sources is comparatively meagre.

One thing is clear: at no time in their recorded history did the peoples of Arabia live in primitive and benighted isolation. Arabia was an integral part of the ancient Middle East and was always in close contact with its neighbours, and duly influenced by them.

The surviving records provide only a shadowy notion of the actual nature, extent and duration of these early contacts, as will be shown in brief outline below.

1.1 Egypt

The name 'Misr' (Mizraim in the Old Testament) was the one by which Egypt was known from very early times. The first historical evidence shows an already developed culture in full vigour, and indeed the country is regarded by many authorities as the grandam of all civilizations.

The navigation of the Red Sea played an important part in the commercial expansion of Egypt, and starting from about 2750 BC Egyptian rulers undertook regular maritime expeditions there. The purpose was to obtain ivory and slaves from Nubia (more easily accessible from the Red Sea than direct from Egypt southwards), gold from Punt (the biblical Phut, probably Somalia), copper from Sinai, and spices and precious metals from Havilah (probably Najran).

Incense and resins for temple services, embalming the dead and burning at funeral rites came from southern Arabia in the Himyar region. Quoting from Egyptian temple records, the Greek historian Herodotus (d. 425 BC) relates that Sesostris I (d. 1928 BC), in order to ensure the safety of his trade routes, proceeded down the shores of the Red Sea conquering the nations on the coast as he went.

By the time of Tuthmosis I (d. c. 1512 BC) of the Eighteenth Dynasty, victorious campaigns were being conducted by the Egyptians across Palestine and northern Arabia as far as Syria and Mesopotamia, so that in their inscriptions on the walls of Karnak the pharaohs were able to claim the Euphrates as the eastern boundary of their empire.

In 1490 BC Queen Hatshepsut revived the copper mines of Sinai, which the Egyptians had exploited some centuries earlier, and from this time on they remained the chief source of the Egyptian copper supply. Hatshepsut also dispatched an expedition to the Red Sea and Punt, to confirm her right of access to those regions.

By this time too the Egyptians had built roads across Sinai and northern Arabia to Mesopotamia. One ran from the port of Akaba through Tayma to the northern borders of Babylonia, and was to lead to a series of confrontations between the Egyptians and the rulers of Mesopotamia.

Later still, an important Egyptian highway went down from Tayma to the Hejaz and Himyar, with halting-stations at places along the way, including the area where Yathrib (Medina) later arose (O'Leary, 1927, p. 36). The name 'Yathrib' is thought to be Egyptian in origin, and equivalent to that of two well-known cities named Athribis, one on the Nile delta and the other in Upper Egypt. Yathrib is the Iathrippa of the classical geographers.

Foreign influence in Arabia is supported by the existence of great dams and irrigation works in southern Arabia which typically belong to a river-valley culture, and so point to an Egyptian – or according to some authorities, a Mesopotamian – presence. Sculptures found in Arabia likewise show Egyptian – or again, Mesopotamian – traits, indicating an early penetration of both these cultures into the country.

Monotheism had come to Egypt with the pharaoh Akhenaten (d. 1362 BC) and may to some degree have influenced the Jews living in Egypt during that pharaoh's reign. Scholars have also noted traces of monotheism in a number of ancient Himyarite (south-Arabian) inscriptions that could point to the impact of Hebrew if not Egyptian religious trends there.

The possibility of the Egyptian pantheon leaving its mark on the gods around the Meccan shrine has also been put forward (see Section 2.12).

1.2 Mesopotamia

The land enclosed by the rivers Tigris and Euphrates was known to the Arabs as Jezira, 'island' – a name later applied only to the northern area – and to the classical writers as Mesopotamia, 'between the rivers'.

This region, like Egypt, had had contact with Arabia from as early as 2500 BC, as revealed in the cuneiform inscriptions of the Akkadians, a Semitic people of the north, and of the non-Semitic Sumerians – originally from central Asia – who inhabited the south of the country.

The Sumerians slowly extended their dominance over the whole of Mesopotamia, which in time had a mixed population of Semitic and non-Semitic peoples which has continued ever since. It is from Erech, one of the city states of Sumeria, that modern Iraq is said to get its name. Another Mesopotamian town south of Erech, called Ur of the Chaldees – from Old Semitic *ur*, 'fort' – was the home town of the patriarch Abraham, ancestor of the Jews and northern Arabs.

The Akkadians and Sumerians were succeeded by the Assyrians and Babylonians, who carried on the contacts made by their predecessors and were in frequent conflict with their neighbours.

The rulers of Mesopotamia sent their merchant ships to Dilmun (Bahrain), Hasa (classical Gerrha) and as far south as Oman. Records of the Assyrian king Tukulti Ninib I (fl. *c.* 1260 BC) list these regions as subject countries, but this may only have meant that they were friendly trading states.

In 854 BC the name 'Aribi' (Arab) is found in an Assyrian inscription which relates that one Gindibu the Arab was a member of a conspiracy against the Assyrian king Shalmaneser III, and provided a thousand camels for the support of the enemy.

A king of the Aribi is also mentioned in an inscription (738 BC) of the Assyrian king Tiglath-pileser III, who occupied the northern Hejaz after defeating Zabiba, queen and high priestess of the Kedar tribe of Arabia. The Kedar were a tent-dwelling and warlike Arab people skilled in archery, often mentioned in the Bible. Their traditional progenitor was Kedar, son of Ishmael (Gen. 25:13). They inhabited a large area south-west of Damascus.

In 715 BC Sargon II of Assyria found it necessary to deal with the tribes of Arabia who menaced the trade routes from Yemen and the Hadramaut. These tribes included the Thamud and the Aribi. Among those who sent gifts of white camels to Sargon were Shamsi, queen of the Aribi in the northern desert, and Yathamar, king of Saba in southern Arabia.

In 703 BC Yati, queen of the Aribi, sent troops under the command of her brother to help the Babylonians in their war against Sennacherib of Assyria, and in 690 BC Sennacherib organized a punitive expedition to Arabia to attempt to subdue the troublesome Aribi.

The Arabs remained recalcitrant, and in 676 BC Esarhedon of Assyria deported the Arab queen Tayl Khunu to Nineveh, along with her sister Tubwa, for their part in aiding Babylon against the Assyrians. Tubwa was given as a wife to Hazayl, king of the Kedar. Subsequently, another Arab revolt under a certain Uabu (Wahab) was crushed by the Assyrians.

In 660 BC Assurbanipal – the Sardanapalus of the Greek writers – the last effective king of Assyria, also mounted a campaign against the Aribi. Then in 648 BC he put down a rebellion of Arab tribes in the region of Ushu (Palmyra), among them the Kedar, whose king, Amuladi, was captured along with his ally Adiya, queen of a neighbouring tribe.

In 612 BC Nabopolassar of Babylon declared his independence from Assyria and founded the Neo-Babylonian (or Chaldean) empire which succeeded Babylonia. In 606 BC he allied himself with the Medes and took part in the sack of Nineveh, the Assyrian capital. Babylon grew in power thereafter.

The Kedar are once again listed with certain other Arab peoples who, threatened by Nebuchadnezzar II in 580 BC, offered to pay him tribute. But the king was now determined to chastise the troublesome Arabs on his borders. Among the Arabs killed on this occasion was their leader Adnan. His son Maad, who escaped the massacre and fled to the Hejaz, was one of the remote ancestors of the prophet Muhammad.

In 552 BC Nabonidus, the last king of Babylon, took the north-Hejaz town of Tayma – later the centre of the Tayi tribe – which he visited in person and made the seat of his power, subduing Arabia as far as Yathrib (Medina). Nabonidus's son Belshazzar was left in charge of Babylon, and was defeated and killed by the Persians in 539 BC.

1.3 The Jews

The Old Testament is basic to any understanding of ancient Arab history. It provides the principal frame of reference not only for the historian but also for the student of religion. Arabs themselves, lacking early records of their own, have to fall back on the Bible, suitably adapted, for the story of Abraham and his descendants and, as we shall see, for the history of the early Arab tribes.

The Arabs, like the Jews, claim descent from the patriarch Abraham, though the traditions relating to Abraham differ in the Jewish and Arab versions, and these differences need to be made clear.

Abraham (fl. c. 1800 BC) was from the Mesopotamian town of Ur of the Chaldees, which he left with his wife, Sarah, to dwell in the land of Canaan in Palestine. A famine drove them thence to Egypt, where Abraham acquired an Egyptian concubine named Hagar, who served as Sarah's hand-maid. Through Hagar, Abraham became the father of Ishmael, the progeni-tor of the northern Arabs. Through Sarah, Abraham later had a second son, named Isaac, the progenitor of the Jews.

On God's command – according to the Arab tradition – Abraham, accompanied by Hagar and their son Ishmael, journeyed to the Hejaz in the region of Mount Arafat near Mecca, and here Abraham proved his devotion to God by showing his willingness to offer up his son as a sacrifice. On his way to the mount of sacrifice, Satan appeared before him at Mount Muzdalifa and tried to hinder him from his purpose, but the patriarch drove him off by pelting him with stones.

Abraham proceeded to Mount Thabir, near Mina, in the hills east of Mecca, to carry out the sacrifice, but at the last moment divine interven-tion miraculously provided a sheep to replace his son. The incident is mentioned in the Koran (37:101), and though the son is not named in this context he is presumed to have been Ishmael.

In Mecca, on the site of a structure said to have been built by Adam but destroyed in the Flood, Abraham and Ishmael raised the shrine known as the Kaaba (22:27). Having completed his work, Abraham returned to his wife, Sarah, abandoning Hagar and Ishmael in the desert.

In her desperate search for water, Hagar ran between the hills of Safa and Marwa near Mecca, and she and her son would have died of thirst had not an angel revealed to them the well of Zamzam, now within the precincts of the shrine at Mecca. The tombs allegedly containing the remains of Ishmael and Hagar lie at the foot of the north side of the Kaaba.

According to the Bible (Gen. 21:14), Abraham abandoned Hagar and Ishmael in the wilderness of Beersheba in southern Canaan, and not near the Meccan hills. The Bible goes on to say (Gen. 21:21) that Ishmael dwelt in the wilderness of Paran, which is in Sinai and not the Hejaz. In the biblical version, the son that Abraham is prepared to sacrifice is not Ishmael, son of

Hagar, but Isaac, son of Sarah. The place of the intended sacrifice is not Mount Thabir, near Mecca, but Mount Moriah in Jerusalem.

There is no biblical warrant for the belief that Abraham and Ishmael had any connection with the region of the Hejaz in general or with Mecca and the Kaaba in particular, nor are the alleged tombs of Hagar and Ishmael mentioned in the traditions of pre-Islamic Mecca. And the Koran story of Ishmael and his mother stems from the later (Medinan) period of Muhammad's mission.

Muslim authorities are divided over these details. Thus, Ibn Ishak, Ibn Masud, al-Baydawi and other commentators state that the son to be sacrificed was Ishmael, while commentators like Ibn Omar, Ibn Abbas and Abdulla ibn Ahmad agree with the biblical version and say that the son was Isaac. In modern times, the Egyptian scholar and statesman Taha Husayn, much to the displeasure of the authorities, questioned whether Abraham had even been in Mecca (Guillaume, 1983, p. 156).

The 'religion of Abraham' assumed prominence after Muhammad, repudiated by the Jews, gave Abraham a new role (see Section 9.1).

Whatever the association between Abraham and the Arabs might have been, it is clear that the Jews and Arabs later developed extensive trade relations. The Bible records that in the days of Jacob – Abraham's grandson – Arab traders carried spices, balm and myrrh from the hills of Gilead to Egypt (Gen. 37:25). Gilead, an important trading area east of the Jordan, was later occupied by the Ghassan tribe.

From Ophir (Zofar) in southern Arabia, King Solomon imported timber, spices, perfumes and precious stones (1 Kings 10:11). In about 990 BC the Queen of Sheba (Saba, also in south Arabia) visited King Solomon bearing royal gifts (1 Kings 10:1–2). The Bible relates that at this time, 'All the kings of Arabia and governors of the country brought gold and silver to Solomon' (2 Chron. 9:14).

In about 880 BC Jehoshaphat, king of Judah, received from the Arabians 7,700 rams and 7,700 he-goats as tribute (2 Chron. 17:11). A few years later, however, in 870 BC, the Arabians 'that were near the Ethiopians' (2 Chron. 21:16), presumably in the Hejaz, invaded Judah (then ruled by Jehoram), plundered the king's house, and carried off his wives and sons, except the youngest son, Jehoahaz. In time the Jews recovered their strength, and in 790 BC Uzziah, king of Judah, defeated the Arabians (2 Chron. 26:7).

In 701 BC, during the reign of Hezekiah, certain Arab tribes were allied with Sennacherib of Assyria in his campaign against Jerusalem. But operations were abandoned when a plague broke out in the Assyrian army, killing thousands of soldiers (2 Kings 19:35).

A century later, in 597 BC, Nebuchadnezzar II of Babylon invaded Judah, captured Jerusalem, destroyed the temple, and carried off most of the inhabitants into captivity in Babylon. Ezekiel, who was taken to Babylon during the deportations, mentions several places in Arabia and lists the many exquisite commodities exported from there by the Arab tribes (Ezek. 27:19–24).

Among the last biblical references to the Arabs there is one that relates how in 445 BC Geshem the Arabian joined others who mocked Nehemiah for attempting to rebuild the walls of Jerusalem and opposed him in the reconstruction of the city (Neh. 2:19).

(For later contacts between Jews and Arabs see Section 3.2 and Chapter 9.)

1.4 India

The discovery of cylinder seals and other neolithic artefacts in the Indus valley and southern Mesopotamia indicates contact between pre-Aryan India and Sumeria from a very early date. In the Babylonian period Indian vessels made the journey from India to the Shatt al-Arab by coasting along the Persian and Arab shores of the Persian Gulf, including those of Bahrain and Oman. Bahrain (ancient Dilmun) was for centuries a transit port in the luxury-goods trade with India.

Seagoing Indian ships sailed from the mouth of the Indus and other Aryan-speaking ports of coastal India, and from the Dravidian-speaking regions of the south. There was trade with south Arabia, the port of Aden being only the largest of many emporia along its coast. The warehouses of south Arabia and the Persian Gulf ports were filled with merchandise from India and Sri Lanka.

The chief exports from Arabia were aromatic herbs and Arabian perfumes. Indian exports to Arabia included gems, ivory, cinnamon, pepper, ginger, rice, sandalwood, camphor, dyes and rare animals (apes and peacocks). Strabo (d. AD 21) refers to 'honey made from reeds without any bees', or raw cane sugar, which came from India.

India's cotton was well known, and Indian cotton fabrics and richly hued textiles were in great demand throughout the Arab world. Silk came from India as well as from China. Indian bows and arrows were well known and highly prized, and were used to deadly effect by the famous Arabian archers. The shafts of the Arab spears were made of bamboo brought from India.

Because of the lack of hard woods in Arabia, Indian timber was in demand from Babylonian times and for centuries thereafter. It is recorded that the third caliph Othman (d. AD 656) in rebuilding the Prophet's mosque in Medina made the roof out of Indian teak.

1.5 Persia

In 539 BC the Persians under Cyrus the Great conquered Babylon and inaugurated the Persian (Achaemenian) empire. Arab mercenaries joined the armies of Cyrus in the overthrow of Babylon, in the course of which

Belshazzar, the last prince of Babylon, was killed. Cyrus then proceeded to extend his domain over northern Arabia, and captured the important trading centre of Tayma, the last outpost of the Babylonian empire to hold out against the Persian invaders.

The conquest of Egypt in 525 BC by Cambyses, the son of Cyrus, was in some measure achieved through the cooperation of the desert Arabs. Herodotus' account of the campaign suggests that it was made across the sands under the security assured by the Arabs, who provided water for the desert march.

Cambyses' successor, Darius I, made further conquests which linked together large parts of the Middle East from the Mediterranean to the Indus. He sent a Greek captain, Skylax, on a voyage (512–510 BC) from the Indus across the Indian Ocean and up the Red Sea to Arsinoe, near modern Suez. An inscription of Darius records the tributary status of the Arabaya (Arabs), a status that continued off and on for two centuries.

In 480 BC the Arabs were among the fifty-six nations who, according to Herodotus, served in the army of the Persian king Xerxes against the Greeks.

In 331 BC Alexander the Great defeated Darius III at Arbela and incorporated Persia within the Macedonian empire. On Alexander's death in 323 BC, the Persian empire fell to the lot of his general Seleucus (see Section 1.9).

In about 250 BC an Iranian people of north-east Persia known as the Parthians, under Arsaces I revolted against the occupying Seleucids and founded their own Parthian (or Arsacid) dynasty (247 BC–AD 224), claiming descent from the old Persian (Achaemenid) kings and, like them, Zoroastrian by religion.

The Parthian empire, under rulers like Mithridates I (d. 137 BC), stretched from the Euphrates to the Indus, virtually confining the Seleucids to Syria. They set up one of their provincial capitals at Ctesiphon (Madain) in central Iraq, on the bank of the Tigris opposite the earlier Greek camp of Seleucia, twenty miles south-east of modern Baghdad.

By the first century AD the Romans had replaced the Greeks in most parts of the Near East, and they now had to contend with the old enemy of the Seleucids. For long Rome and Parthia were face to face, fighting for supremacy. When in the second century the Sassanian empire – also Persian, and Zoroastrian – was established, Rome had to reckon with the same foe under a new guise.

In the course of their early contacts, the Persians introduced into Arabia a new method of irrigation that became known as the Persian wheel, a water-wheel worked by a camel, and an ingenious system of underground canals (kanats) They also introduced the so-called 'Arab' steed, which had first been tamed in the grasslands of Bactria more than a thousand years before, and which was the ancestor of both the Libyan (Arabian) and the

Mongolian strains. Persian horses were highly valued in war and peace, some being bred for battle, some for racing.

Horse-racing was a favourite pastime of the ancient Arabs. Horses were run without riders, as in harness racing in Rome at the Corso, riders being brought in much later. In war, men on camels led the horses riderless to battle and would mount them only when they reached the battleground. In a hadith, Muhammad curses those who neglect native horses and prefer Persian (Goldziher, 1967, p. 156).

Arab poets sang the praises of the excellent swords and beautiful sword-sheaths that came from Persia. Coats of mail (from which the hauberk evolved) and iron helmets (plates of iron clamped together with studs) were also imported from Persia before Islam, later to be adopted by the 'Saracens', Turks and Crusaders.

1.6 Abyssinia

From pharaonic times Abyssinia – the Cush of the Bible – was inhabited by the Cushites, a Hamito-Semitic people, the Semitic element made up mainly of Arabs coming in over the centuries across the Red Sea from southern Arabia.

In the Egyptian hieroglyphic texts the dominant tribe of the region was called the Habasha (or Ahabish). In about 800 BC a Habasha chief claiming descent from Menelik I, son of King Solomon and the Queen of Sheba (she was known to the Arabs as Bilkis), founded the kingdom of Abyssinia.

From the sixth century BC on, the Abyssinians began to foster stronger links with Saba, Himyar and the Hejaz on the Arabian mainland. Their close ties with neighbouring Egypt had remained constant, and from the last century BC they began increasingly to be influenced by the Hellenized Egyptians.

By the beginning of the Christian era, under their ruler or negus (*najashi* in Arabic), the various tribes were united to form the kingdom of Aksum. The port of Adulis on the Red Sea handled cargoes from India, East Africa and the Persian Gulf, and trade relations between Aksum and the south-western states of Arabia continued to prosper.

Aksum reached the peak of its power during the reign of Ezana (AD 324–42) the 'Constantine of Abyssinia'. In AD 330 he was converted to Christianity by Frumentius – known to the Abyssinians as Abba Salama – who was named first bishop of Aksum by St Athanasius in Alexandria. Christianity, adopted in its Coptic (Monophysite) form, became the state religion. The country also became a close ally of Byzantium.

Around AD 345, during the reign of Alamida, the Abyssinians invaded and asserted their authority over certain parts of Himyar, bringing Christianity with them. This occupation lasted for about thirty years, until AD 375, when they were ousted by an Arab chief converted to Judaism (see Section 3.2).

In 525 King Kaleb (Elasbeha) of Aksum sent an army to protect the Christians of Najran from persecution by the Jewish king Dhu Nuwas, and left a viceroy behind to govern the region. Some fifty years later, in 576, the Abyssinians were once again supplanted, this time by the Sassanian Persians.

It should be noted that just before the beginning of Muhammad's mission there was a small colony of Abyssinian merchants and mercenary workers in Mecca, and that during the persecution of the first Muslims in AD 615 the Abyssinian ruler Ashama (Arma) gave asylum to many of the early Muslim converts (see Section 5.20).

1.7 The Aramaeans

From about 1300 BC Syria was inhabited by the Aramaeans, a Semitic people who, in the biblical genealogy, are descended from Aram, son of Shem (Gen. 10.22). They had migrated from northern Arabia and settled in Syria. The early-Greek term for Syrian was 'Aramaean'.

The Aramaeans established autonomous states in Damascus (which in ancient times was called Aram), Palmyra (the biblical Tadmor), Aleppo, Edessa (Urfa in modern Turkey), Carchemish on the Euphrates, and other places. They are mentioned in the Egyptian, Akkadian, Assyrian and Babylonian records, and frequently in the Bible. For years they were a thorn in the side of the Assyrians and suffered mass deportations and exiles as a result.

They were known to be a roving people, with widespread mercantile activities, but lacked an original and creative culture. Their large and mixed pantheon was taken from many foreign peoples, their principal deities being the storm-god Hadad, the sky-god Alaha, and the goddess Athargatis.

Aramaean power began to decline from about 700 BC, as they fell successively under the sway of the Assyrians, Babylonians, Persians, Macedonians, Seleucids and Romans.

Their enduring and outstanding contribution to Middle Eastern culture was the Aramaean script, adapted and simplified from the Phoenician alphabet and developing a set form some time around 850 BC. The Aramaean language – Aramaic – spread rapidly across adjacent borders, until by 400 BC it had become the lingua franca of a region extending from Syria to Mesopotamia, from Egypt to Asia Minor and the Caucasus, from Persia to the Punjab, being used for both official and trading purposes. Aramaic was one of the languages used by the Indian king Ashoka (fl. c. 232 BC) in his trilingual (Aramaic, Greek and Prakrit) rock edicts and proclamations.

Some portions of the Old Testament were written in Aramaic, and Aramaic was the language spoken by Jesus and understood by the people of Palestine. Hebrew, Arabic, Palmyrene, Nabataean and several other regional languages owe their alphabetic forms and large parts of their vocabulary to Aramaic.

Related to Aramaic and derived from it is Syriac (Christian Aramaic), spoken in Syria from the second to the twelfth century AD. It was the language of many early churches and, like Hebrew, acquired the status of a divine language. It survives to this day as a liturgical language in certain eastern Christian churches.

From about the middle of the fourth century AD, many religious, philosophical, medical and scientific texts began to be translated from Greek and Latin into Syriac, and these in turn were translated into Arabic during the early Muslim period and contributed in no small measure to the spread of learning in the Muslim world (see Section 13.10).

1.8 The Nabataeans

Traditionally, though disputably, regarded as the progeny of Nebajoth, first-born son of Ishmael (Gen. 25:13), the Nabataeans were an important group of Semitic peoples who some time before the fifth century BC had settled in Arabia Petraea, the region around the Sinai peninsula.

Sinai – the home of the Edomites of the Old Testament and the Idumaeans of the New Testament – was one of the chief ancient sources of copper supply. It lay on the caravan route linking Egypt, Palestine, Syria and Mesopotamia, and for centuries it remained a prosperous country with a thriving economy, trading in incense, spices and silver. In 312 BC Antigonus I, one of the successors of Alexander the Great, sent an expedition against the Nabataeans to secure their territory, but without success.

The Nabataean seaport was Ayla (biblical Elath, modern Akaba), and among the important commercial towns was Bostra, where the boy Muhammad was to meet the monk Bahira who foresaw his mission. The Nabataean capital Sela (that is, the 'Rock', of Edom), known in Latin as Petra, was described by the English divine John Burgon (d. 1882) in the oft-quoted phrase as 'a rose-red city, half as old as time'. The present ruins at Petra include a great theatre, and temples with 'crescent' or horned altars, all carved out of multicoloured, largely red, rock.

The Nabataeans are said to have been 'one of the most gifted peoples of history' (Glueck, 1966, p. 3). Their domain once extended from Damascus to the Hejaz; and places like Hijr, Tayma, El Ola, Duma and Dedan were Nabataean by 25 BC. Wherever they ruled they left evidence of a brilliant Hellenistic culture, with impressive ruins that survive to this day. Their skilled irrigation techniques in places like the Negev have 'excited the admiration of modern engineers' (Irvine, in Wiseman, 1973, p. 296).

Famous rulers include Aretas IV (d. AD 40), whose governor in Damascus imprisoned St Paul (2 Cor. 11:32), and Rabbal II (d. AD 106), whose famous 'Arabian' archers assisted Titus in reducing Jerusalem.

Arabic was the speech of daily life, for which the Nabataeans evolved a script of twenty-two letters derived from Aramaic, which became the direct ancestor of Arabic writing (see Section 4.2).

The Nabataeans venerated many of the deities worshipped by their neighbours, including Hadad, a Syrian god; Elh, Alh or Allah; Hubal; the goddesses Allat, Ozza and Manat; Kayis; Aziz; Nasr; Wadd; Sowa; Dhu Ghabat, 'He of the Thicket'; Dhu Shara, 'He of the Highlands', worshipped in the form of a black stone; Shay al Kaum; Ara; Baal Shamim; and Rahman, honoured in conjunction with Rahim.

A gradual transformation of some of these deities took place with the coming of Christianity. The church historian Epiphanius (d. 403) wrote that in Petra they would sing hymns in Arabic to the Virgin, calling her by the Arabic name of Chaabos (Arabic *Kaab*, 'Virgin'), and to her son Dusares (Dhu Shara), the only begotten Lord.

In AD 106 the Roman legate to Syria, Cornelius Palma, annexed Nabataea on behalf of the emperor Trajan and brought Nabataean political rule to an end. Nabataea became the Roman province of Arabia, with its capital at Bostra. For over three centuries after the fall of the kingdom, the Nabataean script continued to be used by Arabic-speaking peoples.

1.9 The Greeks

There are frequent references to the Arabs in the classical writings. The Arimoi and Eremboi of the Homeric poems are thought by some scholars to refer to the Aramaeans and to the Arabs.

Epigraphic and numismatic evidence shows that by about 350 BC Greek culture had penetrated as far as Saba, and had made itself felt in other parts of southern Arabia as well.

In about 325 BC Alexander the Great sent his admiral Nearchus to sail from the Indus along the Persian Gulf. Nearchus built a port at Charax, near modern Basra, though no trace of it remains today. Another of Alexander's admirals, Anaxicrates, sailed up the Erythraean Sea (the Arabian Sea and along the Red Sea), through the Bab el Mandeb. Alexander was also credited with making plans for the invasion of southern Arabia, and the emissaries of his espionage service were already familiar with the southern ports of that country.

After Alexander's death in 323 BC his empire was partitioned between his two generals Ptolemy and Seleucus. The kind of Grecianized civilization that the Ptolemies (323–30 BC) and the Seleucids (323–64 BC) introduced into their colonial territories, extending from Egypt across the Middle East to central Asia, is known as Hellenistic, to distinguish it from the Hellenic or 'Attic' civilization of Greece.

A common form of Greek (Koine Greek) became the international language of the eastern Mediterranean and western Asia, and as a result of

Greek commercial enterprise many of the coins used in these regions, including Arabia, for centuries bore the impress of the Athenian owl.

Ptolemy I, surnamed Soter (d. 283 BC), who obtained Egypt, established his capital at Alexandria, and his successors, the Ptolemies, ruled Egypt for 300 years. Throughout this period they maintained close ties with the Arab rulers, to keep open the desert trade routes, like the profitable incense route to the south through Yathrib (Medina). During the reign of Ptolemy I the Greek botanist Theophrastus wrote a detailed account of the aromatic shrubs of Arabia, incorporating information gathered by Alexander's own botanists.

Ptolemy's successor, Ptolemy II Philadelphus, founded the Museum and Library of Alexandria, filling it with hundreds of thousands of manuscripts later to be inherited by the Muslims. In 265 BC he dispatched a naval squadron to the Red Sea to establish a base on the coast above Yenbo, the seaport of Yathrib. This was followed by a trade agreement with the Lihyanites of Dedan. He also restored a road from Coptos near Thebes in Upper Egypt to the port of Berenike on the Red Sea. Coptos became, according to Strabo, 'a town common to the Egyptians and the Arabians'.

In 190 BC Eratosthenes, the librarian of Alexandria, knew the outline shape of the Arabian peninsula, the course of the chief inland trade routes which criss-crossed the region, the emporia which dotted them, and the location and movements of the chief tribes.

In 140 BC Ptolemy VIII Euergetes equipped an expedition under the Greek navigator Eudoxus of Cyzicus to sail from Egypt through the Pillars of Hercules (the Straits of Gibraltar) and then along the coast of Africa to find the sea route to India. On the first voyage he managed to reach the west coast of Africa, returning with a few natives of the place and other proofs of his journey. He made a second attempt, but failed to return.

In 116 BC, during the reign of Ptolemy IX Lathyros, the historian and grammarian Agatharchides left a description of the Red Sea and the peoples and animals of southern Arabia.

With the death of Cleopatra in 30 BC the Ptolemaic empire fell to the Romans.

To Seleucus I, surnamed Nicator (d. 280 BC), fell Alexander's Asiatic conquests. He founded the kingdom of Syria (312 BC), established a military settlement in the town of Antioch on the Orontes, and founded Seleucia on the Tigris. The last-named town, somewhat south-east of present-day Baghdad, became an important focus of Greek culture. The empire of Seleucus included Syria, Palestine, Asia Minor, Babylonia, Persia, Bactria, Media and Parthia.

In about 250 BC the Parthians freed themselves from the Seleucid yoke and founded the Parthian empire. This slowly encroached upon the domains of their former rulers, so that within a century the Seleucids were left only with Syria, parts of Palestine, and a few outposts elsewhere.

In 64 BC the Romans under Pompey deposed Antiochus XIII Asiaticus, the last of the Seleucids, reduced Syria to a Roman province, and extended their influence as far as Gerrha (Hasa) in the Persian Gulf.

Many towns that later became famous as Islamic centres, like Damascus (one of the oldest cities in the world, mentioned in Genesis 14:15), Alexandria, Palmyra, Mosul, Emesa (Homs), Nisibis, Carchemish, Edessa, Antioch, Aleppo and others, had long historical links with the Hittites, Assyrians, Egyptians, Mitanni, Armenians, Persians, Greeks (Ptolemies and Seleucids) and Romans.

When the Arabs embarked on their own career of conquest in the seventh century AD, Egypt, Palestine and Syria were largely Hellenized (and Mesopotamia somewhat less completely so), having been exposed to and absorbed Hellenistic influences for nearly a thousand years.

Also, from the beginning of the Christian era many of these same places became important Christianized towns, notably Damascus, Nisibis and Antioch, which were famed as theological and educational centres. By the time Islam took them over they had been Christian for nearly six centuries.

St Addai, the traditional evangelizer of Mesopotamia, who founded a church in Edessa during the reign of King Abgar V (d. AD 50), was only one of many zealous Christians who were active in these areas. Large parts of Syria and Palestine came under the jurisdiction of the Byzantine emperor and of Christian tribal principalities like the Ghassan, to be considered later.

The impact of Hellenistic culture not only on the outward features of Islam but also on the development of Islamic thought (see Section 13.15) cannot be overestimated. Bernard Lewis writes, 'So great is the Hellenistic influence that Islam has been described as the third heir, alongside Greek and Latin Christendom, of the Hellenistic legacy' (1966, p. 134). Certain Muslim scholars regard the encounter of Islam with Hellenistic thought as having had a deeper and more far-reaching influence on their religion than the Crusades or the Mongol invasions.

1.10 The Romans

The Romans were slowly to gather up much of the Middle East into their own empire. They started their conquests with the Hellenized world of the Seleucids, completing the annexation of Syria and the adjacent territories by 65 BC, only to find themselves confronted by the Parthians. In 53 BC they suffered one of the most crushing defeats of their history when in a battle against the Parthians the Roman consul Crassus was routed and slain at Carrhae (Harran) in northern Mesopotamia.

Their fortunes were soon restored, but they were glad to have the Arabs of the Syrian Desert as a buffer between their eastern provinces and Parthia.

Further to the west the Romans gained control over the Ptolemaic empire by 30 BC, on the death of Cleopatra.

In about 24 BC, during the reign of the emperor Augustus, the Roman prefect of Egypt, Aelius Gallus, took a Roman army from the northern shores of the Red Sea to Marib and Sanaa in the south. The geographer Strabo accompanied the expedition and left a useful account.

Owing to the ignorance of the Nabataean guide, who led them over a long and circuitous route, the Romans took six months to reach the borders of Najran. The city of Najran fell to a single attack, and Aelius Gallus went on to Saba, ruled by Ilasarus (Il-Shar). But only two days' march from his planned destination – the famous incense country of the Hadramaut – he was compelled by lack of water to abandon the enterprise. He returned to Najran, and carried on to Khaybar, then Hijr, and so back to Egypt. The return journey took two months. The greater part of the Roman army had perished from disease, famine and thirst, but only seven were killed in battle.

By the end of the first century BC the Romans had extended their mercantile interests in the Red Sea and Indian Ocean. Aden (known to the Greeks as Arabia Eudaemon, and to the Romans as Attanae) was a flourishing emporium which controlled the entrance to the Red Sea and the Somali coast, as well as the route to the Persian Gulf.

When the local ruler tried to hinder Roman enterprise in this area, the Romans in about 15 BC took over the warehouses in Aden and started to dismantle the port, and were then granted the right to establish a trading post with garrison there. The Romans also had commercial ties with the rulers of the coastal ports of Ocelis and Kane, situated west and east of Aden.

During the centuries of Roman rule over the Grecianized provinces of the Ptolemies, Greek navigators and scholars continued their work of exploration and discovery. In about AD 50 a Greek sailor named Hippalus first made known to the western world the regular alternation of the monsoon winds. This discovery facilitated and made safer the shipping route to India, as a result of which Arabian commercial supremacy in eastern trade, and especially the Arab monopoly on trade with India, came to an end.

Around AD 80 an unknown Greek sea captain who had settled in Egypt wrote a work known as *Periplus of the Erythraean Sea* (*Circumnavigation of the Arabian Sea*). Written in Greek, it is a seaman's guide to the Arabian Sea and its main ports, with data on river mouths, harbours, merchandise and trade. Eleazos (El-Azd) is mentioned as king of the Hadramaut.

The Greek astronomer Ptolemy of Alexandria (d. AD 160) had at his disposal several works on Arabia written by Greeks. Drawing on material from these and other works – notably one called *Arabica*, in five volumes, by a certain Uranius (fl. *c.* AD 50), and another on Arabian 'archaeology', in four books, by a certain Glaucus (fl. *c.* AD 90) – Ptolemy produced a famous geographical treatise containing a catalogue of places with their latitude and longitude. He also constructed maps, including a map of Arabia and a map of the world.

In the meantime Rome continued to extend its eastern boundaries. Trajan (d. AD 117) led an expedition against Parthia and annexed parts of Armenia and Mesopotamia, though not without occasional reverses.

A Syrian-Arab line of Roman emperors was inaugurated with Septimius Severus (d. AD 211), an African who was born in Leptis (a Phoenician city in Tripolitania (Libya) and died in Eboracum (York, in England). He married a Syrian named Julia Domna, daughter of the Arab priest-king of Emesa. Their son, the cruel and licentious Caracalla (d. 217), was assassinated at Edessa.

Caracalla was succeeded by Heliogabalus, Syrian by birth and grand-nephew of Septimius Severus and Julia Domna. Heliogabalus sought to introduce into Rome the worship of the Phoenician god Elogabal of Emesa – after whom he was named – represented by a coarse black conical stone. Infamous for his debaucheries, he was murdered by the praetorians. Alexander Severus (d. 235), cousin and adopted son of Heliogabalus, was the last of the Syrian-Arab line of Roman emperors.

Between AD 244 and 249 the emperor of Rome was Marcus Julius Philippus, a native of Arabia, born in Arabia, and known as Philip the Arabian. In April 248 he celebrated the thousandth anniversary of the founding of Rome. He made peace with Persia, but both he and his son were killed in battle against the anti-Christian Decius, who succeeded him. Philippus was honoured by early church writers as the first Christian emperor.

By about this time the Sassanian Persians became the chief rivals of Rome for supremacy in the Middle East. In AD 265 Odhaina (Odenathus), an Arab chieftain of Palmyra, defeated the Sassanian king Shahpur I and pursued him to the very walls of his capital, Ctesiphon. In reward, the Roman emperor Gallienus made him master of the Roman legions of the east.

Odenathus was succeeded by his ambitious widow Zenobia. She tried to assert her independence by founding her own empire, whereupon she was attacked and defeated in AD 272 by the Roman emperor Aurelian and was led captive behind his chariot at his triumph through the streets of Rome. Thereafter she was kept in easy captivity.

1.11 The Sassanians

In AD 226 a group of Persian nobles led by Ardashir, grandson of a Zoroastrian priest named Sasan, rose up against their Parthian overlords and established the Sassanian dynasty of Persia, and in a way continued the dynastic traditions of their Zoroastrian predecessors, the Achaemenians and Parthians.

The Sassanians built their capital not on the Iranian plateau but at Ctesi-phon on the Tigris, formerly a Parthian military camp on the opposite bank to the earlier Hellenistic settlement of Seleucia. Together the twin towns of Seleucia and Ctesiphon were also known as Madain, 'the Cities'.

The language of the Sassanians in its written form was called Pahlavi (Middle Persian), and their religion remained Zoroastrian. The followers of Zoroaster were commonly known as magi, the Majus of the Koran (22:17), and in the early Islamic annals they were classed among the hanifs – those who had abandoned idolatry.

Zoroastrian communities seem to have been established in Arabia from very ancient times. Their fire-temples are mentioned in some early Arabic texts, and one of them was situated in Muzdalifa, a 'station' of the Kaaba pilgrimage. The sacred well of Zamzam near the Kaaba was also sacred to the early Zoroastrians. The Black Stone within the Kaaba is reputed to have been a relic left by them. Zoroastrian angelology and demonology have influenced Judaism, Christianity and Islam.

For centuries the Sassanians remained a thorn in the side of Rome, and after the division of the Roman empire (AD 395) they became a threat to Byzantium and its chief rival for supremacy in the Middle East. At its height Sassanian rule covered an area stretching from central Asia across Iran to lower Mesopotamia. Among the Arab tribes, the vassal kingdom of Hira was the Sassanians' principal ally, and through Hira Sassanian suzerainty spread for a time as far as south-west Arabia. By the second half of the sixth century the Sassanian ruler exercised control over Medina, appoint-ing an administrator to ensure peace and collect taxes.

The long conflict between Sassanian Iran and Byzantium ultimately came to an end with the defeat of the Sassanian king Khosro II Parviz at Nin-eveh in 627. Khosro fled the field, to be deposed and put to death by his own army, and his son and successor Kobad II sued for peace. This disastrous Persian defeat left the way open for Arab expansion. The last Sassanian king, Yazdagird III, was routed by the Muslims at the battles of Kadisiya on the Euphrates (636) and of Nihavand (641) in Media.

1.12 Byzantium

In 667 BC a small settlement was established in north-eastern Asia Minor by colonists from Megara in Greece led by Byzan (or Byzas), after whom the place was named Byzantium. Here, nearly a thousand years later, the Roman emperor Constantine the Great, finding that from its seven hills it commanded the approaches to both Europe and Asia, founded the city of Constantinople in AD 328. He had embraced Christianity in 313, and it became the official faith of the empire.

By the end of the fourth century the Roman empire was divided into two parts: the western (Roman) empire, with capital in Rome, and the eastern (Byzantine) empire, with capital at Constantinople. Rome was generally hostile to Constantinople, because of political rivalry, jealousy over its mercantile power, and the deep doctrinal differences between the Latin church of Rome and the Greek church of Constantinople.

Under Justinian I (r. 527–65) the Byzantine domain included Asia Minor, Syria, Palestine, Egypt, North Africa to the borders of Morocco, southern Spain, Italy (southern Italy remained part of the Byzantine empire till the eleventh century) and the Balkans. Justinian ordered the building of the church of St Sophia (Haghia Sophia, 'Divine Wisdom'), a stupendous edifice and a marvel of architecture. He also codified the Roman law, which exercised a great influence on European (and to some extent Islamic) law.

Between them, the Byzantines and the Sassanians virtually controlled the whole of the Middle East, Byzantium exercising sway over Syria, Palestine and upper Mesopotamia. From about the middle of the fifth century they vied for power over the contiguous Arab principalities, which were drawn into their rivalries: the kingdom of Ghassan paid allegiance to Byzantium, as did Hira to the Sassanians.

Inevitably the two great powers became involved in wars, and these lasted off and on from AD 430 to 630. The final phase of the prolonged struggle between them moved towards a climax after 615, when the Sassanian king Khosro II defeated the Byzantine emperor Heraclius. After a further series of reverses, in 625 the Byzantine army started to gain the initiative, and in 627 Heraclius won a final victory over Khosro at Nineveh, not far from Arbela, the scene of Alexander's victory over Darius III in 331 BC.

These events took place during the early days of Muhammad's prophetic career, and the first setback of the Byzantines and their subsequent victory are both referred to in the Koran (see Section 5.16). In general the pagan unbelievers in Mecca who opposed Muhammad were inclined to favour the Sassanian Persians, whereas Muhammad and his followers inclined towards Byzantium.

The organization of the Byzantine empire reveals a basically Hellenistic bias that did much to shape the culture of the countries of the Middle East both before the advent of Islam and for some time after. During the Muslim period Byzantium remained the only infidel power for which the Muslims had some regard. They were impressed by the glory of the Byzantines' civilization, by their academies of learning, and by the great advances made by them in architecture and the arts, science and medicine, and law and administration, and they borrowed extensively from them. There is hardly any area of Muslim culture where the impact of Byzantium is not in evidence (see Chapter 13).

2

THE ANCIENT ARABS

Certain early texts speak of an aboriginal population of 'lost Arabs' (*Arab al-bayda*), who may have been primitive tribes of mixed Hamito-Semitic descent – some perhaps cave-dwelling. Among them were the Jadis (the Jodicitae of the classical writers); the Wibar (the Jobaritae); the Tasm and Bahm, mentioned by the early poets; and the Rass, Ad and Thamud mentioned in the Koran (25:40). Little is known about these tribes, and no trace of them remains. They were probably exterminated or absorbed by intermarriage with other Arab tribes.

The Arabs of the historical period are, like the Jews, a Semitic people, descended from Shem, son of Noah. They are divided into two great races: the Kahtan or southern Arabs, descended from Joktan of the Bible, and the Adnan or northern Arabs, descended from Ishmael, son of Abraham and his concubine Hagar.

The Arabs were spoken of at different times as bedouin or people of the desert; nomads living in 'houses of hair'; Skenites (Greek: 'tent-dwellers'); Ishmaelites, descended from Ishmael; Hagarites, descended from Hagar; and later as Saracens or 'desert folk'.

There were also many Arab communities outside the Arabian peninsula. Some tribes were nomadic pastoralists who lived in tents. Others were settled and lived in unwalled settlements or larger towns; many of these towns engaged in international commerce. Although not remote from the influence of other peoples and civilizations they tended to be conservative, and adhered to their own way of life.

All Arabs belonged to tribal groups, and each tribe had a number of branches (sub-tribes, clans or septs). Tribal and clan rivalry was endemic in Arab society, and the raid (*ghazwa*) or pillaging expedition (*razya*) was a common occurrence, in which one tribe would attack the camp or caravan of another tribe. Tribal traditions often reflected tribal rivalries, many of which existed centuries before Islam, and these were to play a significant part in the life and career of Muhammad.

As the name of a man is often linked with his father by the prefix *ibn*, 'son of', so the name of a tribe has the plural prefix *Banu*, 'children of'. Thus the Banu Kinda signifies the Kinda tribe.

2.1 The Kahtan Arabs

The Kahtan race was the elder line of the Arabs who, in the Arab tradition, were said to be descended not from Abraham but from Kahtan, the biblical Joktan (Gen. 10:25), himself descended from Noah. The Kahtan are regarded as the indigenous Arabs (*Arab al-ariba*), or the original Arabs (*mutariba*).

The Kahtan migrated from Mesopotamia to southern Arabia, and were spoken of as southerners. Semites of pure stock, they were of darker complexion than the northern Arabs. Until well into Abbasid times (*c.* AD 850) it was considered a sign of pure Arab descent to be swarthy (*akhdar*) and to be able to trace one's ancestry to a family from the southern region of Arabia.

The Bible (Gen. 10:30) says that the sons of Joktan (Kahtan) dwelt between Mesha (Mayin) in the south-west and Sephar (in Himyar) in the south-east. In time the area of their occupation stretched from Yemen on the Red Sea to Oman on the Indian Ocean.

They used a language commonly called Himyarite, which was related to Akkadian, Ethiopic (Abyssinian) and Sabaean, with a script found in numerous south-Arabian inscriptions that was deciphered by European explorers and scholars only at the end of the nineteenth century.

The southern tribes were generally settled agriculturists and town-dwellers. They depended for their livelihood on raising their crops and breeding livestock. A high mountain ridge along the south-west coast served with the monsoons to ensure a plentiful supply of rain. Owing to its rich and flourishing economy, the south came to be known to Roman writers as Arabia Felix – that is, 'fertile'.

From the time of ancient Egypt, the region was famous for its incense, resins and spices. Herodotus writes that the best frankincense, myrrh, balsam and cassia came from this land. The air of the place was so balmy with the perfume of aromatic plants that the Romans spoke of it as Arabia Odorifera. The trade in the 'perfumes of Araby' annually depleted the Roman treasury of millions of denarii.

The Kahtan south was for centuries the transit area for long-distance trade, both internal and overseas. According to the Roman (Syrian) historian Ammianus Marcellinus (d. AD 390), its coasts had many anchorages and safe harbours, with trading towns in an uninterrupted line. It had always been in close mercantile contact with Egypt, Mesopotamia, Persia, India, and the ports along the Red Sea and the east-African littoral. Recent studies point to a close association between the south-Arabian civilizations and the Greek, Hellenistic and Roman worlds.

Philby writes that, for at least two millennia before the birth of Muhammad, Arabia had outstanding commercial and cultural achievements to its credit. From a very early period a number of highly organized Kahtan principalities and city-states began to arise in southern Arabia, their names being found in the Bible, in Egyptian, Mesopotamian and south-Arabian inscriptions, and in the writings of the Greeks and Romans. But few reliable records of pre-Islamic Arabia survived the coming of Islam, as they were largely expunged or modified to conform with the orthodox faith.

Each city-state was ruled by a dignitary (*mukarrib*) who combined the functions of king, judge and priest, though there was also a separate hierarchy of priests, who wielded considerable power and supervised the worship at the various shrines. The treasurer (*kabir*), an important state official, looked after trade and taxes. In the enlightened Kahtan social order, women enjoyed a considerable degree of independence.

The political interrelationship of these early states is not clear, but over the centuries there was much rivalry and conflict over trade monopolies and the control of ports and commercial and religious centres. The ruling families intermarried, borders were altered and capitals changed with conquest.

No coherent historical record of southern Arabia for this early period can be constructed from the material currently available, but there are indications of a culture going back to the twelfth century BC. The chief city-states are listed below.

Mayin, biblical Mesha (Gen. 10:30), the Minaea of the classical writers, situated near the Red Sea, was the northernmost of these early kingdoms, with its capital at Karna. It long (1200–700 BC) continued as a group of city-states, achieving a semblance of political unity for limited periods only.

Saba, the biblical Sheba (Gen. 10:28), famous for the queen who visited King Solomon, was first mentioned as early as 1200 BC. It retained its identity till about 75 BC, and its capital was first at Marib (the Mariaba of the Greeks) and later at Sanaa. An important town was Sirwa. In about 650 BC a prince of Saba, with the help of Egyptian or Babylonian engineers, built a great dam at Marib, replacing an extensive, earlier and more primitive system of irrigation canals, sluices and reservoirs, in order to check and utilize the flow of the river Adana (Dana) and its tributaries during the rainy season. Generations of Sabaean and Himyarite rulers improved and reinforced the dam, which became famous in Arabian legend.

Ophir was named from the son of Joktan (Gen. 10:29). Although no state in Arabia is specifically known as Ophir, it appears in the Bible as the place from which Solomon obtained gold and precious stones (1 Kings 10:11). Its location has been identified with places in India, Africa, the Persian Gulf, and especially southern Arabia, whose ports had easy access to gold-producing countries.

The name 'Ophir' is thought to be related to Zofar, a name borne, in its many variants, by numerous towns in southern Arabia: Dhofar (or Zafar or Sephar), Taphar, Thafor, Sapphar, Zafir, Sephir. Some think it is etymologically related to the Semitic word *sepher*, 'writing', and that these towns were so named because of rock inscriptions or other epigraphic records in or around their area. Compare Kirjath-sepher, 'city of books', in ancient Canaan (Josh. 15:15).

Kataban, south of Saba, had its capital at Zofar. The religious centre at Timna had sixty-five temples, as well as statues distinctively Hellenistic in style. Kataban was in frequent conflict with Saba and Himyar.

Hadramaut, the biblical Hazarmaveth (Gen. 10:26), the Atramitae of Pliny, was also earlier known as Raydan. The capital was Shabwa; the principal port, Kane, was situated along the coastal strip of Mahra.

Dhofar or Zafar, the biblical Sephar (Gen. 10:30), had settlements as early as the twelfth century BC. For a time it was a colony of Hadramaut, but little is known of its history. In the twelfth century AD the region fell within the political sphere of Oman.

Himyar, the Homeritae of classical writers, grew to be the dominant Kahtan state from the first century BC, and in time it exercised control over Kataban, Saba and Hadramaut. Its capital was Zofar, taken over from Kataban. Another important town was Ausan, near Aden. Both classical and Arab writers often used the term 'Himyar' as a general name for southern Arabia, and in the Arab tradition Himyar was regarded as 'the cradle of the Arabs'. In AD 525 it was occupied by the Abyssinians, and in 575 by the Persians.

In more recent history the emphasis shifts from the city-states to the Kahtan tribes.

The eponymous ancestor of the southern tribes was Jerah (Gen. 10:26), son of Joktan, known in the Arab tradition as Yereb. Only the descendants of Yereb are true Arabs. The designation of the country they inhabited as Arabia 'is an innovation of the Greeks' (Irvine, in Wiseman, 1973, p. 290).

One of Yereb's descendants was Yeshed, the legendary founder of Marib, the site of the famous dam. Yeshed's son Abd Shams Saba had two sons, Kuhlan and Himyar, whose descendants ruled alternately. They became the progenitors of the Kahtan tribes.

From the beginning of the first century AD breaks began to appear in the walls of the Marib dam. As a result of general neglect and the poor quality of repairs, the structure suffered progressive deterioration, bringing with it increasing loss of arable land and a recurrent migration of people, many of whom left for central Arabia and further north and east. A number of tribes who occupied Mesopotamia, Palestine and Syria came originally from southern Arabia during this steady migration. The development of Roman shipping in the Red Sea also led to a gradual loss of caravan traffic and trade with the south.

In about AD 350 (the date is variously given) the dam finally burst, causing the great 'flood of Irim' mentioned in the Koran (34:15). The result was the virtual break-up of the southern kingdoms and city-states, the acceleration of tribal movements (see Section 2.3), the decline in importance of southern Arabia, and the widespread economic and political changes in the whole of the peninsula.

2.2 The Adnan Arabs

The Adnan tribes of the Arabian peninsula were nomadic pastoralists, originally from Palestine. These northern Arabs were the Arabized descendants of the Egypto-Jewish Ishmael and the nomad and other Arab and non-Arab tribes with whom their ancestors intermarried. Lighter complexioned than the Kahtan branch, they were regarded as mixed Arabs (*mustariba*).

Their language was related to Canaanite, Phoenician, Hebrew, Aramaic and Syriac. According to the Bible (Gen. 25:18), they dwelt between Havilah (Najran) and Shur (the Syrian Desert), going on to occupy most of north and central Arabia, including Yamama and Nejd. Branches were later to spread through most of the Middle East, Egypt, Syria, Palestine and Mesopotamia. Their political relationship was generally with Palestine and Syria, and later with Byzantium.

The origins of the Adnan tribes are preserved in Arab legend. It is related that the patriarch Abraham came to the Hejaz, in the environs of Mecca, and here he abandoned Hagar and Ishmael. Thus from an early period the chief Adnan tribes are associated with Mecca and the Kaaba shrine.

On Hagar's death her son Ishmael was brought up by the Jurham, a Kahtan tribe descended from and named after Hadoram (Jurham) son of Joktan (Gen. 10:27), and settled in and around Mecca. Ishmael married Rilah, daughter of Mudad, a chieftain of the Amr ibn Adi, a clan also of the Jurham tribe.

In the Bible and in the later Islamic tradition, twelve sons of Ishmael are named and are said to be the progenitors of the twelve great Adnan tribes, though the names of the tribes are not the same in the two versions, nor is the precise relationship or history of the tribes clear or consistent.

Among the sons of Ishmael (Gen. 25:13–15) were Nebajoth, ancestor of the Nabataeans; Hadar, identified with the prophet Hud; Tema, founder of Tayma in northern Hejaz, occupied by the Tayi tribe; Dumah, whose name is preserved in Duma, later capital of the Kalb tribe; Jetur, ancestor of the Ituraeans, who settled in northern Palestine; and Kedar, from whom the principal Adnan tribes claimed descent.

Adnan (fl. *c.* 580 BC), who gave his name to the Adnan race, was a direct descendant of Kedar. Adnan's son Maad escaped the massacre of Nebuchadnezzar II (see Mesopotamia) and settled in the Hejaz near Mecca. Maad's son, by a Jurham woman, was Nizar.

The progeny of Nizar were to join in the centuries-old struggle that went on among the tribes for supremacy in Mecca and guardianship of the Kaaba.

Among the earliest to win control of the region, if only briefly, were the Amila, who later settled in the Sinai. They were displaced by the Jurham, whose suzerainty was of longer duration.

It is only through the tenuous links of Ishmael and Nizar with the southern Jurham that the northern Adnan tribes – including the Kinana (Koraysh) branch, to which Muhammad belonged – can claim their slight admixture of pure Arab blood; otherwise they are closer kinsmen to the Jews. Indeed, the early bedouin spoke of certain important tribes, like the Kedar and the Thakif, as Jews.

Because they were related by intermarriage to the tribes of Ishmael, the Jurham claimed from a very early date to be the rightful guardians of the Kaaba. They took over the Kaaba from the Amila and rebuilt it. Tradition has it that the Jurham remained custodians of the shrine for several centuries, but then began to commit acts of sacrilege and vandalism. They extracted the Black Stone (see Section 2.7) from the wall of the Kaaba and threw it into the well of Zamzam, and then filled the well with the sacred utensils belonging to the shrine.

The Jurham were finally driven from Mecca by severe maladies and 'perished utterly'. In another account, they were displaced in about AD 330 by the Khozaa, after which they migrated northwards, joined the Kodaa tribal confederation, and settled in Sinai and southern Palestine, and are believed to be identical with the Judham tribe.

The Khozaa tribe, who displaced the Jurham, also belonged to the Kahtan race. They were led by Luhay ibn Amr, who seized the government of Mecca and took charge of the shrine. Luhay was responsible for adding several foreign idols to those already placed around the Kaaba. He, or his son, also brought from the Nabataeans the image of the god Hubal which was set up as the principal idol of the Kaaba.

As we shall see in Section 2.4, the Khozaa in turn were displaced by the Koraysh, a tribe that played a dominant role in the early history of Islam.

2.3 Tribal Disruption

The movement of tribes in the Hejaz that was to lead to the ascendency of the Koraysh was part of the larger movement of populations following the bursting of the Marib dam in the fourth century AD. It led to the gradual disruption of the tribal system and brought about fundamental changes in the tribal structure of the Arabian peninsula and beyond. This is generally true of all Arab tribes, whether settled, bedouin or nomad, whether pagan, Jewish or Christian.

A comparative study of demographic maps tracing tribal settlements every half-century from the time of the Marib catastrophe shows a constant migration of peoples, the obliteration of tribal boundaries, the weakening of old tribal bonds and the formation of new tribal alliances. In the mêlée the distinction between even the two major Arab 'races' – southern Kahtan and northern Adnan – became confused.

Certain regional features – such as modes of dress, diet and speech – distinguished some of the tribes at first, for example the Kayis (northern) and the Kinda (southern), but, with the closer contacts brought about by tribal movements, tribal habits altered and these ceased to be the distinguishing characteristics of tribal identity.

Tribes detached themselves from their genealogical group and joined others to form another larger group with a common interest, and a new tribal confederation (hilf) came into being. Old tribal names often served as a collective designation for disparate elements brought together in this manner.

The name 'Maad', which is a distinctive northern-Arab tribe name, appears in later genealogies as southern. Similarly, the question whether the Kodaa and Khozaa belonged to the northern or to the southern branch was long debated. The position of a number of lesser tribes remains equally uncertain, though they achieve a tribal status by claiming, and being accepted into an advantageous relationship. In practice such a claim is all that matters, and has no bearing on actual kinship.

Tribes therefore came into being not only through common descent but through common settlement. And, because of tribal rivalries and changing alliances, some tribes who had previously been classed as Adnan later claimed to belong to the Kahtan group, to obtain the support of the southerners in the area where they sought to settle.

In the light of these facts it would seem that the usual classification of tribal groups showing the origin and relationship of the Arab clans – which had never been consistently tabulated by the earliest authorities – represents an attempt to reconstruct and systematize a confused and chaotic tradition stretching over many centuries. Tribal identity and kinship had long been lost or become hopelessly confused and could not be clearly disentangled.

Some scholars believe that, by a process of 'working back', tribal and family genealogies and the legends relating to tribes have been largely 'Islamized' and invented to establish élitist clan connections. They represent the speculations of Muslim theorists and are largely fictitious.

Later, non-Arab Muslim writers of the nationalist movements (see Section 13.2) liked to satirize Arabs' pride in their so-called tribal identity. Since genealogy and tribal affiliation depended on descent, it is clear that they could not be established unless paternity could be confirmed. Doubts about a woman's virtue were a frequent theme of Arabic satire (Goldziher, 1967, p. 178). God alone knows, it was said, who a person's father is, for women are weak and a man may have one among many fathers. Sometimes whole tribes were stigmatized in this way.

The rise of Islam and the wars conducted within Arabia by the first caliph, Abu Bakr, as well as the expansion of the Muslim empire outside Arabia and the conversion of foreigners during the Muslim conquests, further speeded up the fragmentation of tribes and the dilution of Arab purity.

Many tribes had moved far from their homelands to fight in foreign countries, or had been transplanted to distant provinces. Others migrated to new lands as merchants or tradesmen and settled down in the newly acquired territories. Influential non-Arab tribes and communities became affiliated to Arab tribes and claimed to be Arabs themselves. This led inevitably to intermarriage and the miscegenation of the Arabs with Persians, Syrians, Egyptians, Greeks, Armenians, Berbers, Turks and other non-Arabs, leading to a progressive racial mixture of the whole population (see Section 13.3). A demographic redistribution occurred so that no pure Arabs can be identified any longer.

In whatever manner the later tribal hierarchy evolved, it is clear that what mattered was not the fictional genealogy or the family fable – that could be rearranged anyway – but which group was in the right place at a particular time. By the end of the sixth century AD the tribe that happened to be in control of the city of Mecca assumed a dominant position in Arabia, not only because of the religious importance of the Kaaba but because of the growing importance of the city, which by then had become a great commercial centre with wide trading interests in many foreign countries.

2.4 The Koraysh

In about AD 350 an influential confederacy of Adnan tribes called the Kinana began to assume importance in the Hejaz. The most prominent tribe of the confederacy were the Koraysh. The name 'Koraysh' signifies shark or other large sea creature, and probably comes from a tribal emblem. Some derive it from the Persian name 'Cyrus' (Kurash).

A century later, in about AD 450, a Korayshi named Kosay, son of Kilab and Fatima – the latter a woman of the Jadara tribe – decided to gain control of Mecca and the Kaaba. The shrine had originally been under the guardianship of the descendants of Ishmael, but from about the fourth century BC it had fallen successively to the Kahtan tribes: the Amila, the Jurham and the Khozaa.

Born in Mecca, Kosay had been raised among the Nabataeans, and on reaching man's estate he made plans for the restoration of the city and the shrine to the Adnan race. He received a promise of support from the Nabataeans, and from the Kahtan tribe of Kodaa acting on behalf of the Byzantine emperor. They were soon able to depose the Khozaa and to establish the rule of the Koraysh in Mecca.

Kosay instituted many of the ordinances relating to the administration of the Kaaba and the government of Mecca. He was said to have brought from the Nabataeans the goddesses Allat, Ozza and Manat. The Kaaba, neglected by the Jurham, needed repair, and soon after his accession Kosay had it demolished and rebuilt on a somewhat grander scale.

Kosay's son and successor, Abid Menaf, encouraged the expansion of business enterprise with foreign countries, and as a result Mecca acquired considerable commercial importance. The descendants of Abid Menaf were among the chief participants in the power struggle for supremacy in Mecca and in the rise and spread of Islam (see Section 5.2).

At the same time the cementing of alliances with the Arab tribes had become a matter of state policy with the Byzantine and Sassanian rulers, the tribe in control of Mecca being of particular interest to both sides. Because the Byzantines had helped the Koraysh to set up their rule in Mecca, Abid Menaf became an ally of Byzantium in the ongoing territorial conflict between the two empires.

The Sassanian monarch at the time was Kobad I, and his Arab ally was Mundhir III, king of Hira in the Euphrates valley. Kobad favoured a new communistic religion then being propagated by a Persian reformer called Mazdak, and he ordered his vassal Mundhir to impose the new faith on the Arabs, and if necessary to capture Mecca, destroy the Kaaba and kill Abid Menaf. But other problems intervened to occupy Kobad, and he did not proceed further in the matter. Mecca was left in peace from foreign interference thereafter.

2.5 Mecca

This thriving metropolis was situated in a valley at the crossroads of two major trade routes through Arabia: the north–south Hejaz road along the coast of the Red Sea, linking Himyar with Palestine and Syria; and the east–west Nejd road, linking Yemen with the Persian Gulf and Iraq. It was a bustling centre of commerce and a regular halting-place with a plentiful supply of water for caravans.

Mecca almost monopolized the entrepôt and transit trade between the Indian Ocean – including East Africa – and the Mediterranean. Through the town were transported large quantities of merchandise to and from the Egyptian, Syrian, Roman, Byzantine, Persian and Indian trading centres.

Leather, gums, frankincense, spices and precious metals formed the staple exports from Mecca itself. There was also considerable trade traffic through Yathrib (Medina) across the desert en route to and from Persia and Iraq – especially in perfumes, skins and textiles – and some of this traffic passed through Mecca as well.

By the sixth century AD most of the neighbouring countries had their trade depots within Mecca. An Egyptian centre (the Dar Misr, or House of Egypt) had been established in AD 500, soon to be followed by a Byzantine trade agency. During the rule of Abid Menaf, Mecca also had close business dealings with the Christian principality of Ghassan, whose local representative was allotted a residence in a circle of houses next to that of the ruling family (Esin, 1963, p. 59).

2.6 The Kaaba

What is best known about the pre-Islamic religion of pagan Arabia centres largely on traditions relating to the Kaaba and its environs. In order to remove its many pagan associations, Muslim writers have given the Kaaba a history of their own. It was said to have been built by Adam, destroyed in the flood of Noah, and rebuilt by Abraham and his son Ishmael. The linking of Abraham with the Kaaba dates from the post-Islamic period.

It is thought that the Kaaba was originally built to house a sacred black stone (see Section 2.7). The place became a centre of worship for the early Arab tribes, who brought the images of their tutelary gods and installed them around the temple. The chief deity of the pagan shrine was Allah, and even before the advent of Islam the Kaaba was known as the House of Allah.

The Kaaba remained a pagan pantheon till AD 630, when Muhammad destroyed the images. But it continued to be Arabia's holiest shrine and the focus of Muslim unity, and it remains the point towards which Muslims turn to worship.

The Meccan valley was carved out by an ancient stream, which in any violent rainstorm may still fill and overflow, flooding the city and the shrine and obliging pilgrims to wade out, as happened as recently as 1950. After one such flood in AD 300 the Kaaba was repaired by Omar al-Jarud, whose descendants thereafter became known as the Jadara or masons.

The Kaaba has been subject not only to periodic flooding but, because of the use of lamps in the shrine, to fire as well. In the course of its long history it has been damaged and destroyed by flood and fire more than a score of times, and has often had to be rebuilt from its foundations up. Many alterations in its shape and size were made centuries before and centuries after Muhammad.

The Kaaba is draped in a richly decorated canopy (kiswa), which is annually renewed. The practice of ceremonially covering the temple was started more than three centuries before the birth of Muhammad, by Asad Abu Karib (fl. c. AD 415), after his conversion from paganism to Judaism (see Section 3.2).

Originally a simple structure the height of a man and open to the sky, the Kaaba is now a cubical building approximately forty feet high, long, and broad. The present structure is not older than the seventeenth century AD (O'Leary, 1927, p. 197).

2.7 The Black Stone

According to the commentator Ibn Abbas (d. 687), Muhammad said that the Black Stone came down from paradise, and at the time of its descent it was whiter than milk; but the sins of men who touched and kissed it caused it to become black. According to an old tradition of the Persians, the stone was allegedly the emblem of Saturn and one of the relics left in the Kaaba by their hero Mahabad (Hughes, 1977, p. 155).

Western scholars believe that the Black Stone was a meteorite that fell from the skies in prehistoric times, and that the Kaaba was built to house it. It was worshipped by the ancient Arabs and continues to be revered by Muslims to this day. One of the main objectives of the Meccan pilgrimage is circumambulation around it. It lies embedded in the eastern corner of the Kaaba, about five feet from the ground.

It may not be the original meteorite. Some time in the third century AD the Jurham guardians are said to have removed it and thrown it into the well of Zamzam. In 603 it was broken into three pieces by the catapults of the Omayyad army (see Section 13.6), and it was later stolen by the Karmathians and allegedly pulverized.

The present stone is an irregular oval some seven inches in diameter, with an undulating surface. It is made up of a dozen smaller stones of different shapes and sizes, apparently not of the same composition, held together in a cement mixture and now well smoothed, the whole being set in a silver mounting.

The Black Stone is the most sacred but not the only sacred stone in the Kaaba. In the west corner another stone, the 'lucky' (asaad), is built into the wall. This is touched but not kissed by pilgrims. Yet another stone, 'the place of Abraham' (makami Ibrahim), the stone on which Abraham is said to have stood while constructing the original shrine, is now covered in a gilded cage and kept in a little building just outside.

Muhammad condemned all forms of idolatry, and the adoration of the Black Stone never became part of the Muslim pilgrimage. Stroking or kissing the stone was therefore not regarded as its worship. The caliph Omar (d. 644) said of the Black Stone, 'I know you are nothing but a stone that neither harms nor helps. If I had not seen the messenger of Allah kiss you, I would never kiss you myself.'

2.8 The Pagan Pilgrimage

The great pilgrimage (hajj) to Mecca and the Kaaba was the highlight of the pagan religious year. The pilgrimage lasted ten days and was hedged in by many taboos, most of which have been retained in Islam, if in slightly modified form. A number of ritual practices and exclamatory formulas now accompanying the Muslim pilgrimage, as well as the ceremonies observed at the various 'stations', can also be traced back to pre-Islamic times.

Profane clothes were not allowed in the temple precincts during the pilgrimage. The pilgrims first put themselves in a state of sanctity (*ihram*) by bathing and donning white pilgrim garb, also called *ihram*. This change of clothes used to take place at the sanctuary of the goddess Manat. Those who could not afford to buy fresh clothes performed the circumambulation of the shrine in the nude (Hughes, 1977, p. 630).

Before entering the shrine, the pilgrim announced his readiness for service (*talbiya*) to Allah, the Lord of the Kaaba, by the intonation (*ihlal*) of the formula 'I arise to perform the religious duties, O Allah. There is no partner with thee.' This ancient formula, called the *labaika*, after the initial phrase 'I arise', is preserved in present usage.

The central rite on entering the sacred enclosure was the circumambulation (*tawaf*) of the Kaaba seven times, in a counter-clockwise direction, keeping the Kaaba always on the left. At each circuit the pilgrim kissed the Black Stone, or bowed or waved towards it.

After the circumambulation the various tribes would pay homage and offer sacrifices to their particular patron deities, whose idols and monoliths surrounded the Kaaba. The pagan Korayshis invoked their own goddesses, notably Allat, Ozza and Manat.

All these ceremonies occupied five days. On the sixth day the pilgrim performed the rite of running (*sai*) seven times between the Meccan hillocks of Safa and Marwa, situated a few hundred yards from the Kaaba. Muslim tradition has it that this was done in commemoration of the desperate search for water made by Hagar for herself and Ishmael when they found themselves abandoned by Abraham.

In pagan times each of these hillocks was surmounted by a stone or copper idol, one of a man and the other of a woman, which were likewise objects of veneration. The pagan Arabs, including the Khozaa and the Koraysh, used to offer libations to them, and touch them to obtain blessing.

According to legend, in ancient times a woman named Nayla and her lover Isaf made love within the holy precincts of the Kaaba and were turned to stone. By order of the ruler, their petrified bodies were placed on Safa and Marwa as a warning against such sacrilege. The story of this couple may conceal evidence about the nature of certain 'filthy activities' that used to be performed at this site and in the Kaaba, and to which the Koran refers (7:27). This seems to be confirmed by it being permissible to make the circumambulation of the shrine in the nude, and by the revelry that marked the end of the pilgrimage (see below). These ancient practices associated with the pilgrimage were not easy to eradicate, and it was said that for at least fifty years after the death of Muhammad there were times when respectable men and women who visited the shrine on a pilgrimage had, for the sake of decency, to perform the circumambulation of the Kaaba separately.

On the eighth day the pilgrims went on to the valley of Mina, three miles east of Mecca, where they spent the night. Early on the ninth day they proceeded to another important pilgrimage point, the small granite hill of Arafat, about thirteen miles east of Mecca, where they remained standing from midday to sunset. Here in pre-Islamic times was the shrine of a deity named Ilal, who used to be worshipped by the Arabs. The rite of standing (*wukuf*) at Arafat was an essential part of the pilgrimage.

On the setting of the sun at Arafat there was a dash (*ifada*) to Mount Muzdalifa, the next pilgrimage point, three miles away towards Mina. Muzdalifa was surmounted by a round tower and was regarded as sacred to the thunder-god Kuza (A. J. Wensinck, in SEI, 1974, p. 124). Here pilgrims would light fires and keep a vigil through the night, raising a great shout from time to time. The pagan practice of lighting fires at Muzdalifa was observed at Muhammad's farewell pilgrimage and continued till the time of the caliph Harun al-Rashid (d. 809).

The concluding rite of the pilgrimage took place on the tenth day in the valley of Mina, an ancient sacrificial site, about halfway back to Mecca. Here seven stones, previously collected at nearby Muzdalifa, were cast by each pilgrim to form a cairn. The purpose of the throwing is not clear, but Muslim tradition relates that it was in the vicinity that the patriarch Abraham encountered Satan and drove him off by pelting him with stones.

The stoning (*rajm*) at Mina removed the pilgrim's state of sanctity, so he could now return to normal life. As a climax to the proceedings a great sacrifice used to be performed at Mina, when hundreds of goats, sheep and camels were offered to the deities. It was also customary to perform a sacrifice at a granite block on the slope of Mount Thabir nearby, the site of Abraham's intended offering-up of his son. The feast of sacrifice (Id al-Azha) is said to commemorate the event and marked the end of the pilgrimage. Mina has ever since remained the great place of animal sacrifice for Muslim pilgrims.

The three-day period, from the eleventh to the thirteenth day, following the end of the pilgrimage was called *tashrik*, 'drying', after the drying of the blood and flesh of the slaughtered animals. It was spent at Mina and was regarded as a well-earned time of rest and relaxation after the rigours of the hajj. From references in early Arabic poetry, it seems that the occasion provided an opportunity for amorous encounters between the young men and women of different tribes. Muhammad was to refer to this period as 'days of eating, drinking and sensual pleasure' (A. J. Wensinck, in SEI, 1974, p. 124).

2.9 Allah

The supreme deity of certain ancient Arab tribes, such as those living in the Hejaz, was Allah (29:61), a name said to be derived from the root *al*, 'god', which itself is based on the phoneme *l*, the nucleus of the divine name in many Semitic languages. The sound is pronounced with the tip of the tongue turned up and back against the roof of the mouth, so that it is full-throated and heavy.

The name Allah itself is cognate with the names of God in several Semitic pantheons: the Babylonian and Assyrian Ilu, the Canaanite El, the Hebrew Elohim, the Aramaean Alaha, the Nabataean Elh or Alh, the Ilah of central Arabia.

A shadowy ineffable deity, Allah was not represented by any image, nor did he enjoy popular cult adoration, as did the lesser gods and goddesses. To distinguish him from the other gods, he was given the title of Allah Taala, 'God Most High'.

He was revered mainly by those pre-Islamic Arabs who tended to monotheism, and even the Arab Jews and Christians of those days referred to God as 'Allah'. His name frequently formed part of the personal name of pre-Islamic Arabs. For example, Muhammad's own pagan father was Abdulla, 'servant of Allah', and the name 'Abdellas' found among Arab Christians – including at least one bishop – is the Greek version of 'Abdulla'.

Allah was worshipped in the Kaaba sanctuary which was his chief shrine, and the Kaaba was known as the House of Allah (Baitullah). In pre-Islamic poetry Allah is spoken of as the 'Lord of the Kaaba'. Pilgrims making the circuit of the shrine addressed their homage to him in the *labaika* formula.

The pagan practice of making offerings to Allah, as well as to an array of secondary gods who were called Companions of Allah (6:137), is mentioned in the Koran. As the Meccans pointed out, Allah did not forbid this kind of worship (6:149).

In his early Meccan period, Muhammad, well aware of the pagan associations of Allah, showed considerable hesitation in adopting that name for the God he proclaimed, and tried instead to use the name 'Rahman'.

One aspect of Allah may have been personified in the god Hubal, who was accorded pride of place among the idols of the Kaaba. The name is said to be derived from the Semitic *Hu*, meaning 'He' or 'He is' (see 3:1), with the suffix *El*, 'God'. He was perhaps an ancient variant of Allah, and his name used to be invoked as a war-cry by the Meccans. Hubal was venerated by the Nabataeans and certain other northern tribes, but is not named in the Koran. In his youth, Muhammad helped with the preparations being made for the ceremonial installation of Hubal in the Kaaba.

2.10 The Titles of God

In the Koran (7:179) it is said that Allah has 'most excellent names' (*asma al-husna*). From its pages the Muslims culled a series of honorifics – ninety-nine in all – which are treated as the titles of God. For example: al-Majid, 'the Glorious'; al-Ghafur, 'the Forgiving'; al-Razzak, 'the Provider';

al-Hakam, 'the Judge'; al-Khalik, 'the Creator'; al-Awwal, 'the First'; al-Akhir, 'the Last'.

Some of these honorifics bear a close linguistic relationship with the names of pagan deities, and to account for this the Muslims maintained that the pagans perversely named their idols after the titles used from earliest times for the one true God (Sale, 1886, p. 127). Thus Allat was derived from Allah; Manat from Mannan, 'Bountiful'; Jibt from Jabbar, 'Preserver'; and so on.

On the other hand it might be suggested that the early Muslims, many of whom still retained a reverence for their old gods, may well have sought to perpetuate the names of their deities by concealing them in the so-called 'most excellent names' bestowed upon Allah. By this strange conversion the names of many heathen deities could have survived within the pale of Islam.

Thus Wadd, a moon-god, was assimilated into and survived in al-Wadud, 'the Loving'; Munim, worshipped in north Arabia, survives in al-Mani, 'the Withholder'; Salm, a deity of Tayma, in al-Salaam, 'the Peace'; Kaus or Kayis, regarded as the consort of Manat, is retained in al-Kawi, 'the Strong'; Aziz of north Arabia is preserved unchanged in al-Aziz, 'the Mighty'. The pre-Islamic designations of God, al-Rahman, 'the Merciful', and al-Rahim, 'the Compassionate', remain conspicuous in Islam.

It is known that the chapters (*suras*) of the Koran were named and arranged in their present form only after Muhammad's death (see Section 7.6), and it is possible that the 'rememberers' of the Koranic text, or those who helped the compilers, gave certain chapters their titles from words in the text that were the same as the names of pagan gods. Thus, Tarik, a stellar deity, is preserved in the title of Sura 86; Nasr, a deity of Himyar, lives on in the title of Sura 110; Shams, a solar deity often personified as a goddess and widely worshipped in the Middle East, is the title given to Sura 91 (see Section 2.16).

2.11 The Daughters of Allah

Three female deities named in the Koran (53:19) – Allat, Ozza and Manat – deserve special brief mention. In the Hejaz these three goddesses, who presided over the planetary bodies, were spoken of as the 'daughters of Allah' (*banat Allah*).

Some scholars suggest that 'Allat' (al-Lat, 'the goddess') may have been the name from which the name 'Allah' is derived, since it preceded the male form of the name. The Nabataeans knew her as the goddess of war. Herodotus mentions her as Alilat, the great goddess of the Arab people.

The two goddesses associated with her – Ozza, the Arabian Aphrodite, to whom cruel blood sacrifices used to be offered in some places, and Manat, goddess of destiny or fate – were also known to the Nabataeans. The pagan

Korayshis used to chant invocations to these goddesses as they circumambulated the Kaaba.

More specifically, Allat was worshipped in Tayif, forty miles south-east of Mecca; Ozza at Nakhla, forty miles east of Mecca; and Manat at Kodayd, not far from Mecca on the road to Medina. In these and other places, they were worshipped as female figures or in the form of a cubical rock or a black stone.

In 616 Muhammad, in an attempt to placate his Meccan opponents, spoke favourably of these three goddesses, but he withdrew his approval not long after (see Section 5.21). Tayif, one of the great centres of pagan worship in Arabia, had sanctuaries for all three goddesses, as well as a large image of Allat, and in 630 Muhammad ordered these shrines and the idol to be destroyed.

2.12 The Pagan Deities

Ten deities of the pre-Islamic Arabs are mentioned by name in the Koran: Allat, Ozza and Manat (53:19); Jibt and Taguth (4:54); Nasr, shaped like an eagle; Yaguth, like a lion; Yahuk, like a horse; Sowa, like a woman; and Wadd, like a man (71:23).

The Arab historian and genealogist Hisham al-Kalbi (d. 820), in his book of idols (*Kitab al-Asnam*), gives more comprehensive lists, as do other Arab writers. Modern scholars have named more than seventy idols worshipped by the pre-Islamic Arab tribes.

Many of the idols around the Kaaba pantheon represented deities worshipped in southern Arabia, Mesopotamia, Palestine, Syria and other places further afield. One writer, Ahmed-Bey Kamal, on no good authority compiled a list of gods which supposedly had been identical in Ancient Egypt and Arabia.

These ancient idols were believed to have formed a circle of 360 monolithic figures around the sacred shrine. Some were tall standing stones; some were crudely fashioned in human or animal shape. Some reputedly were prehistoric, dating back to the antediluvians of Noah's time.

It is also thought that many of the pillars in the colonnade now surrounding the Kaaba were installed on the original site of the earlier stone uprights. During the great annual pilgrimage to Mecca the desert Arabs would sacrifice animal victims at the altars of these deities. (From Islamic times the shedding of blood within the Kaaba precincts has been prohibited.)

Long before the birth of Muhammad, one of the monoliths was said to have been taken to Somnath in western India, where it was worshipped as the linga of Shiva. It was eventually destroyed in 1024 by the Muslim conqueror Mahmud of Ghazni.

Among the other gods venerated by the Arab tribes, the following are named in various Arabic texts. Most of these probably also had shrines dedicated to them around the Kaaba.

Gadd a god of fortune was a deity of Dedan. Rodha, an idol of the Rabia tribe, symbolized the evening star. Saad, worshipped by one of the Kinana tribes, was a long rock to which blood sacrifices were offered. The Kodaa worshipped Okaysir, a large quadrangular unhewn black stone. The tribe of Munhib ibn Daus worshipped Dhul Kafayn, 'He of the Two Palms [of the hand]'.

An idol of the pagan Tayi was Fals, carved in the form of a man. Ali, whom Muhammad sent to destroy the idol, brought back a magnificent sword specially forged and donated to the shrine. Ali kept this celebrated weapon, known as Dhulfikar, as his personal sword. Another famous idol, Dhul Khalasa, carved out of white quartz, was situated at Tabala between Mecca and Sanaa. Arrows of divination would be used at his shrine. Muhammad said that one of the signs of the end of the world would be the revival of Dhul Khalasa's worship (see Section 14.15).

The gods of the southern Arabs included Haubas, a moon-god; Athtar (Ishtar), a moon-goddess; Samawi, a sky-god; and Dhat Baadan a sun-goddess, all of Himyar. Talab and Riyam were two tree-deities at whose shrine oracular communications used to be received. The latter idol, in Sanaa, was destroyed by the tribespeople in about AD 410, on their conversion to Judaism (Faris, 1952, p. 10).

The patron deity of the city-state of Mayin was Nakra. Wadd, already mentioned above, was the patron deity of the city-state of Ausan, in the region of Aden. The chief deity of Saba was Almaka, on whose altars oblations of frankincense and myrrh used to be laid. Amm, 'uncle', a moon-god, and tutelary deity of Kataban, had a shrine near Marib.

Chief of the hosts of evil was Satan (Shaytan), also known as Iblis, a name derived from the Greek diabolos. Under him were several lesser satans. In addition, there was a class of evil entities called afrit, of monstrous size, full of malice and inspiring great dread.

Better known were the jinn (singular: jinni, 'genie'), a word derived from the Avestic jaini, 'wicked spirit', and taken over into Aramaic and later used by Aramaic-speaking Christians to designate all pagan gods, reduced to the status of demons. Like Satan, the jinn were created from the element of fire. They could take on animal or human shape and were believed to haunt the air, inhabit the hills and trees, and infest dark and desert places. They were not usually malevolent, but were very mischievous and troubled mankind.

The jinn give their name to one of the suras of the Koran, where it is related that a company of jinn once listened to the Koran and became believers (72:1).

2.13 Nature Worship

Like other peoples of the ancient world, the Arabs worshipped natural objects like the heavenly bodies, stones, trees and wells. The Sabians were star-worshippers, the people of Himyar worshipped the sun, the tribes of Asad and Kinana the moon. The Kaaba is thought to have been dedicated to the Great Goddess, or to a lunar deity (see Section 2.14).

According to al-Shahrastani, (d. 1153), an opinion prevalent among the Arabians was that the circumambulation of the Kaaba originally symbolized the motion of the planets (Rodwell, 1915, p. 455). The three goddesses Allat, Ozza and Manat presided over the moon, the planet Venus and Sirius (the Dog Star) besides other celestial bodies. The Koran refers to Allah as 'Lord of Sirius' (53:50).

The patron deities of many pagan tribes were associated with stones. The Arab reverence for the Black Stone was a form of litholatria or stone worship, a kind of fetishism found in all parts of the world, in which stones of strange shape, size or colour were regarded as sacred. Such stones were touched, stroked or kissed by the worshipper, who thereby acquired some of a stone's holiness by contagion.

The Nabataean god Dhu Shara and the sun-god Elogabal of Emesa (now Homs, in Syria), on the Orontes, both had the form of a black stone. (The Emesa stone was smashed by the Muslims when they took the town in AD 636, lest it be equated with their own, and the leading Christians living there were exiled.)

Many kinds of tree-deities also received homage. Sometimes an actual tree was held sacred, like the date palm in Mesopotamia, and in other cases the tree was represented by a stone which the deity was believed to inhabit. In common with other Semitic peoples, the Arabs had a particular reverence for the acacia tree. The shittim tree of the Bible, out of which the Ark of the Covenant was made, was an acacia. A famous acacia tree sacred to Ozza grew on the Tihana coast west of Mecca.

When Muhammad made his followers take the oath at Hodebiya (see Section 6.13), he took up his stand under an acacia tree. The tree thereby acquired a renewed sanctity and was visited by pilgrims, until cut down by the caliph Omar.

The best-known of the sacred wells in Arabia is the well of Zamzam, south-east of the Kaaba, which an angel was said to have revealed to Hagar. It was also sacred to the early Zoroastrians, as seems to be indicated by a line in an old Arabic poem about the Persians muttering their prayers there with a low buzzing sound, after which the well was named. About a century before Muhammad's time the well had become choked with silt, and it remained blocked until cleared by Abdul Muttalib, Muhammad's grandfather.

The well is still regarded with great reverence by Muslim pilgrims, who drink from its waters and carry away small quantities to take home with them. The water is sipped by the dying and is thought to bestow blessing.

2.14 The Feminine

It is interesting to find, as a curiosity of symbolism, how far the esoteric concept of the Feminine pervaded Arab life and belief. As in many other religions of the ancient Middle East, there was a strong feminine bias in the early religion of Arabia. This seems to have centred principally on the worship of an underlying feminine principle, like the Great Goddess common to several ancient mythologies.

Female deities like Allat, Ozza and Manat predominated in importance over male. Even the sun-deity Shams was treated as female by some Arab tribes. The moon (see below), though often ruled by a god, was regarded as the feminine orb *par excellence*.

The Kaaba was first erected to provide a suitable sanctuary for the Black Stone, which is believed to have been a token of the Great Goddess. The name 'Kaaba' itself, traditionally said to be derived from a word for 'cube', is more accurately traced back to the ancient word *kaab*, meaning 'virgin', cognate with the Old Semitic root QBA meaning female pudenda. Even today the border surrounding the Black Stone is shaped like the vulva, while the shrine itself is set in an ovoid space. John of Damascus (d. 749), who lived in the capital of the Arab empire, connected the word 'Kaaba' with Kubar, or the Star of Aphrodite.

Another symbol of the Great Goddess was the full lunar orb, and the moon-goddess was one of the deities to whom the Kaaba was dedicated. In fact the mystical association of things lunar with important events in Arab or Islamic annals has been remarked on by more than one writer, as if the moon were guiding the destinies of the Arab people. For example, the most critical battle in Muhammad's career occurred at a place called Badr, which means 'full moon' (Frieling, 1978, p. 48).

The number seven, one quarter of the number of days in a lunar month, is a lunar number. Herodotus mentions the use of seven stones by the Arabs when taking solemn oaths. The historian Masudi (d. 956) records an old belief that the Kaaba was dedicated to seven heavenly bodies. In pre-Islamic times the Kaaba was to be circumambulated seven times, keeping the Kaaba on the left, the sinistral or feminine side. The pilgrim had to run between the hills of Safa and Marwa seven times. Seven stones were thrown by each pilgrim at Mina, and so on. Some of these practices, as we have seen, have lasted to the present day.

Muhammad forbad the use of any metal but silver, the moon metal, for signet rings. Pigeons, like doves, are the birds of the Great Goddess. They abound in the Kaaba, and no one may kill them there or in any part of the sacred city.

The preferred Muslim colour, green, associated with vegetation rites, was the favoured colour of the Great Goddess. The standard (*liwa*) of the early Muslim armies was green in colour, and sometimes triangular in shape (Hughes, 1977, p. 607), again suggesting the female. As white became the colour of the Omayyads, and black of the Abbasids, so green became the colour of the Fatimids, the descendants of the Prophet.

The most frequently employed of all Islamic invocations is the *tasmiya*, in which Allah is designated 'the Merciful' and 'the Compassionate', both regarded as feminine qualities (see Section 10.6). Most of the Koran was traditionally said to have been received through the angel Gabriel, who is connected with the spirituality of the moon. Muhammad also received some verses of the Koran through the inspiration of what is known as the Sakina, the female aspect of the spirit of God.

It is to be noted that the lunar crescent or the sickle of the new moon, as distinct from the full orb, was originally a symbol of the planet Venus and of the goddess Ishtar, and was later adopted by the Christians as a symbol of the Virgin Mary. From the ninth century on, the crescent was widely used in Venice, Naples, Constantinople and other places by Christian princes and chivalric orders under the protection of the Virgin. When Constantinople fell to the Ottoman Turks, in 1453, the Byzantine device was taken over by the conquerors, as a sign of victory over the Christians. From Turkey, the use of the crescent as an emblem on banners and flags spread to other Islamic countries.

Most of the pre-Islamic Arab tribes followed a lunar calendar, which Muhammad retained and which Muslims still use. Friday, a day dedicated to the moon in many pagan communities, was the day appointed for public assembly (*juma*) among the ancient Arabs, and was subsequently adopted as the 'sabbath' of the Muslims. The first day of the Muslim era was a Friday.

In Islamic times the attendants who served at the greater mosques were sometimes eunuchs. As late as the fourteenth century the Moroccan traveller Ibn Batuta recorded that the servants of the Mosque of the Prophet in Medina were eunuchs, headed by an Abyssinian who was treated like a great emir. This is reminiscent of the eunuch hierophants in the temples of the Great Mother in Phrygia, Ephesus and elsewhere.

Death, funeral and related obsequial rites were among the services conducted in the shrines of the Great Goddess. Analogous rituals are found associated with the Arabian temple. Prophets numbered in their hundreds are said to be buried around the Kaaba (A. J. Wensinck, in SEI, 1974, p. 197), and it is known that till recent times corpses before interment used to be carried in procession around the shrine.

Again, fertility rites, in conjunction with ritual nudity, temple prostitution, sodomy and other libidinous practices, often attended the idolatrous ceremonies at the temples of the Great Goddess. Before Islam such practices were known to have taken place in the vicinity of the Kaaba. It appears that such activities continued – though intermittently and to a lesser degree – even after the establishment of Islam, and were denounced by the scandalized pilgrims and roundly condemned by the orthodox. They continued to be reported from time to time till the nineteenth century by both Muslim and non-Muslim travellers.

John Lewis Burckhardt, who visited Mecca in 1814, wrote, 'The Holy Kaaba is rendered the scene of such indecencies as cannot with propriety be more particularly noticed. They were not only practised here with impunity, but almost publicly'.

Writing of Medina in 1882, Charles Montagu Doughty speaks of 'carding, playing, tippling in arak, brutish hemp smoking, ribald living'. It was only the strong, if sometimes puritanical, hand of the Saudi rulers that put a stop to these excesses.

2.15 Women before Islam

The tradition of renowned queens and redoubtable female warriors was not unknown in the Middle East – the semi-legendary Semiramis of Nineveh, the Queen of Sheba, and Cleopatra of Egypt are examples.

The Arabs too have a long record of intrepid female rulers and tribal chieftains. Such were the previously mentioned queens Zabiba, Shamsi, Yati, Tayl Khunu, Tubwa and Adiya, who long resisted the Assyrian kings. The Lihyanite realm, too, boasted a queen. Then there was Nayla – known as Zabba, the 'Heavy-Browed' – queen of the Kodaa confederacy, who in about AD 270 established herself on the Euphrates somewhat north of Babylon. (Zabba is not to be confused with the ill-fated Zenobia of Palmyra.) Zabba's sister, known by the diminutive 'Zubayba', ruled a town on the opposite bank of the river. When Jadhima ibn Fahm, a leader of the Tanukh tribe, a branch of the Kodaa, tried to make incursions into her territory, Zabba inflicted a heavy defeat on him in a battle in which he lost his life. The exploits of this queen were celebrated in early Arabic poetry.

From the poems and legends of pre-Islamic Arabia it is clear that the women of those days enjoyed a high status and had a great deal of social and sexual freedom. Pre-Islamic society in Arabia was predominantly matriarchal and matrilineal. It was more important to know who a child's mother was than the father. Belief in the existence of ancient Arab matriarchies was held by early-twentieth-century scholars like W. Robertson Smith, though it is not endorsed with the same emphasis today.

In ancient Arab society, the child belonged to the mother's family and lived in the mother's house. In much of Arabia, both in the towns and among the bedouin, descent was traced back to the female ancestor, and men and women were reckoned as belonging to the mother's clan. The head of the household was often the matriarch, and on her death the headship passed to another female. Property, inheritance, communal administration and social status were all matters in which the mother, sister, daughter, maternal aunt or other female relative figured prominently.

Al-Bukhari (d. 870) relates that Muhammad was thrice asked by a man to state which parent had the first claim on a person, and Muhammad thrice replied that it was the mother. Only after he was asked the same question a fourth time did he say that the father had a claim, implying that the mother's claim was considerably greater than that of the father.

Women entered general society, and went about unveiled. They used the veil only as a means of dalliance, to indicate bashfulness, or when they wished to hide their identity; otherwise they walked about freely and with the face uncovered. Romantic courtship was a recognized institution. Fornication (zina) was not regarded as sinful, but could be treated as a legal infringement of family property rights (J. Schacht, in SEI, 1974, p. 658).

Although young unmarried girls did not always have freedom in the selection of their husbands, they had the choice of rejection, and could suggest preferences. Married women were regarded as the equals and companions of their husbands. They could return to their own people if ill-treated or displeased. Indeed, on getting married a woman did not have to leave her home, and her husband might visit her for longer or shorter periods.

Divorce was easy and common in Arabia, and women had equality with men in all divorce proceedings. Young widows or divorced women among the bedouin could live in their own tents, where they received suitors as they felt inclined (Glubb, 1979, p. 28). They could determine the choice of their next husband. In Muhammad's case, the proposal which led to his first marriage came not from him but the widow Khadija.

A woman could usually have only 'one husband at a time', but in some cases where forms of polyandry were permitted she could have two or more husbands concurrently. Women could marry frequently, and often did. And this custom seems to have been so strongly rooted that it was apparently never abolished.

Speaking of conditions prevailing at the beginning of the twentieth century, the Begum of Bhopal, herself an orthodox Muslim, said that the women of Mecca frequently contract as many as ten marriages, and those who had been married only twice were few in number. A woman could put away her husband because he was growing old, to take another who was young, good-looking and rich (Muir, 1912, p. 294).

The Roman (Syrian) historian Ammianus Marcellinus (d. AD 390), who travelled widely in the Middle East, writes of the custom, among the Arabs of his day, of contracting temporary marriages – a form of union that remained legal in certain Muslim countries till recent times. Burckhardt adds that it was the custom of the early Arabs to assign some female of the family, most commonly the host's own wife, to a traveller who became their guest for the night. This custom of the 'hospitable widow', as the woman given to the guest was euphemistically called, long persisted among the desert tribes.

Because of such laxity the Arabs acquired the reputation, widely held by the neighbouring peoples of Syria and Egypt, of being subject to inordinate sexual appetite which they were unable to control. Ammianus Marcellinus remarked on the ferocity with which the two sexes among the Arabs abandoned themselves to fornication. A Talmudic doctor, Rabbi Nathan, wrote that nowhere in the world was there such a propensity to fornication as among the Arabs.

Many women were well educated, and some took part in public debates and poetical contests at the annual fairs, such as those at Okaz near Mecca. Among the more distinguished women poets was Khansa (real name Tomadir), who died (c. 616) just when Muhammad's career was beginning.

Women also took an active part in commerce, sending their merchandise to Palestine, Syria and Persia. Muhammad's great-grandmother Salma was a merchant who directed her own affairs; she married Hashim only on condition that she remained mistress of her business concerns and retained the power of divorce. Khadija, the first wife of Muhammad, had large business interests. The mother of Abu Jahal, an opponent of Muhammad, ran a lucrative trade in perfumery. Hind, wife of Abu Sofyan, another opponent of Muhammad, sold her merchandise among the Christian tribes of Kalb on the Syrian border.

All in all, Arab women were known to be fearless, independent and brave. They often accompanied their husbands to battle, usually as camp-followers, stationed just behind the lines, and encouraged them as the battle was joined. In the event of retreat or defeat they hooted and jeered at their men like furies, sometimes rushing into the fray themselves. The tradition of such female warriors continued till the time of Muhammad, and it is known that some women, like the 'feminist' Nosayba, even took part in Muhammad's battles.

2.16 Pagan Survivals

Basically, the religion of Abraham as preached by Muhammad signified the worship of one God, and Muhammad did not interfere with any of the time-honoured elements of native paganism where these did not entail poly-theism or idolatry. He was careful not to undermine the foundations of the original Arab faith, and made substantial concessions to his pagan contemporaries. Where change was needless he made none.

He altered nothing in the pre-Islamic calendrical system or in the sacred months of the pagan Arabs, and they still remain (9:5). Mecca, the sacred city of pagan worship, continued to be the 'mother city' (42:5) and the spiritual focus of the new faith, and remains central in the prayer and pilgrimage of all Muslims.

The deity proclaimed by Muhammad was given a local name, 'Allah' – the name of the supreme deity of the Arabs, pagan and non-pagan, before Islam. The deity was also given a local habitation in the Kaaba. The Koran urges Muslims to 'worship the Lord of this House' (106:3) – the 'House' meaning the Kaaba – and at no time did Muhammad make any attempt to alter the status of the pagan fane.

He also retained, almost intact, all the old pagan ceremonies, and to this day the rites of the Kaaba hang like an incongruous shroud around the living faith of Islam. And then the great iconoclast, who sought to banish idolatry root and branch, made the near-veneration of the Kaaba fetish – a black stone worshipped by the ancient Arabs – the central rite of the Muslim pilgrimage.

Both in Mecca before the Hegira (see Section 6.2) and later in Medina, many ostensibly earnest followers of Muhammad were known to be of doubtful faith (see Section 6.4). But, besides these, there were others who tended to a kind of qualified monotheism, holding that the acceptance of Islam need not mean the total abandonment of older beliefs. Monotheism, as we have seen, was not a novel idea among the Arabs of Muhammad's day: centuries of contact with Jews and Christians, and with their own hanifs, had already familiarized them with the idea of there being only one God. At the same time they saw no incompatibility in worshipping both the Almighty God and various lesser deities. Many Arabs, including the pagans of Mecca, believed in Allah as the supreme God, the creator of the heavens and the earth (29:61) who was not represented in their temples by any image. Yet they also believed in the existence of subordinate deities, both male and female, who were regarded as the 'companions' or the 'daughters' of Allah, and who were fashioned as idols in their places of worship. Some were intercessors with the supreme deity and helped in bringing worshippers closer to Allah (39:4). Devotees would set aside a share from the produce of their fields for Allah and a share for the subordinate gods (6:137).

Converts holding such indulgent views could well have included the amanuenses who took down the Koranic messages, or who were subsequently associated with the collection and compilation of the Koran and with the growth of the new religion. Reverence for the old deities was deep-rooted and strong, and among those who accepted conversion there were some who still retained an affection for their lost idols, whose names, in disguised form, may have been preserved in Islam.

However extreme such speculations might appear, it is useful to remember that old gods die hard, as the Jews learned when they entered Canaan (Leslie, 1936, and many other books). Some of the ancient Egyptian deities are known to have become the saints of Coptic Christianity (Goldziher, 1971,

p. 297). When in AD 596 Pope Gregory I, 'the Great', sent the Benedictine prior Augustine (later St Augustine, archbishop of Canterbury) along with Hadrian the Negro and other monks to convert the English, he instructed them to break the pagan idols but to preserve the temples and convert them for Christian use. The story of the survival throughout Europe of pagan gods as Christian saints, of pagan fanes as Christian churches, and of pagan celebrations as Christian festivals forms the subject of a considerable literature.

The pagans of Arabia did not renounce their deities with good grace. The people of Tayif, when forced to abandon the old faith, pressed hard for the preservation of their idols (see Section 6.18). In fact, after Muhammad's death – when the threat of being raided and the prospect of booty had gone – most of his one-time allies among the Arab tribes promptly withdrew from Islam and reverted to their ancestral faith (see Section 12.1). We learn too from the annals of early Islam how frequently and with what nostalgic yearning the Arabs spoke of pre-Islamic (*jahiliya*) times, when they could worship as they pleased, drink wine and listen to music and poetry.

To the present day, Muslim pilgrims in North Africa and India visit the shrines of alleged Muslim saints, many of which are known to be places of ancient pagan pilgrimage. The English traveller C. M. Doughty, writing in 1888, told of finding at Tayif stone blocks called Allat, Ozza and Manat, as well as Hubal, at which people still secretly sought help in case of illness (F. Buhl in SEI, 1974, p. 287).

Finally, Muhammad left intact most of the customary law of the pagan Arabs, which has been embodied in the Muslim sharia.

2.17 Customary Law

The fundamental principle underlying all law was known to the pre-Islamic Arabs as *sharia*, or 'right way' (45:17), derived from a term meaning the assigned path or beaten track (5:52) leading to a watering place. This is the path that people have to follow in the regulation of their lives, both as individuals and as members of the society to which they belong.

From the general principle of sharia flows the *sunna*, 'custom', another term used by the pre-Islamic Arabs to denote the ancestral usage or model pattern of behaviour established by the forefathers of the tribe (Rahman, 1966, p. 44) and the consensus (*ijma*) of the tribal assembly, and thus embodying the beliefs and practices of the whole community.

The 'lore' incorporating and codifying these principles and practices handed down from generation to generation was known as the *hadith*, also a term of pre-Islamic usage, meaning 'story' or 'report', commonly translated as 'tradition'.

This customary law was fairly uniform among all Arab tribes, and was almost universally accepted and observed by them. Its precepts were directed towards the cultivation of the civilized virtues (*muruwa*) of sincerity, truthfulness, courage, resignation, self-respect, liberality, kindness to one's kin and charity. Details concerning their application are referred to in ancient Arabic poetry and the early traditions.

In practice, customary law covered those observances required by nature (*fitra*), including personal hygiene; ablutions (private and religious, and after certain kinds of defilement); the care of hair, moustache and beard; cleaning teeth and paring nails; conduct in sickness; and death and burial.

It covered social behaviour: the laws of hospitality; forms of salutation, notably the salutation of peace (Salaam); conversation and listening; eating and drinking; approved wearing apparel; entertainment; gambling; divination by lots, arrows and other means; celebration of feasts and fasts; lunar observances; pilgrimage; and abstinence during the month of Ramadan, which, says the Koran (2:179), 'was prescribed to those before you' (see Section 3.1).

Special laws dealt with matters relating to women: menstruation and puberty; fornication; marriage; dowry; adultery; divorce; polygamy; concubinage; children; adoption; and circumcision.

Fairly uniform too were the laws concerning the structure of the tribal community (*umma*): jurisprudence (*fikh*, 'understanding'); oaths, vows and evidence; politics; assemblies; taxation; property and inheritance; bequests and endowments; murder, theft, wounding and slander; economic matters relating to buying, selling and barter; commercial contracts; and usury and interest.

Additional laws governed military matters; the correct use of the bow and arrow, and the sword; the taking of hostages; the treatment of male, female and child prisoners; peace treaties; raids; blood feuds; retaliation and vendetta (*thar*); fighting during the sacred months; and slaves, their acquisition, treatment and manumission.

The historian Abul Fida (d. 1331) writes, 'The Arabs of the time of ignorance [before Islam] used to do things which the religion of Islam has adopted.' This was inevitable, for Islam was deeply rooted in the past, and, with the coming of the new dispensation, much of the existing conceptual framework, along with the old terminology, was incorporated into the new order – with the necessary amendments – and has been perpetuated therein. Some of the material was embodied in the Koran, and much of it entered by way of the hadith.

3

THE MONOTHEISTS BEFORE MUHAMMAD

Muslim writers speak of the period in Arabia before Muhammad as the time of 'ignorance' (*jahiliya*), and generally tend to describe the state of pre-Islamic Arabia in very sombre terms, so as to highlight the blessings brought by the Prophet.

But, centuries before Islam, powerful religious influences, including monotheism, had operated across the peninsula and had left a considerable, though largely understated, impression on the people of Arabia. Islam may be regarded as one stage of a long period of development in the religious and social life of western Asia and the Middle East that is still going on.

Despite the Koran stating more than once that no prophet had appeared in Arabia before Muhammad (32:2; 36:5), it also speaks of certain prophets sent by God in earlier times to proclaim monotheism to the Arab tribes and reform their society. All these early prophets brought the message of the one true God, spoke out against idolatry, and tried to prevail upon the people to abandon their old ways; and all suffered persecution as a result.

One such prophet was Shoayb, who came to the tribe of Madyan (7:83) in north-west Arabia, to urge them to follow the path set by Allah. The people rebuffed Shoayb, and because of their recalcitrance they perished in an earthquake. The inhabitants of Madyan were said to have been the Midianites of the Bible (Exod. 2:15), and Shoayb is identified by some commentators with Jethro, the father-in-law of Moses.

Another prophet was Hud, who was sent to the tribe of Ad (7:63) in southern Arabia, between Oman and the Hadramaut. Here again the people refused to listen; they were punished by a drought. Hud is identified by some with Eber, ancestor of the Jews and Arabs, and by others with Hadar, son of Ishmael (Gen. 25:15). There is a shrine to Hud in the Hadramaut, where reputedly he is still held in reverence (Bethmann, 1953, p. 115).

One of the early rulers of the Ad tribe was the impious Shadad, who ordered the construction of a city called Iram (89:6), having great buildings with marble columns to rival paradise. When it was completed, the presumptuous king and his courtiers set out to see it, but while still a day's journey from the place they were destroyed by a tornado which buried them all in the sand. Iram, it is said in legend, still stands in the desert but remains invisible. Some have identified the people of Iram with the Aramaeans, and Shadad with the Syrian monarch Benhadad (1 Kings 15:18–20).

A third prophet was Salih (7:71), who went to the Thamud, a tribe of western Arabia mentioned in the inscriptions of Sargon II in 715 BC as subject to Assyria. Certain authorities have suggested his possible identity with Salah, son of Arphaxad (Gen. 10:24), and others with Sheleph, son of Joktan (Gen. 10:26).

In terms anticipating the Korayshi's rejection of Muhammad, the Koran relates how the people of Thamud rejected Salih, saying he was only a man like themselves who could make no claim to revelation, a foolish impostor (54:25), a man bewitched (26:153), for whom they would not give up the religion of their fathers (11:65). They too were punished with a severe earthquake.

The region occupied by the Thamud – the Thamudaei of Pliny the Elder – was Hijr, whose capital was the city of the same name, identified with the biblical Dedan (Jer. 25:23), situated in the northern Hejaz between Medina and Syria. Another name of Hijr was Madain Salih, meaning 'the cities of Salih'. Hijr is also the title of Sura 15 of the Koran.

The Thamud were followed in this territory by the Lihyan – the Lechieni of Pliny – who ruled here and westwards along the Red Sea for about 150 years. Their chief town, El Ola, lay some eighty miles south-west of Tayma. Eight Lihyan rulers are listed, among them a woman. One of the rulers was called Tulmay, 'which suggests that they belonged to the Ptolemaic period' (Irvine in Wiseman, 1973, p. 299). In and around El Ola are found rock hewn chambers in Hellenistic style, statuary with Hellenistic features, and rock inscriptions in south-Arabian characters. These inscriptions are of a monotheistic nature, which may suggest Hebrew influences.

Lihyan rule was brought to an end in about 90 BC by the Nabataeans, and the later Lihyanites became affiliated as a clan to the Hodayl tribe.

3.1 The Hanifs

The pre-Islamic monotheist was commonly spoken of as a 'hanif' – a Syrian-Christian loanword – signifying one who had moved away from idolatry. In the early Islamic period the term generally embraced four religious groups: Zoroastrians, Jews, Christians and Sabians, all of whom receive special recognition in the Koran (22:17). (The Sabians are to be distinguished from the Sabaeans, the people of Saba.)

The term 'Sabian' was loosely used for several categories of peoples: those who followed the ancient religion of Seth, Enoch (Idris), or Noah; a Judaeo-Christian baptizing sect of Gnostics in southern Iraq who still exist in the same region and are known today as Mandaeans; and those who had left their faith for another, such as Muhammad himself and his first converts, who were called Sabians by their pagan contemporaries (Hughes, 1977, p. 551).

Commonly the term 'Sabian' is applied to an ancient Aramaic-speaking people of Harran in northern Mesopotamia – a town often mentioned in the Bible (e.g. Gen. 11:31) – who worshipped the stars and venerated angels.

During the Seleucid period these Sabians came under Hellenistic influence – Harran was known to the Church Fathers as Hellenopolis – and were devoted to scientific studies. They long survived under Islam, making many important contributions to Islamic civilization. Harran had a large Christian (Monophysite) community under a bishop.

The term 'hanif' was more specifically applied to those indigenous reformers who under Jewish or Christian influence began to appear among the Arab tribes from about the fifth century AD. The hanifs and those who followed their disciplines or believed in what they taught were especially prominent in the urban areas of the Hejaz, including Mecca, Yathrib (Medina) and Tayif, right up to Muhammad's own day.

A Christian historian of Gaza named Sozomenus (d. 443) wrote of certain Ishmaelites (Arabs) who, proud of their descent from Abraham, wished to do away with the pagan corruptions that had crept into their ancient faith. They were openly critical of the idolatrous religion of their people and desired to reform it so that the 'religion of Abraham' (*millat Ibrahim*) might thereby be restored.

Ardent souls in search of truth, the hanifs proclaimed the unity (*tauhid*) of the Supreme Being, the Lord of Heaven. They addressed God by such titles as al-Rahman (the Merciful), al-Rabb (the Lord), and al-Ghafur (the Forgiving). They believed in the resurrection of the body and the Last Judgement, and spoke of future happiness in the Garden (Paradise) for the virtuous. They also warned of the punishment reserved in hell for the wicked.

According to Ibn Ishak, the hanifs believed their fellow Arabs had drifted away from the religion of their father Abraham, and that indeed they had no religion at all. They inveighed against polytheism, against the worship of deities like Allat and Ozza, and against the worship of the Black Stone. 'What is the stone', they asked, 'that you should circle around it? O people, seek for yourselves a faith, for by God, you are based upon nothing.'

They condemned other pagan customs, such as the burying alive of unwanted baby girls, and as a result of their teachings this custom was fast dying out. They preached human responsibility, advocating a pure religion and a better moral life, and put their higher ideals into practice by giving alms, helping the sick and the poor, caring for orphans, protecting widows and those who were helpless or in need, and buying slaves in order to free them.

Following the example of Christian monks, the hanifs performed regular prayers at fixed times every day. Some covered their heads in a mantle (*dithar*) to assist meditation and, it is thought, to induce revelation. Again, following the Jewish practice of abstinence for ten days in the month of Tishri, and the ascetic disciplines of Christian monks during Lent, the hanifs underwent a routine of self-denial. Every year during the sacred month of Ramadan they would go through a period of withdrawal (*tahannuth*) from worldly activity, lasting from a few days to the full month, abstain from sex and alcohol, and fast from sunrise to sunset each day. Ibn Hisham and certain other authorities derive the term from *ta-hannuf*, signifying the performance of hanif-like disciplines.

During Ramadan the hanifs of Mecca would retire into the hills and caves around the town, where the solitude and silence of the desert worked on their spirits and brought to them a closer realization of the divine presence. Among those who followed this practice was Abdul Muttalib (d. 578), Muhammad's grandfather-to-be, who used to seclude himself in a cave – the cave of Hira, according to the biographer al-Zuhri (d. 742) – where he would fast and meditate.

It seems clear that for a considerable time before the advent of Muhammad some of the basic concepts of Islam were already 'in the air' and influencing thoughtful people in Mecca and elsewhere. Wellhausen says the hanifs were 'evidence of a mood widely current in Arabia before Muhammad, which characterized many of the noblest spirits'. According to Sprenger, 'Islam is the fruit of the hanif tradition', a well-rooted tradition that continued to grow till Muhammad's day.

Muslim chronicles cite twelve of Muhammad's 'companions' who at first were hanifs, but there were other hanif contemporaries as well. Among them were the following, of whom details are given elsewhere in this book: Othman ibn Huwayrith, of the Asad tribe; Zayid ibn Amr, whom Muhammad met in 595; Waraka, who encouraged Muhammad in his mission; Koss ibn Sayda, of the Iyad tribe, one of whose sermons Muhammad heard in about 610; Obaydulla ibn Jahash, who took part in the Abyssinian Hegira; Omayya of Tayif, an opponent and rival of Muhammad; and Abu Amir, who also opposed Muhammad; Abu Kayis, leader of the Aus tribe, who became a vigorous opponent of the Prophet after his migration to Medina and remained hostile till his death, though later accounts speak of his conversion to Islam.

Of these hanifs, four were related to Muhammad: Othman ibn Huwayrith, Zayid ibn Amr, Waraka and Obaydulla. And some were also Christians: Othman ibn Huwayrith, Waraka, Koss ibn Sayda, Obaydulla, and possibly Abu Amir.

Muhammad himself applied the term 'hanif' to Abraham, since he was thought to be the original exponent of monotheism (21:52). In the Koran the faithful are enjoined to follow the religion of Abraham (3:89), who was neither Jew nor Christian (3:60) but a hanif (16:121), sound of faith.

For a time the term hanif was used for all Muslims, but, because it did not apply exclusively to the followers of the Prophet, it passed out of favour with them.

3.2 The Jews before Islam

According to Arabian tradition, the Jews first settled in northern Arabia in the time of Moses, followed in the course of time by many others who sought refuge in the country when fleeing from persecuting conquerors: Nebuchadnezzar, the Seleucids and the Romans.

Historically, however, the Jews entered Arabia about three centuries before the birth of Muhammad. After the destruction of the temple of Jerusalem by the Romans under Titus in AD 70, many Jews came to live among the peoples of northern Arabia. During the succeeding centuries large and small Jewish communities were to be found scattered all over the peninsula, including Himyar in the south, and some proselytizing was done by them.

When in AD 345 the Abyssinians occupied Himyar, the Himyarite ruler (*tubba*) and his family took refuge in Yathrib (Medina), which at the time had the largest community of Jews in Arabia. The Abyssinian occupation was not of long duration, and in 375 one Malik Karib, an Arab convert to Judaism and related to the former tubba, expelled the foreigners and restored the Arab dynasty.

His son and successor Asad Abu Karib (d. 415) travelled to Yathrib to be formally received into the Jewish faith, and on his return in 400 he proclaimed it to be the official faith (Philby, 1947, p. 117). Asad Abu Karib then marched north to attack Yathrib, to rid the place of its pagan inhabitants so that, with its large Jewish population, it would become a wholly Jewish town. He was dissuaded from taking this barbarous step by two rabbis of the Korayza tribe.

When the king proposed storming Mecca instead, the same rabbis counselled against it because, they said, it was a city of ancient sacrosanctity and it would not be proper to destroy it. The king then visited Mecca in person and gave orders for the Kaaba to be decked out in striped Yemeni fabric, and it was from this time that the practice was started of covering the shrine in a *kiswa* or 'robe' (Esin, 1963, p. 51).

Jews and Christians lived peacefully together in southern Arabia till 524, when another Jewish king of Himyar, a descendant of Asad Abu Karib known as Dhu Nuwas, 'He of the Hanging Locks', invaded neighbouring Najran, which had a flourishing Christian community established by Fimiyun, and began a persecution of the Christians there, killing their king, Haritha (the St Aretas of Eastern hagiography), and throwing those who refused to apostatize to Judaism into a burning trench.

It is thought that the Koran refers to this incident in an early Meccan sura which says, 'Cursed be those who constructed the pit and provided the fuel, and sat around to witness what was done to true believers' (85:7). Because this interpretation would imply the Koranic acceptance of Christians as 'true believers', other interpretations were later put on this verse, some suggesting it referred to the three Jews cast by Nebuchadnezzar into the fiery furnace (Dan. 3:20).

One of the victims of Dhu Nuwas's persecution, a man named Daus Dhu

Thalaban, escaped to the court of the Byzantine emperor Justin I and, holding up a half-burned Gospel, called for retribution. At the emperor's request, an army of the king of Abyssinia in 525 crossed over from Abyssinia, defeated Dhu Nuwas (who was later murdered by his subjects), and left a viceroy named Sumyafa to rule over the kingdom. Sumyafa was in turn to be overthrown by an opponent named Abraha.

3.3 The Christians before Islam

It is related in the New Testament (Acts 2:11) that on the day of Pentecost the Arabians were among those present in Jerusalem who heard the Apostles preaching to them in their own language. St Paul writes (Gal. 1:17) that shortly after his conversion he went to Arabia, but nothing more is mentioned about his visit there. The place referred to may have been Arabia Petraea, the region in and around Sinai.

There were Arab converts to Christianity from a very early period, a few of whom attained some renown. The Gnostic teacher Monoimus (d. 180), and the ascetic Valerius (fl. c. 250), a disciple of Origen and founder of the Valerian sect, were two among a score of Arab Christians who have left their mark on church history. St Simon Stylites (d. 499), the pillar hermit, was an Arab, and crowds of desert Arabs visited the outskirts of Antioch for a sight of their famed countryman as he preached the Gospel from the top of a high column.

Missionaries and monks, some sent officially and some on their own initiative, spread across the whole of the Middle East, many settling among the Arab tribes and communities. Wherever they settled they built churches and monasteries, made converts, and encouraged literary and cultural activity, exercising a considerable influence in and around the regions they occupied. Besides missionaries, Christian traders and craftsmen were soon to be found in most of the larger Arab towns. They were regarded as peaceful, industrious and dedicated to their faith.

There were several Arab bishoprics in the chief towns of Syria, Palestine and Mesopotamia, and many of the bishops retained their Arab names. More than three centuries before the time of Muhammad, Christianity had also penetrated deep into the heart of the Arabian peninsula, and was widely diffused there. In the north, churches were founded by missionaries of the Byzantine empire; in the south, along the Hadramaut and Oman, by missionaries from India; in Yemen and the Hejaz by missionaries from Abyssinia. By the middle of the sixth century Arabia was fairly central in the geographical dispersion of Christianity.

For well over a century before Islam the traditions concerning Jesus and the disciples who followed him were well known throughout the Middle East, including Arabia. The Christians used as their scriptures the various Gospels current at the time in Syria and Palestine, including the books containing the apocryphal sayings and stories about Jesus. The common language of the Christians in these regions was Syriac (Christian Aramaic), and it was in this language that many of their texts were written.

The Christians of Arabia were aware of the obscure and often bitter controversies – with their excommunications and anathemas – that were taking place between the different factions in Alexandria, Rome, Constantinople and other centres of Christian theological conflict. Indeed, the Syrian-Christian term for faction (*shia*) passed into Arabic with the meaning of party or 'sect'. But on the whole the Christian communities in Arabia were not generally affected by these dissensions.

Christianity appeared in the eastern churches in its Monophysite (Syrian, Coptic, Abyssinian), Diphysite (Nestorian), Anti-Monophysite (Melchite), Arian, Gnostic and Manichaean forms.

The Manichaean sect, tinged with dualism, was founded by Mani of Ecbatana (d. 276), and its missionaries spread into Central Asia – where Manichaeism became the state religion of the Uighur Turks in 762 – then eastwards into Tibet (Hoffmann, 1961, p. 52) and westwards to North Africa, where it made a notable convert in St Augustine (d. 430).

There was a Manichaean centre in Hira, Mesopotamia, and the ideas of Mani would certainly not have been unknown in a place which had so lively a commerce with Hira as Mecca. Mani's claims that he was the Paraclete whom Jesus had promised, that he was the last and final prophet in a prophetic succession, that he received his revelations from a heavenly being, that Jesus was not crucified but another was put in his place: all may well have influenced Muhammad.

The Manichaean adept was known as *siddik*, 'truthful'. Muhammad gave this title to Abu Bakr, the first caliph, and also used the term in the Koran (19:57) to describe Idris or Enoch. Manichaeans were extensively employed by the Muslims, who respected their zeal, their integrity, their devotion to study, their knowledge of astronomy, medicine and mathematics, and their proficiency in the arts.

The Christian sect founded by Nestorius (d. 451), bishop of Constantinople, flourished exceedingly in Persia, where they had fled from Byzantium after being denounced by the theologians of Constantinople for their insistence on the dual nature of Christ: that he was both human and divine. They were welcomed in Persia as opponents of Byzantium, and received encouragement from many of the Sassanian kings. The Nestorian university established in AD 531 in Jundishapur in south-west Persia became a model the early caliphs were to copy (see Section 13.9).

The Nestorians carried their religious doctrines far and wide, and the great trade routes from Ctesiphon (near Baghdad) to Beijing were marked by their shrines. They set up religious schools and centres of learning in India and Ceylon, and in the Kurdistan highlands, Persia, Bactria, Parthia, Sogdiana, Scythia, Turkestan and the Mongolian tribal lands. They also sent missionaries to China and Japan (Rice, 1964, p. 12); a Nestorian mission that arrived in the Chinese capital in 635 is mentioned in an imperial edict promulgated by the Chinese emperor (Diringer, 1947, p. 286).

3.4 The Monks

Many devout Christians in the Middle East gave time to good works, acts of charity, and the care of the poor and the sick. A man named Sasaa, of the Christian Tamim tribe in central Arabia, used to buy female babies to save them from being buried alive. His grandson Farazdak, a famous Christian poet of the Omayyads, used to boast that he was descended from one who gave life to 'those who were buried'.

Christians of more intense religious fervour retired from the towns to live in small monastic communities, dedicating their lives to God. The deserts of Egypt, Asia Minor, Syria, Palestine, Mesopotamia and Arabia were dotted with their sanctuaries, several of which are mentioned in the pagan and Muslim chronicles. In later years most of these were taken over and converted to Muslim use.

The Arabs used the Syriac word (*dayir*) for monastery, and most of the populace knew of the devotion of those who lived in such places. They knew about the recluses who dwelt in solitude in a cave or other lonely place, devoting themselves to prayer and meditation. Arab poets wrote of the solitary desert cell and the monk who prays through the night with only the stars to witness his vigil and hear his prayers.

Along the caravan routes in the desert, the twinkling light of a hermit's retreat could be seen in the darkness from afar. Hermits broke the tedium of the journey and assured the traveller of welcome, shelter and hospitality. A pre-Islamic poet wrote, 'Their nature is not like that of other men. Their bounty never fails. They are girded with chastity and their hope is set on nothing but the world to come.'

The Arabs were acquainted with the meditative practices of the monks. During prayers the monk did not cover his head, for this was a Jewish custom, and 'it dishonoureth the head' (1 Cor. 11:4). But if he wished to meditate he would wrap himself in a mantle or cover his head with a piece of cloth, so that he might not be distracted by external sights and sounds.

The monk had five periods of daily prayer, and sometimes he prayed far into the night, believing that 'prayer is to be preferred to sleep' (Archer, 1924, p. 67). Prayers were accompanied by reverential postures: standing with the palms together, bowing down, kneeling, and sitting on the heels.

Some practised prostrations with the forehead touching the ground, a form of worshipful salutation known in Arabic as the *sajda*, a term of Syriac derivation (see Section 10.5). Among the Syrian Christians the marks on the forehead caused by such prostrations were often regarded as proof of a monk's piety (Andrae, 1960, p. 89). The Koran too refers to similar marks on the forehead of those who pray (48:29).

These deep prostrations were performed from a kneeling position, care being taken to ensure that, as the forehead touched the ground, the 'unclean back parts' were not raised. This manner of praying was ridiculed by the Jews, as it was known to have been of ancient Canaanite provenance, and many church leaders also discouraged it. The practice was gradually abandoned by Christians, though it is still used on occasion, as during a penitential pilgrimage.

In the view of Macdonald, Archer and other authorities, Islam drew much of its spiritual inspiration from the Christian anchorites, with their long vigils and night prayers. During the early years of his mission Muhammad had met and conversed with several Christian monks and spoke appreciatively of them. He knew their manner of life, and their nocturnal devotions, and was impressed with their humility (5:85). He was referring to them when he said that among the 'people of the book' are an upright folk who devote themselves to God during the night watches, and enjoin justice and do good works (3:109–10).

Although Muhammad did not sanction the monastic life which, he believed, the Christians had invented themselves (57:27), during his search for a vital faith he was clearly influenced by the commitment and discipline of the Christian monks. Like other truth-seekers of his time, he adopted some of their practices, such as covering his head during meditation, praying several times a day and making deep prostrations during the prayer ritual. The Muslim formula (known as *taswib*) in the muezzin's morning call to devotions, 'Prayer is better than sleep', is reminiscent of the monastic precept of the desert anchorite.

3.5 The Christian Tribes

Besides individuals and small groups, many larger communities and even entire Arab tribes were Christian, or had substantial Christian populations. Like their pagan compatriots (see Section 2.3), the Christian tribes were often made up of shifting units who ranged over wide areas, and precise details of tribal locations, affiliations and movements are not consistently recorded and not always clear.

These tribes were to be found in regions extending from Syria to southern Arabia, and from the Mediterranean to the Persian Gulf. Many of their rulers were known for their devotion to literature and the arts, and their encouragement of poetry. Christians were to make a great contribution to the creation and dissemination of the Arabic script and language, and to learning in general.

Among the numerous tribes and clans of Syria, Palestine, Mesopotamia and the Arabian peninsula, several deserve special mention as they played a significant part in history, both before and after the advent of Islam. The text below indicates the location of the Christian tribes roughly between AD 300 and AD 600.

Syria and the north-west territories of Arabia were occupied by several branches of the great Kodaa confederation, once widespread in southern Arabia and by the second century AD dispersed through the Hejaz and Mesopotamia.

The best-known among them were the Tanukh tribe, who settled south of Palmyra, near Lebanon, under their chief Numan ibn Amr ibn Malik (d. 270). Probably the most famous of the Tanukh rulers was Queen Mawiya (d. 375), whose chief propagandist of the Christian cause was her bishop, the monk Moses, with a diocese covering many of the nomad tribes in Mawiya's time. As a result of the efforts of missionaries like Moses, most of the Syrian tribes were converted to Christianity.

Related to the Tanukh were the nomadic Bahra tribe, who wandered between Palmyra and Damascus. The area south of Damascus, known as Ituraea, was occupied by the Salih. The ruling clan of Salih was converted to Christianity in about AD 365. Another branch of the Kodaa confederation, known as the Udhra, inhabited the land east of modern Amman and gave their name to a genre of Arabic love poetry. These and other related tribes all had their own bishops.

Somewhat further to the north, in upper Palestine, were a tribe belonging to the large and widespread Azd confederation who, bringing with them the idol of their deity Ayim, had likewise migrated from the south in the second century AD, spreading eastwards towards Oman and north towards, and then beyond, central Arabia. This tribe, called the Ghassan, came to rest in the Transjordan in about AD 250. They fought a famous battle on what became known as the Day of Halima, defeating the Syrian Arabs and taking over their territory.

The royal house of Ghassan embraced (Monophysite) Christianity and ruled (AD 292–640) over parts of Palestine and the western side of the Syrian Desert, with a capital near Damascus and a second capital at Bostra, once a Nabataean centre and now under a bishopric. The Ghassan built many churches and monasteries, and Christianity continued in the dynastic line down to its close. Under the quickening impulse of Hellenistic culture they reached a high degree of civilization.

With the coming of Islam the Ghassan played a significant part in the spread of learning in and around their territory. As a Muslim chronicler described them, 'They were Lords in the days of ignorance [before Muhammad], and Stars in the time of Islam.'

Off and on for long periods the Byzantine-supported Ghassan were involved in a struggle for influence over the Arab tribes, their rivals being the Persian-backed kingdom of Hira ruled by the Lakhmid kings (see below). In 529 the Byzantine emperor Justinian bestowed on the Ghassan ruler

Harith III ibn Jabala the rank of *phylarch*, the highest Byzantine rank below that of emperor.

The last Ghassanid prince, Jabala II (d. 637), was sheltered by the Byzantine court, where he was greatly honoured. The Byzantines continued to give asylum to other notables who sought refuge from the Muslims, such as Zarr ibn Sardus of the Tayi tribe. In about 710 a certain al-Wabisi of the Korayshi clan of Makhzum, unwilling to remain a Muslim, went to Byzantium, became a Christian, married, and died there. Many other Arabs continued to take the same route to safety. A Saracen named Samonas became a friend of the emperor Leo VI (d. 912) and later entered a monastery.

South of the Ghassan principality were the Bali tribe of the Kodaa confederation, who occupied certain areas of central Palestine around Galilee. Like the Amila and Judham (below), the Bali were largely Christian, and all three are listed among the tribes who fought against Muhammad's army at the battle of Mota.

The Amila are said by some scholars to be of Aramaean origin; some identify them with the Amalekites of the Old Testament (Num. 13:29); others believe they are descended from Abimael, son of Joktan (Gen. 10:28); and still others believe they may be related to the Jurham, who overcame them in the Hejaz, after which they settled in central Palestine.

The widespread Judham tribe (also known as the Amr ibn Adi) belonged to the Kodaa confederation, and are thought to be related to, if not the same as, the Jurham, though this is disputed. Driven from the Hejaz, they settled around the area of Hijr and westward along the coast of the Red Sea and the southern part of Sinai, with their capital at Ayla (Akaba). In about 350, under Nabataean influence, the Judham were converted to Christianity. The area in the environs of Sinai was dotted with their church buildings. Their church leaders in the middle of the fifth century included the bishops Abdulla (Abdellas) and Haritha (Aretas).

The leading tribe of the Syrian desert were the Kalb, who came to be regarded as the supreme representatives of the Kahtan (southern) Arabs, as the Christian Kayis were of the Adnan (northern) Arabs. They too belonged to the Kodaa confederation and migrated north, establishing their capital at Duma. In pagan times Duma had been the seat of a line of Arab queens or high priestesses, whose chief deities were Atar (Ishtar), Dai, Abirillu and Nuhai.

In Duma the Kalb tribe adopted the Christian faith. Among the more notable members of this tribe was Zayid ibn Haritha, the adopted son of Muhammad. In October 630 Muhammad sent an armed force against the Christians of Duma.The Kalb later became the chief supporters of the Omayyad caliphate, and the caliph Muawiya took a wife from that tribe, who became the mother of Yazid I.

South of the Banu Kalb territory were the Banu Tayi, also of Kahtan stock. Though largely nomadic, they settled in large numbers in and around the ancient town of Tayma, founded, according to tradition, by Tema, son of Ishmael (Gen. 25:15). Tayma, as we have seen, was famed from the time of the ancient Egyptians and Mesopotamians as a beautiful and prosperous oasis on the desert route between the head of the Red Sea and the head of the Persian Gulf, and controlled the trade route from the Hejaz to Syria. It had a large population of non-Arabs, including some Jewish settlements.

The Banu Tayi were said to have 'passed their lives in idolatry', until their conversion to Christianity. One of their members was Hatim Tayi (fl. c. AD 590), who lived before Muhammad and whose name in eastern legend is proverbial for hospitality. Muhammad said that when he heard a people praised he found when he actually met them that they fell short of his estimate. The exception were the Banu Tayi, who exceeded his highest expectations in possessing the most excellent virtues. Their name was so well known that the inhabitants of Arabia were at times referred to by outsiders as the Banu Tayi. With the coming of Islam most were forced to convert.

The Buyan clan, an offshoot of the Tayi, were renowned for their literary skills and for a new type of writing elaborated by them. The invention of the Arabic script is ascribed to three Buyan scholars.

Among the pagan tribes of the northern Hejaz were a community of Christians, mainly from the Judham and Tayi, who had settled in the hill-girt oasis of El Ola in the region once occupied by the Thamud and Lihyan tribes. Another group, also from Tayi, had set up hermitages in the Wadi al-Kora, 'Valley of Villages', made up of an almost continuous line of oases. Situated north of Medina and west of Khaybar, the valley also contained Jewish settlements.

In a remote part of the Medinan oasis dwelt the Christian tribe of Ganim – part of the Azd confederation – who were related to the (non-Christian) Aus and Khazraj tribes of Medina. In AD 630 their place of worship was burned down on Muhammad's orders.

There was also a small Christian community in Medina itself, but the chief settlements were Jewish, and Judaism had a powerful impact on the social structure prevailing there (Muir, 1912, p. 116), both before and during Muhammad's time.

Ranging over an extensive area between the Hejaz and Nejd were the Christian clan of Asad, related to the (non-Christian) Koraysh tribe (Trimingham, 1979, p. 263). Among the more important members of the Asad clan were the reformer Tolayha; Khadija, the first wife of Muhammad; Waraka, a cousin of Khadija; and Othman ibn Huwayrith.

Ibn Hisham and others relate that Othman ibn Huwayrith, a leading Meccan and also a cousin of Khadija, appalled by the idolatry prevailing in the Kaaba, went to the Byzantine court, where he was honourably received and was converted to Christianity. In about 605, some time before Muhammad's mission began, Othman returned to Mecca and, on the strength of an imperial grant, laid claim to the government of the city, intending to reform the pagan religion. Opposed by the ruling Meccans, he fled to Syria, where the Meccans were able to procure his assassination two years later. In later Muslim tradition he was often classed as a hanif.

Several scattered tribes, large and small and mostly nomadic, occupied the Jezira, northern Mesopotamia. The tribes of that region and of the Syrian steppe seem to have been almost entirely Christian (Kennedy, 1986, p. 20).

Chief of these tribes were the Taghlib (also known as the Banu Hind), who originally came from Nejd in central Arabia. The first batch of Taghlib migrants to the north settled along the upper Euphrates around AD 450, shortly after which they were converted to Christianity. The remaining Taghlib clans in Nejd became involved in a forty-year war with the tribe of Bakr, which ended in AD 534. This war was famous in ancient poetry as the War of Basus. After the war, the remnants went north to join the other members of the tribe.

The Taghlib were conquered by the caliph Omar but refused to pay the *jizya* (the tax levied on non-Muslims), saying that, as Arabs, they should be exempt. They were therefore taxed like Muslims. The historian Yahya ibn Jarir (d. 1079) records that the Taghlib still remained Christian in his time, more than 300 years after the Prophet's death.

Somewhat south of the Taghlib were the Iyad tribe (or Iyad ibn Nizar), originally from Yamama and claiming desent from Maad, son of Adnan, ancestor of Muhammad. In the course of their migration northwards, their forbear Iyad (from whom they derive their name) raised a sacred tower in Mecca, probably in the style of a Mesopotamian ziggurat. They were also said to have built a cubical edifice, known as the Kaaba, in Sindad, between Kufa and Basra (Faris, 1952, p. 39).

They finally came to rest along the upper Euphrates valley, setting up their capital at Anbar, which had been an important town from the time of the Parthians. By AD 420 Anbar had become a Christian stronghold whose people had a reputation for learning and were famous for the use of a lapidary form of writing (see Section 4.2).

The Lakhmid tribe belonged to the Kahtan (southern) branch of Arabs, but had strong Adnan (north-Arab) affiliations as well. They ruled (AD 268–605) an area between Syria and Mesopotamia, with their capital at Hira (from Syriac *herta*, 'camp'), situated along the lower Euphrates. The site around Hira was a place of age-old sacrosanctity, revered in folklore as the burial-place of Adam and Noah.

As the Ghassan rulers, with territory extending over large parts of Syria, were favoured by the Byzantines, so the Lakhmids, whose domain extended over much of modern Iraq, were favoured by the Persian Sassanians. In

AD 325, Shahpur II of Persia granted the Lakhmid ruler Imru al-Kayis the title of 'King of all the Arabs', a title that was enshrined in an inscription at Namara dated AD 328, which is the oldest inscription in the Arabic language (Rodinson, 1976, p. 27).

The Lakhmids reached a high degree of cultural development, and in AD 410 Yazdagird I of Persia entrusted Numan I, the ruler of Hira, with the education of his son Bahram Gur, the great hunter celebrated in Persian legend. At the end of his reign Numan I renounced the world to become an anchorite.

From AD 510 Hira was the seat of a Nestorian bishopric, but not all the Lakhmid kings were Christian, and two were known never to have relinquished their allegiance to the goddess Ozza. But they married into Christian families, and their subjects were generally Christians, and so were many of the smaller tribes living in Lakhmid territory.

Hind, wife of Mundhir III (d. 554) of Hira, founded a monastery with a commemorative inscription that described her as 'daughter of a king, mother of a king, and bondmaid of Christ'. The monastery was long remembered in Islamic annals.

The Numan dynasty of Hira is frequently mentioned by Arab historians, and the court was known as the rendezvous of the poets and intelligentsia of the day. Like the Persian nobles, prominent Arabs would send their sons to the Christian schools of Hira if they wanted them to learn how to read and write.

The Arabic language, the Arabic script, and Arabic poetry all owe a great deal to this the most extraordinary of all the Christian states of pre-Islamic Arabia (see Chapter 4). Indeed, it was in Hira that a poetic and literary language was born that was to evolve into the language of universal usage among intellectuals throughout the peninsula.

From the middle of the sixth century the Sassanian kings began to treat Hira more and more as a vassal state, and the rulers of Hira in turn began to seek stronger alliances with their own Arab people. Numan IV (d. 602), another Christian ruler famed in Arabic poetry, aroused the suspicion of the Persians because of his increasing association with other Arab leaders, especially the Christian tribe of Bakr, and consequently he was overthrown and slain by Khosro II Parviz and the Lakhmid dynasty was abolished.

The fall of this buffer state – combined with the victory of the Bakr tribe over the Persians three years later – greatly facilitated the Arab conquest of the Persian empire. Several centuries after Islam, considerable numbers of the inhabitants in and around Hira remained attached to their Christian faith. The town of Najaf, famous in Shia history, grew out of the town of Hira.

In the area a little to the north of Hira there were thriving Christian communities locally known as the Ibad al-Masih, 'slaves of Christ', who eventually constituted a clan called the Ibad. In time they took over a nearby pagan shrine dedicated to the goddess Ozza (to whom animal and, it was said, human sacrifices once used to be offered) and built a church there. Here by the Euphrates in around 560 they established their capital, known as Akula, which had its own bishop.

As the town of Hira had formed the nucleus for the Muslim town of Najaf, so Akula was to grow into the town of Kufa (Trimingham, 1979, p. 171), famed for its learned men and its school of grammarians and jurists. In AD 635 Kufa received a large influx of Christians, expelled from Najran. The fourth caliph destroyed the Kufa church in 660, and made Kufa his own capital, bringing marble pillars from buildings in nearby Hira.

One of the main sources of information about the extent of Christian influence in the whole of this area was a book by the Arab historian Hisham al-Kalbi (d. 820), entitled *The Churches and Monasteries of Hira and the Genealogies of the Ibadis*. The original is lost, but was often quoted by later geographers and historians.

South of the Banu Ibad were the Ijl, who had set themselves up between Hira and Basra. This mainly Christian tribe had settlements further to the south as well.

In the Tigris–Euphrates delta lay the Arab principality of Charax, with its capital at Obula, near the Persian Gulf – a site once occupied by Alexander's Greeks and later by the Parthians. In the fourth century AD, Arabs from Hira built a small monastery some miles east of Obula. Situated amid groves of date palms, it was a pleasant spot in an otherwise inhospitable climate.

Here in 638 the Muslims founded Basra, the town of Sinbad the Sailor. In time this town was to become as famous in Muslim history as Kufa. The scholars of Basra became the best readers and exponents of the Koran, and made signal contributions to the growth of the Arabic language. In literature, theology and politics, Basra and Kufa were to play a more important role than most other cities of the Muslim world. Watt writes that in the early Abbasid period Basra was the scene of important intellectual advances, notably the acceptance of certain aspects of Greek thought (1990, p. 87).

In south-western Iraq lived the Adnan tribes of Rabia, Namir and, further to the south, Mudar – predominantly Christian, and all with their own churches. One branch of the Mudar was the non-Christian Kinana group, to which the Koraysh tribe of Muhammad belonged. The Rabia and Mudar were frequently in conflict, especially after their conversion to Islam. Both tribes played a decisive part in the conquests made during the Omayyad caliphate.

The coast along the Arabian side of the Persian Gulf, once known as Bahrain (called Dilmun in Sumerian inscriptions), was a hive of Christian missionary activity. Till the early Islamic period Bahrain embraced a coastal area larger than the island of Bahrain today. It started where the 'two rivers' (*bahrain*) meet in southern Iraq to form the Shatt al-Arab (O'Leary, 1927, p. 10) and continued along the coast to Hasa (ancient Gerrha), Kuwait and the peninsula of Qatar.

Christian enterprise was not confined to the coastal regions but was also to be found inland from the littoral, both in the villages and among the nomadic tribes. Hasa, Hajar, Qatar and the territory between Qatar and Oman each ranked as a Nestorian diocese.

Chief among the Christian tribes in these areas were the Bakr (or Bakr ibn Wayil), who in AD 502 threatened the borders of Syria until the Byzantine emperor Anastasius I made a treaty with them and bought them off. They later achieved considerable renown when in 605 they inflicted a severe defeat on the Persians at Dhu Kar, near Kufa – a victory long celebrated by Arab poets and writers. As already stated, the demise of the Lakhmid buffer state and the defeat of the Persians by the Bakr armies opened the way for the Muslim conquest of Persia.

Another tribal group related to the Bakr were the Kayis (or Abdul Kayis), once of Najran, who had settled around Bahrain, Qatar and the adjacent areas. In AD 575 a bishopric was established in Bahrain to administer their churches. Inland from Bahrain and somewhat to the north and west of the Kayis were the Christian tribe of Ayub.

By about the middle of the third century AD scattered groups of yet another Christian tribe, the Mazun (Mazon, Magan), belonging to the Azd confederation, had penetrated into the region of Oman (Muscat), an ancient source of copper supply. There was soon a flourishing community of Christians there, and in about 424 a bishopric was established in Oman, with its capital at the important textile and trading centre of Sohar on the coast. When the Muslims took over Oman they allowed the Mazun to remain Christian only on condition that they surrender half their lands and property. Many of the Mazun did, and continued in their faith.

Further south, beyond the borders of Oman, the state of Dhofar also had a large Christian community, with a bishop at the port town of Moscha.

The Christian tribes of Nejd and Yamama were strongly influenced by Nestorian missionaries. One of these tribes, the Tamim, related to the Ayub, were spread over large parts of eastern Arabia. They had been instrumental in establishing the dominant position of the Koraysh in Mecca, but in about 450 BC they were accused by the other tribes of having robbed the Kaaba. The Koraysh, grateful for the help they had received, invested them with important religious and judicial duties.

From an early date the Tamim had assumed charge of the annual poetry festival that used to take place at Okaz. This function they continued even after their conversion to Christianity, presiding over the contest as judges. Two famous poets of the Tamim tribe were Jarir and Farazdak, both Christians.

Because of the beauty and cultural attainments of the women of Tamim, they were favoured as wives by the men of the aristocratic families among the Koraysh. The famous and much maligned female reformer Sajaz came from the Tamim, and in the course of her controversial career she received much support from the members of her clan. During Muhammad's time some members of the Tamim reluctantly accepted Islam, but after his death they fell away, only to be forced back into submission.

One of the Tamim clans was the Najia. Also Christian, and also compelled to accept Islam, they staged a Kharijite revolt against the caliph Ali. Many returned to the Christian faith and boasted of their Christianity to Ali's troops when captured (Trimingham, 1979, p. 279).

Still further south were the influential Hanifa, a branch of the Bakr tribe (Muir, 1912, p. 457), Christian, and widely dispersed in Yamama. Hauda ibn Ali, one of the Christian rulers to whom Muhammad sent a letter urging conversion (see Section 6.14), and his successor, the reformer Musaylima, belonged to this tribe. Following their conversion to Islam, several members of this and other Yamama tribes became famous as Koran reciters.

South of Nejd lay the region of Najran. Its capital, also called Najran, was on an important caravan route connecting southern Arabia with the Hejaz and the Mediterranean, and eastwards across Nejd with the Persian Gulf and beyond.

The Persian-born Arab historian al-Tabari (d. 923), recounting an earlier history, tells of a wandering Syrian ascetic named Fimiyun (Phemion? Euphemius?) who supported himself by trade as a builder. He was captured by the bedouin, taken to Najran, and sold into slavery, probably some time in AD 460. Here he converted many of the Arabs to Christianity, and founded the first Najran church.

The town of Najran was the venue of an annual fair that was as significant for the south as the fair at Okaz, near Mecca, was for the Hejaz. At the Najran fair, monks would take the opportunity of preaching to the heathen Arabs. As a result of their efforts, practically all the population of Najran had become Christian by the end of the fifth century (Glubb, 1979, p. 51). There was a period of disruption when in 524 Dhu Nuwas, the Jewish ruler of Himyar, invaded Najran and started a persecution of the Christians, until he was defeated by the Abyssinians – allies of Byzantium – in the following year.

The historian Ibn Hisham refers to Najran as having the 'religion of the king' – that is, the Byzantine emperor. Najran had a cathedral, described as a very splendid edifice, with striped marble and mosaics donated by the Byzantine sovereign (O'Leary, 1927, p. 144). The Christian communities in Najran, owning large leather industries and textile factories producing the famous 'Yemeni garments', constituted perhaps the wealthiest population in Arabia.

Najran had a far more developed political life than any other contemporary Arab state of the time. It was governed by a *sayid* ('exalted one'), who dealt with external affairs, commerce and defence; an *akib*, who was his deputy and generally looked after internal matters; and a bishop, who looked after the clergy and church affairs. (The term 'sayid' was later used for a descendant of the Prophet.) The aristocracy of Najran, headed by the Dayan family, made generous contributions to the church and its works, and poets spoke of them as being 'the noblest of the Arabs'.

There were two great tribes in Najran, each with a large proportion of Christians. One was the Harith, who had settled in the north-west and were responsible for building a 'kaaba' in Najran – a large monastic establishment extolled in Arabic writings as an asylum for the oppressed. It also served as a place of pilgrimage for Arab Christians.

The second great tribe was the more widely diffused Kinda, who had spread throughout southern and central Arabia, some even migrating as far as Palestine and Syria and forming alliances with the Maad and other Adnan tribes of the north. The Kinda tribe were ruled by a Christian dynasty notable for its patronage of poets and its dedication to learning. The Islamic philosopher Yakub al-Kindi (d. 868), known to the West as Alkindus, and Abdul Masih al-Kindi (d. 915), an Arab Christian author of an anti-Islamic apologia (*risala*), were both descended from the royal family of Kinda.

Najran remained Christian until the caliph Omar forced its Christians' conversion and then exiled many of them to Kufa (see Section 10.19).

Still further south, along the foot of the peninsula (Yemen, Himyar, Hadramaut), Christian influences had entered both from Najran and from Abyssinia. In his history of the church, Philostorgus (d. 439) relates that in 342 the Byzantine emperor Constantius sent an embassy headed by a bishop, Theophilus the Indian, bearing rich gifts, including two hundred Cappadocian horses, to obtain permission from the Himyarite king to build churches in his kingdom. Sanction was given, and one church was built in 'the Roman market of Adanon' (Aden), another at Hormuz (probably Kane, named after Hormuz in the Persian Gulf by Persian traders) and the largest at Zafar, south of Sanaa, which was adorned with marble and mosaic also presented by the Byzantine emperor.

In about 345 the Abyssinian negus gained control of certain south-Arabian provinces – under the title (preserved in an inscription) 'King of Aksum, Himyar, Saba and Raydan' – and attempted to establish Christianity as the state religion. This first occupation (345–75) was brought to an end when the Abyssinians were overthrown by an Arab chief who founded a Jewish kingdom.

There was said to have been another brief period of Christian rule in Himyar, when a Christian usurper named Abd Kelal set up a short-lived regime (455–60) in Saba, but the facts about this, as indeed about other matters relating to this period, were never clear and still remain confused.

In any event, it would appear that Christianity continued to thrive in many parts of the south, with several active churches by the end of the fifth century.

The Abyssinian governor Sumyafa, installed during the Abyssinian occupation in 525 after the death of Dhu Nuwas, acknowledged the over-lordship of the negus and ruled the south, from the capital at Sanaa, as governor on behalf of his Aksumite sovereign. Sumyafa is known from at least four south-Arabian inscriptions, one of which is dedicated 'in the name of the Merciful [al-Rahman] and of his son, Christ Triumphant' (Philby, 1947, p. 121).

(It was some time after this, in about 550, that Christian missionaries probably from Himyar travelled to the Nubian state of Alodia on the Nile, whose capital, Soba, was situated near present-day Khartoum, where Christianity became established as the state religion in 580 (Trimingham, 1979, p. 302).)

In 530 an ambitious official of Syrian origin named Abraha displaced Sumyafa and, after a fruitless attempt to set up independent rule, obtained recognition as viceroy of the negus. He carried through a scheme for reconstructing the Marib dam, and it is to this circumstance that we owe one of the most famous of all south-Arabian inscriptions. Marked by a cross, it records the major repairs undertaken, beginning with the words 'By the might and majesty and mercy of the Merciful [al-Rahman] and of his Mes-siah and of the Holy Ghost, I Abraha, recorded this inscription.' It also tells of an epidemic, probably smallpox, which prevailed in the Marib district at this time.

Abraha received the envoys of many distinguished rulers who came to offer congratulations. They included those from his own sovereign, the negus of Abyssinia, from the Byzantine emperor Justinian, from the Persian king Khosro I, and from the Christian Arab kings of the northern borders, namely Mundhir III, ruler of Hira, and Harith III ibn Jabala, ruler of the Ghassan kingdom (Philby, 1947, p. 122).

In Sanaa, Abraha built a magnificent church known as the Kalis (from Greek *ecclesia*, 'church'), which was hailed as the wonder of the age. His hope was to make it a centre of pilgrimage for the south, much as the Kaaba was for the Hejaz. A group of Meccans, resenting this attempt to divert pilgrim traffic from Mecca, came to Sanaa and defiled the church by defecat-ing in it. In another account, they assassinated one of Abraha's allies.

In reprisal, Abraha marched to Mecca in about 550 with a large army of Arabs and Abyssinians. One of the things that left an impression on the Meccans was the presence of elephants in Abraha's army, and Abraha's route became known as the Elephant Road. On the way Abraha also seized two hundred camels belonging to Abdul Muttalib (Muhammad's grandfather-to-be), who at the time was the most influential person in Mecca.

Abdul Muttalib sought a meeting with Abraha, who assured him that he had not come to make war. Abdul Muttalib said, 'By God, we seek not war, in which we are not skilled. I only want my camels.' The astonished Abraha said, 'What! Do you speak of your camels, and fail to speak of the temple venerated by you and your fathers which I have come to destroy?' Disconcerted, the Meccan replied, 'The camels are mine, but the temple belongs to another and is his to defend. Only give me back my camels' (Nicholson, 1969, p. 67). The camels were restored to Abdul Muttalib, who then tried to plead the cause of the Meccans and persuade the invader to turn from his design.

As it happened the invading army was stricken with smallpox, and Abraha was forced to retire. The word for smallpox in Arabic also means 'little stones', in reference to the hard pustules that form in the disease, and the Koran in referring to the incident (105:1) speaks of flocks of birds hurling stones at the invaders.

In a later tradition Muhammad was said to have been born in the 'year of the elephant' (am al-fil), the year of Abraha's invasion, in order to establish a portentous connection between the birth of the Prophet and the failure of Abraha to take the holy temple. In fact Muhammad was born some two decades later. According to al-Zuhri (d. 742), Muhammad was born eighteen years later; according to Ibn al-Kalbi (d. 820), twenty-three years after the year of the elephant.

Abraha died on his return to the south, and the despotic rule of his two successors prompted a local Himyar leader named Sayif ibn Dhu Yazan to appeal to the court of Hira, through whose help he obtained the intervention of the Persians.

A seaborne expedition from Persia drove out the Abyssinians in 756, and turned part of Himyar into a Persian province. And so it remained for more than fifty years. The Persians appointed local rulers to govern their own districts, all under a succession of Persian satraps residing at Sanaa.

The last satrap was Badhan, who ruled during the reign of the Sassanian monarch Khosro II Parviz, and he submitted to the Muslims in AD 628. Two years later the Himyarites were coerced into accepting Islam.

4

ARABIC BEFORE ISLAM

The important part played by Christians in the development of the Arabic language, in the creation of the Arabic script, and in laying the foundations of Arabic poetry, grammar and lexicography still remains to be explored in detail, and can be referred to only briefly in this book. It need hardly be said that the possession of a common language was of vital importance in the writing of the Koran, the propagation of Muhammad's message and the subsequent expansion of Islam.

4.1 The Arabic Language

Arabic, one of the Semitic group of languages, was in a fairly advanced state of development before Islam, and was popularly understood in most parts of Arabia by about AD 480. Poets were composing in this medium, and reformers like Koss ibn Sayda and Omayya of Tayif were using it in their teachings.

The language owed its advancement largely to the patronage of the Christian principalities of Arabia, notably the Lakhmids of Hira, who were the first to adopt it as their official language. This they did in 520, and by the end of the sixth century it had spread over almost the whole of the peninsula through the work of poets and wandering minstrels.

This literary Arabic, with its refinements of grammar and its wide vocabulary, contained a large admixture of non-Arabic words borrowed direct from foreign tongues, mainly Aramaic, Syriac (the spoken vernacular of the Christian communities best-known to the Arabs), Hebrew, Pahlavi (the language of Sassanian Persia), Ethiopic (mainly shipping and nautical terms) and Greek, including the Greek of Ionia (Yunan) and Byzantium ('Roum').

The new language grew rapidly all the time, with alterations taking place in its structure, vocabulary and forms of expression. The Hejaz, being at the crossroads of international trade, was exposed more than any other part of Arabia to foreign influences, and it was here that what later came to be known as Koranic Arabic evolved; all the properties of Koranic Arabic were familiar in the Hejaz before Muhammad appeared on the scene.

After Islam, further progress in the development of Arabic was made by writers and scholars who came principally from once-Christian centres like Najaf (formerly Hira), Kufa (once Akula), and Basra (raised on an earlier Christian foundation). Both Kufa and Basra were especially famed for the eloquence and correct speech of the inhabitants, who carried on, in a now Muslim environment, the cultural traditions of the Lakhmid dynasty.

4.2 The Arabic Script

Long before the Arabic script was invented, different forms of writing were used for the many regional vernaculars spoken in Arabia, some going back centuries before the Christian era. They are found in various inscriptions graven or scratched on rocks, of which the earliest examples, in south Arabia, are in the Mosnad script, employed for writing the Himyarite, Sabaean, Minaean and other southern dialects.

There are also pre-Islamic inscriptions in Thamudic, Lihyanite, and Safaite (named after Safa, south-west of Damascus) – mainly variations of south-Arabian scripts. Other noteworthy examples, written in the Mosnad, Aramaic, Nabataean, Syriac and Greek scripts, are found at Hijr (AD 267); Namara (AD 328); Zabad, south-west of Aleppo (AD 512); and Harran (AD 568).

It is thought that some rudimentary form of writing allied to the south-Arabian scripts was probably used in the Hejaz as early as AD 520, though no evidence of this survives. Both Hebrew and Syriac were also known to have been used in the region.

The early history of the Arabic script remains obscure and confused; reliable references are lacking and sources are fragmentary. Many of the old traditions on the subject, first compiled by Hisham al-Kalbi (d. 820) and Haytham ibn Adi (d. 821), supplemented with material from an account given by Baladhuri (d. 892), were put into a semblance of order by the Bactrian historian Ibn Khalikan (d. 1282).

It is said that about AD 510 three persons of the clan of Buyan of the Christian tribe of Tayi adapted the letters of the Aramaic alphabet – used by the Nabataeans since the second century AD – to produce the main outlines of the Arabic script, consisting of twenty-two letters. This script was later improved by Moramir ibn Morra of Anbar, capital of the Christian tribe of Iyad. 'Moramir' is the Arabized name of a Syriac scholar called Mar Amer, and he added six more letters, making a total of twenty-eight.

The shape of the new letters was adapted from an angular model of the early Syriac, and was perfected in the course of time by the Christian calligraphers of Akula of the tribe of Ibad, who themselves had acquired it from the Iyad tribe. This was a lapidary form of writing, also known as the monumental style, which had been used by Christian stone-cutters for engraving scriptural verses on the walls of churches. In time, the town of Akula where this development took place was renamed Kufa, after which this style of writing came to be known as *Kufic*; it was employed mainly for monumental purposes, and was later adapted for the ornamental writing of the Koran.

The Kufic alphabet in its modified form was brought to Hira, and it was here that a cursive or flowing style of writing called *naskhi* was developed by copyists and used in transcribing manuscripts. The scholar al-Suli (d. 946), in tracing the beginnings of the Arabic alphabet, tells how the Arabs learned the art of writing from the people of Hira (Grunebaum, 1961, p. 344).

It was from Hira too that the words for book (*kitab*) and writer (*katib*) were spread among the Arabs. Other words related to writing that entered Arabic were those for scroll (*sijili*), tome (*sifr*), reed or pen (*kalam*; Greek *kalamos*), page (*sahif*) and parchment (*kirtas*).

In about 560 a Christian prince of Kalb named Bishr ibn Abdul Malik – elder brother of Okaydir, ruler of Duma – who had acquired his writing skills in Hira, visited Mecca and taught *naskhi* to Harb ibn Omayya, father of Abu Sofyan. Harb in turn introduced the new skill to others, and it soon displaced the older forms of writing in use till then.

This Arabic script, first created and propagated by Arab Christians became the script through which the Koran was eventually to be transmitted.

There were still several drawbacks in the script as it had evolved so far, and these drawbacks were present at the time the Koran was compiled. At first, all the letters of the Arabic alphabet (in common with other Semitic scripts) represented only consonants (Diringer, 1947, p. 275), the signs to indicate vowels being introduced much later. For long, therefore, early written Arabic remained a kind of imperfect shorthand.

Many Arabic words are made up of triliteral (three-letter) roots, and often a number of related words are formed from the same root. So, in the absence of vowels, the root QTL, 'kill', may read QaTL, 'killing', QaTaLa, 'he killed', QaTiL, 'a killer', and so on – a situation that left room for erroneous readings.

Furthermore, just as in English the consonants HRD (without vowels) may be read as HaRD, HeRD, HoRDe, HoaRD, HeaRD, HeRoD, HiReD, so also in Arabic words made up of consonants alone may have entirely different and unrelated meanings.

Again, just as in English the letter *c* does service for two sounds, *k* (come) and *s* (cent), so in the old Arabic script – which did not adequately distinguish between letters of the same shape, like *ba* and *ta*, *jim* and *he*, *sin* and *shin*, and so on – identical letters, lacking as they did any marks to distinguish them, might indicate more than one consonantal sound.

As Nicholson points out, 'It is possible to read the same combination of consonants, bnt, nbt, byt, tnb, ntb, nyb, and in various other ways' (1969, p. 201). Words made up of such consonants become clear in meaning only from the context in which they occur, or from the way in which they are vocalized.

In brief, Arabic at this time was written with consonants alone; there were no points to differentiate between consonants of the same shape; there were no signs to indicate vowels; there were no diacritical marks of any kind.

Finally, the words in early Arabic sentences were often joined together, with no spaces between them and with nothing to indicate pauses or to separate sentences, the reader having to guess the necessary divisions as he went along. All this was to become highly significant for the accurate reading and interpretation of the Koran.

Some of these shortcomings were subsequently remedied as a result of innovations based on Nestorian Christian practice (see Section 7.9).

4.3 Poetry

Among the early Arabs, prose or the language of everyday life was not regarded as worthy of perpetuation or remembrance, and no noteworthy prose from the pre-Islamic period has come down to us. Poetry, on the other hand, was taken more seriously, for it embodied the power of the inspired word, which was not manifest in prose. But opinion on the subject was divided, and Arabs tended to vary in their attitude towards poets.

Generally, the poet was thought of as half-insane. He depended for his inspiration on powers from the unseen, which might be malevolent. He was looked upon as a sorcerer or magician (sahir). He might be bewitched (mashur) or even possessed by jinn (majnun). Evil spirits might use him for communicating messages which were false and intended to deceive (see Section 5.14).

Poetry was seen as the language of incantation and magical formulas, and the aid of a poet was frequently sought by individuals or tribal groups for execrations and maledictions. Often the poet would cover his head in a mantle (burda), as if secretly summoning spirits to give him a revelation. Like the sorcerer, the poet used 'oathing formulas', swearing by things on earth and in heaven to lend support to his pronouncements and call down the potency of the things named.

The concept of the poet as a necromancer or a man possessed had a special relevance to Muhammad's personal views on poets and the nature of what they said.

There was, however, another and more favourable view of poets. It was believed that during his inspirational moods the poet might be regarded as a knower (shayir), or a diviner and soothsayer (kahin), whose ecstatic raptures were worthy of serious reflection. Also, the poet was capable of extemporizing verses suitable for any occasion. When called upon to do so he could invoke blessings, and as such was deemed a benefactor. But, although his improvisations were sometimes recognized as prophetic in character, he never achieved the status of a prophet in the Old Testament sense.

Arab poets of old, and especially the court poets, were preoccupied with form and style, the melody of words, the rhythms of balanced phrases, the music and harmony that emerged from the interplay of vowels and consonants, and the beauty of expression. They discovered new metres and new rhythms, developed to the full the opportunities their language offered for poetic eloquence, and set standards of excellence that later poets were long to emulate.

Even before the emergence of Islam, many types of complex prosody and subtle rhythms, along with a grand oracular style, rhetorical declamations, parallelism, assonance, alliteration, startling imagery, prosodic repetition and measured verse, had been virtually fixed and perfected.

Several kinds of verse were used, among them the *saj*, a form of rhymed and rhythmic prose made up of short phrases, which was the special mode adopted by sorcerers in pronouncing their curses and for conveying every kind of esoteric lore. Other forms were the *kasida* or ode; the *rajaz*, in iambic form; and the *ghazal* or love lyric, later perfected by the poets of the Christian tribe of Udhra. Some modes, such as the cursing rhymes, were believed to be extremely potent to harm and hurt, and the *hija* or satire could be devastating in its effects. There were also celebratory verses, eulogies, war poems and laments.

At first most of the early poetry was preserved by oral tradition through the professional reciter (*rawi*), who remembered, repeated and handed it down. Every professional poet – including those who could write – had a rawi to whom he committed his poems and who in turn transmitted them to others. Imru al-Kayis, the famous pre-Islamic poet (see below), had himself been the rawi of another poet. The poet Dhul Rumah (d. 638) could neither read nor write, but rawis took down the poems he dictated to them.

The rawi was expected to know the genealogy of the poet, to understand the allusions in the poem he took down, to relate the circumstances that prompted the poem, and to clear up any difficulties the poem presented.

In the early days regular contests in poetry, in rhymed prose and in extemporaneous rhetoric, followed by debates, used to be held at fairs in various places, such as the town of Najran in the south, at Majna not far from Mecca, at Dhul Majaz at the foot of Mount Arafat and, most famous of all, at the prosperous market town of Okaz near the valley of Nakhla, east of Mecca.

The great seven-day national gathering at Okaz was held in the month of Dhul Kada, one of the sacred months when fighting was forbidden and hostilities between any warring tribes were suspended. It was held under the aegis of the Christian tribe of Tamim, and the winning verses would be displayed near the temple shrine. The Okaz fair was the centre of old Arabian social, literary and political life. Free and fearless debate on all manner of subjects used to take place between members of different tribes, and the nature of the discussions and the results of the contests would be carried to all parts of the peninsula. 'What Okaz says today', ran the popular view, 'all Arabia will repeat tomorrow.'

The work of the early poets represents the only pre-Islamic Arabic 'literature' there is. With the coming of Islam a great deal of the material was ignored or perished through neglect, and it is indeed surprising that so much has survived.

Not long after he attained power, Muhammad put an end to the contests at Okaz, partly because of his distrust of poets (see Section 7.15) but also perhaps because the public discussions that followed might have proved inconvenient and damaging to his rising claims.

Muslim theologians too had no sympathy with the sentiments expressed in the pre-Islamic writings. The poet's praise of wine, the free expression of his love for women, his manner of living and his outlook on life, his glorification of the benighted (*jahiliya*) days before Islam, and the fact that he sometimes invoked the pagan deities did not endear him to the orthodox. It was said that anyone who later quoted the ancient poets took care to ensure that they were suitably amended to accord with Muslim sentiment – with 'Allah' substituted for 'Allat', with the old objectionable traditions expunged, and with the remaining material reshaped.

The Egyptian scholar Taha Husayn, writing in 1925, said that little of any genuine pre-Islamic literature had survived, and that whatever did had little to do with the pre-Islamic period but represented the notions of Muslims and was 'simply fabricated after the coming of Islam' (Kritzeck, 1964, p. 60). This extreme view, it must be said, needs qualification, and most scholars have no doubt that much of what has survived does represent the original work of the ancient poets.

Christians played a considerable part in the development of Arabic poetry, the patronage of the Christian princes of Arabia being especially significant. The royal courts of Ghassan, Hira and Kinda, for instance, were well known to the wandering minstrels – Christian and non-Christian – who flocked there in search of patronage and remuneration.

The court of Hira, where the art of writing had been developed earlier than in any other part of Arabia, became the favourite rendezvous for the aspiring bards of the day, and it was in Hira that the oldest written poetry in the Arabic language was produced.

Many of the famous pre-Islamic poets were Christians, or belonged to Christian tribes, or were patronized by Christian princes, and they made major contributions to the creation of new poetical forms and the development of Arabic metrical devices. Because of their Arab common background, they also shared ideas in common. Thus the poems even of non-Christians were impregnated with Christian ideas or terms of Christian connotation.

Among the poets named in the early traditions was Ayub ibn Mahruf (fl. *c.* 480) of the Tamim tribe, who, according to Ibn Arabi, was the first of the Christian Arab poets. The warrior-poet Muhalhil ibn Rabia (fl. *c.* 500) belonged to the Christian tribe of Taghlib and was said to have composed the first Arabic ode. Bistam ibn Kayis (fl. c. 510), another warrior-poet, belonged to the Christian Bakr tribe. Juhaya ibn Mudarib (fl. c. 520) came from the Christian tribe of Kinda.

The poet Samawal (Samuel) ibn Adiya (fl. c. 535), a convert to Judaism, became a byword for loyalty among the desert Arabs because he refused to surrender goods left in his custody by the poet Imru al-Kayis (who was then in Constantinople), even though his own son was put to death before his eyes. Mutalamis (d. 570), a great lover of wine, whose real name was Jarir ibn Abdul Masih, was a Christian of the Tamim tribe, attached to the court of Hira.

The poet Adi ibn Zayid (fl. c. 587) of the Ayub clan was in the service of the Persian king Khosro I, and was also patronized by the Lakhmid court of Hira. A Christian, he is chiefly remembered for his wine songs. The deep feeling that some of these poets had for their own Arab tradition is found reflected in a line from an ode by Adi in which he invoked 'The Lord of Mecca and of the Cross'.

The early accounts speak of seven outstanding odes called the Moallakat, 'esteemed'. This word is also said to signify 'suspended', because the odes – between 60 and 100 couplets each – were said to have been inscribed in letters of gold on rolls of Coptic cloth and hung on the curtains that adorned the Kaaba. They represented the most treasured verses collected over the years. To these seven odes two others were added later, making nine in all. Among these honoured verses were several composed by Christians. The following are the poets of the Moallakat.

Imru al-Kayis (d. 540), a prince of the Christian house of Kinda who spent much time at the Byzantine court, is reckoned among the greatest of the pre-Islamic poets of Arabia. The caliph Omar, who seldom praised poets, and Ali, the Prophet's son-in-law, both extolled his genius. His ode was the most honoured among the Moallakat.

Amr ibn Kulthum (d. 570), of the Christian tribe of Taghlib, the grandson of Muhalhil mentioned above, and Harith ibn Hiliza (d. 570), of the Kalb (or Bakr) tribe, resident poet at the court of Amr ibn Hind of Hira, were two other ode writers greatly esteemed for their work.

Tarafa (d. 560), a Christian of the Bakr tribe, like his maternal uncle Mutalamis before him (mentioned above), was also attached to the court of Hira. The bitter tongue of the youthful Tarafa enraged his royal patron Amr ibn Hind and led to his death by execution at the early age of twenty-four.

Antara (d. 590), an Arab-Negro warrior-poet of the Abs tribe, tried his hand at all forms of poetry and on a variety of subjects, but complained that his predecessors had left him nothing new to say and no new way of saying it.

Nabigha (d. 610), of the Lakhmid tribe, spent much time at the courts of both Hira and Ghassan. He was well acquainted with Christianity, and there is a tradition that he was a Christian, though this is denied by some.

Zuhayr (d. 625), another member of the Lakhmid tribe, may also have been a Christian, though this too is denied by some authorities. He lived to a great age and met the Prophet but did not accept Islam. 'Allah knows what is hidden and has stored it in a scroll,' he said, 'and will reveal it on the day of reckoning.'

The two poets whose odes were added to the odes of these seven were Asha and Labid. Asha (d. 629) stands in the first rank of Arab poets. It is said that Ibadi wine merchants taught him the Christian religion. He too spent much time at Hira, becoming the boon companion of one of the Lakhmid princes and a close friend of the bishop of Najran.

Labid (d. 662) belonged to the last generation of pre-Islamic poets who received the patronage of the Lakhmid rulers. He embraced Islam in 631, after which he ceased to compose. He was said to have died aged 110 years.

Pre-Islamic Arabic poetry was rooted in the life of the common folk and helped to formulate the views and outlook of the people. The poets dealt with a wide range of subjects: the wonders of nature, the pleasures of the chase, the delights of wine, romantic love, social justice, and reflections on life and death. Many were troubadours who wandered from one end of Arabia to the other, enthusiastically welcomed by tribespeople keen to hear their ballads. 'The words of the poet', it was said, 'flew across the desert faster than arrows.'

Poetry created an invisible bond between the different desert communities, and by extolling the qualities of sincerity, bravery, hospitality, resignation and other noble traits, and by commending devotion to the deities, often with an emphasis on monotheism (the power and mercy of Allah), it contributed towards reinforcing the social, moral and religious consciousness of the Arab nation.

The rich material in these poems provided the people with a link with their own past. Poets were called 'the archives of the Arab'. Their verses tell of the lost races of Arabia, like the Tasm, Jadis and Bahm; of the ancient tribes and their relationships; and of long-forgotten battles about which nothing else is known. There is a great deal about the beliefs and customs of the ancient Arabs, and about tribal lore, folk traditions and race history, which would have been completely lost but for the poems.

The study of these early poems involved tracing the lives of those who wrote them and of the peoples about whom they wrote, and an understanding of the historical and social background in which the poets lived. This in turn stimulated the writing of genealogies, biographies and histories, which in the course of time became independent branches of study.

The wide vocabulary, syntactical modes, verse structure and grammatical forms employed by the early poets became the primary sources for Arab

scholars who wished to study the origins of their language and the derivation, meaning and usage of words. Similarly, Arab scholars who later com-
mented on the origins of Islam and interpreted the text of the Koran were
of necessity drawn back to the bards and ballads of earlier times.

It is important to bear in mind that the standard of literary Arabic was
set not by the Koran but by the pre-Islamic poets, and that the study of
Arabic philology, lexicography and grammar was based not on the Koran
but on this ancient poetry (Gibb, 1974, p. 39), which supplied the most
authentic models of Arabic in its original form.

Abdulla ibn Abbas (d. 687), a cousin of the Prophet and founder of
Koranic exegesis, used to refer back to pre-Islamic poetry in order to clarify
the meaning of certain obscure words and help him in understanding the
Koran.

When a learned follower of Muhammad named Abu Aswad al-Duali
(d. 688) conceived the idea of having a simple word-book and grammar on
Koranic usage, such as Christians had devised and used for their own
scriptures, he engaged as his assistant a poet and scholar from the Christian
tribe of Abdul Kayis.

It was again from the early poets that the Arab philologist and grammarian Khalil ibn Ahmad (d. 790), of the Mazun tribe of Oman, deduced and
systematized the rules of Arabic prosody in a work that has never been
superseded.

A huge lexicographical tome of difficult and obscure words was compiled
from the works of past Arab writers – mainly the pre-Islamic poets – by the
theologian and scholar Abu Obayd al-Kasim Sallam (d. 839), the son of a
Greek slave from Herat.

5

THE MECCAN PERIOD

The pre-Islamic Arabs did not have a historical or biographical tradition (see Section 13.12), and information about the ancestry and early life of Muhammad seems to have been pieced together by his first biographers from the professional storyteller (*kass*) and tribal sources.

This information had been transmitted orally for more than a century before being committed to writing, so that no Muslim biography of Muhammad has come down to us that can be dated before one hundred years after his death. Not a single one of the known biographers had any personal acquaintance with the Prophet. There are no Gospels in Islam.

All those who passed on the story of the Prophet's life, as well as most of the early chroniclers, seemed to have had three objectives in mind: (1) to sort out the details of Muhammad's antecedents and family history and formulate a consistent account from the often conflicting material; (2) to provide a record of Muhammad's raiding expeditions and military campaigns (*maghazi*), in which they appear to have been more interested than in his religious development, so that he became the inspiration of Muslim conquerors; (3) to explain or provide a context for the many ambiguous passages in the Koran (see Section 7.12).

The order of events in Muhammad's life was not always clear, and in none of the early biographies was a serious attempt made to arrange the material in chronological sequence. Dates are mentioned anecdotally, referring to events which themselves cannot always be dated – 'six years after the death of Amina' or 'eight years after the death of Abu Talib', for example.

The date of Muhammad's birth is unknown. The dates and details of his early youth and religious development must remain only partially known. Muhammad at that time was an unimportant figure, and no one thought it worth while to take notice of what he said or did. The date of his first revelation is approximate. All dates before AD 622, when Muhammad, aged about fifty-two, left Mecca to take refuge in Medina, and which marks the beginning of Muslim chronology, are matters of dispute.

Besides the lack of a fixed chronology, there is insufficient information about many features of Muhammad's personal and public life. Thus the first two-thirds of his life are known mainly in broad outline (Dermenghem, 1958, p. 5), and there are varied and even contradictory traditions of what happened at many important stages in his career, including the circumstances of his death.

It is known that biographical data was sometimes received from individuals who themselves claimed to have received it from earlier sources. These persons then put up their knowledge for sale, and what they had to disclose was determined by what was offered materially in return. This practice was not unknown elsewhere: the Koran makes a reference to those who made corrupt extracts of the Pentateuch to sell for a small price (2:73).

The business of selling material on Muhammad's life continued long after his death. One notorious pedlar was Shurabil ibn Saad (d. 740), who had compiled lists of people associated with the Prophet in any way. If an enquirer did not agree to reward him suitably, he would, for instance, deny that any of his ancestors had been present at the Battle of Badr or some other prestigious enterprise. Most of the early historians, including Ibn Ishak, would have none of him.

What was finally recorded by any historian in writing, from the material obtained from oral testimony, was a selection made at his discretion. The relevant parts of his work were in turn accepted or rejected by other writers as they thought fit. Each author sought to improve on his forerunners and supersede them as a standard authority.

Many of the events found recorded in the Prophet's biographies originate in hearsay and popular tradition. The early biographers were aware that not all the narratives recorded by them were to be taken as authentic, and that they might have been wrongly informed on certain points. They sometimes frankly indicated their doubts by adding the comment 'God knows whether this is false or true.' Pious embellishments and sectarian additions and omissions cannot be ruled out in such compilations.

The first biographer of Muhammad, Ibn Ishak, was accused by one of his contemporaries, Malik ibn Anas (d. 795), of conveying false traditions. Another biographer, Ibn Hisham, frankly confesses that he omitted many items from his work for a variety of motives. The problem of what is to be accepted and what rejected in the various biographies of the Prophet seems never to have been resolved.

5.1 Muhammad's Biographers

The first to compile a biography (sira) of Muhammad was Ibn Ishak (d. 768) of Medina. His grandfather Yasar was a Christian of the Namir tribe, who had been captured in 633 in a church in Ayn al-Tamar in Iraq and brought to Medina as a slave by the Muslim general Khalid ibn Walid.

Ibn Ishak's work was generally regarded by his immediate successors as a trustworthy account. It contained many details of Muhammad's appearance, daily life and habits, as well as a record of his military campaigns which Ibn Ishak had obtained from his contemporary al-Zuhri, who had assembled the various traditions about them. Al-Zuhri belonged to the Zuhra clan, to which Muhammad's mother, Amina, belonged. Ibn Ishak's original biography is lost, but it survives in large measure in the work of his successors, who quoted him extensively.

Omar al-Wakidi (d. 823) was also a Medinan, and his life of the Prophet also laid much emphasis on his military exploits. Al-Wakidi is regarded as the least truthworthy of the Prophet's early biographers. Ibn Hisham (d. 834), of Basra, edited and in part altered and amplified the work of Ibn Ishak, adding some fresh material. Ibn Saad (d. 845), secretary to al-Wakidi, wrote a work of dubious historical worth, full of genealogical and biographical detail about Muhammad and his contemporaries. Abu Jaafar al-Tabari (d. 923), a Persian-born historian, also wrote a life of Muhammad, which is often quoted by later writers.

Many Western scholars have raised doubts about the historical value of these, the most basic of all biographies of the Prophet. Some, like Henri Lammens, have held the extreme view that, while some of the exegetical material, clarifying certain Koranic texts, may be genuine, almost all the historical material was invented. Others are of the opinion that nothing can be said for certain about the Prophet's life, except what is confirmed by the Koran, which itself is a poor source of biography.

In addition to the Muslim texts mentioned above, some slender information on the Prophet's life is found in certain non-Muslim sources, some of which even pre-date the Muslim works. There is a small body of writings in Greek and Syriac dated between 634 and 643; a Hebrew text contemporary with the conquest of Jerusalem (638); and an Armenian chronicle of the 660s, which gives us the earliest narrative account of Muhammad's life to survive in any language (Cook, 1983, p. 73). These differ from the Muslim accounts in several respects, and if they are correct in any significant degree it would suggest that the traditional material is 'seriously misleading' on important aspects of Muhammad's life, 'and that even the integrity of the Koran as his message is in some doubt' (Cook, 1983, p. 76).

These non-Muslim sources, it should be noted, are seldom drawn on in writing Muhammad's life, and his biographers, both Muslim and non-Muslim, confine themselves to the Muslim sources.

5.2 The Ancestry of Muhammad

As already stated (Section 2.4), by the middle of the fifth century AD the Koraysh leader Kosay had gained control of the city of Mecca. He was succeeded by his son Abid Menaf, who himself had four sons.

The wide-ranging interests of the Korayshis at this period are brought out in the traditional account of these four sons, each of whom cultivated trade relations with different countries, as follows: Al-Muttalib with Yemen, Nofal with Iraq and Persia, Abid Shams with Abyssinia, and Hashim with Syria and Mesopotamia.

Abid Shams and Hashim were twins, joined together at the shoulder,

Abid Shams being the first to emerge from his mother. The twins were separated by being cut apart.

In the half century before Muhammad the two most powerful Korayshi clans were those named after Hashim, son of Abid Menaf, and Omayya, son of Abid Shams. Between the family of Hashim (to which Muhammad belonged) and that of Omayya (progenitor of the Omayyad caliphs) there was much rivalry and a long struggle for power.

Hashim was invited to the court of the Byzantine emperor and was granted a letter of safe conduct for the merchants of Mecca to take their merchandise to Syria. The Hashim clan also had guardianship of the Kaaba and were responsible for the welfare of pilgrims.

Hashim married a woman of Medina named Salma, and the couple became the parents of Abdul Muttalib, who in time took charge of dispensing water to pilgrims and feeding them. He also cleared the choked-up well of Zamzam in the courtyard of the Kaaba. Like other religious-minded men of Mecca, he would retire to the hills around the city every year and observe a period of abstinence. In 550 he tried to dissuade the Abyssinian governor of Yemen, Abraha, from attacking Mecca.

Abdul Muttalib married Fatima, daughter of Amr ibn Aidh of the Korayshi clan of Makhzum, and they became the parents of Abdulla, who married Amina, daughter of Wahab of the Zuhra clan, also belonging to the Korayshi tribe. Their son Muhammad, the prophet-to-be, was born about four months after Abdulla's death. According to tradition, Muhammad was born, as he was to die, on a Monday, but the precise date of his birth is not actually known, and is variously said to be between AD 567 and 573, the commonly accepted date being 570.

The fact that Muhammad had tribal links both with Mecca and with Medina was to play an important part in his life. By the time the boy Muhammad had grown to manhood, the clan of Hashim had been ousted from their place of authority in the Korayshi hierarchy and the guardianship of the Kaaba had passed from them to the rival clan of Omayya, whose forceful leader Abu Sofyan was to become an opponent of Muhammad.

5.3 Childhood and Youth

Although in later apocryphal accounts many miracles were said to have accompanied Muhammad's birth and childhood, few facts are historically known about his infancy or youth.

His first nurse was Umm Ayman, a Christian from Abyssinia, still in her early teens. (She later married Zayid ibn Haritha, Muhammad's adopted son.) Muhammad's second nurse was Thuwayba, who looked after him for a few weeks.

His third nurse was Halima, from the Banu Saad, a bedouin clan of the (non-Korayshi) Hawazin tribe. Muhammad's widowed mother entrusted the four-year-old boy to her so that he might be away from the insalubrious climate of Mecca and benefit from the healthier life of the desert. The Prophet later attributed the purity of his Arabic speech to his early upbringing with the Banu Saad. Halima took the child back to his mother when in his fifth year he had an attack of what she feared might be the falling sickness (see Section 5.13).

When Muhammad was six years old his mother died, and he was thrown upon the care of his grandfather Abdul Muttalib, who was said to have taken the orphan to the Kaaba to be presented to the shrine deity Hubal. On the death of the grandfather, two years later, Muhammad's uncle Abu Talib, an influential man of Mecca, took charge of him.

These early years were uneventful, and Muhammad was employed, like other lads, in tending the goats and sheep of Mecca in the neighbouring hills and valleys. In about 582, when he was twelve, Abu Talib took him to Syria on a business journey lasting several months. They passed through Petra, Jerash, Amman and other famous towns, and came into contact with Christian communities established there.

On the return journey to Mecca they stopped at Bostra in Syria – a big junction on the caravan route, a meeting-place of five major roads, and also a great Christian centre with a fine cathedral. In Bostra, a Christian monk named Bahira was said to have perceived an aura of greatness about the lad, which he confirmed from a mark between Muhammad's shoulder-blades. Bahira conversed with the boy and predicted that he would be the prophet of the Arabs, lead them away from idolatry, and clean up the temple of the Kaaba.

Between the ages of seventeen and nineteen Muhammad used to join his uncles in the local skirmishes that periodically flared up between the Arab tribes during the long sacrilegious (fijar) wars, so called because they often took place during the sacred months when fighting was prohibited. His duty was to pick up the spent arrows of the enemy and hand them to his own side to shoot back.

Throughout his youth, until he was over twenty years old, Muhammad continued to travel with Abu Talib on his caravan treks to northern Arabia, Palestine and Syria, where he came across many different peoples and became acquainted with their way of life. At the same time he gained first-hand experience of foreign trade and realized its economic value for the prosperity and survival of a country. He himself carried on a small trade with Abyssinia, in skins and leather, his trading partner being Al-Sayib of the Makhzum clan (the clan to which Muhammad's grandmother Fatima belonged), and their merchandise used to be stored in a warehouse owned by Al-Sayib in Mecca.

In about 594, when Muhammad was twenty-four, an accidental fire followed by a flash flood so damaged the Kaaba that it had to be razed to the ground by the Korayshis. At the time the Kaaba was still a low roofless structure, and it was now intended to raise its height. But neither wood nor labour was locally available to build it.

The timely wreck at Jedda on the Red Sea of a Greek ship carrying timber for the construction of a church in Abyssinia, as well as the presence of a

Coptic Christian woodworker and artist named Bakum (Pachomias?) among the crew, provided what was needed. Muhammad joined the men who went to the hills to obtain stone for the structure, and he helped to install the Black Stone, which had been dislodged from its niche. According to legend, he settled a dispute among the tribal leaders about who should put the stone in position. Placing the stone in the middle of a blanket, he instructed each to lift a corner, and when it was at the required height he personally set the meteorite in its place. Then the idol of the great god Hubal, carved of red agate, was restored to its original position over the pit in the centre of the edifice, after which the Kaaba was for the first time provided with a roof.

Throughout this period Muhammad remained faithful to the idolatrous practices of his fathers, taking part in the annual pilgrimage in its unchanged form along with the other pagan worshippers. According to a statement of the Prophet, quoted by the historians Kalbi and Yakut, Muhammad once sacrificed a ewe to the goddess Ozza and partook of the meat, and he continued to eat the flesh of animals so sacrificed in keeping with popular custom.

Before Muhammad received the revelations that altered the course of his career, he was well acquainted with the work of the hanifs and religious reformers of the Hejaz, some of whom had a formative influence on his life. These deserve special notice.

5.4 Zayid ibn Amr

A Korayshi, and uncle of Omar – who later became the second caliph – Zayid ibn Amr is classed as a hanif. He called himself a follower of Abraham's religion, wrote poetry expressing his views on the heathenish practices of his tribe, and condemned female infanticide and idolatry. Every year he would spend the month of Ramadan in retirement in a cave in Mount Hira.

In about AD 595 Muhammad met and conversed with Zayid, and offered him some meat he was carrying, prepared from the flesh of an animal sacrificed to idols. Zayid refused the food, upbraided Muhammad for idolatry, and rebuked him for eating the flesh offered to pagan gods (cf. Acts 15:29). Muhammad later said, 'After that I never knowingly stroked one of their idols nor did I sacrifice to them.'

Zayid used to sit in the courtyard of the Kaaba and pray, 'O God, I do not know how you desire to be worshipped. If I knew, I would worship you.' Mocked by the people, he went to Syria and Iraq to question the rabbis and monks. On his way back, in AD 608, he was killed by bandits. He lies buried at the foot of Mount Hira.

In his teachings Muhammad was later to consign all unbelievers to the flames of hell, but he was said to have invoked God's merciful grace on Zayid, saying that, although he was not a Muslim, God would pardon him.

The Prophet said of him, 'On the last day Zayid will rise again, a community in himself. He is one of those destined for paradise. I have seen him there.'

5.5 Koss ibn Sayda

A Muslim tradition relates that, some time before Muhammad's mission began, the bishop of Najran – Koss ibn Sayda, of the Iyad tribe – preached in the market-place of Okaz near Mecca. He spoke 'as though in ecstasy', chanting the rhymed prose (saj) commonly used by poets of the day, in a style reminiscent of the early suras of the Koran. So striking was the sermon, it was said, that it was 'preserved in people's memories', and fragments survive.

It started, 'O ye people draw near,/And hear, and fear./Signs are read/Not to be gainsaid;/Stars that set and rise,/Sea that never dries,/And roofed above, the skies./On earth below that lies:/Rain is shed,/Plants are fed,/Male and female wed./Time flying and time fled./O mortals say,/Where are the tribes today/That once did disobey/The rules of goodness,/Where are they?/Verily doth Allah give/Light to those who seek to live.' Koss then went on to preach about human frailty, the grace of God and the coming Judgement.

Muhammad, who was present, heard 'as though spellbound' and was deeply moved. The sermon agitated his mind and stirred his soul. The Mutazili freethinker Jahiz (d: 869) records a tradition about Muhammad himself recalling how vividly he remembered the scene, the man, the eloquent words and the persuasive message.

Years later, when a deputation from the Iyad tribe visited Mecca, Muhammad enquired about Koss, and was informed that he had died (c. 613). The Prophet spoke kindly of him, as one who had preached 'the true universal faith'.

5.6 Omayya of Tayif

A reformer of the Thakif tribe of Tayif, Omayya ibn Abu al-Salt (d. 629), a somewhat older contemporary of Muhammad, was a poet and seeker after religious truth who became an opponent and rival of the Prophet. His poems have points of contact with the Koran. He spoke of himself as a hanif, and declared that the religion (din) of the hanif, which was the true faith, would survive the resurrection at the world's end.

During his trade journeys to northern Arabia, Nabataea, Palestine and Syria, he had made a study of the doctrines of the Jews and Christians, and he spoke with approval of the schools set up by Christian tribes like the Iyad.

The Christians of Nabataea used a formula taken from Jewish practice, based on references in the Torah to the Lord God as 'merciful and gracious' (Exod. 34:6). This formula, known in Arabic as the tasmiya, 'naming', or the basmala, invokes the name of God in similar terms. Omayya of

Tayif acquired this formula and taught it to the Koraysh (Rodwell, 1915, p. 19). Muhammad also adopted the formula and used it constantly. The *tasmiya* reads, 'In the name of God [Bismillah], the Merciful [al-Rahman], the Compassionate [al-Rahim]'. It is to be noted that the term *Rahman* had strong Christian connotations.

The *tasmiya* became the most hallowed of all Muslim formulas, and is found at the start of every sura of the Koran except the ninth – the omission there occurring because the ninth sura originally formed a continuous sura with the eighth. The *tasmiya* is repeated before prayers, ablutions and other religious functions, as well as before meals, on going on a journey, making love and similar occasions.

The *tasmiya* is not used before the slaughtering of animals, or at the start of battles or a jihad, the attributes of mercy and compassion being omitted in such cases. Instead, Muslims utter the formula which reads, 'In the name of God, God most great'. The latter part of the phrase (*Allahu Akbar* in Arabic) is known as the *takbir*.

5.7 Khadija

Muhammad had requested his uncle Abu Talib for the hand of his daughter Umm Hani, but, although Abu Talib had a great affection for his nephew, he refused, because of Muhammad's poverty.

When Muhammad was twenty-five years old, Abu Talib recommended him to a rich widow of the Koraysh tribe. Khadija, daughter of Khuwaylid, was already twice widowed and the mother of two sons and a daughter by her former husbands. Muhammad entered her service and was entrusted with the management of her trading enterprises, and as her steward he made several journeys to various parts of Arabia and Syria, including Damascus and Aleppo. His shrewd business sense was a great asset to her.

In 595, shortly after joining her service, Muhammad married her, and thereafter till his flight to Medina in 622 (see Section 6.2) he lived in her house. Brought up in straitened circumstances, he was now freed of the burden of economic insecurity, if not actual destitution. A verse in the Koran reads, 'Have we [God] not relieved you of the burden that galled your back?' (94:2). According to another verse, 'Did the Lord not find you needy and enrich you?' (93:8). He could now devote more time to the reform of Arab paganism, to which both he and Khadija were committed.

Khadija was generally said to have been forty years old at the time of her marriage to Muhammad, but one writer, Ibn Habib, records that she was twenty-eight. This seems more likely, since she bore Muhammad two sons, Kasim and Abdulla, both of whom died in infancy (Muhammad was often called Abul Kasim, 'Father of Kasim', after his son), and four daughters: Zaynab, who married Abul As, a nephew of Khadija; Rokaya; Umm Kulthum; and Fatima. Only Fatima survived the Prophet, and it was only through her that the line of the Prophet was perpetuated. All the present descendants of Muhammad and all the great imams of the Shias are descendants of Khadija.

Little is known about the fifteen years of Muhammad's life between his marriage to Khadija and his first revelation, in a cave in Mount Hira (see Section 5.9), but the direction she gave to his life can scarcely be denied. The guidance given to the Prophet when he had been 'wandering in error', as stated in one of the earlier verses of the Koran (93:7), is thought to have come from Khadija.

It was to her that he went for solace in his troubles. She was the first to believe in his mission, assuring him of her faith in him. She often accompanied him when he retired to the desert to meditate. She strengthened his sense of vocation and inspired him to stay firm in his beliefs. She belittled the opposition, pointing out the futility of their babble. She comforted him during his moods of deep depression, and in his darkest days she remained his chief counsellor and support.

Khadija died in 619. Her tomb, in the valley just above Mecca, is still visited by Muslim pilgrims. Her death was one of the severest blows of Muhammad's life, and for long he remained inconsolable. Years after her death, and after he had remarried, he retained a deep affection for her. When he heard a voice that sounded like hers, and sometimes even when he heard her name pronounced, he would be overcome with grief and tears would come to his eyes.

One of his later wives, the young and beautiful Ayesha, deeply resented the tender memories he cherished of Khadija, and was more jealous of the dead woman whom she had never seen than of all his living wives and concubines. When she once boasted that Allah had replaced 'that toothless old hag' by a better, Muhammad angrily retorted, 'No, Allah has not replaced her by a better. When I was poor, she shared her wealth with me. When I was rejected she believed in me. She declared I spoke the truth, when others called me a liar. And through her Allah granted me children, while withholding those of other women.'

Khadija was the person who had the single most important influence in the life of the Prophet. She was perhaps the most extraordinary woman in the annals of Islam, and was rightly given the title of 'Khadija the Great' (Khadija al-Kubra). Muhammad spoke of her as one of the four perfect women in the history of the world, the other three being Asiya, the daughter of the pharaoh who brought up Moses; the Virgin Mary, mother of Jesus; and Fatima, his daughter by Khadija.

Little is known about Khadija's religious beliefs, but according to al-Tabari she had read the scriptures and was acquainted with the history of the prophets. She was familiar with Christian writings, knew a great deal about Christianity, and may have been a Christian herself.

She certainly had firm links with the Christian faith. Othman ibn Huwayrith, a convert to Christianity who sought to reform the faith of

Mecca, was Khadija's cousin. Another cousin, Waraka, was also a Christian. Her second husband, Abu Hala, belonged to the Christian tribe of Tamim. To her third husband, Muhammad, she presented a Christian servant named Zayid ibn Haritha, whom the Prophet was to adopt as his own son.

She may have been among those who related to Muhammad the stories of Christ's life that imbued many of his revelations. Being a literate woman, she may have been among the first of those who took down his inspired dictations. She must have insisted – and she was in a position to do so, for he never opposed her – that he observe the Christian custom of monogamy, for during their twenty-four years together he never took another wife.

It may have been she who brought to his notice the need to reform the idolatrous religion of the Arabs and put a stop to certain of their social customs, including the practice – against which many hanifs had already spoken out – of killing female babies.

Although it is said that Khadija was the first of Muhammad's converts to Islam, it would be equally true to say that she was responsible for his conversion in the first place.

5.8 The Merchant

Before he received the call – which was to come around AD 610 – Muhammad had been associated with trade and commerce off and on for more than twenty-five years. He came from a business community, and started to learn about things commercial from the age of twelve under the tutelage of Abu Talib. He assumed charge of Khadija's business at the age of twenty-five, and after they were married he continued to manage her affairs. To earn his own livelihood he must have carried on his occupation of buying and selling for some years after Khadija's death.

He had an excellent knowledge of business matters, caravan traffic and foreign markets, and was fully aware of the importance of trade routes in the life of a commercial community. The Koran is filled with trading references, illustrative trading metaphors and commercial terms, which are used to express fundamental points of religious doctrine. Many of these terms have been collected in a book (1892) by an American author, Charles Torrey.

Thus the Koran speaks of caravans for the winter and summer trade journeys, of things being recorded in a ledger, of the Last Judgement as a reckoning, of each person receiving his due account, of a balance being set up, of the deeds of each person being weighed, of each soul being held as a pledge against deeds committed, of the support being given to the Prophet as a loan to God.

Muhammad's shrewd understanding of trade relations came in useful at many points in his career. His decision to send a group of his supporters to Abyssinia in 615 was prompted, in part, by the desire to forestall his Meccan opponents in dealings with that country. His move to Medina, where he set up his base in 622, was made with the intention of disrupting Meccan commerce. Medina was strategically well placed to suit his policy of intercepting and harassing the caravans of his opponents and hampering and eventually controlling their trade. His continual attacks on Meccan caravans and the plundering of their merchandise over the years were calculated to weaken and coerce the Koraysh into accepting his mission and acknowledging his leadership.

5.9 The Cave of Hira

Muhammad was a man of pensive disposition and somewhat melancholic temperament, and towards his late thirties he became more and more reclusive, showing at times a morbid tendency. He had a deep feeling for his people and began to be tormented by doubts about the faith of his fathers, and wondered what he should do to bring it more in accordance with the religion of the Jews and Christians.

During the month of Ramadan he would sometimes retire, accompanied by Khadija, to the hills around Mecca, taking only the necessities of life with him, as his grandfather Abdul Muttalib and other pious Meccans, as well as the hanifs, were in the habit of doing.

One day (c. AD 610), when Muhammad was about forty years old, he withdrew alone to a cave at the foot of Mount Hira, a stony hill about three miles north-east of Mecca. It was the very cave to which the hanif Zayid ibn Amr used to retreat. That same night, the twenty-seventh night of Ramadan, called in the Koran (97:1) the Night of Power (laylat al-kadr), while rapt in meditation, he heard a voice that commanded him saying, 'Read [ikra],' and Muhammad asked, 'What shall I read?' (Compare: 'A voice says, "Cry" [Hebrew kara, 'read']. And I said, "What shall I cry?"' – Isaiah 40:6.)

Muhammad said that he was not a reader, at which point he felt himself squeezed so that he could barely breathe. The voice repeated, 'Read in the name of Allah who created man from a clot of blood. Read, for the Lord is beneficent and has taught man the use of the pen [kalam].'

This was said to have been the first revelation made to Muhammad, and the verses he heard then formed the beginning of the earliest chapter of the Koran (96:1–4).

Profoundly shaken by the experience, Muhammad returned home, worried that he might be possessed, and said to Khadija, 'Cover me, cover me! I am filled with anxiety for myself.' She questioned him about what had happened, and to set his mind at ease she sought a means of testing whether the spirit that had spoken to him was good or evil.

She asked him to tell her when the visitant came to him again. In the account of Ibn Ishak, when the vision next appeared to him Khadija asked Muhammad to sit first on her left thigh and then on her right thigh and then on her lap, and each time Muhammad confirmed that the presence was still there. Then, while he remained sitting on her lap, she exposed her form and drew her husband inside her shift, at which time Muhammad informed her that the vision had gone.

Presumably, the evident modesty of the apparition enabled Khadija to confirm that the visitant was 'an angel and not a satan'. She was certain that Muhammad had been chosen by God to lead the people of Arabia away from idolatry. 'Be of good cheer,' she assured him, 'truly, by the Lord in whose hand lies the soul of Khadija, I hope you will be the prophet of his people.'

According to a tradition reported on the authority of the biographer Musa ibn Okba (d. 758) and others, Khadija took Muhammad to see Addas, a Christian from Nineveh who had settled in Mecca, and Addas explained to them what he knew about the angel Gabriel.

5.10 Waraka

Khadija then went to see her cousin Waraka ibn Nofal, also of the Koraysh tribe. He was a learned man of wide experience, descended from the tribal priesthood charged with looking after the shrine of the goddess Ozza not far from Mecca. A convert to Christianity, he knew Hebrew, had made a study of the Jewish and Christian scriptures, and had translated some of the Christian writings, including portions of the Gospels, into Arabic. Waraka's sister is also mentioned as being knowledgeable in the Christian writings and a regular reader of the Gospels (Glubb, 1979, p. 68).

When Waraka heard Khadija's story, he replied, 'If you have been given a true account of what has occurred, then, O Khadija, there has come to Muhammad the spirit of the Namus [from the Greek *nomos*, 'Law'] which appeared to Moses, and Muhammad will be the prophet of his people. Bid him therefore be of good heart.' Khadija returned to Muhammad and related what she had been told.

Shortly after, Muhammad himself sought out Waraka and repeated his experience to him, and Waraka once again confirmed that Muhammad had been vouchsafed a promise of the Law for the Arabs. 'But', he added, 'people will vilify you, and treat you spitefully. They will call you a liar, reject you, fight against you and expel you from the tribe. If it is God's will that I should still be alive I shall help you in such a way as the Lord directs.' He then kissed the forehead of Muhammad, and Muhammad returned to his house, relieved of his worry and strengthened in his convictions. This word of encouragement, it has been said, must have been of great importance in his inner development (Watt, 1953, p. 51).

In the same year (610), not long after this meeting, Waraka died, a Christian. In many Islamic books he is treated as a hanif, or a follower of the true religion.

5.11 The Interval

After the first revelation in the cave of Hira a considerable period elapsed before Muhammad received any further enlightenment. This interval (*fatra*) of inaction and uncertainty between the first message (Sura 96) and the next was said to have lasted seven months, according to some chroniclers, or seven years, according to others, a period of three years being taken by many authorities as most probable.

According to al-Tabari, the people mocked Muhammad, saying that his so-called Lord (*Rabb*) or Companion (*Sahib*) had deserted him. One woman – some say Umm Jemil, wife of his uncle Abu Lahab – called out, 'Your Satan [Shaytan] has forsaken you and hates you.'

In the beginning the uncertainty of his position caused Muhammad great mental anguish. He suffered black moods of deep depression, and even thought of committing suicide (18:5). The commentators Ibn Hisham and al-Bukhari state that he sometimes wanted to end his life by throwing himself from the cliffs. He doubted the reality of his mission, and wondered whether he had been deceived.

From these crises of doubt and despair he was restored to an equable frame of mind only by the constant reassurance of Khadija, who pressed on him the need for trust and patience, and encouraged his efforts to acquaint himself more thoroughly with the monotheistic faiths. During this time he continued to visit members of the Christian communities who lived around Mecca, and listened attentively to what they had to say (see Section 10.2).

There is a conflict of scholarly opinion about the exact sequence of the next three revelations, but they are generally thought to have occurred in this order. One day in AD 613 the long silence was broken when Muhammad received a message of divine support, in which he was assured that the Lord (*Rabb*) had not forsaken him and was not displeased with him (93:3). Soon after, as he lay on a carpet, covered with a mantle, he had two more revelations, both beginning with the words 'You enwrapped in your mantle', one bidding him to stand up and pray (73:2), followed by another urging him to arise and preach (74:2). From then on he received a series of revelations, and these were memorized and taken down by associates and afterwards collected to form the body of the Koran.

5.12 The Illiterate Prophet

The significance of the words of the first revelation given to Muhammad in the cave of Hira and the precise nature of what he was commanded to read have been much debated by scholars. During this first vision the Prophet was shown a page from the heavenly book and ordered to read the fiery words inscribed upon it. He was also divinely provided with the facility to do so, for he was said to be illiterate.

In the Koran, Muhammad is referred to as the 'unlettered' (*ummi*) prophet

(7:157). He could not read any book, nor write one (29:47). It was asserted by Muslim theologians that Muhammad was not to be regarded as a man of book learning, expressing what he had acquired from other writings. It was necessary to have a prophetic vessel unpolluted by 'intellectual' knowledge of scripts, in order that a pure scripture might be produced. The illiteracy of the Prophet thus confirms the miraculous origin of the Koran.

A story is related that when one of Muhammad's early enemies, Ibn Siyad, was asked by Muhammad, 'Do you bear witness that I am the prophet of God?' Ibn Siyad replied, 'I bear witness that you are a prophet of the illiterate.'

Western scholars generally reject the idea that Muhammad could have been illiterate. He belonged to an influential family in charge of the most sacred shrine of pagan Arabia. He travelled for years on business to foreign countries, and must have been well acquainted with his own Arabic at least, if not with other languages as well (see Section 7.10).

His wife Khadija was a successful businesswoman, and came from a literate family. Even if we assume that Muhammad was illiterate when he married her, it is unlikely that during their twenty-five years together she would not have persuaded her husband to learn how to read and write. He was later keen enough about literacy to allow some of the Meccans captured at the Battle of Badr to earn their ransom by teaching the Medinans to write.

Muhammad may have felt that the Arabs lacked a revealed book, and in that sense it was the Arab people who were 'unlettered' (62:2), as would seem to be confirmed by Ibn Siyad's retort that Muhammad was the prophet of an illiterate people.

The vision in the cave of Hira has also been interpreted as a command emanating from Muhammad's own subconscious, to read and study the holy books of the Jews and Christians, whose scribes had been given pens to write down the truth of God's dispensation in their scriptures, which the Arabs lacked.

The textual accuracy of the Koran would also depend on the literacy of the Prophet, rather than on that of his numerous amanuenses, not all of whom were equally literate or competent in Arabic. According to some scholars, Muhammad personally arranged some of the verses and revised them. During the drafting of the treaty of Hodebiya (see Section 6.13) he altered certain words in his own handwriting. On his deathbed he was said to have called for writing material so that he could settle the matter of his succession, though this request was denied him.

5.13 Seizures

From his childhood Muhammad had been subject to spells of vertigo, when he would collapse unconscious to the ground. It first happened when he was four years old and in the care of his nurse Halima. He was walking with her son at some distance from the bedouin encampment when he suddenly fell down in a faint. Fearing that the boy was possessed by the devil (Nicholson, 1969, p. 147), Halima took him back to his mother.

The seizures continued off and on through much of his life, and have been variously described and accounted for. They would usually start with a headache and a sense of great mental agony, with an unaccountable fear coming over him. He had a desire to hide himself, knowing an attack was imminent. His eyes would begin to roll from side to side, his head would sway and fall forward, and he would drop whatever he was holding.

Even on a cold winter's day, beads of sweat would appear on his forehead, and soon he would perspire so profusely that his whole body was bathed in sweat. Then came a sense of suffocation and physical constriction, as though his body were being squeezed tight, causing him great pain. His lips would start to twitch and his whole body would tremble from head to foot. His breathing would become laboured; he would groan and blow out heavily, make raucous sounds, and 'cry out like a camel colt'.

He would bite his tongue, his mouth would fill with froth, and his face would become red, as if he were apoplectic. Then the blood would suddenly drain from his face and his colour would 'bleach', changing to white. He would sink or fall heavily to the ground as if intoxicated (Andrae, 1960, p. 50), writhing in convulsive spasms, and then lie unconscious and still, in a cataleptic trance. Describing the experience, he once said to Abdulla ibn Omar, 'I hear a loud voice and then I seem to be struck by a blow, and feel as if my soul were being torn from me.'

At other times he would hear peculiar sounds outside and about him, and noises within his head: rustlings in the wind, the humming of bees, the rushing of wings, whisperings and wandering voices (hatif), and, most disturbing of all, the reverberation of bells. The bell sounds had the strangest effect upon him: he found them most unpleasant, and the hardest to bear, and 'they well-nigh rent his heart in pieces'. Even the everyday sound of bells affected him strangely. They made him anxious and uneasy, sending him into a state of near-panic. For this reason he rejected the use of bells for calling the faithful to prayer.

Some of Muhammad's followers explained the childhood attack by saying that angelic beings had rendered the boy unconscious, so that his heart might be removed and the drop of original sin that it contained could be squeezed out (see Section 11.13).

Based on the evidence, the view of his contemporaries might well have been that Muhammad had the 'falling sickness', or epilepsy. The Arabs of the time, like many ancient peoples, regarded epilepsy as a sacred disease which sometimes afflicted persons under divine blessing. Like the epileptic, Muhammad often had an 'aura' or premonitory warning of an attack, and would try to hide or wrap himself or cover his head in a mantle. These and other symptoms described in the Arabic writings have given support to the hypothesis of epilepsy. Whatever it might have been, Muhammad's pagan opponents in the early days offered to obtain treatment for his condition.

Subsequently, writers like al-Wakidi preferred to explain the attacks as a 'fever', or an 'ague', or 'migraine', and some have stated that they induced a condition of 'holy trance', when Muhammad had ecstatic visions and became the recipient of divine revelations, which he dictated while in this state. And indeed, in the beginning of Muhammad's prophetic career, the seizures often did presage a revelation.

The seizures varied in duration, from short blackouts to longer periods of unconsciousness. They also lessened in frequency as time went on, and there are few instances of seizures during the later Medinan period. It has further been suggested that Muhammad's sickness, though mild to begin with, had been left untreated, and as a result led to a slow process of mental deterioration which is reflected in the marked differences between the Koranic passages dictated at Mecca and those dictated later in Medina.

The fact that during the Medinan period consciousness was retained has led certain authorities to conjecture that, while some of the trances were genuine, the later ones, though apparently spontaneous, were sometimes under his control and were self-induced for a specific purpose (Torrey, 1967, p. 59). Muhammad may have felt that the declining frequency of the sacred trances might lead his followers to believe there was a similar decline in the inspirational nature of his utterances. The state of dissociation and ecstatic trance could have been simulated or achieved in good faith, through self-suggestion, at any time he desired to come out with one of his oracular pronouncements.

Muslim scholars dismiss all such speculations as prejudiced and without foundation. No Arab record exists of Muhammad having suffered from epilepsy. At no time did he show any evidence of the so-called symptoms of progressive deterioration, and not a single one of his companions ever referred to him as mentally unbalanced. To pacify and tame the wild tribal factions in Arabia, to draw so many disbelieving Arabs into the fold of Islam, to be the recipient of such sublime revelations as we find in the Koran: these provide the clearest evidence, they say, that Muhammad was rational, clear-headed and sane, and remained so to the end of his life.

5.14 The Possessed

Belief in demonic possession was common among almost all peoples of the past. Muhammad's childhood seizures would therefore not unnaturally lead to the supposition among the primitive bedouin that the child Muhammad was possessed. Later, various theories were put forward about the nature of his sickness. It could be that he was under the spell of women with the evil eye (*isabat al-ayn*), who create mischief because of envy (*hasad*) and contrive their wickedness by knotting. Muhammad was aware of the prevalence of such practices among the Arabs (113:4–5).

There were those who believed that Muhammad himself possessed the evil eye. His wife Khadija did not like to feel that he might exercise this power, and used to send for an old woman to charm it away. When Muhammad began to receive his messages, he dispensed with this woman's services (Guillaume, 1960, p. 7).

Muhammad's opponents would not have allowed the symptoms that accompanied his mysterious paroxysms to pass unnoticed. His claim that the angel Gabriel was communicating messages to him from Allah could easily be used to confirm their view that evil entities were responsible for his visions and made him hear hallucinatory voices. Like sibyls, diviners and shamans under the influence of their demons, Muhammad was the mouthpiece of spirit powers, a man possessed (44:13).

Some identified the possessing entities as jinn (52:29) who prompted his duplicity. Some called him a man bewitched (25:9) and under the spell of malicious beings. Some said he was a magician (37:15) or a soothsayer (69:42). Aswad ibn Abdul Yaguth of the Zuhra clan, who was the Prophet's cousin on the maternal side, accused him of being a sorcerer and a madman, and even tried to hire assassins to kill him (Thaalibi, 1968, p. 90).

Muhammad believed that Satan and the lesser satans were bent on seducing and misleading mankind. They enter a person's mind during prayers and at night, and put specious thoughts into him that are contrary to the teachings of the true faith. Satan deceived Adam so that he was cast from paradise (2:34). He insinuated false words into the messages of all the great prophets of past times. On one memorable occasion Muhammad himself had been temporarily misled in this way (see Section 5.21).

It was said by Muhammad's detractors that evil powers endowed him with the faculty of ill-wishing, which he exercised, and which accounted for the number of people who mocked or opposed him coming to a bad end. Five of Muhammad's scoffers perished in a single day. He cursed his uncle Abu Lahab, and he died not long after the Battle of Badr.

During this battle Muhammad reputedly used the words and gestures that commonly accompany a malediction. He first retired to his tent to meditate, then emerged and in a ritual gesture threw a handful of pebbles in the direction of the enemy, crying out, 'Evil seize their faces.' At the Battle of Honayn he performed the same gesture, casting a handful of gravel towards the opposing forces and shouting, 'Ruin seize them. I swear they are discomfited.'

In another curious incident it is related that when a Christian delegation from Najran visited Muhammad and they became involved in a discussion about the merits of their respective religions, he suggested they settle the matter by a contest of cursing (3:54). This the Christians declined to do (see Section 10.19).

According to the Muslim chroniclers, Muhammad was indeed able by his words to influence events, but this power came not from evil entities but from Allah, who guided him through life and worsted his enemies and those who stood in opposition to him.

5.15 Zayid ibn Haritha

The second of Muhammad's converts, after Khadija, was Zayid ibn Haritha (580–629), born in southern Syria of the Christian tribe of Kalb. He had been kidnapped by bandits and sold as a slave to one of Khadija's nephews, and was brought up, still with strong Christian affinities, under Khadija's protection.

When Khadija married Muhammad she presented her husband with the boy Zayid, who must have been about fifteen years old at the time, as his servant. On being offered the chance of returning to his tribe, Zayid expressed a desire to remain in the household. Moved by his devotion, Muhammad went with him to the Kaaba, publicly freed him from slavery, and announced that he was adopting him as his own son. The youth was thereafter known as Zayid ibn Muhammad.

Zayid has the distinction of being the only one of Muhammad's companions whose name is mentioned in the Koran (33:37). Muhammad arranged for Zayid to marry his first nurse, the Christian woman Umm Ayman – also known as Baraka – fifteen years older than Zayid, and she bore him a son called Osama. Zayid later married Muhammad's cousin, the beautiful Zaynab, whom he was later to divorce so that she might be free to marry Muhammad (see Section 6.10).

Zayid was about thirty-one years old when the Koranic messages began to come to Muhammad. A literate person, well versed in Arabic, he was among the amanuenses who took down the Prophet's early messages. His influence on the Prophet's religious development may have been considerable. During Muhammad's rise to power and authority Zayid came to be highly esteemed, since he was trusted by the Prophet. It has been said that, but for his premature death at the Battle of Mota in 629, he might have succeeded Muhammad (Watt, 1961, p. 157).

5.16 The Early Converts

One of the most important of the early converts to Islam was Abu Bakr, a wealthy merchant only two years younger than Muhammad. He was to become the father-in-law of Muhammad, and the first caliph, or successor, of the Prophet. Abu Bakr in turn prevailed upon Othman ibn Affan, a Korayshi of the powerful Omayyad clan, to join the company. Othman was to become the third caliph.

Other converts at this time included Zubayr ibn Awwam, a nephew of Khadija and a distinguished warrior. (Zubayr's son Orwa was to become a distinguished authority on the early traditions of Islam.) There was also Abdulla ibn Umm Maktum, again related to Khadija, whom Muhammad initially turned away because he was blind, but later accepted (80:1). He was to serve twice as governor of Mecca. The Prophet's uncle Hamza first opposed the new faith, but was moved to his nephew's defence when he heard him being reviled by a group of Meccans. He too became a convert.

Another early believer was Ali – son of Abu Talib, Muhammad's uncle – whom Muhammad had taken into his household when Ali was thirteen years old. Ali was to marry Fatima and so become Muhammad's son-in-law, and later the fourth caliph, as well as the first of the Shia imams.

In the beginning the new religion had to be practised with caution, for fear of arousing the scorn and antagonism of the Koraysh. Goldziher writes that the early Muslims had to keep their prayers more secret from the pagan Meccans than any other aspect of their faith (1967, p. 42). And even after Islam began to be practised more openly their ritual prostrations gave rise to considerable opposition and ridicule, the postures being regarded as degrading and obscene.

According to one tradition, Abu Talib came unawares upon his young son Ali and Muhammad performing their prayers in a glen near Mecca, and asked them what they were doing. Muhammad replied that he was following the teachings revealed to him, and invited Abu Talib to join Islam. In a version that comes from Ayesha, the old man replied that he could not give up the faith of his fathers nor, he added, could he join in devotions which 'necessitated his placing his backside above his head' (Glubb, 1979, p. 98). Later, the townspeople of Tayif agreed to join Islam if they could be exempted from the 'degrading prostrations', but this request was denied (see Section 6.18).

What greatly added to the courage and confidence of the early believers was the conversion of Omar ibn al-Khattab, fiery and quick-tempered, 'a man of blood and iron' and once a bitter opponent of the new faith. Hearing that his own sister Fatima and her husband Sayid (son of Zayid the hanif) had both become followers of Muhammad, he came to their house while the slave Khabab (see below) was reading aloud a part of the Koran from a manuscript. In a rage he struck his sister, causing her to bleed. Overcome with remorse, he was persuaded by Khabab to read the verses concerned (from Sura 20) and hear about the new religion, and eventually he became a Muslim himself. Omar was later to become the second caliph.

Muhammad used to meet his early followers not in his own dwelling but in the house of a young man of the Koraysh clan of Makhzum named Al-Arkam, which was situated in a quiet spot on the outskirts of Mecca. For centuries afterwards certain Muslim families used to boast that an ancestor of theirs had embraced the faith 'while Muhammad was in the house of Al-Arkam'.

The various authorities give different lists of the early converts and the order of their conversion. Neither Abu Bakr nor Ali thought fit to honour Khadija and Zayid ibn Haritha as the first among the believers. Perhaps Khadija could not be mentioned because she was a woman. But Zayid could not have been ignored because he had been a slave, since other slaves are named. Perhaps both were excluded as alien Christian elements who could not properly figure among the true converts to Islam.

Among the former slaves named with the early converts was Khabab, already mentioned, a confederate of the Zuhra clan working as a blacksmith, whose mother was a professional circumciser. Another was Ammar ibn Yasir, who used to visit the house of Al-Arkam. He had contact with Christianity through his mother's second husband, a freedman of Greek origin and hence presumably a Christian.

Abu Bakr once ransomed a slave named Bilal who was being cruelly treated by his Meccan master. Bilal was the son of an Abyssinian slave girl, and as such acquainted with Christianity. He joined the household of Abu Bakr and later fled to Medina with the other Muslims. Because of his stentorian voice, he became the first muezzin, calling the faithful to prayer from the roof of the highest house near the mosque.

When in October 630 Muhammad received John, the Christian prince of Ayla, at Tabuk, he commanded Bilal to entertain him with all hospitality, possibly because Bilal knew the ways of the Christians.

Muhammad had granted Bilal a portion of land as a gift, but on the Prophet's death Omar, the second caliph, a man of strong Arab feeling and unable to forget Bilal's slave origin, confiscated the land, saying that Bilal had failed to cultivate it. With Omar's permission, Bilal left Medina for Christian Syria, and here he made the call to prayer for the last time when Omar came to Damascus in 639 and said he wished to hear him. In one account he died in Damascus, where his alleged tomb is still shown. In another account he moved from Damascus to Christian Tarsus in Anatolia, and died and was buried either there or in Aleppo.

It is notable that among the new converts, about forty in number, several belonged to the lower social scale, of either Abyssinian or Byzantine origin. A number of the Prophet's close associates in Mecca were Christians or came from a Christian background, some converted in the house of Al-Arkam.

Christians were also among Muhammad's first amanuenses. In these early Meccan days he felt closely drawn to the Christians, including the Greeks (Byzantines). At that time Byzantium controlled Syria and Egypt and was an ally of Abyssinia. When in AD 615 the Persian ruler Khosro II Parviz defeated the Byzantine armies under Heraclius, the Meccan opponents of Muhammad rejoiced because the Persians, like themselves, were regarded as 'idolators', being fire-worshippers, with whom Islam had little in common (Rodwell, 1915, p. 210).

But the sympathies of the Prophet were with Byzantium, and he had a revelation as follows: 'The Greeks have been defeated in a land nearby. But after their defeat they shall defeat their foes' (30:1–2). Ten years later, in 625, there was much rejoicing in the camp of the faithful when the Byzantines dealt the Persians a crushing defeat, thus fulfilling Muhammad's prophecy. It is said that when tidings of the Byzantine victory became known many people embraced Islam.

5.17 The Meccan Opposition

From about the time of the conversion of stalwarts like Hamza and Omar around AD 615 can be dated the more open and public preaching of Muhammad.

The radical ideas he disseminated aroused the hostility of the Meccans (Korayshis). Muhammad was accused of being a trouble-maker, and of propagating a fresh (*muhdat*) religion (21:1), not in conformity with Arab beliefs, and contrary to the way of the ancestors. (Among other matters, the ancestors knew nothing of paradise, hell, or the Day of Judgement.) It was feared that the monotheism on which Muhammad laid such emphasis would undermine the importance of Mecca as the chief religious centre of the Arabs, and in consequence have an adverse effect on Meccan trade. In 617 the Meccans decided to impose an economic and social boycott on the Muslims.

During this period of Korayshi opposition, Muhammad continued to enjoy the protection of Abu Talib, his uncle and adoptive father. A Meccan delegation was arranged to visit Muhammad at the house of Abu Talib in order to reason with him. It was headed by Amr ibn Hisham, chief of the Makhzum clan of the Koraysh, who was surnamed Abu Hukm, 'Father of Justice'. He was to become known in Islamic annals as Abu Jahal, 'Father of Foolishness', because of his bitter opposition to Muhammad.

Abu Jahal asked Muhammad what it was the Meccans had to do or say to make him desist from his preaching, and Muhammad replied, 'Say only, "There is no God but Allah."' At this time Muhammad made no claim to being an apostle of Allah (see Section 11.12), but in some accounts he is said to have added, 'And Muhammad is the messenger of Allah.' Abu Jahal refused to comply, and the delegation left.

Abu Jahal regarded Muhammad as a charlatan, and derided his message as the invention of a madman. When he was slain at the Battle of Badr some ten years later, Muhammad exulted over his severed head. In the Koran Abu Jahal is referred to as a man who disputed about God without knowledge or direction, and was consigned to hell (22:8–9).

The Meccans now urged Abu Talib to use his influence to stop his nephew from creating tribal dissension and defaming the Meccan religion. Abu Talib, old and sick, summoned Muhammad and endeavoured to persuade him to abandon his preaching, as it was bringing disgrace to the family and trouble to Mecca. According to one pious tradition, Muhammad replied, 'If you gave me the sun in my right hand and the moon in my left on condition that I alter my course, I would not abandon it.'

Although much is made in the Muslim records of the oppression of the early converts at the hands of the Korayshis, such persecution as occurred was generally mild in character (Watt, 1953, p. 123) and its extent has been exaggerated. The boycott was not strictly enforced. The poorer and unprotected converts occasionally suffered harassment for their faith, but on the whole this amounted to little more than ridicule, taunting and petty irritations. Hardly any case of real persecution is mentioned in the Koran.

In 619 Abu Talib succeeded in persuading the Korayshis to lift the ban they had placed on commercial and social relations with the followers of the new faith.

5.18 Abu Sofyan

The head of the Omayyad clan at this time was a wealthy and respected Meccan named Abu Sofyan, grandson of Omayya and, as a Korayshi, distantly related to Muhammad. A man with notable gifts of leadership, he was also head of the Meccan senate (*mala*), custodian of the Kaaba keys, and keeper of the shrine standard (*liwa*) and hence virtually general-in-chief of the Korayshi state forces.

As one of the principal merchants of Mecca, Abu Sofyan was a powerful and influential person. In AD 606 he headed a party of merchants on a visit to the Persian capital and was admitted to the presence of Khosro II Parviz, the Sassanian monarch. He also spent some time at the court of Hira, and Thaalibi suggests he may have acquired his heterodoxy from the Christians of Hira (1968, p. 92).

According to a tradition recorded by al-Baladhuri, Muhammad had at one time invested in some of merchandise carried by Abu Sofyan's caravans to Syria, and reaped some profit from the trade.

During his subsequent rise to power, Muhammad had to reckon with Abu Sofyan, who now led the Meccan campaign against him and came to be regarded as 'the arch-enemy of Islam'. At the Battle of Badr (AD 624) Abu Sofyan's eldest son and heir, Hanzala, was slain by the Muslim forces. In the same battle Abu Sofyan's wife Hind also lost her father, Otba ibn Rabia, as well as her brother and uncle, all of which only served to increase her and her husband's hostility towards Muhammad. Hind never disguised her intense hatred for the Prophet.

Failing to convert or even conciliate Abu Sofyan, Muhammad in 628 sent an agent to kill him, but the would-be killer failed in his attempt. Muhammad's personal enmity towards his kinsman is thought to have been irrecoverably perpetuated in the Koran, where he is referred to as 'that Satan' (3:169).

Abu Sofyan's sister, Umm Jemil, was the wife of another opponent of the Prophet, Abu Lahab (see below). Abu Sofyan's son-in-law Obaydulla became a Christian during the Abyssinian exile (see Section 5.20). Another son-in-law, Orwa, treated Muhammad with scant respect when the latter was trying to negotiate for permission to return to Mecca in 628 (see Section 6.13).

Even after his conversion to Islam in 630, reluctantly and under duress (see Section 6.17), Abu Sofyan retained his hostility to Muhammad and Islam. Although he was present on the Muslim side at the Battle of Honayn

(630), he was secretly delighted at the first defeat of the Muslims and whispered to a fellow Meccan, 'Nothing can stop their flight.' He was also present, again on the Muslim side, at the Battle of Yarmuk (636) against the Byzantines, and could not conceal his joy at every advantage gained by the enemies of Islam during the encounter.

Though a cousin of Abu Sofyan, Othman, became the third caliph, he continued in his own way the family antagonism against Muhammad's tribal branch (the Hashim). Muawiya, the son of Abu Sofyan, became the first caliph of the Omayyad line, and he and his successors were notable for their many covert acts of hostility to the Prophet's clan.

5.19 Abu Lahab

In the year 619, when Muhammad was forty-nine years old, he lost his faithful wife, Khadija. A few weeks later his uncle Abu Talib became very ill. Muhammad visited him on his deathbed, and pleaded with him to profess Islam, but the old man remained firm, saying he could not give up the religion of his people. Also, he considered the visions of Muhammad a delusion and his religion a cause of tribal dissension. With the death of Muhammad's two chief protectors, the risk of personal danger from his enemies was greatly increased.

Abu Talib was succeeded as head of the Hashim clan by his younger brother, Abdul Ozza, 'Servant of Ozza', better known as Abu Lahab, who, though he mistrusted Muhammad's visionary claims, came forward with a promise of support and protection. Some time later, anxious about rumours he had heard, he asked the Prophet whether, according to his new teaching, Muhammad's grandfather Abdul Muttalib and his uncle Abu Talib, both of whom had helped and protected him, were now in hell because they had not been his followers. Muhammad confirmed that such was indeed the case. The ancestors of all the Meccans were suffering in hell because they had lived in idolatry and died infidels.

Shocked and furious at this want of gratitude and family feeling, and appalled at the barbarity of the new teaching, Abdul Ozza denounced Muhammad's mission, withdrew his protection, and departed, calling out, 'May you perish! I shall never cease to be your enemy.' Muhammad called back, 'Let him perish! Let him burn in the fiery flame!' Following this incident, Abdul Ozza acquired the surname of 'Abu Lahab', 'Father of the Flame'. Muhammad received a divine revelation consigning both Abu Lahab and his wife Umm Jemil – the sister of Abu Sofyan – to the flames of hell (111:3). Abu Lahab died of grief and vexation in 624, one week after the Battle of Badr. His body remained unburied for several days.

Muhammad's daughters Rokaya and Umm Kulthum were wedded to Otba and Otayba, the two sons of Abu Lahab. Otba later divorced Rokaya and embraced Christianity (J. Barth, in SEI, 1974, p. 11), and Muhammad gave his freed daughter in marriage to Othman ibn Affan. When, in September 624, Otayba divorced Umm Kulthum, Muhammad married her to Othman too.

5.20 Abyssinian Exile

Close commercial and social links existed between Abyssinia and the Hejaz in Muhammad's day. Abyssinian merchants and artisans plied their trade in Mecca, and the richer Meccan merchants employed Abyssinians as mercenaries, to police their homes and warehouses.

From his business experience, Muhammad knew that Abyssinia represented a lucrative market for the Korayshis, and he was aware of the strategic importance of that country in any trade war with Mecca. An alliance with Abyssinia would not be difficult, since Muhammad believed that the religious doctrines of Islam and Christianity were essentially the same. This he felt would be useful in securing any such alliance, for the negus would prefer to deal with him rather than the Korayshi idolators.

At about this time, when antagonism towards him and his adherents was gathering momentum, there occurred an episode of some importance, though, like much that has been written about this period, there is some confusion about the facts.

Under material inducement or threat of social boycott, a number of converts, especially among the poorer classes who were without tribal protection, had recanted and withdrawn their allegiance to Muhammad. Before he lost any more of his followers in this way, Muhammad thought it would be expedient to send them to Abyssinia, where they could remain until it was safe for them to return. 'It is a Christian country,' he told them, 'the king rules with justice, the people are friendly, and no one is wronged.'

The emigrants included not only the poor and vulnerable, but also influential people belonging to prominent Meccan families and under no personal threat – people whom the Korayshis would not have dared harm, for fear of provoking a tribal feud. This group included a number of Muhammad's strong-minded associates who tended to go their own way and create dissent, and Muhammad perhaps did not want to have them around while he was trying to establish his authority in Mecca, where he himself remained.

How these people were induced to go is not clear. Muhammad may have been able to convince them that the emigrants needed competent leaders to assist them in settling in Abyssinia until the crisis was over, and also that they were in a better position to negotiate with the Abyssinians concerning any problems that might arise.

Accordingly, early in 615 and over the next few months, the emigrants set out in small groups (so as not to arouse suspicion) for Shoayba, the ancient port of Mecca not far from Jedda, and from there they crossed the

Red Sea in separate Abyssinian vessels. Early Muslim writers, including Ibn Ishak and Ibn Hisham, refer to this exodus as the First Hegira (or emigration) in Islam, the more important one being the Great Hegira to Medina seven years later in which Muhammad himself took part.

This first migration is said to have comprised eighty-three men in all, many of them accompanied by their wives and children, making a total of about 150 persons. They received a kind welcome in Abyssinia and spent their exile in Aksum, the capital of the country. The names of some of those who took part are listed in the chronicles, and the principal ones are listed below.

The leader of the emigrants was Jaafar, son of Abu Talib, a cousin of Muhammad and older brother of Ali. He later rejoined Muhammad and died at the Battle of Mota (629). Jaafar was accompanied by his wife Asma bint Omayis. After Jaafar's death she married Abu Bakr, and on his death Ali.

Zubayr ibn Awwam, Khadija's nephew, and cousin of the Prophet, also returned to rejoin Muhammad. He died at the Battle of the Camel (656) after Muhammad's death.

Othman ibn Affan, of the Omayyad clan, was accompanied by his wife Rokaya, a daughter of Muhammad. Othman was later to become the third caliph.

Abu Salama, ten years older than Muhammad, was accompanied by his wife. He was present at the Battle of Badr and died in 625, of wounds received at Ohod. Muhammad married his widow, Umm Salama. Abu Salama is to be distinguished from Abu Salama son of Abdul Rahman, mentioned below.

Khalid ibn Sayid was an early convert who had been turned out of his father's house and lived with Muhammad. While in Abyssinia he made himself an iron ring plated with silver and inscribed, 'The truth is only with God.' On his return, Muhammad took it from him and gave him his own gold ring in exchange. This iron ring became the Prophet's signet ring, and was handed down to his successors, only to be lost by the caliph Othman.

Othman ibn Mazun, of the Korayshi clan of Juma, was accompanied by his two sons. He tended to asceticism and later took a vow of chastity about which his wife complained to Muhammad's wife Ayesha. Neither Abu Bakr nor Omar liked his extreme views. A man of independent opinions, he gathered around him a group of like-minded believers.

Hattab was accompanied by his wife Fukayha, daughter of a Christian named Yasra. The Korayshis claimed that Muhammad received religious instruction from Yasra (see Section 10.2).

Musab ibn Omayr, a zealous Muslim, had tried to convert his pagan mother, but she replied, 'I shall never make myself a fool by entering into your religion. Begone, I wash my hands of you and cleave steadfastly to my own faith.' Musab went to Abyssinia accompanied by his wife Hamna bint Jahash, sister of Obaydulla ibn Jahash (see below). On her mother's side, Hamna belonged to the Christian tribe of Asad. On Musab's return to Mecca in 620, Muhammad sent him to instruct the new converts in Medina. Musab fought at Badr and was killed at Ohod.

Abdul Rahman ibn Auf, of the Zuhra clan and ten years younger than Muhammad, was an early convert. On his return from Abyssinia he joined Muhammad in Medina. He became a wealthy merchant and fought in several battles. In 627 he married Tomadir, daughter of the Christian chief of the Kalb tribe. They became the parents of Abu Salama, a famous juris-consult. (He is not to be confused with the Abu Salama mentioned above.)

Sakran ibn Amr, a Korayshi, was accompanied by his wife Sauda bint Zamaa. With them was her brother Malik ibn Zamaa. Sakran became a Christian and died in Abyssinia; in 619 his widow returned to Mecca and married Muhammad the same year.

Obaydulla ibn Jahash, whose mother, Omayma, was a daughter of Abdul Muttalib, thus making him a cousin of Muhammad, was accompanied by his wife Umm Habiba, daughter of Abu Sofyan. He became a fervent Christian in Abyssinia, and Ibn Ishak records that he used to tell the Prophet's companions, 'We see clearly, but your eyes are only half open.' He died in Abyssinia in 628 in the profession of his faith. Muhammad married the widow by proxy, before her return. Muhammad also married Obaydulla's sister Zaynab bint Jahash.

The Meccans, who had trading relations with Abyssinia, were alarmed that Muhammad's party might seek to undermine their trade with that country. Accordingly, a two-man delegation was dispatched to Ashama, the negus, to ask for the repatriation of the leading refugees. The Meccan delegation was led by Amr ibn al-As, later the conqueror of Egypt.

The negus refused the request but said he would like to hear what the refugees had to say, and he invited them to present their case. Their spokes-man, Jaafar, explained to the negus and the bishop and priests who were present that they had once been idolators but Muhammad had shown them the right path. He was then asked to read one of the revelations of Muham-mad, and Jaafar recited Sura 19, entitled 'Mary', which tells the story of the birth of John the Baptist and the miraculous birth of Jesus.

Only the first thirty-five verses were read out, for verse 36 starts with the words 'It is not proper for God that he should beget a son', and this would imply that Muhammad rejected the Sonship of Jesus and would have offended the negus. Some authorities believe that this sura then actually contained only thirty-five verses and ended where Jaafar had stopped. The remainder of the sura has a different rhythm, style and rhyme and is more polemical in tone, and must have been added at a later date, as a result of Muhammad's growing opposition to the Christians in Arabia.

In any event Ashama was satisfied – perhaps under the impression that the Muslims were a Christian sect (Glubb, 1979, p. 122) – and he categorically refused the deputation's request to send the refugees back to Mecca. This greatly relieved the Prophet when the news reached him.

Some months after this incident Muhammad received news of the negus's death. He then summoned his followers, ranged them in ranks behind him and cried out four times, 'God is great!' and offered prayers for Ashama. When his followers asked him why he had done this, he replied that it was to remember the kindness of the departed negus. In one account, some onlookers exclaimed, 'He is praying for a dead Christian whom he has never seen.' Ayesha, the wife of the Prophet, preserved a tradition that a light was always seen over the grave of the negus.

The refugees spent variously between several months and thirteen years in Abyssinia, in comfort, peace and security. Some died in exile; a few, as we have seen, became Christians and remained in the country of their adoption. About thirty families returned to Mecca within a year when they learned that the Korayshis were now more kindly disposed towards the Muslims after Muhammad's concession to them (see Section 5.21). One group of fourteen men, including Jaafar and Othman ibn Affan, accompanied by their families, returned just before the Great Hegira in 622. After Muhammad had established himself in Medina, thirty-two men with their families came to Medina in 628, crossing the Red Sea in two ships provided by the then reigning negus.

5.21 The Satanic Verses

The pressure on Muhammad to make concessions to the pagans of Mecca continued to increase, and, according to al-Tabari, he himself was keen to make it easier for the Meccans to accept his message. With this in mind, in 616 he tried to come to some reconciliation with the polytheists in respect of the deities Allat, Ozza and Manat, the three most popular goddesses of Mecca and the neighbouring towns, and decided to admit them as worthy of honour.

He went to the Kaaba and, in the presence of the elders of Mecca, recited the verses still found in the Koran (53:19–20) calling attention to the three goddesses. He then added the words 'These are the exalted damsels [*gharanik* – variously translated as 'females', 'birds', 'swans', 'herons', 'cranes'] mounting upward to heaven, whose intercession may be sought.'

The idolators were delighted with the new trend in Muhammad's revelation, which was taken as bestowing divine status upon these deities and authorizing their worship, and, although some scoffed at his so-called monotheism, there was general relief that the tension had been eased. The reconciliation seems to have lasted long enough for the exiles to receive the news in Abyssinia, and for some of them to return to Mecca.

But, after a time ('the same evening', according to some; 'weeks' or even 'months' according to others), Muhammad realized that the compromise was ineffectual. He then retracted what he had said, explaining that the additional verses had been placed on his tongue by Satan and had been uttered by him under delusion. Accordingly the 'satanic verses' were excised and replaced by others. The substituted verses now read, 'What, shall men have male progeny, and God female? This is a most unfair distinction' (53:21-2). The implication after this change seems to be that if the three deities had been male instead of female the objection to them would be overcome, or at least lessened. This appears to be strengthened by another verse: 'Would God choose daughters rather than sons?' (37:153).

In any event, the opponents of Muhammad were not slow to point out that, if the excised verses had been inspired by Satan, how could one be sure that other parts of the Koran, if not the whole of it, were not the result of satanic prompting (wiswas) rather than divine inspiration (wahi)? In response, Muhammad declared that Satan had tampered with the revelations of past apostles too, but 'God brings to nought that which Satan has suggested' (22:51). As for his teachings, he emphasized, they could not be the doctrines of an accursed Satan (81:25).

The story of the satanic verses has been the subject of endless and bitter controversy. Historians and commentators like al-Wakidi, Ibn Hisham, Ibn Saad, al-Tabari, al-Zamakshari, al-Baydawi and Jalaluddin, are among those who have mentioned the incident. Later theologians began to deem it heretical to believe that Muhammad should have suffered such a lapse, 'after he had received the truth', and the incident was seldom recorded in the later biographies of the Prophet and is denied by many Muslims to this day.

5.22 The Tayif Sojourn

Daunted by the extent of the animosity he faced in Mecca, Muhammad now sought a place of sanctuary, but tribe after tribe, it is said, refused to help him, for fear of incurring the displeasure of the Korayshis. In 619 he finally decided to go to Tayif, in the company of his adopted son, Zayid ibn Haritha.

Tayif, a green hillside town about forty miles south-east of Mecca, was famed for its orchards and vineyards. A busy commercial centre, it was inhabited by the Thakif tribe and by a few rich Meccan merchants who would go there in summer to escape the dust and heat of Mecca. It was also the centre of a small wine trade, the wine being made and sold by Jews and Christians.

Muhammad stayed in the town for ten days and met some of the leading men there. He sought their help, and proposed ways of removing Meccan control over their affairs. He also spoke about his own mission and called upon them to worship God. His words provoked both indignation and amusement.

Some of the merchants, mindful that his retraction of the 'satanic verses' concerning Allat, the tutelary deity of Tayif, might have meant the loss of pilgrim revenue for the town, would have nothing to do with him. Tired of his preaching, they finally hired men to drive the intruders out of the town.

In a sad frame of mind, Muhammad and Zayid took shelter near one of the famous vineyards about two miles outside Tayif. Here a Christian slave named Addas brought out a tray of grapes and other refreshment for the wanderers, and received Muhammad's blessing for his courage and kindness.

The two men returned to Mecca, having been assured of their safety by one of the Korayshi chiefs, Motim ibn Adi of the Nofal clan, but Muhammad's position was still far from easy.

During the next few months he took the opportunity provided by various fairs to preach to visiting nomadic tribes: the Kinda, Kalb, Hanifa and Amir. The first three, who were either wholly or partly Christian, did not respond to his preaching. The Amir likewise were not interested, though they did join him at a later date.

5.23 The Night Journey

Many religions feature accounts of the visit of a prophet or seer to the heavenly and infernal regions, either alone or guided by an angel, and by means of either a ladder or a vehicle. Such episodes include Jacob's Ladder (Gen. 28:12), which is called *maareg* in the Ethiopic *Book of Jubilees*; Elijah's translation to heaven in a chariot of fire (2 Kings 2:11); Enoch's ascent to the various heavens and hells, described in the Ethiopic and Slavonic *Books of Enoch* (c. 50 BC); the ascension of Christ (Luke 24:51); St Paul's transport to the third heaven (2 Cor. 12:2); and the ascent made to the heavenly realms, assisted by an angel, described in the *Ascension of Isaiah* (c. AD 80).

The visits of certain other patriarchal figures to the heavens and hells are also described in the early Gnostic writings. There is said to be a Pahlavi text, written some four centuries before Muhammad, which tells of the ascent to heaven of the priest Arta Viraf, guided by the archangel Sarosh, till he stands before the deity Ormazd, and then of his visit to the nether regions.

Muhammad and other religious-minded Korayshis may well have been acquainted with at least some of these stories. According to the Koran, Muhammad's opponents declared that they would never believe in his mission until he 'ascended by a ladder to heaven' (17:95).

Once, while staying at the house of Umm Hani, daughter of Abu Talib, in 621, Muhammad claimed to have had the desired experience. It has been suggested that this may have been his attempt to proclaim the miracle expected of him to convince the Meccans that he was a prophet.

A verse in the Koran states that Muhammad was 'carried by night from the sacred temple of Mecca to the temple that is more remote' (17:1). The 'more remote' (al-aksa) temple is not named, but is said to be in Jerusalem, and later a mosque was raised on the alleged site on Mount Moriah. (Jerusalem is never mentioned anywhere in the Koran.)

Many elaborations have been woven around this 'night journey' (isra), for which there is no Koranic warrant. According to the accepted version, the story is as follows. One night in Mecca, several months before the Hegira, while the Prophet was in a state 'between sleep and wakefulness', the angel Gabriel appeared to him with a majestic horse called Burak, which was described as woman-faced, peacock-tailed and white, and 'whose every stride', wrote Ibn Ishak, 'carried one as far as the eye can reach'.

The Prophet mounted the creature and was transported to Mount Moriah in Jerusalem. Here he caught hold of the lower rung of a golden ladder (miraj) suspended from heaven and, accompanied by Gabriel, ascended to the seven heavens one by one, meeting at their gates the prophets Adam, Enoch, Joseph, Moses, Aaron, Abraham and Jesus in turn. He finally stood 'two bows' length' from the outermost veil concealing the thousand-veiled God, beyond which neither Gabriel nor he could approach. As the Koran says, 'God does not speak to man but by vision or behind a veil' (42:50).

Before returning, Muhammad was also vouchsafed a glimpse of the infernal regions. The whole episode took no more than a fraction of a second.

It was said that, when Muhammad related his experience to the household the following morning, Umm Hani was greatly disturbed, and begged him not to disclose it to the people and expose himself to ridicule and damage his reputation. He did however tell the most faithful of his followers the story. Abu Bakr was prepared to believe it, but to most it caused great embarrassment and consternation, and some found it so ludicrous and incredible that they abandoned their faith (Glubb, 1979, p. 136). As expected, Muhammad's proclamation in the public square that during the night he had been translated to Jerusalem and back (the journey to heaven was withheld) evoked nothing but mirth and doubts about his sanity.

To mitigate what in the view of the hard-headed Korayshis was the absurdity of the story, a tradition speaks of Muhammad saying, 'My eyes were sleeping but my heart was awake.' Another tradition tells of Ayesha explaining, after the Prophet's death, 'The apostle's body remained where it was, but God removed his spirit by night.' Subsequently, many Muslim theologians stated that the night journey of the Prophet was no more than a mystical experience, and others declared that it should be accepted only in a symbolical sense.

6

MEDINA AND AFTER

The town of Yathrib, known from the time of the ancient Egyptians, lies about 230 miles north of Mecca. The Jewish name for Yathrib was Medina, from the Aramaic word for 'city' (*medinta*). There is no truth in the claim that the place was named from the phrase *Medinat al-Nabi*, 'the city of the Prophet' (Rodinson, 1976, p. 139).

According to tradition, the chief Arab tribes, like the Aus and Khazraj, who had settled in Medina belonged to the Kahtan race, originally from southern Arabia, and were thus of a different stock from the Meccans, who belonged to the northern or Adnan racial group.

Mohammad had personal connections with Medina. There was a Nabataean market in Medina, and here Hashim, Muhammad's great-grandfather, would come to trade. It was during one of these business trips that he met and married Salma, daughter of Amr, who was a member of the Najjar ('carpenter') clan of the Khazraj of Medina. Muhammad's grandfather Abdul Muttalib was born and grew up in Medina. His father, Abdulla, used to go on trading ventures there, and on one such visit he died and was buried in Medina. When Muhammad was a child his mother, Amina, took him on a visit to see his relations there, and she died on the way back.

The Prophet was making no progress with his mission in Mecca and the cause had stagnated. It has been suggested that it was not violent persecution – of which there is scant evidence – but Muhammad's failure to make any headway with the Meccans that made him consider moving to Medina and bringing commercial pressure to bear on the Meccans from there.

He did not wish to leave Mecca and was bitter about having to do so, and made out that he was being banished from his home city by the Meccans. The Koran therefore forbids Muslims from making friends with the people of Mecca who drove the Prophet from his home (60:9).

Muhammad's subsequent success in Medina persuaded him to adopt Medina as his new home. He was to live there for the rest of his days, and made it the headquarters of all his operations, military and religious. There he would die, and there he would be buried, behind his mosque.

6.1 The Pledge of Akaba

During their annual pilgrimage to Mecca in 620, a group of six men from Medina belonging to the Khazraj clan – to which Muhammad was related – met and conversed with the Prophet. They thought he might be of help in the problems – social, commercial and especially tribal – they were facing in their own city. If he had a religious lesson to impart, so much the better.

In 621 a group of twelve persons – ten from the Khazraj tribe and two from the tribe of Aus – met Muhammad at a place called Akaba, in the Mina gorge north-east of Mecca, and entered into a formal agreement with him. They took an oath not to worship idols, or lie, or commit adultery, or kill their infant daughters, and to obey Muhammad. This was known as the First Oath of Akaba. They returned to Medina with a disciple of Muhammad named Musab ibn Omayr to teach them the Koran.

The following year (622) the pledge was renewed by seventy-three men and two women from Medina, with the additional promise that they would defend with their lives any Muslims who should go to Medina. This was the Second Oath of Akaba. The pledge was confirmed in the Semitic fashion (Prov. 17:18) by the *bayia*: Muhammad held out his hand, palm up, and the men filed past him and struck his palm with theirs. The women took a simple oath.

From among these men Muhammad chose twelve disciples, saying, 'Moses chose from among the people twelve leaders, and Jesus twelve apostles. You twelve shall be my sureties for the rest' (Muir, 1912, p. 130).

The Medinans then returned to their city with some of Muhammad's adherents, to prepare for his coming and propagate the new teachings. They were followed by small groups of Meccan converts, about 150 in all, and in this way Muhammad's influence in Medina gradually increased. Soon the only Muslims left in Mecca were Muhammad himself, Abu Bakr, Ali and a handful of close associates.

6.2 The Hegira

Some time in June 622 (the authorities are not agreed on the exact date), Muhammad, having made arrangements for his reception in Medina, left Mecca by night. He took with him Abu Bakr and the few remaining converts, leaving behind only his twenty-year-old cousin Ali and a companion who were to follow some days later. This event is known as the Hegira (Arabic *hijra*, translated, 'emigration', 'departure', 'expulsion' or 'flight').

The story of the Prophet's escape from Mecca and the Meccan pursuit is much embellished in Muslim chronicles. For example, Muhammad and his party are said to have taken refuge in the cave of Thaur, about three miles outside Mecca. Here a spider spun a web over the mouth of the cave, and this led his pursuers to believe that no one was inside. From there the fugitives made their way to Medina in stages with the aid of a bedouin guide, taking about nine days to complete the journey and arriving around 28 June 622.

When Muhammad and his party reached the village of Koba, about three miles south of the oasis of Medina, they were sighted by a Jew who immediately informed the Medinans that the person they were expecting had arrived. On hearing the news, the Muslims came out to welcome the Prophet. He invited them to build a mosque at Koba in honour of his deliverance. It was a simple structure, part of which Muhammad helped to put up, and it became the first public place of worship for the new religion.

Three days later Muhammad remounted his camel, al-Kaswa, 'the Ear-Cropped', and rode towards the centre of Medina. He dropped the reins of the camel, having decided to go wherever the animal led him. It stopped in an empty field covered with graves. Here Muhammad purchased a plot, and set about getting a house built for himself and his family. Here also a mosque, the Mosque of the Prophet (Masjid al-Nabi), was built.

Muhammad had received a hero's welcome in Medina, and, except in certain quarters, his influence grew rapidly, until within a short time he was to become the virtual ruler of the city.

In 638, six years after the death of the Prophet, the caliph Omar, having investigated the customs of the Greeks and Romans, decided to establish an era to begin with the migration of Muhammad from Mecca to Medina. The era was fixed to begin from the first day of the lunar year in which it took place. In 622 this day fell on Friday 16 July 622, and this date marks the start of the Muslim calendar and is the first certain date in the history of Islam.

The calculation of equivalent Muslim (lunar) and Christian (solar) dates is complex. The Muslim year, which is made up of twelve lunar months of 354 days, is eleven days short of the solar year of 365 days. In thirty-three solar years there are thirty-four lunar years. Each Christian century consists of about 103 Muslim years. For international convenience, almost all Muslim countries now use the Gregorian (solar) calendar.

6.3 The First Muhammadans

The Meccan converts of Muhammad who participated in the Hegira – traditionally said to have numbered seventy persons – were known as the 'exiles' or 'refugees' (muhajirs; Arabic plural muhajirun – from the same root as hegira). In time the term came to include all the early converts who left Mecca after the pledge of Akaba, those who accompanied and followed him in the Hegira and those who joined him later in Medina, before his conquest of Mecca in January 630.

The early converts at Medina who rendered help (nasr) to the new arrivals from Mecca became known as the Ansars, a term first used in the Koran for the disciples and helpers of Christ (3:45). These Medinan helpers were drawn mainly from the two rival tribes controlling the Medinan oasis: the Khazraj, related to Muhammad through his great-grandmother and whose chief was Saad ibn Obada, and the Aus, once associated with the Jews, whose chief, Saad ibn Muad, later turned against them.

Those designated as the Prophet's 'companions' (ashab; singular sahab – origin of the Western term sahib) included a miscellaneous category of adherents, ranging from close intimates to those who had simply spoken to or even heard the Prophet or who just lived in his vicinity during his lifetime. For a time his followers called themselves 'Steadfast' (hanif, the pre-Islamic term for monotheist); later they came to use the term 'the Faithful' (muminun, singular mumin), and also spoke of themselves as belonging to the 'Party of Allah' (hizb-i-Allahi).

Muhammad had once said that, of the many Muslim sects that would arise after his death, only one would consist of the true adherents of the faith. All others would be infidels. From the very beginning the doctrine preached by Muhammad bore his name. Even before the Hegira the Prophet's followers were known as the 'community of Muhammad' (umma Muhammadiya), and this usage continued for centuries.

In the course of Muslim history many sects have claimed to belong to the pure community of Muhammad. There were also mystical groups who spoke of themselves as pilgrims along the 'Muhammadan path' (tarika Muhammadiya), to indicate their adherence to the law as laid down by the Prophet himself, as distinct from the corruptions that had crept in. In India the 'Muhammadan way' was initiated by reformers such as Ahmad Sirhindi (d. 1624). The Urdu poet Khaja Mir Dard (d. 1785) also did much to advance the process in that country. In more recent times a Muhammadiya movement has become prominent among the Muslims of Indonesia.

The designation 'Muhammadan' was in general use even among Muslims and in the West till the beginning of the present century. It was, and still remains, the only distinctive name for the religion promulgated by the Prophet.

In recent times Muslims have tended to object to the term 'Muhammadan' on the ground that it might imply that the faith was the creation of the Prophet, or even that Muhammad was the object of worship. The term 'Musalman' (or 'Mussulman'), the once universally used Persian form of 'Muslim', is now also falling into disuse.

Muslims prefer the term 'Islam' for their religion and 'Muslim' for an adherent of Islam. As we shall see, both of these terms originally came from pre-Islamic Christian usage (see Section 10.5), and were first used by Muhammad in a general sense, for the religion and the followers of all the prophets from Abraham to Jesus.

6.4 The Hypocrites

Muhammad was aware that some of his followers who had ostensibly accepted the new doctrine were persons of dubious faith, and they form the subject of Sura 68 of the Koran.

Some people, says the Koran, pretend to accept, but inwardly they lie, and their hearts are sealed. They vacillate and remain uncertain in their fidelity. They are irregular in their duties and cannot be relied upon in times of crisis. They waver, grumble, criticize and secretly harbour unbelief. They doubt the revelations and deny the faith. In the Koran, a person of this category, whether sceptic or freethinker, is dubbed a 'hypocrite' (*munafik*; Arabic plural *munafikun*). The Koranic term is of Ethiopic origin, and means 'scoffer'.

Many of these munafiks derided the fasting and prayer rituals of the new religion and were cynically outspoken on other matters about which Muhammad's followers were generally hesitant to speak. Two such scoffers, named Rafaa ibn Zayid and Sowayd ibn Harith, were among those who embraced Islam yet secretly ridiculed it whenever they could, which made them very popular with certain sections of the Prophet's following.

Genuine converts, Muhammad knew, were difficult to find. As he once confessed, 'I have never invited anyone to accept Islam but he has shown signs of reluctance, suspicion and hesitation, except Abu Bakr.' The people were not strong in their faith, dissent was frequent, and loyalty fragile. During the time of the so-called persecution quite a number of converts renounced their faith. Others of his more articulate companions expressed their own views more forcefully than was desirable in an infant community. Many more turned their backs on him when he claimed to have been miraculously transported from Mecca to Jerusalem. Even the stalwart Omar was to feel like leaving after what he thought was the humiliating treaty Muhammad accepted at Hodebiya (see Section 6.13).

6.5 Hasan ibn Thabit

Not long after Muhammad's arrival in Medina he became the object of attacks by Arab poets who ridiculed his claims and satirized his mission. They declared that the Koran was Muhammad's own poetical composition. They boasted they could tell stories as good as his, and accused him of ambition and falsehood. Muhammad was extremely sensitive to these attacks and reacted with force. As a result, several of his detractors paid for their temerity with their lives.

Muhammad hated to think that his Koranic inspirations might be regarded as the utterances of a mere poet (see Section 7.15), and more than once he made it clear that he abominated poetry and detested the whole fraternity of poets. One hadith credits him with saying, 'A bellyful of purulent matter is better than a bellyful of poetry.' He referred to Imru al-Kayis, the greatest of the early poets, as 'their leader to hell-fire'. He abolished the annual poetry contests held at Okaz. But, in order to counter the attacks on him, he himself engaged poets to glorify his military exploits and respond to the polemical tirades of his enemies.

His chief poet was Hasan ibn Thabit of the Khazraj clan. Descended from a long line of poets, Hasan had spent many years in the entourage of the Christian prince of Ghassan, and he wrote a glowing account of the luxury and magnificence of the Ghassan court. Like most Christian poets of his time, he wrote in praise of wine, 'which turns us into kings'.

The Prophet presented him with Sirin, one of two Christian girls sent to him by the governor of Egypt (see Section 6.14), reserving the other, Mary the Copt, for himself. The fact that Muhammad provided a Christian girl for Hasan suggests the poet might have been a Christian himself. After Muhammad's death Hasan became an adherent of Othman, the third caliph, and favoured Muawiya for succession to the caliphate after Othman's death.

6.6 The First Battles

In February 623, a few months after he had settled in Medina, Muhammad organized his first raiding expedition (*razya*) against a Meccan caravan. This was followed by several others, some of which he led personally, the purpose being to obtain booty, harass the Meccans, and help the trade of Medina.

In January 624, during one of the Arabian sacred months when fighting was prohibited, Muhammad's men carried out a raid on a Meccan caravan in the valley of Nakhla, in the course of which one Korayshi was killed and two others were taken prisoner. The caravan was brought back to Medina as booty. There was an outcry in the city at this breach of an ancient tradition forbidding fighting at such a time, but Muhammad duly received a revelation justifying warfare in the sacred season if carried out in the cause of God (2:214). The leader of the expedition, Abdulla ibn Jahash, was given the title of 'Commander of the Faithful' (*Amir al-Muminin*) – a title later to be borne by the caliphs.

Historically, the most momentous of the encounters between Muhammad and the Korayshis took place on 15 March 624. Muhammad had learned that a large Meccan caravan of several hundred richly laden camels on its way back to Mecca from Syria would pass by a place called Badr, twenty miles from Mecca, and here Muhammad planned to ambush it. The caravan was led by Abu Sofyan, the Omayyad chief.

Muhammad proceeded to Badr and, on the advice of a Medinan citizen, filled in all the drinking wells, except one, where he took up position, intending to deprive the Meccan caravan of access to water. Destroying wells was a serious crime in a desert community, but the Prophet believed it was warranted in the circumstances.

Abu Sofyan came to learn of the plan to waylay him, and sent a messenger named Damdam to tell the Meccans to send a force to ward off the attack. By making a detour along the Red Sea coast, Abu Sofyan was able to bring his caravan safely home.

In the meantime the Meccans assembled a force and proceeded to Badr to confront the raiders. There a bloody battle ensued which is described in great detail in the Muslim chronicles. Muhammad himself took no active part, but directed operations from a shelter of palm fronds that had been erected for him. Behind the shelter swift-running camels had been kept in readiness by the chief of the Aus, who told the Prophet that, in the event of defeat, 'you could escape on your camels to Medina' (Glubb, 1979, p. 184).

From his shelter Muhammad kept up a constant prayer to Allah, and these ceaseless pleadings so troubled Abu Bakr that he felt constrained to protest, 'O messenger of God, your repeated entreaties will only annoy your Lord, for surely he will fulfil his promise to you.' Throughout the conflict Muhammad remained highly strung, and once, during a moment of intense excitement, he suffered a paroxysm and collapsed in a faint.

While the fighting was in progress, a sudden brief squall whipped up a cloud of sand into the faces of the Meccans, and with prophetic sight Muhammad cried out, 'A thousand angels are falling upon the enemy.' This incident is also referred to in the Koran: 'If you are steadfast and fear God, and the foe come upon you, the Lord will help you with five thousand angels' (3:121).

In the Muslim traditions it is said that the Meccans were supported at Badr by Satan, who took the guise of Joal ibn Soraka, a chieftain of the tribe that controlled the surrounding countryside. He had assured the Meccans of victory, but as the tide of battle turned he ran away. On being questioned why, he replied, 'I see that which you cannot see' (8:50) – meaning the angels fighting on the side of the Muslims.

According to the chronicles, 700 Meccans fought against 350 of Muhammad's men at Badr, and the battle ended in a victory for Muhammad's side. The Prophet lost fifteen men and the Meccans fifty. Among the dead were Abu Jahal and other prominent Meccans, including the eldest son of Abu Sofyan. The battle was notable not so much for the brutal deeds committed by both sides as for the way in which Muhammad's party dealt with their captured enemies, who were only trying to defend their caravans against predatory attack. Muhammad was present at the executions that followed.

In July, September and October 624 Muhammad followed up the advantage gained at Badr by leading three more expeditions against Meccan caravans, taking rich spoils. The Meccans finally reorganized themselves under Abu Sofyan, now commanding three thousand men, and on 23 March 625 they invaded Medinan territory near Ohod, a hill about six miles north of the city, and here engaged with Muhammad and his supporters.

The ranks of the Muslims – only seven hundred strong according to the chronicles – were soon broken. Muhammad tried to halt his fleeing men, crying out that he was the apostle of God, and exhorting them to return, but to no avail. A detachment of Meccans now bore down upon the Prophet, who inflicted a spear wound on a Meccan from which the man later died. Muhammad himself was struck by a stone which split his lip and broke two of his teeth. He also received wounds in the cheek and leg, and a rumour soon spread that he had been killed. His life was saved only through the devotion of a small group of followers, who surrounded him and bore him away to the safety of a hollow. Thus concealed, they washed his face and attended to his wounds.

Much of the credit for the Meccan victory was attributed to the brilliant and ruthless commander Khalil ibn Walid of the Makhzum clan. Khalid later joined Muhammad and won renown as the greatest of the Muslim generals.

The Battle of Ohod, with seventy-four of Muhammad's men killed (including his uncle Hamza) for only nineteen Meccans, was a setback for the Muslims. The people were dismayed, especially in the light of the divine assurance that 'twenty steadfast men will vanquish two hundred; one hundred will vanquish a thousand' (8:66). Having been told to regard the victory at Badr as a mark of God's favour, it was difficult to explain the defeat at Ohod. But the answer was vouchsafed in the next revelation (3:120–200): God had allowed the defeat as a test.

The Meccans did not immediately follow up their victory, and from April 626, after a respite of a year, Muhammad resumed his attacks on merchant caravans. Such raids became increasingly productive, with Muhammad's party growing rich in camels, slaves, and captive women and children. A number of other tribes joined Muhammad's plundering forays, partly as a safeguard against attack by him and partly at the prospect of a share in the booty.

For some time Muhammad had contemplated taking over the flourishing settlements of the Jews, and he now set about doing so. From 624 he began to attack them one by one, until by 628 no important Jewish clans remained in Medina or its environs (see Section 9.2). Throughout this period the battles against other non-Jewish tribes continued unabated, and with increasing success. In all, Muhammad organized well over 100 raiding expeditions (see Section 14.4).

6.7 Salman the Persian

In April 627 the Meccans, having made preparations for a decisive attack on Medina, now advanced towards the city, this time with an army of seven thousand men, including allies among bedouin clans like the Ghatafan and Asad, who were smarting from the onslaughts made on them by Muhammad's marauders. The situation looked grave, and in his dire predicament Muhammad turned to one of his companions, Salman the Persian.

By means of a Persian-type fortified trench – called by its Persian name *khandak* – which was dug around the weaker section of Medina's perimeter, Salman was able to defend the city. The Arabs, unfamiliar with trench defences, did not know how to proceed. In what became known as the Battle of the Ditch, the faltering Meccan attack was easily repulsed and the day was saved for Muhammad.

Salman was a Christian from a Zoroastrian (magian) family; he had studied in the Nestorian college at Jundishapur in Persia, and then spent many years in Syria with Christian anchorites of the Kalb tribe, before going to Medina. He is not named as one of Muhammad's amanuenses, but it is said that he used to have long talks with Muhammad, and it was probably from him that certain eschatological notions and much of Muslim angelology and demonology, as embodied in the Koran, are derived.

So impressed was the Prophet with the wisdom of Salman that he once laid his hand on the Persian and said to his followers, 'If knowledge were attached to the Pleiades, the men of his race would stretch out and reach for it.' Muhammad's opponents named Salman among those from whom the Prophet received some of his teachings, as well as help in the composition of certain parts of the Koran.

Whether Salman ever became a Muslim himself is not clear. After the death of the Prophet he left Medina – he did not approve of Abu Bakr as successor, preferring Ali – to live among the Muslim converts of the once-Christian tribe of Rabia in Mesopotamia, and he was said to be buried either in Ctesiphon or in Jerusalem.

Salman came to play a great part in the gnosis of later Shia sects like the Nosayris, who almost deified him – including him in their mystical Trinity, along with Ali and Muhammad. Sometimes, indeed, he was accorded a higher rank than the other two (G. Levi della Vida, in SEI, 1974, p. 501).

6.8 The Wives of Muhammad

The facts concerning Muhammad's private life are given in great detail by Ibn Ishak, Ibn Hisham, Ibn Saad, Ibn Hanbal, al-Tabari and other chroniclers, as well as in the hadith. In one hadith Muhammad is reported as saying that three things gave him the greatest delight: prayer, perfume and women. The Koran too hints at his susceptibility to the charms of women (33:52). According to Ibn Arabi, the Prophet had stated that he perceived divinity in woman, 'who was made lovable to me by Allah' (Schuon, 1976, p. 185). According to the Turkish-born scholar Nabia Abbott, Muhammad, 'the prayerful and perfumed prophet of Islam, was avowedly a great lover of the ladies' (1985, p. xv).

It is said that Muhammad once told his young wife Ayesha that if she died before he did he would give her a splendid funeral. 'Yes,' she replied, 'and then you would go straight off and amuse yourself with your other

women; after which you would arrange for a wedding with a new wife.'
Upon hearing this, Ibn Ishak writes, the Prophet smiled.

Muhammad's seeming preoccupation with women and the frequency of
his marriages aroused comment among his contemporaries. His opponents
accused him of giving himself up to female company, which was not in
keeping with the character of a prophet, and of pretending he received
divine guidance and inspiration for his marital problems.

The Jews, who held it as a maxim that carnality precludes prophecy,
declared that if Muhammad were a prophet his interests would not so inces-
santly be directed towards women. 'What kind of prophet is this man', they
asked, 'who only thinks of marrying?' (Andrae, 1960, p. 188). And the
doubtful circumstances in which he acquired some women for himself, such
as Rihana and Safiya (see Section 9.2), were thought to be incompatible
with the status and conduct of a person claiming to be divinely guided in
whatever he did.

Some Muslim writers regarded this side of Muhammad's nature as a sign
of superior virility, and indeed went on to say that he could satisfy all his
wives in a single night. They justified his polygamy on several grounds: that
he wished to secure the allegiance of certain communities by marrying into
their tribe; that he wished to secure the loyalty of certain individuals by
marrying into the family; that a plurality of wives was required for reasons
of social prestige; that he married to provide a husband for widows and a
father for orphans; and that he wished desperately to be the father of a boy
and remove the stigma of being sonless.

The Koran allows a believer to have four wives, but a special revelation
allowed Muhammad to exceed that number. In the common account,
Muhammad had eleven wives, but according to some traditions he had
twenty-two (Hughes, 1977, p. 400). Some of the twenty-two marriages were
invalid because the contract had not been fulfilled; some were never
consummated; some ended in divorce; some of the girls elected to leave
him; some marriages were intended but were broken off at the last stage;
and some were temporary.

Thus, Muhammad contracted two marriages in 630. One was to Asma
bint Numan of the Kinda tribe, but he sent her back because of a hysterical condition. The other was to Amra, daughter of Yazid of the Wahid
tribe of the clan of Kilab. She, however, had been reluctant to marry the
Prophet, because her father had been killed by the Muslims, so he divorced
her too. There is also a tradition that the Prophet once saw the child Umm
Habib, daughter of Ibn Abbas, crawling about, and remarked that if he were
alive when she grew up he would marry her. But he died while she was still
a child (Guillaume, 1960, p. 55).

Each of Muhammad's regular wives who were with him in Medina had a
one-room apartment adjacent to and along the eastern courtyard of the

mosque, and as his harem grew the number of rooms increased. The commonly accepted wives of Muhammad are listed below.

(1) Khadija, Muhammad's first wife, died while he was still in Mecca. Muhammad's fidelity to her for twenty-four years is thought to be due in part to the love and respect he had for her, but it may also have been determined by his need of the wealth, influence and security she provided, and she was in a position to insist that he remain monogamous. However, his strong masculine drive, of which Arab writers speak with approbation, may have overridden grief and convention, for about one month after the death of Khadija he married again.

(2) Sauda bint Zamaa, widow of Sakran of the Abyssinian exile, was married to Muhammad in 619, when she was about thirty years of age. As she grew older Muhammad neglected her, and in 630 he divorced her. On her plea that she wished to avoid the disgrace of being a rejected woman, he took her back.

(3) Ayesha, Muhammad's favourite wife (see Section 6.9), was the daughter of Abu Bakr, who became the first caliph. She played a significant part in the early history of Islam.

(4) Hafsa, the daughter of Omar, who became the second caliph, was the seventeen-year-old widow of Khonays, an early convert to Islam, when Muhammad married her in January 625, after the death of her husband at Badr. In the harem she was an ally of Ayesha. She died in about 670.

(5) Zaynab bint Khozayma was the widow of Muhammad's cousin Obayda, who was also killed at Badr. She was thirty when Muhammad married her in January 626. She died eight months after the marriage.

(6) Umm Salama, of the Makhzum clan, was the wife of Abu Salama of the Abyssinian exile. When Abu Salama died in 625, of wounds received at Ohod, Abu Bakr and Omar, both fathers-in-law of Muhammad, and Muhammad himself, sought her hand. To Muhammad she said that he already had four permitted wives – Sauda, Ayesha, Hafsa and Zaynab bint Khozayma. It was to allow Muhammad to marry more than four wives that a revelation was sent down to permit him to do so (33:49). Muhammad married her in March 626, when she was twenty-nine years old. In the harem she was an ally of Fatima, wife of Ali. She survived Muhammad.

(7) Zaynab bint Jahash (see Section 6.10) was the wife of Muhammad's adopted son, Zayid ibn Haritha, who divorced her so that Muhammad could marry her.

(8) Juwayriya was the daughter of Harith ibn Abu Dirar, the chief of the Mustalik tribe (a branch of the Khozaa), and the widow of a man of that tribe. She was captured during Muhammad's expedition against the Mustalik. Muhammad ransomed her from a citizen and married her in January 628. She was twenty-two years old at the time, and full of grace and beauty.

(9) Umm Habiba (d. 665) was the daughter of Abu Sofyan and the wife of Obaydulla of the exile in Abyssinia. On Obaydulla's death in that country

in 628, Muhammad decided to marry her, and when the mourning period was over the marriage was performed by proxy before the ruler of Abyssinia. She joined Muhammad in Medina in 628. She was thirty-five years old at the time. She was an ally of Fatima.

(10) Safiya married Muhammad after he had captured the Jewish settlement of Khaybar. She was an ally of Ayesha. She died in 672.

(11) Maymuna, daughter of Harith, sister of Umm al-Fazl and sister-in-law of Abbas, Muhammad's uncle, was a comely widow of twenty-six whom Muhammad married in 629 during his pilgrimage to Mecca. She survived him, dying at the age of eighty-one. She was the aunt of the famous Khalid ibn Walid, the recently converted 'Sword of Allah'.

6.9 Ayesha

In 621, before Muhammad left for Medina, he was betrothed to a seven-year-old girl named Ayesha, daughter of his faithful follower Abu Bakr and his wife Umm Ruman. To strengthen his own ties with Muhammad, Abu Bakr had broken off her betrothal to a young man named Jubayr ibn Mutam, in order to accommodate Muhammad. Jubayr's parents, who were pagans, were only too glad to end the engagement, as they feared the marriage might lead to the boy's conversion to Islam.

In 623, about nine months after the migration to Medina, when Ayesha was nine years old and, as the sources comment, still interested in playing with her toys, Muhammad, then fifty-two, consummated the marriage. Ayesha was the only virgin bride of Muhammad, and there were no children by the union. After the deceased Khadija, Ayesha became the great love of his life, and she remained his favourite to the end. It was in her room and with his head on her lap that he breathed his last.

According to Ayesha, whenever Muhammad went on a journey he would decide by the casting of lots which wife was to accompany him. During his raiding expedition against the Mustalik tribe in December 627 he took Ayesha with him. On the return journey the following month, a halt was made in the evening, the last stop before Medina. Before dawn, while it was still dark, Ayesha left her litter to answer a call of nature, and while so occupied her shell necklace fell off without her noticing it. When she returned and the men had begun to strike camp, she realized that her necklace was gone. She went back and felt about in the sand until she found it.

On returning, she saw that the caravan, with her litter, had moved off without anyone noticing that she was not in her usual place. She wrapped herself in her cloak and waited, thinking that her absence would soon be noticed and someone would be sent back for her. As it happened, a young man, a member of the raiding party named Safwan ibn Moattal, of the Solaym tribe, had straggled behind. Seeing Ayesha and recognizing her as the wife of the Prophet, he made his camel kneel and asked her to mount.

Then, taking the head-rope, he walked ahead, leading the animal. Ayesha remained silent, veiled and properly covered throughout.

On rejoining the main party in Medina the next morning, she explained what had happened, but the people drew their own conclusions and malicious rumours were soon spread about. Hamna bint Jahash, sister of Muhammad's wife Zaynab, even alleged that Ayesha and Safwan had known each other for some time, and spoke of earlier meetings between them. Among Ayesha's other accusers were Abdulla ibn Obayi, chief of the Khazraj tribe, and Muhammad's poet, Hasan ibn Thabit. Muhammad's son-in-law Ali told the Prophet, 'Women are plentiful. All you have to do is change her.'

Muhammad, not knowing what to think, and dismayed at the magnitude of the scandal, stayed away from Ayesha, but he found the separation from his wife more than he could bear, and after a month he was vouchsafed a revelation (24:11) that placed her innocence beyond doubt and settled the unpleasant affair. But he never took Ayesha alone on any future expeditions. Some of the rumour-mongers among the men, including Hasan ibn Thabit, were flogged, although Abdulla ibn Obayi was spared because of his status.

Ayesha's apartment opened out directly into the courtyard of the Medina mosque where the Prophet used to discuss political and social affairs with individuals and groups, and she was thus particularly well placed to listen to what was going on. It is believed she would inform her father, Abu Bakr, of anything of political significance, which may have helped to advance his political career.

It was further said that Ayesha tried to influence Muhammad's views through her power in the harem. Two main rival factions had formed within the female quarters, with bitter hostility between them. One was led by Ayesha, who was joined by Hafsa, daughter of Omar, and the Jewish wife Safiya. The other was led by Fatima – daughter of Muhammad and Khadija, and wife of Ali – and her two allies Umm Salama and Umm Habiba.

According to al-Bukhari, Ibn Hanbal and Ibn Saad, Muhammad received the inspiration for many of his suras while in Ayesha's presence. When Umm Salama complained to him about the favouritism shown to Ayesha, he dismissed her, saying, 'Trouble me not about Ayesha. She is the only one in whose company I receive any revelations.'

It is also significant that over 2,000 hadiths have been ascribed to Ayesha, and, although most of these have been rejected by knowledgeable scholars, more than 170 are accepted as authoritative and are thought to have been given to Ayesha by the Prophet himself.

Young as she was, Ayesha had acquired a good understanding of Muhammad and the general trend of his teachings. There is a tradition that during his absences from Medina he would instruct his followers to consult her if they had any religious problems (Armstrong, 1991, p. 240).

Ayesha was eighteen years old when Muhammad died, and was both intelligent and beautiful, but like all his wives she was precluded by Koranic decree from ever marrying again. She remained active in political affairs to the end of her life. She opposed Othman, the third caliph, as well as the fourth caliph, Ali, and was an involved observer when her allies fought against Ali at the Battle of the Camel almost twenty-five years after the Prophet's death.

She died in 678, aged sixty-four, of an unspecified illness. Nabia Abbott says that, reading the accounts of her last illness, 'one is struck by the absence of any joyous note of spiritual victory, or of heavenly anticipation' (1985, p. 216). Indeed, she wished she had never been born, and hoped she would sink into complete oblivion. She expressly forbade the burial of her body near Muhammad's, and she was laid to rest in the Baki cemetery outside Medina.

6.10 Zaynab bint Jahash

The Ayesha affair was not the only matter relating to Muhammad's wives that caused adverse comment among the Muslims: another incident had taken place some eighteen months earlier. This was his controversial marriage to his cousin Zaynab bint Jahash, a sister of Obaydulla ibn Jahash (of the Abyssinian exile), and at the time the wife of Muhammad's own adopted son, Zayid ibn Haritha.

Muhammad had warned his followers never to visit the houses of men who were away from home. In August 626 he himself visited Zayid's house and finding him absent he was on the point of leaving when, as al-Tabari relates, he accidentally caught sight of the ravishing Zaynab, who happened to be scantily clad. He looked away, but smitten by her beauty he looked again and exclaimed aloud, 'Praise be to Allah who turns the hearts of men as he wills!' (Later he was to warn men never to look twice at any woman, 'for the first look is excusable, but verily the second is unlawful'.)

Returning home at once, he slept with his fifth wife, Zaynab bint Khozayma. In a hadith, he declared, 'When one of you sees a woman and is attracted to her, he should hurry to his wife. With her it would be the same as with the other one' (Mernissi, 1975, p. 11).

Zaynab bint Jahash was a haughty woman who resented the fact that she was married to an ex-slave. When her husband returned, she told him what had happened and what Muhammad had exclaimed upon seeing her. Knowing she had attracted the Prophet, the woman gave her husband no peace until he decided to part with her in favour of Muhammad and divorced her.

After waiting the required four-month period, Muhammad married her in March 627. She was thirty-two years old when she became the Prophet's seventh wife; she died in 641.

The union of a man with the wife of his adopted son was forbidden by

Arab custom, and, as Ibn Hisham says, the event caused much unfavourable comment and earned the censure of the Medinan Muslim community, who saw the marriage as incestuous.

But the problem was resolved when Muhammad became the recipient of a specific revelation, embodied in the Koran: 'Zayid having settled the matter concerning her divorce, we [God] have married her to you. No blame attaches to the Prophet when God has given him permission' (33:37). Much to the annoyance of Ayesha, Zaynab would later boast that she had been married to Muhammad by the express command of Allah, who was her matchmaker. It was this revelation that prompted Ayesha to remark caustically to her husband, 'Your Lord seems to have been very quick to gratify your desires.'

6.11 Mary the Copt

In addition to his wives, Muhammad had two concubines. One was Rihana, whom the Prophet took into his household in 627 after the massacre of the Jews of Korayza (see Section 9.2). The other was Mary the Copt, one of two Christian slaves sent to Muhammad in 628 by the governor of Egypt (see Section 6.14).

Mary the Copt was a fair and curly-haired girl whom Muhammad used to visit frequently by day and by night. On one occasion Hafsa caught Muhammad and Mary together. Not only were they in Hafsa's own private apartment and in her bed but – as his wives came to him in rotation – it was also on Ayesha's 'day'.

Muhammad pleaded with Hafsa not to tell Ayesha, promising to forgo Mary's company altogether. Hafsa agreed, but reported the matter to Ayesha anyway, and a scandal spread through the harem. The Prophet found himself received by his wives with coldness and reserve for his infringement of harem rules.

To free him from his rash promise never again to see Mary, to whom he was deeply attached, he received the following revelation: 'Why, O Prophet, do you hold that to be forbidden which God has made lawful to you, from a desire to please your wives. God has released you from your oaths, and God is your master' (66:1–2).

Hafsa and Ayesha continued to tax Muhammad about his visits to Mary, upon which the Prophet lost patience and threatened to divorce them, again through divine inspiration, warning them that, if he did put them away, Allah would give him in exchange 'other wives, better than you, virgins as well as those who have known men' (66:5).

The warning had the desired effect of silencing his wives, but he thought it wiser to separate Mary from them, so he found her lodgings in another quarter of Medina, where he continued his visits. He was extremely jealous of her, and when gossip started that her cousin Mabur used to visit her regularly he sent Ali to investigate. When Ali spied Mabur approaching Mary's house he took out his sword and gave chase. Mabur ran off, but in the course of his flight he tripped and fell and Ali noticed that he lacked male organs. Ali sheathed his sword and reported back to Muhammad, who gave thanks to Allah, but ordered Mabur never to see Mary again.

In April 630 Mary became the mother of a son whom Muhammad called Ibrahim (Abraham), a name he held in the highest esteem. But in January 632, during a partial eclipse of the sun, when he was only fifteen months old, the boy died, to Muhammad's great grief.

His first wife, Khadija, and Mary the Copt were the only women of Muhammad's household who bore him children. Mary died about five years after Muhammad.

6.12 The Harem Crisis

By Muhammad's mid-fifties trouble had begun to brew among the inmates of his harem, and as he approached his sixtieth year the problem was getting beyond his control. Some of the new brides would have preferred a more satisfactory marriage than with an ageing man, whatever his status. It was said that the regular wives taught the newcomers stratagems by which they could avoid his embraces. One such was to quote the Koranic verse 'I seek Allah's protection from you' (19:18). How often these were used is not known (Abbott, 1985, p. 62).

Muhammad's expanding harem, his advancing years and his declining strength made it impossible for him to satisfy the needs of his wives with impartiality, as Allah required (4:3). Besides Mary the Copt, he had favourites, such as Ayesha and, to a lesser degree, Umm Salama and Zaynab bint Jahash. Another revelation was received (33:51) exempting him from treating his wives with impartiality.

His wives often plagued his life with their complaints and demands. There were disputes about their rights and the 'days' allotted to them. They quarrelled about their status. They grumbled about the growth of his harem and the shorter time each could spend with him. Lacking other satisfaction, they demanded at least the pleasure of fine clothing and other luxuries. A harem crisis threatened.

The problem, complicated by the impasse over Mary the Copt, reached such a pitch and Muhammad found the situation so intolerable that he separated himself from all his wives and, following a revelation, offered them a choice between an 'honourable dismissal' (divorce) and remaining with him (33:28).

Rumours of the threatened divorce spread, and a potentially serious situation might have arisen, for divorce would have given grave offence to certain powerful relations of the women concerned, including Abu Bakr (father of Ayesha), Omar (father of Hafsa) and Khalid ibn Walid (nephew of Maymuna). It is thought that some of the lesser wives may have chosen divorce, but Ayesha and eight of the others remained with him (Watt, 1961, p. 226).

It was at this time, in response to the behaviour of his wives, that Muhammad started to receive a series of revelations limiting their freedom. He did not wish them to be as independent as women were in the days of 'ignorance' (*jahiliya*), before Islam (33:33). Muhammad began to be troubled about the looks his wives received, and may have returned, when outsiders were present. Al-Baydawi relates that Muhammad may have instituted the segregation of women when he noticed at a common meal that the young Ayesha's hand touched that of one of the guests.

In yet another revelation, males not of the household were ordered not to engage in conversation with the Prophet's wives except from behind a curtain, otherwise it would cause the Prophet uneasiness (33:53). Those of his wives guilty of lewdness would receive a double punishment (33:30), but those who obeyed God and the Prophet would receive a double reward and an honourable place in paradise (33:31), for they were not as other women (33:32).

Ibn Saad records a tradition according to which Talha ibn Obaydulla, cousin of Abu Bakr, was heard to say that he would marry Ayesha when Muhammad died. Muhammad heard about this, and may have begun to wonder what would happen to his many beautiful wives. He received a revelation that no one could marry any of the Prophet's wives after his death (33:53). To strengthen the prohibition, they were all placed under a taboo by being accorded the title of 'Mothers of the Faithful' (33:6).

A story is related that a woman known to be one of Muhammad's widows later married Ikrima, son of Abu Jahal, much to the annoyance of the Muslims, who regarded the marriage as a slight on the Prophet's memory. But Abu Bakr assured them that the woman's marriage with the Prophet had been broken off and had not actually been consummated.

As compared with the days before Islam, the freedom of women was greatly curtailed by Muhammad, and it was felt by many that the principal Muslim laws governing the status, seclusion, veiling and general conduct of women were all largely determined and set down by the ageing Prophet following his own experience with his young wives.

6.13 The Treaty of Hodebiya

Muhammad had made up his mind to visit Mecca on a pilgrimage, his purpose being to test Korayshi opposition there. In March 628 he set out from Medina with fourteen hundred men, along with animals to be offered as a sacrifice.

Halfway to Mecca, he paused at Abwa, where he visited the grave of his mother, Amina. Al-Baydawi states that the Prophet sought God's permission to pray for the salvation of her soul, but this was forbidden by God, in a verse revealed to him (see Section 14.16). Muhammad then resumed his journey.

When news of his approach reached Mecca, the Koraysh resolved to be firm. They were aware of Muhammad's growing power and the strong bargaining position he had acquired through his control of the caravan routes. They knew that hostilities with him would irretrievably damage their trade. But they were determined to deny him the privilege of entering the city, and not to give him the impression that he was free to make the pilgrimage whenever he wished. The citizens of Mecca, joined by some of the surrounding tribes, took up arms and awaited him just outside the town.

Forewarned of this, Muhammad left the main road and camped at Hodebiya, seven miles from Mecca. Emissaries were sent from the Koraysh informing him of their determination to resist, despite his protestations that he had come in peace only to perform the pilgrimage. One of the emissaries, a chief from Tayif named Orwa, son-in-law of Abu Sofyan, was quite blunt: 'The people of Mecca will not suffer your motley rabble to enter the city.' He then stretched out his hand to take hold of the Prophet's beard, but was restrained by the other members of his party.

Muhammad then decided to send his own emissaries to Mecca. His first envoy was roughly handled by the Meccans. Muhammad then desired that Omar should go, but Omar declined, saying there was no one in Mecca to protect him from danger. Othman, who was an Omayyad and a cousin of Abu Sofyan, then offered to go.

When several hours passed and Othman did not return, there was fear in Muhammad's camp that he had been killed. It now looked as though Muhammad's own position might be one of great danger. In the circumstances Muhammad was determined to fight to the last in case of attack. Taking his stand under the shade of an acacia tree (48:18) he exacted from his followers an oath of loyalty and a promise that they would defend him to the death. Later, it was to be regarded as an honour to have had an ancestor who had made the famous 'pledge under the tree'.

As it happened, Othman returned safely, with a Korayshi proposal for a treaty to be concluded between the two parties. The Korayshi embassy was headed by Sohayl ibn Amr.

Muhammad summoned his son-in-law Ali and began to dictate the terms of the treaty: 'In the name of God [Bismillah], the Merciful [al-Rahman] . . .'. At this point Sohayl stopped him, saying he objected to the name 'Rahman' being used as a name of God in the treaty, as he did not know of any God called by that name. The name 'Rahman' was accordingly deleted, and Muhammad resumed his dictation: 'This treaty is between Muhammad the Apostle of God [Rasul Allah] . . .'. Sohayl now objected again, saying Muhammad's claim to be an apostle of God was presumptuous and unacceptable. 'Just write your name and the name of your father,' said Sohayl. Al-Bukhari and Muslim ibn al-Hajaj both quote traditions to the effect that Muhammad then took the pen from Ali and struck out the words 'Apostle of God', substituting in his own handwriting the words 'son of Abdulla'.

According to the terms of the treaty, there would be ten years of peace. If any Meccan went over to Muhammad, Muhammad would have to send him back. But if a Muslim went to Mecca, the Koraysh would not be obliged to return him to Medina.

As for the pilgrimage, the Muslims were now to go back to Medina, but they could return the following year for the lesser pilgrimage (omra). They could remain in Mecca for only three days. They were to come armed with only sheathed swords.

These grudging concessions created a sense of deep humiliation amongst Muhammad's followers. The Prophet tried to pacify them, but Omar refused to be convinced and could barely conceal his indignation. Al-Wakidi records Omar as saying afterwards that had he found a hundred like-minded men he would have abandoned Islam (Andrae, 1960, p. 160).

Muhammad and his party sacrificed the animals they had brought at Hodebiya, and returned to Medina. On the way back the Prophet was inspired by God to declare that a manifest victory had been achieved (48:1).

6.14 External Contacts

To strengthen his position further, Muhammad now sought to make alliances with other Arab tribes, with a view to securing his trade routes to Syria. In the autumn of 628 he approached certain tribes, mostly Christian, like the Judham in southern Palestine and the Kalb in Syria, and made agreements with them.

At the same time, Muhammad decided to proclaim his prophethood as far afield as possible, and sent out communications to the heads of the larger Arab states, the kings of Yamama, Oman and Bahrain, summoning them to embrace Islam.

The replies from Oman and Bahrain were non-committal. Hauda ibn Ali, head of the Christian Hanifa tribe of Yamama, the most powerful man in central Arabia, replied as follows: 'Excellent is the revelation to which you invite me. Grant me a share in the rule and I will associate myself with your enterprise.' On receiving this reply Muhammad cursed Hauda, who, it is said, died the following year.

Missives demanding their conversion were also sent to foreign rulers on the same date. The story goes that Heraclius, emperor of Rum ('Rome' – that is, Constantinople), having read the letter commanding him to abandon the idolatrous worship of Jesus and Mary and summoning him to acknowledge the mission of Muhammad, cast it aside as the effusion of a harmless lunatic. The chroniclers add that the Byzantine empire was soon to lose extensive territories to the Muslim armies.

The message to Harith VII, prince of the Christian tribe of Ghassan, who was the Byzantine governor of Bostra in Syria, likewise ordered his conversion. Again the messenger was dismissed as the emissary of a madman. Harith died the following year, and his territory, the chroniclers point out, would shortly come under Muslim rule.

The Persian ruler Khosroz II died before the letter reached him, but his successor, Kobad II, on reading the contents, tore it in pieces. When the Prophet was informed of what had happened, he exclaimed, 'Even thus, O Lord, rend his kingdom!' And so it was to be.

The envoy to the Roman governor (*mukaukis*) of Egypt was received with courtesy and returned with a friendly answer, along with the customary gift of two slave girls. Muhammad took one of these – Mary the Copt – for himself, presenting the other to his poet, Hasan ibn Thabit.

The message to the negus of Abyssinia was also courteously acknowledged. From his understanding of Islam, the negus believed that the new religion was a form of Christianity. In a second letter sent by the same bearer, Muhammad informed the negus that it was now safe for the remaining Muslims (about sixty in number) who had sought refuge in Abyssinia to join him in Medina.

Western historians give little credence to the legends of these missives and the demands made by Muhammad for the conversion of foreign potentates. Copies of the letters and their replies preserved in the Muslim chronicles are considered to be largely apocryphal. These chronicles give conflicting descriptions of the letters: the dates of their dispatch, the persons to whom they were addressed, and the precise wording of their contents. The claims are inconsistent with Muhammad's situation at the time.

At the time of the alleged dispatch of these letters, Muhammad's power extended little beyond Medina. Even Mecca was not yet under his authority. He was in no position to demand or enforce the conversion of any independent ruler, and he was too pragmatic to attempt to do so. He may have sent envoys with friendly letters to the rulers of the surrounding countries to establish closer relations with them. He may also have put forward his own account of what was taking place in his part of Arabia, to forestall Meccan appeals for assistance against him. The polite replies from Egypt and Abyssinia would appear to confirm that the letters could have done little more than this.

The legend of these historic missives, it is thought, was fostered to counter the disasters of the seventh year of the Hegira, which ended with a tragic defeat at Mota in September 629 (see Section 6.16). It also helped to lend a prophetic touch to the success of the Muslim armies in the decades following the death of the Prophet.

6.15 The Lesser Pilgrimage

In February 629 Muhammad, accompanied by two thousand followers, returned to Mecca to perform the *omra* or lesser pilgrimage. (This is to be distinguished from the *hajj* or greater pilgrimage.) According to the terms agreed in the previous year at Hodebiya, the Korayshi forces left the town and camped on the surrounding hills.

Muhammad and his followers then made the seven circuits of the Kaaba and the seven runs between Safa and Marwa, and then sacrificed the animal victims they had brought.

While in Mecca, Muhammad tried to become reconciled with the members of his clan, the Hashim. The former chief of the clan, his uncle Abu Lahab, had died in 624, and the present head was Abbas, another uncle, who was a banker. An idolator and a long-time opponent of Islam, Abbas had fought against Muhammad at Badr, although he subsequently decided to take a more neutral attitude.

Now, seeing that the power of his nephew was in the ascendant, Abbas declared himself ready to accept Islam. To seal the renewed alliance, Muhammad married Maymuna, the sister of Umm al-Fazl, Abbas's wife. Shortly after, the great general Khalid ibn Walid, who was Maymuna's nephew, also joined the Muslim ranks.

Wishing to make a friendly gesture, Muhammad asked the Meccans if he could remain in the city for a few days, so that they might sit down with him at the wedding feast. But the Meccans with pointed discourtesy told him they had no need of any food he might offer them. Then, reminding him that his three days allowed for the pilgrimage had elapsed, they hurried him off.

Abbas remained in Mecca to carry on Muhammad's work there. (He was eventually to become the eponymous ancestor of the Abbasid caliphs.)

6.16 The Campaigns

Concurrently with his raids on merchant caravans, the Prophet organized numerous expeditions against neighbouring tribes and towns. Between the years 624 and 628 he had completed his conquest of the most powerful Jewish communities (see Section 9.2); he now turned his attention to wider conquests.

However, most of the expeditions against the Arab tribes mounted in 629, the seventh year of the Hegira, ended disastrously. In February a party of Muslims sent out towards Fadak against the Banu Murra was cut to pieces. (Muhammad avenged this loss a few months later, when his forces defeated the Murra.) In April a party sent against the Banu Solaym was routed, and most of its members were slain, the leader escaping only with some difficulty. In June an expedition against the Banu Layth on the road to Mecca also suffered great loss of life, the remnant being forced into rapid flight.

In July Muhammad sent a detachment to Dhat Atla, near the Syrian border, to call the people to embrace Islam. They were answered with a shower of arrows. The Muslims fought back but were slaughtered, only one man being spared to take back the tale.

In September 629 Muhammad sent an emissary to one of the princes of Ghassan. On his return journey the man was waylaid and killed by bedouin tribesmen. A Muslim force was thereupon dispatched under the Prophet's adopted son, Zayid ibn Haritha, with Khalid ibn Walid as next in command. They advanced up to the frontier of the Byzantine empire, where they were met by a contingent of Christian and pagan auxiliaries and were heavily defeated at Mota. Among the dead were Zayid ibn Haritha, Jaafar – the brother of Ali, only recently returned from Abyssinia – and the warrior-poet Abdulla ibn Rawaha.

The surviving Muslim army, now led by Khalid ibn Walid, returned to Medina – to be met with mockery and abuse. The people pelted them with dirt and shouted at them for fleeing from the scene of battle. The Prophet eventually managed to pacify the populace, and the next morning assured them that he had seen the martyrs of Mota reclining on rich cushions in the pavilions of paradise.

(The defeat of Mota was to be avenged in July 632, some weeks after Muhammad's death, when Osama, the son of Zayid ibn Haritha and Umm Ayman, marched to Mota, ravaged the land, slew many of the inhabitants, and brought the rest back as captives.)

The military campaigns continued in 630 and 631. Many of the allied ranks who were called upon to take part in these campaigns were becoming disaffected, and some refused, in defiance of Muhammad's express command. Those who did participate grumbled about their disproportionate contribution to the armed strength. They were also beginning to find the marches long, tedious and often unnecessary. Above all, they complained about the unfair allocation of booty.

On one occasion the men crowded around Muhammad, loudly demanding a more equitable share-out of the spoils. So rudely did they jostle him that his mantle was pulled away and his clothes were torn, and he was forced to take shelter under a tree. On the way back to Medina they even plotted to murder him by pushing him over a cliff (Rodinson, 1976, p. 277).

It was because of such unhappy incidents that Muhammad decided never to lead any expeditions in future. The last one in which he personally took part was that to Tabuk in October 630, where he made a treaty with the Christian tribes. He followed this by directing a series of operations against them (see Section 10.19).

6.17 The Conquest of Mecca

Not long after the defeat at Mota, hostilities broke out between the Muslims and the tribes allied to the Korayshis. Muhammad took this as an infraction of the treaty of Hodebiya, secretly welcoming it as opportunity of ending the ten-year truce with Mecca agreed to less than two years previously. From his journey to Hodebiya in 628 and the lesser pilgrimage in 629, he had gathered that Mecca could not hold out against a large force, and he started preparations for a march on the city.

The Koraysh sent Abu Sofyan to negotiate with Muhammad. The old man first visited his daughter, Umm Habiba, Muhammad's wife, to solicit her intervention. But she refused even to let him sit down in her room, and rolled up the carpet laid down on the floor. Abu Sofyan exclaimed, 'My dear daughter, either I am too good for the carpet, or the carpet is too good for me.' 'It is the Prophet's carpet,' she replied, 'and you are an unbeliever.' 'Truly', the aggrieved father remarked, 'you have changed for the worse since you left me.'

When Abu Sofyan saw Muhammad in the street and paused to speak to him, the Prophet passed him without looking in his direction. Having failed in his attempt to obtain an interview, Abu Sofyan mounted his camel and returned to Mecca.

On 1 January 630 Muhammad set out towards Mecca with an army which, including his bedouin auxiliaries, comprised about ten thousand men. They eventually camped a day's march from the city. The Meccans panicked, thinking the city was going to be captured. Muhammad's uncle Abbas, who had remained in Mecca as his agent, came out to meet his nephew. Soon after, Abu Sofyan also appeared, seeking an interview with the Prophet, which was arranged for the following day.

At the meeting Abu Sofyan was asked whether he now believed that there was only one God, and that Muhammad was his prophet. Abu Sofyan, now almost seventy years old and unwilling to abandon the faith of his fathers, hesitated, and then replied that he was prepared to accept the first part of the declaration but in his heart he had doubts about the second.

At this point Omar drew his sword and threatened him with summary execution, whereupon the old man began to recite in a low voice, 'There is no God but Allah,' and after a pause added slowly, 'and Muhammad is his prophet.' Later he was to remark privately to Abbas, 'Truly your little nephew has become a man of some importance.'

Abu Sofyan was then sent back to prepare Mecca for Muhammad's public entry into the city. The Meccans were to be assured that the lives and property of all those who submitted would be spared. They were to lay down their arms and remain in their houses.

Muhammad entered Mecca on 11 January 630. He visited the Kaaba and, for the second time since the Hegira, participated in the lesser pilgrimage.

He then ordered all the 360 idols in and around the Kaaba to be destroyed, and the paintings on the walls and pillars of the Kaaba to be erased. He himself destroyed a wooden pigeon, regarded as one of the Korayshi deities that hung from the roof of the shrine.

At the same time Muhammad sent his general Khalid ibn Walid to tear down the pagan temples of the neighbouring tribes. (The Jazima tribe, when asked to say, 'We are Muslims,' said instead, 'We are Sabians,' whereupon Khalid slaughtered the whole tribe.)

Muhammad then offered prayers at the tomb of his first wife, Khadija, before visiting Safa, where he sat on a rock, once the site of a pagan idol, while the erstwhile pagans of the Koraysh filed past to pay him homage. He adopted a conciliatory attitude towards those who had formerly opposed him, and in general he did much to placate those people of Mecca who had assembled to take an oath of allegiance to him.

When he addressed the women of Mecca, though, he was repeatedly heckled. One woman in particular refused to be silenced. Asked to identify herself, she did so. She was Hind, the wife of Abu Sofyan, a formidable woman who had fought alongside the other Korayshi women at the Battle of Ohod, in which Muhammad had been defeated. Abu Sofyan's hostility to Muhammad was exceeded only by the hatred with which his wife regarded the Prophet. For political reasons, however, Muhammad took no action against her.

Muhammad left Mecca to the great relief of the inhabitants, having stayed in the town for two weeks.

6.18 The Submission of Tayif

When Muhammad left Mecca, with an army now consisting of twelve thousand men, ten miles north-east of the city, at Honayn, he found himself confronted by a force of the Hawazin tribe, who were joined by a contingent of Thakif tribesmen from Tayif, totalling about four thousand men. Muhammad's warriors were confident of victory, because of their numerical superiority, but they were soon driven back by the ferocity of the Hawazin attack and forced to flee. The Koran refers to this incident, to Muslim pride in their numbers, and to their subsequent flight before the enemy onslaught (9:25).

Calling for victory, Muhammad threw a handful of gravel in the direction of the attackers and with some difficulty was able to rally his forces. As a result of divine help, the Muslims regrouped and, after a fierce battle, pursued the Hawazin and Thakif to the valley of Autas, from which they were eventually dislodged. But the Muslim victory at the Battle of Honayn, on 1 February 630, was gained only after great loss of life on both sides.

Muhammad then pushed on to Tayif. Remembering the treatment he had received in the city in 619, he was determined to have his revenge. He had been instructed by Salman the Persian in the use of the catapult, and he now brought this weapon into operation. But after twelve of his men had been killed by archers from the walls of Tayif he abandoned the attempt to capture the town. Instead, he gave orders for the despoliation of the Tayif orchards and vineyards that lay just outside, and this was done before he returned to Medina.

As more and more tribes surrounding Mecca submitted to the Prophet, a Tayif chief of the Thakif tribe named Orwa ibn Masud, the son-in-law of Abu Sofyan who had been uncivil to Muhammad in Hodebiya, now visited Muhammad in Medina and embraced Islam. On returning to Tayif he tried to persuade the townsfolk to accept the new faith, but they shot him to death with arrows.

A few months later, however, the Thakif decided that their acceptance of Islam could no longer be safely postponed, and in December 630 a six-man delegation arrived in Medina to negotiate with Muhammad the conditions under which they would accept his religion.

They asked to be allowed to keep the image of their tutelary goddess Allat for three years, then reduced the request to one year, six months and finally one month, but each time the Prophet refused. Then they asked that her image be destroyed by an outsider, so that they might be saved the disgrace of doing it themselves. Abu Sofyan was delegated to perform the task, but he stayed outside the shrine, refusing to have anything to do with the destruction of a revered idol, and this was carried out by another Muslim, amid the cries and wails of lamentation of the women of Tayif.

Next the Thakifites asked for the preservation for their own use of the forest of Wajj, a place famous for wild game. This was granted. Also granted to them was leave to observe the fast of Ramadan somewhat less strictly than other Muslims. They were denied permission to drink the delectable wines of their own renowned vineyards.

They asked to be exempted from saying prayers, but Muhammad insisted that worship was an essential requirement of Islam and refused to allow this. Finally, they asked that they be exempted from the more degrading obligations of the prayer routine, namely the low prostrations, which they deemed undignified and humiliating. The traditions are divergent and often contradictory about what happened next (Kister, 1980, XI, p. 1).

In one account, when this demand was made, Muhammad remained silent, as though he might agree. The men of Tayif looked at the Prophet, waiting for an answer. Omar, who felt that it would be humiliating for other Muslims if the Thakif were exempted from the prostrations because they thought it undignified, drew his sword and said to the delegation, 'You have burned the heart of the Prophet, O men of Thakif, and may God burn your hearts.' To this, says al-Zamakshari, the Thakifites replied that they had come to listen not to him but to Muhammad.

The Koran is thought to record the Prophet's hesitation and his near-acceptance of the Thakif demand, as well as Omar's intervention. The relevant verse reads, 'And truly they [the men of Thakif] were very near to seducing you [Muhammad] from what we revealed to you, and then they would have taken you for a friend' (17:75). This last clause has also been rendered, 'But at the right moment a friend [Omar] reprehended you' (Rodwell, 1915, p. 170).

Muhammad therefore insisted on the prostrations and, says Ibn Hisham, the Thakifites agreed, saying, 'We shall perform the prayer, though it be a degradation.'

No text of the agreement between the Prophet and the Thakif survives, but it is known that, like the treaty of Hodebiya, it named Muhammad simply as the son of Abdulla, without mentioning his status as 'Messenger of Allah' (Rodinson, 1976, p. 270).

6.19 The Year of Deputations

The ninth year of the Hegira (AD 631) is known as the Year of Deputations. The chroniclers relate that Muhammad's war on idolatry and polytheism soon became known throughout Arabia, and his capture of Mecca clearly showed that he had the power to enforce his will.

Representatives of Arab tribes from all parts of Arabia, including the most distant provinces, came hurriedly to make peace, acknowledge Muhammad, submit to his claims, offer allegiance and accept Islam. Moved, it is said, by the power of his personality, the sincerity of his utterances and the simplicity of his life, they voluntarily made their submission to him and acknowledged his spiritual and temporal authority. Those who came to dissent found their objections melt away when confronted by him. Those who were unfriendly found their hostility vanish in his presence.

Modern scholarship finds that much of this is not quite in keeping with the facts and the truth bears a somewhat different complexion. By the time of Muhammad's death the following year, large parts of Arabia were still pagan, or non-Muslim. Most of the tribes simply ignored his mission. Only little groups submitted, and quite a number rejected his demands (F. Buhl, in SEI, 1974, p. 403).

His converts were found mainly among the tribes between Medina and Mecca, and a few others scattered along the trade routes to Syria and towards Najran and Yemen. And among these many submitted for fear of bloody reprisals, for hopes of security from his raids, or from greed – expecting a share of the plunder.

That the conversions were frequently more a matter of expediency and not so much of faith or conviction is shown by the fact that, as we shall see, immediately after Muhammad's death most of the converted tribes apostatized, and had to be reconquered and reconverted by force (see Section 12.1).

6.20 The Farewell Pilgrimage

On 20 February 632 Muhammad left Medina for Mecca, to perform the greater pilgrimage (hajj). He was accompanied by all his wives and a large crowd of the faithful, along with a hundred camels for sacrifice. He was clearly unaware that this was to be his last visit to Mecca, but tradition makes him give many indications that he knew it to be so.

He performed what became known as the Farewell Pilgrimage (hajjat al-wadaa) on 9 March 632, and in doing so he set the seal on the hajj, giving sanction to the retention of many pre-Islamic practices, including some of the archaic formulas used by the pagans. Except that the shrine was cleared of idols and now dedicated to Allah alone, the rites were retained unchanged and have never been completely depaganized.

These clear relics of an idolatrous past were difficult to reconcile with a religion so rigorously monotheistic and iconoclastic as the one consistently preached by Muhammad, and this did not escape comment. From the beginning of the Islamic period and through the centuries, some Muslims, especially the Sufi mystics, have expressed reservations about the propriety of certain of the observances, and have even doubted the need for undertaking the pilgrimage at all. Some, including Omar, found the veneration of the Black Stone particularly abhorrent.

At the end of the pilgrimage Muhammad delivered a farewell address to the assembled multitude from the top of Mount Arafat, which Ameer Ali calls a Sermon on the Mount (1965, p. 114). He started by saying, 'O ye people, hearken to my words, for I know not whether, after this year, I shall ever be amongst you here again.' The speech ended with the Koranic' verse 'This day have I perfected your religion, and appointed Islam to be your faith' (5:5). Then, lifting up his face to heaven, he said, 'O Allah, I have delivered my message. I have finished my work.'

Once again, modern scholarship has expressed doubt and tends to be sceptical about the textual authenticity of the farewell sermon. While in Mecca, Muhammad had numerous private talks and made several public speeches, giving advice and instruction. Over the decades, it is thought, the contents of these were recollected, gathered together and embellished by pious writers in the form of one great valedictory discourse.

The speech summarized many ideas about the equality of all Muslims, social justice, righteousness and the unity of the community, along with other matters relating to the sacred months, the lunar calendar, the abolition of usury, the ending of blood feuds, the rights of husbands and wives, the stoning of those who violate wedlock, the condemnation of those who make false claims – the curse of God and the angels is called down upon them – and the treatment of slaves, all representing many current ideas, and foreshadowing many of a later date.

Soon after the pilgrimage Muhammad left for Medina, never to see Mecca again.

6.21 The Death of Muhammad

There are several accounts of Muhammad's death, and the details given by the Sunnis (the orthodox), by Ayesha, by the Shias (the party of Ali), by the party of Abbas and by other factions differ, and indeed contradict one another, in many important particulars.

There were occasions when Muhammad despaired of unity among the Muslims, and before his death he referred in the following terms to the quarrelsome tribes he had tried to unite: 'As I have lived among them, they have never ceased to wrangle, pulling at my garments, covering me with their dust, until I wished that God would give me rest.'

Towards the end of May 632, some ten days before he died, he went to the Baki cemetery accompanied by one of his followers, and stood for a time silently among the graves. Conscious of the partisan feuds taking place even then, he addressed the dead, saying, 'O people of the grave, you are surely much better off than men here. Dissensions have come like waves of darkness to flood the community, each worse than the preceding, like the successive hours of a sombre night.'

He returned home with a severe headache and a fever, and collapsed in a faint while in the apartment of his wife Maymuna. His fever lasted for about a week, after which he felt well enough to talk to his followers, though he asked Abu Bakr to lead the public prayers. On 6 June he felt his fever returning, and went to the apartment of his wife Umm Salama, where two other wives, Ayesha and Umm Habiba, were also present.

During the night he moaned aloud, and Ayesha suggested he might seek consolation for his suffering in the lessons he had so often taught others in sickness. She said, 'O Prophet, if any of us had moaned thus you would surely have reprimanded her.' 'Yes,' he replied, 'but I burn with the fever-heat of any two of you together.' He then added, 'Suffering is an expiation for sin,' and went on to mention the names of prophets who had suffered before him.

The next day, 7 June, a pain in his side was so intense that he became unconscious. Umm Salama suggested that he be given a decoction after an Abyssinian recipe, and this was done. Reviving from its effects, he became very suspicious and angry about what he had been made to drink, and forced all the women in the chamber to take the medicine. Accordingly, in the presence of the dying Prophet, the medicine was poured into each woman's mouth.

The conversation of the women turned from the Abyssinian remedy to Abyssinia itself. Umm Salama and Umm Habiba, both of whom had been exiles in that country, spoke of the beautiful cathedral of Maria there, and the wonderful pictures on its walls. Overhearing this, Muhammad cried out, 'The Lord destroy Jews and Christians. Let the Lord's anger be kindled against them. Let there not remain throughout Arabia any faith except Islam.' This was to be carried to its conclusion by Muhammad's immediate successors, notably Abu Bakr and Omar.

The following morning, Monday 8 June, 'that accursed woman Ayesha', as the Shia records describe her, entreated the Prophet to move into her apartment, which he did, believing, as she claimed, that it was her 'turn' to be with him, though there was some dispute about this. It was rumoured that while they were together she tried to persuade Muhammad to appoint her father, Abu Bakr, as his successor (caliph).

By this time some other companions of the Prophet had entered the room. According to the Shias, Muhammad desired Ali to succeed him and, though growing steadily weaker, he called for pen and ink to seal the succession. This incident rests on the authority of Ibn Abbas, and is reported by al-Bukhari and Muslim ibn al-Hajaj. The tradition states that Omar, fearing just such an outcome, since he too favoured Abu Bakr, called to the men who had gone for the writing material, 'Come back. He is delirious. The Koran is sufficient for us' (Hughes, 1977, p. 386).

Others insisted that pen and ink be brought, and a noisy argument broke out among those gathered around the bedside of the dying man until Muhammad silenced them, saying he would have no bickering in his presence. He said nothing further, except to call for a toothpick, and a thin sliver of green wood was given to him, which he raised to his mouth to clean his teeth. Having done so, he lay back again.

Muhammad died, aged approximately sixty-two years, at noon on Monday 8 June 632, with his head on the lap of his eighteen-year-old wife Ayesha. As she described it, 'The Prophet died in my arms, his head in my bosom, and during my turn. I had wronged no one in regard to him.'

The news of his death spread rapidly through Medina, and the shocked and bewildered Muslims were, as one contemporary expressed it, 'like sheep on a rainy night'. Some expressed concern about the propriety of his sudden demise. He himself had hardly expected his career to end so suddenly, for he had planned and was preparing for another campaign.

The people were incredulous. How could the Prophet have received no intimation of his death? How could Allah have failed to warn his messenger? How could he have passed away in so unedifying a manner, in the lap of his wife? How could he die without leaving a male heir, or 'sonless' (abtar), which even the Koran regards as a sign of divine punishment (108:3)? How did Allah permit him to leave this world without making his succession clear?

Some believed that the Prophet was simply in a state of 'holy trance' and would soon regain consciousness. When this bodily resurrection did not happen, many were disappointed. Omar, frantic with grief, drew his scimitar and rushed through the crowd shouting that he would strike off the head of any person who dared to say the Prophet was dead. He had simply been taken to heaven, 'as Jesus was' (Kazi and Flynn, 1984, p. 18), but only for a short time, and would return again like the risen Christ (Esin, 1963, p. 118).

Abu Bakr, who at the time of Muhammad's death was away at Sunh, the other side of Medina, returned when he heard the news. He calmed Omar, and went on to address the populace: 'O ye people, if anyone worships Muhammad, let him know that Muhammad is dead. But if anyone worships Allah, let him know that Allah is alive and immortal for ever.' He then continued, quoting from the Koran, 'Thou truly shall die, O Muhammad, as will the others' (39:31). And again, 'Muhammad is nothing but an apostle, and apostles have passed away before him. Yet if he die or be slain, will you turn back upon your heels?' (3:138).

It was later alleged that no one, including Omar, had any recollection of these texts, the implication being that Abu Bakr had invented them for the occasion and inserted them into the Koran, but most scholars do not consider this as likely.

6.22 The Burial

There is as much confusion in the accounts of what happened immediately after Muhammad's death as in those of the circumstances of the death itself.

As indicated, discord about the succession had begun even as the Prophet lay dying. Shortly after he died, and while his body was still warm, further discord set in. The corpse, which remained in Ayesha's room, was visited through the afternoon by the mourners of Medina. Because of the presence of men, Ayesha retired to share the room of one of the other widows.

Two of Muhammad's fathers-in-law, Abu Bakr and Omar, were in Ayesha's room when news was brought to them late in the afternoon that Saad ibn Obada, leader of the Khazraj tribe, had called a meeting in a house of one of their clans, the Banu Sayida, to decide on the succession and other matters arising from the Prophet's death.

The two men decided that time should not be spent in saying the customary prayers, so, leaving Muhammad's family, led by Ali, to attend to the body, they rushed with unseemly haste to the meeting. As a result of this, according to one account, the corpse remained neglected for a whole day. Ali and his supporters knew nothing about the meeting, and no one bothered to tell them (Zakaria, 1989, p. 44). Ayesha, who had been informed of the meeting by her father, Abu Bakr, sent a message saying that it had been the Prophet's dying wish that Abu Bakr should succeed him.

Two main parties were represented at the assembly of electors. One was made up of the Medinan helpers (Ansars), led by the Khazraj chief Saad ibn Obada. The other comprised the Meccan emigrants (Muhajirs), led by three of Muhammad's close associates, all Korayshis: Abu Bakr, Omar, and Abu Obayda. They had Medinan allies in the tribe of Aus, who joined them only because they did not want their rivals, the Khazraj, to assume the leadership.

The meeting went on through the evening and night of the Monday on which the Prophet died. From the outset there were heated disputes about the succession. The Ansars declared that a man from Medina should be chosen to succeed the Prophet. But Abu Bakr insisted that only a man from the tribe of Koraysh would be acceptable to all the Arabs, and, with the connivance of Omar and the behind-the-scenes indication already given by Ayesha, he himself was eventually elected caliph.

Then followed a long discussion about the burial of the Prophet. The Meccan Muhajirs wanted to take the body back to Mecca where Muhammad's people had lived and where he had spent most of his life. The Ansars wanted him to be buried in Medina, because that was where he had established himself and where he had died. A few suggested he be taken to Jerusalem, because that was where other prophets had been buried. Finally, for reasons of convenience – there being other matters to attend to – it was agreed that he should be buried in Medina.

The town having been decided on, a controversy now arose about the most suitable site in Medina for the burial. Some felt it should be in the Baki graveyard outside Medina, where the Prophet's son Ibrahim, his daughter Rokaya and so many companions of the Prophet had been laid to rest. Others believed it should be in the mosque close to his pulpit, or at the spot where he had led the public prayers. No one present was aware that preparations for the burial were already in hasty progress elsewhere.

In one account the body of the Prophet remained on a bier for twenty-four hours. Abu Bakr and Omar returned after the meeting to offer prayers and make their orations, after which the body was buried in Ayesha's apartment on the evening of Tuesday.

In another account it was said that news of Abu Bakr's election was brought to Ali late in the evening of Monday as he sat in silence beside the body of his father-in-law. With him were Abbas, the Prophet's uncle; Fazl, the son of Abbas; and Osama, the son of Muhammad's adopted son, Zayid ibn Haritha.

Ali, determined to avoid a ceremony in which Abu Bakr would inevitably take the lead, decided to bury Muhammad without further delay, on the spot where he had died – in Ayesha's room. Accordingly, the body of the Prophet was hastily washed and prepared for burial, after which it was enshrouded in three cloaks. Then a grave was dug, and it was only then, says Ibn Hisham, that the widows of Muhammad, hearing the sound of pickaxes breaking the soil, became aware that he was going to be interred. Early on the morning of Tuesday 9 June the body was lowered into the bottom of the hole and the earth was shovelled over it. Neither Abu Bakr nor Omar was present (Dermenghem, 1958, p. 54).

(Beside the tomb were to be laid, in due time, the bodies of Abu Bakr and Omar. An adjacent space is said to be reserved for Jesus, who, Muslims believe, will again visit the earth, and die and be buried in Medina – see Section 10.16.)

The election of Abu Bakr was opposed by Abu Sofyan and was never accepted by the Shias, the party of Ali. The dispute thus begun continued during the subsequent weeks, months and years, with other, lesser, disputes proliferating in the course of time, until Islam was rent with schism and religious feuds. Some were minor disagreements, but those relating to succession, doctrine and practice have never been resolved to the present day.

7
THE KORAN

The Koran, the holy book of Islam, is regarded by pious Muslims as coeval with God, eternal and uncreated, and bearing a revelation that is complete, unalterable and final.

The Original Koran is believed to be inscribed in rays of light upon a tablet everlastingly preserved (85:22) beside the throne of God. This archetypal text existed in heaven long before the creation of the world, and is spoken of as the 'mother of the book' (umm al-kitab), the heavenly prototype of all revelation (13:39).

By the grace of God, portions of the book were communicated section by section in the form made known to Muhammad in the course of twenty-three years. This was effected through the angel Gabriel, at both Mecca and Medina, and together the material so delivered makes up the text of the Koran.

The Koran is a miracle (29:50), written in the purest Arabic, the language of God and the angels. Every sura, every, or chapter (114 in number), verse (between 6204 and 6239), every word, every syllable and every letter (the numbers of verses, words, syllables and letters vary in the different reckonings of the Muslim authorities) is inspired by God. When verses are quoted from it they are often introduced by the phrase 'God has said' (kala Allahu), for the author is God.

The Koran, it is said, gives an authentic account of the history of the world and the lives of the patriarchs and prophets of old; it provides material about certain early kings and the true facts concerning Jesus and also the destiny of the human race, of which only incomplete versions are to be found in the Jewish and Christian scriptures. It is a compendium of universal wisdom. Indeed, some hold that every aspect of human knowledge, including all sciences and skills, has its root in the Koran and could be known to those with sufficient insight to comprehend the book's mysteries.

The Koran is unalterable. It is not subject to change or amendment. After the proclamations recorded in the holy book, the pen of revelation has dried up, the heavenly inspiration has ended, and nothing more remains to be said. Nothing can be added to it or taken away from it. It contains all that is needful for the guidance of men and women in every activity. It constitutes not only the religious but also the social, cultural, commercial, ceremonial, military, legal, civil, criminal and administrative codes of Muslims, covering every aspect of life.

7.1 The Angel Gabriel

The intermediary in all the revelations made by God to Muhammad was
the angel Gabriel, the 'illustrious messenger' (81:19) who communicated
God's message to the Prophet. (The Greek *angelos*, 'angel', also means 'messenger'.) This is made clear in order to emphasize the impersonal character
of the Koran, and to refute the allegations of Muhammad's Meccan
opponents that his messages were all his own invention.

No mention of Gabriel occurs in the Koran until the Medinan period,
and then he is named only twice: as the angel through whom the Koran
descended (2:91) and as a helper (66:4). He is referred to, though not by
name, in other verses. Thus, Gabriel was seen by Muhammad 'in the highest point' (53:7) of the 'clear horizon' (81:23), and he then approached
until he was two bows' length away (53:9). On another occasion (53:13)
Muhammad saw a vision near the sidra tree (or lote tree) marking the
boundary between this world and the next.

According to the different traditions, inspiration was received from other
sources as well. At times it came from the Holy Spirit, who brought it down
from God (16:104). At times it came from the Sakina, which in the cabbalist writings is the female aspect of God.

In one account Muhammad said, 'The angel sometimes takes the form
of a man for me.' Asked to describe him, Muhammad replied that his beard
and face resembled those of a handsome young man of Mecca, and he wore
an embroidered turban and rode a white mule with a brocaded saddle. This
young man was identified as Dahya ibn Khalifa, who belonged to the
Christian tribe of Kalb (Glubb, 1979, p. 249).

According to another tradition, reported on the authority of Musa ibn
Okba, after Muhammad's first vision in the cave of Hira, Khadija took him
to see a Christian monk named Addas of Nineveh, who had settled in
Mecca. She told him about Muhammad's vision of Gabriel, and the monk
asked in surprise, 'O lady of Koraysh, how is Gabriel mentioned in this
country of idol worshippers?' He then explained to her that Gabriel was
the angelic guardian sent by Allah to guide the prophets.

According to al-Tabari, one of the reasons why the Jews were not disposed
to accept the revelations of Muhammad was that they were received through
Gabriel, who was the angel of destruction, and not through Michael, who
was the guardian angel of the Jews (Dan. 12:1). The Jews believed it was
Gabriel who inspired Muhammad to carry out his terrible campaign against
the Jewish tribe of Korayza (see Section 9.2).

Muhammad himself likened Gabriel to Noah, Moses and Omar, who
administered stern justice, and compared Michael to Abraham, Jesus and
Abu Bakr, advocates of mercy (Muir, 1912, p. 231). In the mystical tradition of the cabbala, Gabriel is connected with the spirituality of the moon,
while Michael is connected with the spirituality of the sun (Frieling, 1978,

p. 47). Gabriel abides near the level of dreams, which are often delusive, and Michael in the level of visions, which are akin to prophecy (Matt, 1983, p. 229).

7.2 The Descent of the Koran

The Koranic revelations given by Gabriel to Muhammad were not always heard by him in the usual manner, but 'descended' by direct inspiration into his heart and mind. This descent (*tanzil*) sometimes came in words, sometimes in visual form which he was enabled to understand, and sometimes in dreams. Muhammad dictated to his amanuenses what had thus been revealed. Often the revelations were heralded by strange sounds and symptoms (see Section 5.13).

In many cases they descended upon him unexpectedly and at odd times: while he was out riding, or having his hair washed, or while eating (A. J. Wensinck, in SEI, 1974, p. 624). Sometimes enlightenment came to him in answer to a question at a public meeting, or when asked an opinion on some matter that he could not avoid answering, or in response to special circumstances for which an instant comment from him seemed called for. Such revelations appeared to be dictated by the needs of the moment, when he had to take decisions that could not be deferred till an inspirational moment. At such times, it was said, he received immediate guidance from God.

Trifling incidents of ephemeral interest, minor local issues of passing concern and other matters of little moment often prompted a Koranic passage. There were passages about personal slights, in which he cursed his opponents (111:1). This was so well known that once, when he accidentally hurt Muhammad's foot, a companion of the Prophet named Abu Ruhm al-Ghifari was overcome with anxiety lest a Koranic verse be received perpetuating for all time the enormity of what he had done.

Some revelations were provoked by the attacks of opponents, and some were received to forestall objections that might be raised concerning his conduct. Some came to meet the demands of a political or social situation; some to release him from his oaths (66:2), or to justify the killing of infidels and unbelievers (47:4). A number of verses represent bulletins on skirmishes and excursions, or orders of the day for his troops, or relate to his peace treaties with tribal chieftains, or the distribution of booty after a raiding expedition (8:42).

Several verses relate to Muhammad's wives, their disputes and demands. This tendency of the Prophet, especially in the Medinan period, to 'come down to earth' during his revelations and to provide endorsement for his views by what appeared to be facile extemporizations, together with the transient relevance and meagre content of certain of the Koranic verses, did not escape adverse comment. It was felt that the Prophet's constant recourse to revelation when he could not silence his adversaries, or control his wives, or deal with a situation on his own, detracted from the authority of the Koran as a work of revelation brought to him through the inspiration of God.

7.3 The Amanuenses

At the start of Muhammad's mission there were said to have been only seventeen men among the Koraysh, the aristocracy of Mecca, who could write. The scribes and accountants employed by the richer merchants were usually Jews, Christians or Abyssinians. In Muhammad's early days in Medina, writers were equally in short supply, so Muhammad used to offer the poorer captives of his raids and battles their freedom if they would teach his followers the art of writing. Not only were writers few in number, writing material was scarce and not always instantly available. It is not known precisely who took down the first revelations of Muhammad in Mecca, but clearly some of the original material was lost (see Section 7.14).

The amanuenses of Muhammad have sometimes been likened to the recorders (rawis) who took down the poetry of the early bards. Some among his first amanuenses were Christians, or people who had strong Christian leanings, like his wife Khadija, the aged scholar Waraka, and Muhammad's adopted son, Zayid ibn Haritha. Others were Muslim members of his immediate circle, like Abu Bakr and Ali. Among his wives, it is known that – besides Khadija – Ayesha and Umm Salama could read, and Hafsa and Umm Kulthum could both read and write, but whether the two latter wrote to his dictation is not known.

As time passed many other writers took down the inspired messages. These included Zayid ibn Thabit, who was to compile the Koran; Othman, who later became the third caliph; Abdulla ibn Saad, Othman's foster-brother (see Section 7.13); Obayi ibn Kaab, who was to make his own Koranic compilation (see Section 7.14); Muawiya, Othman's cousin, who became the first Omayyad caliph; and also a Jewish amanuensis (Sale, 1886, p. 46). By the time of Muhammad's death, more than forty scribes had been engaged in recording the revelations.

Considering the manner in which the revelations came down and how they were received, the question later to be raised by the Mutazilis and other Arab critics was: How did the amanuenses know when the Prophet was 'under inspiration' and when he was simply expressing his own views? And how did they know when to start and when to stop?

It is only to be expected that some of the material taken down by the amanuenses, perhaps of widely varying competence, would have been subject to the natural errors of all copyists. If Muhammad himself could neither read nor write, as has been claimed, then the textual accuracy of the Koran would have had to depend on the degree of competence of

Muhammad's many amanuenses. The view that Muhammad sometimes revised and corrected the material he dictated has therefore been held by some scholars.

7.4 The Meccan Suras

Scholars make a distinction between the suras of the Koran which Muhammad dictated while he was in Mecca and those he dictated later, after he had established himself in Medina. In later Arabic copies of the Koran, each sura often had a heading to indicate whether it was Meccan or Medinan.

The early or Meccan suras show a tolerance for other faiths, even for the pagan Arabs. They are full of high idealism, prompted by religious conviction and deep spirituality, in consonance with the Jewish and Christian traditions. God is generally referred to as al-Rahman, 'the Merciful'.

These suras consist of religious teachings, moral principles, brief homilies and other inspired sayings of the Prophet. Their message is delivered in a short and simple rhapsodic style, full of visionary power and poetic fire, usually in rhymed and rhythmic prose (saj).

These glowing and impassioned verses, with their striking images and stately rhythms, their mystical beauty and religious insight, were known as the 'terrific suras', because they were often preceded by spells of unconsciousness. Their withering effect was said to have hastened the onset of the Prophet's grey hairs.

The Meccan suras, embodying the faith of Abraham for the Arab people, comprise about one-third of the whole Koran, and would make up a slender volume. Many of these suras, in whole or in part, were on the lips of Muhammad's followers. Despite being transmitted orally, they generally remained unchanged and uncorrupted, to form the nucleus of the faith and the foundation of early Islam. Much of the material had a hymnic or psalmic character, making it suitable for liturgical purposes, so it was also used in public worship and on other religious occasions.

It would seem that before Muhammad left Mecca for Medina the basic beliefs and practices of the early Muslim faith had already been laid down in the early suras, albeit in rudimentary form in some cases. These early passages were referred to as the Koran or 'readings', and served as Bible and prayer-book.

When Muhammad was preparing for his migration to Medina, he sent Musab ibn Omayr to Medina to instruct converts and enquirers there. The reason why Musab was sent was because he could 'recite the Koran', which would seem to confirm that the essential body of the Koran was regarded as being already complete.

The great Scottish authority Richard Bell, after careful scrutiny of the Koranic texts in minute detail, concluded that the Koran was 'definitely closed' about the time of the Battle of Badr (AD 624), less than two years after the Hegira (Watt, 1970, p. 138). At that time the Koran comprised virtually only the Meccan suras.

7.5 The Medinan Suras

In Medina, as Muhammad's status rose and his power increased, a change appears to have taken place in his character (see Section 11.11) and in the nature of the Koranic message. This change is reflected in a marked alteration in both the style and the content of his utterances. The long passages in the Koran that Western critics have pronounced tedious, pedestrian and toilsome to read are almost exclusively suras composed in Medina.

In Medina there is a marked decline in the religious enthusiasm and poetic fervour that illumine the Meccan revelations. The visionary becomes a preacher; the prophet a theologian. Few of the suras bear the marks of divine influence. Muhammad's energy begins to spend itself; his inspiration falters, with only an occasional flash of the old fire. Discursive prose takes the place of ecstatic utterance. Some passages underline his own importance, or deal with personal problems, and show a growing intolerance and hostility to those who oppose him.

The Medinan suras are clearly the product of the Prophet's conscious mind. They consist of exhortations, appeals, regulations and proclamations. The texts begin to resemble doctrinal sermons and take on a more didactic and legalistic tone. The inspired 'readings' become little more than a 'text'. In the Medinan period the term 'Koran' is used less frequently, the term 'al-Kitab', the Book, being used instead.

Unlike the popular Meccan suras, the verses composed in Medina were less familiar to the people, as little of the Medinan material is suitable for recitation in public worship. The fact that the bulk of the Medinan suras remained largely unknown offered scope for alterations and additions to be made to the Koran after Muhammad's death (see Section 7.17).

The differences between the Meccan and Medinan suras were known to Muslim commentators from early times and have frequently been discussed by scholars ever since. In modern times the Iranian writer Ali Dashti made a distinction between the messages received by Muhammad in Mecca and those received by him in Medina. After the Islamic revolution in Iran Dashti was arrested, charged with impiety, imprisoned and severely beaten, and died as a result of this treatment in January 1982. The Sudanese theologian Mahmud Muhammad Taha, in an attempt to find common ground for the different religions in the Sudan, emphasized the distinction between the later Medinan suras, which form the basis of the sharia, and the early or Meccan suras, which in his view had a more universal appeal and were better suited for Islam in the modern world. This distinction did not appeal to the Sudanese authorities and he was arrested on a charge of apostasy and was executed by hanging in January 1985.

7.6 Compilation

At the time of Muhammad's death in 632 the Koran did not exist in anything like its present form. Portions of it, ranging from single verses to entire suras, had been taken down in writing and kept in private hands. Much of the material had simply been memorized by various companions, close associates, 'rememberers' and reciters (*kurra*). There are several conflicting versions of how this material was finally assembled.

During the sanguinary wars undertaken in 633 by the caliph Abu Bakr to reclaim apostates and backsliders, some of those who knew the Koranic texts by heart were killed. More serious was the death during the Battle of Yamama, in the following year, of thirty-nine companions of the Prophet who were among the principal rememberers and reciters of the Koran.

Omar, the father-in-law of the Prophet, fearing that if more of the rememberers died much of the Koran would be irretrievably lost, counselled Abu Bakr to make a collection of the available material and what else remained of the Koranic text. The idea was not well received by the faithful. Many raised objections on the ground that it would be sacrilegious to attempt to do what the Prophet might have done but had not. Even Abu Bakr was doubtful, for this was a task for which he had received no authority from Muhammad.

In the end he gave his approval, however, and he commissioned one of Muhammad's secretaries, Zayid ibn Thabit of the Khazraj tribe, to carry out the sacred duty. In addition to Arabic, Zayid knew Persian, Greek, Ethiopic, Coptic, Syriac and Hebrew, and had read the Jewish scriptures.

Zayid collected all the scattered fragments he could find from the individuals who had preserved them in various ways. Tradition has it that these included writings on scraps of parchment, palm-leaves, flat stones, wooden tablets, pieces of leather, the shoulder-blades and rib-bones of camels and goats, and 'the breasts of men' – that is, the memories of the faithful.

By the end of 634 as many of the fragmentary portions as could be traced and collected were laboriously copied on to separate sheets (*suhuf*), unedited and without critical selection or regard for chronological sequence, and with all their repetitions, discrepancies and dialect variations. Some Muslim authorities say that copies of Zayid's first compilation were made and sent out to various scholastic centres, but others deny this.

The collected material, possibly in Kufic characters, was handed to Abu Bakr, and on his death was committed to the custody of Omar, the second caliph. After Omar's death it passed to his daughter Hafsa, the Prophet's widow.

In the meantime, various extracts of the Koran, from whole chapters to brief fragments, had already been circulating in the provinces where Islam was spreading. Owing to the deficiencies that then existed in the Arabic script, variations occurred in both the reading and the interpretation of these texts, each of which was regarded as authoritative by its exponents.

In the expeditions against Armenia and Azerbaijan, disputes arose amongst the Muslim troops of Syria and Iraq concerning a number of deviations in the passages and readings of the Koranic texts in use. These disputes were serious enough to prompt the general, Huzayfa, to lay the matter before the third caliph, Othman, advising him to interfere and 'stop the people before they differ regarding the scripture as the Jews and Christians differ in theirs'. The situation brought out the urgent need for having a uniform and authoritative edition in place of the conflicting readings in the various rival versions in current use.

Othman therefore decided on a second, more comprehensive and definitive, redaction, to fix the canon once and for all. Once more Zayid ibn Thabit was entrusted with the task, along with three Koryshi helpers: Abdulla ibn al-Zubayr, Saad ibn al-Aas, and Abdul Rahman ibn al-Harith. (There are lists of other helpers who were also said to have made their contribution to the task.) This time they were to call in all existing copies, chapters or fragments of the Koran, compare the material so gathered with the earlier collection in Hafsa's keeping, and prepare a final version of the book, deciding what was to be included and what omitted, and to work out the composition, number and order of the suras.

Othman's commission was faced with several problems: the chronological sequence of the suras, the arrangement and collation of the conflicting texts, and the choice of language from the various dialects in which the Koranic verses had been taken down. To settle the problem of language, Othman instructed Zayid ibn Thabit – who belonged to the non-Koryshi Khazraj clan – to give preference to the dialect of the Koryshi in case of language variation (see Section 7.10).

Since much of the Koran had been dictated in brief passages, rather than the form that now makes up the separate sections, there was no authoritative way of solving the problem of textual arrangement, so the commission recast and put together the suras as best it could from the unconnected fragments. Little attempt was made to avoid repetitions or to connect abrupt transitions.

As it was impossible to determine the chronological sequence of the suras with accuracy, it was decided to start with the auspicious section known as the *fatiha*, 'commencement', which is couched in the form of a brief prayer. 'It is specially noteworthy', says Frants Buhl, 'because of its lack of any distinctively Muslim thought and the presence of Jewish and Christian terminology' (SEI, 1974, p. 280). Thereafter the longest chapter was placed first, with the others following roughly in order of diminishing length. This in fact reverses the order of the revelation, for in general the shorter (Meccan) suras were received first and so predated the longer passages.

As a result of this attempt at order, verses were sometimes transposed out of their original contexts, or isolated fragments for which no place could be found were inserted at random into a sura, or haphazardly joined together despite their disparate subject-matter. Occasionally verses from the Meccan and Medinan periods were dovetailed together, although they had been dictated at different times. Most of the longer suras, such as the third sura, are collections of passages belonging to different periods. Even the shorter suras are sometimes composite.

It is not known who arranged and named the suras. It has been suggested that the Prophet himself gave them their titles, but, since most of them were not collated in their present form till a quarter of a century after Muhammad's death, this would seem to be unlikely. It is thought that he may have named a few, but this is impossible to determine. There was no rule for the choice of a name. The compilers named a sura from some keyword in the text or from any striking word that might identify it. In some cases a sura was known by two titles, one being later dropped.

When the commission had completed its work, Hafsa's original collection was returned to her. All other available copies and remnants, along with any discrepant and contradictory versions, were consigned to the flames. Many Muslims at the time regarded as sacrilegious the wanton destruction in this manner of the leaves and other treasured fragments on which the Prophet's revelations from Allah had been inscribed with such devotion by the faithful.

After Hafsa's death in 670, the governor of Medina, a man named Marwan ibn Hakam – who was Othman's secretary and who subsequently became caliph as Marwan I – obtained the material that had been in her possession and destroyed that as well, so that no evidence of any alternative readings of the canon and proof of changes might remain in existence.

The first uniform text of the Koran was fixed in about 655, some twenty-five years after the death of the Prophet. (It is to be noted that still later dates have been suggested for the final recension – see Section 7.17.) From the newly arranged master-text a number of copies were then made and distributed to the main Islamic centres: one was retained in Medina, and others were sent to Kufa, Basra and Damascus, and possibly to Mecca. Owing to the mistakes of copyists, slight differences crept into these official copies, mainly affecting orthography, dialect, and sura and verse divisions.

Othman's recension was not the only codex made of the Koran. From an early period Muslims had been writing down as much as they could of Muhammad's message and making their own private compilations of the sacred verses. These remained current for centuries, and some acquired special authority. Scholars drew up lists of more than a dozen of such codices (*masahif*; singular *mushaf*), of which one list, made by Ibn Abu Dawud (d. 928) still survives.

These pre-Othmanic collections of the Koran differ extensively from the standard text of Othman (Watt, 1970, p. 45). Some contain non-canonical material; others differ in the words used, in punctuation, in vowel and consonant variations, in the order of the suras, and in some cases by the exclusion of certain Koranic chapters and the inclusion of chapters not in the Koran.

7.7 The Prefixed Letters

Twenty-nine suras of the Koran, mostly Medinan, begin with certain letters of the alphabet. These are known to be part not of the text but of the editing. The significance of these letters is unknown and no satisfactory explanation of their meaning has ever been found, but they have been invested with hermetic mystery and much fanciful speculation abounds.

Like the combinations of letters that make up words in the Koran, these sura headings were subjected to interpretation through various systems of letter mysticism. Each letter (*harf*) of the Arabic alphabet was believed to have a hidden meaning, and this meaning – like the letter's shape – changed according to whether the letter was at the beginning, middle or end of a word. Combinations of two juxtaposed letters, or of the three letters of an Arabic root-word, added further complicated refinements. In some systems (the *abjad*) each letter was also assigned a numerical value and its meaning worked out on the principles of gematria used in the Greek and Hebrew systems.

The prefixed letters were variously said to be abbreviations of the titles of God, or his attributes, or decrees; or of the disused titles of the suras. Some believe they represent the initials or private marks of the amanuenses who took down the Koran, or of the rememberers and reciters, or perhaps of the original owners of the Koranic fragments or suras given to Zayid ibn Thabit, or of those who collected these, or of those who compiled the Koran.

Certain letters are more specifically explained. Thus the letter N that prefixes Sura 68 stands for *nun*, 'fish', signifying the sea-monster Behemoth. The letter Q prefixed to Sura 50 stands for Qaf, the ring of mountains that encircles the earth. The letters KHYAS were said to have been prefixed to Sura 19 by Muhammad's Jewish scribe, and stand for *Kohyas*, meaning 'Thus he [Muhammad] has commanded'.

Again, the letters may preserve the names of pagan deities. Thirteen of the twenty-nine suras mentioned begin with the letters AL. Out of these, six begin with ALM, five with ALR, and one each with ALMS and ALMR. The letters AL may signify Al, 'God', with the name of a pagan deity concealed in the remaining letters. The Mesopotamian sun-god Sin, worshipped in Arabia as far as the Hadramaut, may be hidden in the letters that head Sura 36, consisting of the letters YS, which in Arabic read Ya Sin. This has been alternatively interpreted as 'ya insan', meaning 'O man!', but it might simply be read as an invocation to the sun-god, 'O Sin!'.

Among modern scholars, Hirschfeld adopted the view that the letter S (*sad*) stood for Hafsa, K for Abu Bakr, and N for Othman, all three of whom were closely associated with the compilation of the Koran. Nöldeke, on the other hand, believed that the prefixed letters were meaningless symbols or magic signs. Otto Loth saw a Jewish influence similar to the cabbalistic mystic symbols. These and similar speculations have been dismissed by many others as implausible and arbitrary, but the letters continue to intrigue scholars and baffle interpretation. Watt, who mentions some of these theories, concludes, 'These letters are a mystery' (1970, p. 61).

7.8 Critics of the Koran

Throughout Muhammad's career, both in Mecca and in Medina, doubts were expressed about the true nature of the Koranic revelations. Nor did the official acceptance of the Koran a quarter of a century after his death end the spate of criticism directed against the holy book. Even among those who professed Islam there were people who believed the prophetic inspirations had often been casually received, haphazardly dictated, carelessly taken down or incompletely assembled.

Many objected to the inclusion of certain verses; others objected to longer passages, which they disapproved of entirely. The leaders of certain sects – several Shia theologians among them – maintained that the Koran had been subjected to tampering by additions, excisions and amendments, and that the current Koran was falsified (Goldziher, 1971, p. 109).

Some asked what need there was for God to take oaths like any mortal being, as when he swears by the fig and olive, and by Mount Sinai (95:1); by the declining day (103:1); and by the stars, the night and the dawn (81:15–18). Above all, they asked why the Almighty had to swear on himself (91:5) – though there was a precedent for this, for God swears on himself in the Old Testament (Gen. 22:16).

Some rejected as false all passages in which Allah curses the opponents of Muhammad, or those in which he consigns Muhammad's enemies like Abu Lahab and his wife to the flames of hell (111:1). Such petty vindictiveness was not worthy of the Almighty and the All-Merciful.

Some refused to accept entire suras as authentic. Thus the Ajarida and Maymuniya sects rejected Sura 12 as unworthy because it contained the story of Joseph and Zulaykha (Potiphar's wife), which has to do with erotic seduction and could not form part of a holy book.

A personal servant of the Prophet named Abdulla ibn Masud, who became a Koranic commentator, had made his own compilation of the

Koran which was held in high esteem in Kufa. This man did not regard the first sura and the last two suras (numbers 113 and 114) as part of the Koran, and omitted them altogether in his text.

Although the Sufis (see Section 13.16) did not generally direct any criticism at the Koran, the unorthodox interpretations they gave to many of the verses indicated that those verses, as they stood, did not have their unequivocal approval, and could be accepted only in a metaphorical sense.

Many found the idea that God was the author of the Koran unacceptable (see Section 7.16). In fact, doubts on this point continued to be expressed by Muslin thinkers for centuries. The orthodox view that the Koran was not created but pre-existed from eternity was likewise dismissed by the sceptics.

Foremost among the early critics of the Koran were the Mutazilis, who became known as the rationalists and freethinkers of Islam. The group was founded by the Sufi mystic Wasil ibn Ata (d. 749), a disciple of Hasan of Basra. The Mutazilis were familiar with Greek and Alexandrian writers, and introduced many Greek concepts, including much of Greek rationalism and scepticism, into Islamic philosophical and religious discussion.

In the Mutazili view, to state – as the orthodox did – that the Koran was eternal and not created was tantamount to saying that it was coeval with God. This, according to them, was a form of dualism, constituting the heresy of partnership (*shirk*), making the Koran equal and eternal with the Almighty.

In their opinion, the deliberate destruction by fire of thousands of original texts entrusted to the compilers made it convenient but not veracious to claim that the Koran had always existed in one unique and unalterable form. There was nothing miraculous in the style and composition of the book. It was not written in the purest Arabic, contained numerous foreign words, and bore incontestable evidence of borrowings and alterations, and of Muhammad's personal opinions. In brief, they held the Koran to be a semi-poetical work of Muhammad's own composition.

The Mutazili contention about the Koran being not eternal but created found favour with the last Omayyad caliph, Marwan II (d. 749), and received official support from some of the Abbasid caliphs, including Mamun (d. 833), who set up an inquisition to enforce it. (Some other Mutazili objections are given in the sections that follow.)

Influenced by the Mutazilis were the Ikhwan al-Safa (fl. c. 900), 'Brethren of Purity', mainly of Basra, who also went back to Greek and Hellenistic philosophy and in their encyclopaedias – consisting of more than fifty treatises on topics from mathematics to theology – raised many questions about Muhammad's doctrines. Extremely liberal, they taught that one should not show hostility to any kind of knowledge, or be fanatical in holding any view. Because of their free interpretation of the Koran and religious precepts, they were detested by the orthodox, who persuaded the caliph

Mustanjid (d. 1170) to burn copies of their encyclopaedias publicly in the market-place.

7.9 The Script of the Koran

As indicated in Chapter 4, the earliest form of Arabic writing was deficient in many ways. At the time the Koran was compiled, says Gibb, Arabic was written in a very imperfect script, 'which was all but unreadable to those who did not possess an exhaustive knowledge of the language' (1974, p. 39).

The canon of Othman had no points to distinguish consonants having the same outline, no marks for vowels (although three consonants, *alif*, *vau* and *ya*, later began to be used as vowels) and no orthographic signs whatever. The earliest copies of the Koran that had been sent to the various cities were written in this very imprecise form of early writing. Disputes soon arose about the text, the spelling of words, their vowelization and vocalization, and their meaning, all of which led to discrepant readings and conflicting interpretations of the scripture. The Muslims of Kufa rejected Othman's recension altogether and used their own version.

During the reign of the Omayyad caliph Abdul Malik (d. 705), copies of the Koran with variant and erroneous readings were quite common, and the free interpretation of the text had become widespread. Abdul Malik's governor, Hajaj ibn Yusuf, an Arabic scholar who began life as a schoolteacher, was ordered to see what could be done to systematize the variant readings. He in turn requested a renowned Sufi scholar, Hasan of Basra, to remove the cause of the perplexities. Hasan of Basra appointed a certain Yahya (John) ibn Yaamar, also of Basra, to solve the matter.

On the basis of the dot system used in their script by the Nestorian Christians, and the diacritical and vowel signs used in Syriac, Yahya first introduced into Arabic writing such aids as points and other marks to differentiate between the short and long vowels, to distinguish between the consonants that had the same form but differed in sound, and to indicate the doubling of consonants. The division of words in a sentence and a method of punctuation were brought in a few years later.

These innovations did not immediately receive universal acceptance or gain wide currency. Where the marks were used, they were not employed consistently, nor indeed was the spelling of words uniform. Interpretation still depended on choice (*ikhtiyar*). Further, the marks were not regarded as belonging to the original revelation but were seen as introducing and perpetuating heretical novelties into the reading of the holy book. The great Sunni traditionalist Malik ibn Anas (d. 795) prohibited their use in copies intended for mosque services. Other scholars, including some of the caliphs and local rulers were also displeased and would have preferred the Koran to remain – like the synagogal Torah – without such marks. It is said that when Abdulla ibn Tahir (d. 844), governor of Khorasan, was presented with a sheet of parchment with elaborate penmanship, he objected to the 'coriander seeds' sprinkled over it – meaning the dots.

The first to write about the need to reconcile the inconsistencies in spelling and to have a uniform vocabulary for the Arabic language was Harun (Aaron) ibn Musa (d. 810), a Jewish convert to Islam. Harun's book prompted the compilation of the earliest Arabic word-books (dictionaries).

All these improvements, it must be said, did not put an end to the difficulties of Koranic exegesis, because the written alphabet continued to present problems. The inadequacy of the script made itself particularly evident as different ways of reading (*kira*) the same Koranic script started spreading in different areas, each with its own school of trained readers (*kurra*; singular *kari*). So many regional variations of reading and pronunciation had become established that the problem could be resolved only by compromise and consensus.

The first step in this direction is said to have been attempted by Ibn Mujahid (d. 936) during the Abbasid caliphate. First ten and then seven 'readings' or schools, founded by famous and devout men of learning – three from Kufa, and one each from Basra, Damascus, Mecca and Medina – were accepted as authoritative, and all their readings, with their recommended pauses and vocalizations, were recognized as orthodox.

This anomalous situation prevailed for centuries. Then, from the end of the nineteenth century, printed and lithographed copies of the Koran, carefully and meticulously produced, and representing a single – if still not a universally accepted – 'reading', began to receive qualified approval and to be disseminated from centres like Constantinople and Cairo.

Both manuscript and printed editions of the Koran made today are often festooned with diacritical marks to ensure accuracy and uniformity of pronunciation. Often there are as many marks as letters. But variant readings of the vowels and consonants continue to be regarded as having equal authority.

A standard critical edition of the Koran, making use of all the material now available, still awaits modern scholarship.

7.10 The Language of the Koran

The Koran, it is claimed, is written in the purest form of Arabic and represents the perfection of language. God himself is cited by Muslims as the authority not only for the message but for the purity of the vocabulary, the perfection of the grammatical forms, and the sublime style of the sacred book.

Muhammad had spent his childhood among the bedouin of Hawazin, a tribe not closely related to his own Korayshi tribe. In his youth and early manhood he made many trade journeys to Palestine and Syria, and may have picked up something of the languages spoken there. He was familiar with several dialects spoken in and around the Hejaz.

The Arabic used by Muhammad in his revelations is hybrid in character, with a mixed vocabulary drawn from several languages, and represents a blending of many vernacular forms. The Koran itself was said to have been revealed in seven different regional vernaculars, or dialects of the Arabic tongue. These were Koraysh, Hawazin, Thakif (the dialect of Tayif) and Hodayl, as well as three dialects of the Kahtan Arabs, namely Tayi, Tamim and Yemeni (Himyarite). Later scholars who wished to study the purer forms of the language were obliged to go back to the poetry of pre-Islamic times.

Some features of the language used by Muhammad had even then passed into disuse further north, and were in decline elsewhere. O'Leary states that the Arabic of the Koran shows a language already giving indications of decay (1927, p. 24). By making use of such a composite language, which could not afterwards be criticized, Muhammad permanently 'fixed' this version of Arabic, and thus created Koranic Arabic – a unique, static and unchangeable form of the language.

(During the expansion of Islam, colloquial Arabic continued to develop and flourish independently, assimilating to itself the grammatical forms and vocabulary of the conquered peoples. This demotic or living Arabic in current use began to be more and more removed from the language of the Koran, which became increasingly remote and unfamiliar (Lyall, 1930, p. xxxviii) and soon ceased to be used. Its obsolescence as a spoken idiom and its being regarded as the language of the 'ancients' necessitated Koranic Arabic being studied as a 'foreign' language.)

There are several traditions of the Prophet's linguistic attainments. According to these traditions, it was Muhammad's habit to speak a few words in their own language to the people who came to visit him from the different tribes and nations, including Persian to Persians (Tisdall, 1911, p. 257).

The diversified vocabulary of the Koran would appear to confirm Muhammad's knowledge of foreign words. Modern researchers have listed over 275 loanwords from foreign languages in the Koran. Among the sources of these are Hebrew, Aramaic, Syriac (or Christian Aramaic, which was the most copious source of borrowings), Nabataean, Ethiopic, Persian and Greek. The Muslim encyclopaedist and polygraph Suyuti (d. 1505), in an excess of fervour, adds 'Indian, Coptic, Turkish, Negro and Berber'.

The earliest Muslim commentators acknowledged the borrowings, but later scholars, under the influence of great divines like Muhammad al-Shafi (d. 820), condemned this as heretical teaching: it suggested imperfection and copying, and implied that Arabic was inadequate as a medium for divine revelation. Each word and letter of the Koran was therefore declared to be inspired by God, and written in pure and uncorrupted Arabic. The holy book was free from all admixture, beyond imitation, perfect and sacrosanct.

At the same time, it was known that Muhammad had expressly permitted people to recite the Koran in their own native dialect (Ameer Ali, 1965, p. 186), so presumably vernacular texts were current in many parts of the Islamic world. The famous school founded by Abu Hanifa (d. 767), a jurist of Afghan descent, sanctioned the recitation of the Koran in a language other than Arabic (Grunebaum, 1961, p. 152).

Yet, some time after the Koran was fixed in its present form, most Muslim theologians banned all other versions and prohibited translations, as it was feared that these might lead to misinterpretation of the text and detract from the essence of the original. For centuries, therefore, most non-Arab Muslims living in foreign countries were obliged to memorize or learn to read the Arabic text without understanding much of it, and this, it was realized, was not in keeping with the spirit of Islam.

The case for translating the Koran was presented by many scholars. The Koran itself teaches that God has provided for each people a law given in the language of the people, so that they can read, study and understand it (41:44). For the Arabs too a law has been sent down, written in their own tongue – an Arabic Koran (12:2). In the light of this, it was argued, one has to assume that the Koran is for Arabs alone. If not, and if those who do not speak or understand Arabic are to accept Islam, the Koran has to be translated into their language.

Translations began to appear, and the Koran has since been rendered into some seventy languages, including Indian and African languages. Although the Arabic version is regarded as the authoritative one, the vernacular translations play an important part in its interpretation.

7.11 The Style of the Koran

There are many variations of style in the Koran, from brief ecstatic verses to lengthy prosaic passages. These stylistic differences have helped scholars to distinguish between those sections dictated in Mecca and those dictated in Medina.

Sonorous verse and rhythmic prose in the early style of the Koran had been composed long before Muhammad's time, both by poets and by religious and social reformers like Zayid ibn Amr, Koss ibn Sayda, Omayya of Tayif and others. Many of these verses were popularly known and admired, and frequently recited by the people – sometimes with spellbinding effect. The Prophet's Meccan opponents, contrasting Muhammad's inspirations with the ancient Arab wisdom and the verses in which they were enshrined, often came out in favour of the older works.

After Othman's recension of the Koran had been completed, the suras used to be recited with deep fervour by trained readers adopting a declamatory manner suitable for the intoning of sacred verses. From infancy, people were brought up to hearing them recited. Verses from the holy book were read out on all solemn occasions and in many moving circumstances, from birth to death, and in course of time they began to evoke a deep response from believing listeners. Passages were learned by heart and treasured in the memories of the faithful.

But from the beginning there were rebels who asserted that the high regard in which the Koran was held for its majesty of style and sublimity of thought was largely overdone.

Accepting Muhammad's challenge to produce ten suras (11:16) or even one sura (10:39) like those in the Koran, and repudiating the theologians' contention of the incapacity (ijaz) of any mortal to produce anything comparable, several poets tried their hand at compositions which, they averred, equalled and even surpassed the suras of the Koran in both style and content. When one of the imitators was told that his work failed to evoke the same ecstatic rapture as recitations from the Koran, he replied, 'Let mine be recited in the mosques for a hundred years, and then see' (Rodinson, 1976, p. 92).

The Mutazilis, among other Islamic freethinkers who sought to undermine the orthodox view of the miraculous nature of the Koran, used to circulate the works of earlier Arab poets and wise men in competition with the Koran, to show that for stylistic beauty and moral excellence they were as good as anything to be found in the Koran. The Mutazili writer and master of Arabic prose Amr ibn Bahr (d. 869) – known as al-Jahiz, the 'goggle-eyed', and the grandson of an Abyssinian slave – said that the Koran represents good writing but not the perfection of Arabic.

Over the centuries several writers claimed to be able to write in the Koranic style. Some paid dearly for their presumption. The poet and translator Ibn Mukaffa (d. 758), a converted Zoroastrian who was the first great prose writer in Arabic and made many important contributions to Arabic literature, was tortured to death for attempting to imitate the Koran.

The Persian-born Arab poet Bashar ibn Burd (d. 784), a freethinker from Basra, stated that any of his verses, if properly declaimed by a competent reader, would be seen to rival the Koran. When he heard a singing girl recite one of his poems, he exclaimed that it was better than a comparable sura (number 59, the Hashr) of the Koran.

The Mutazili recluse Abu Musa al Mozdar (d. 840), the Karmathian satirist Mutanabbi (d. 965), the blind poet Abu Ala Maari (d. 1057), and the freethinker Muhadabuddin al-Hilli (d. 1205) were the best known among the writers who privately claimed – or it was privately claimed on their behalf – that their work equalled the Koran in diction, style, beauty of language and moral quality.

Most Western scholars who have gone to the Koran in order to acquaint themselves with its contents, and not in any spirit of hostile criticism, have found the greater part of it, as Andrae says, 'the most boresome reading that can be imagined' (1960, p. 115) – though the same could be said of most scriptures.

The best-known of the nineteenth-century champions of Muhammad and his message, Thomas Carlyle, called the Koran 'a wearisome confused jumble, crude, incondite' and complained of its 'endless iterations, long-windedness, entanglement . . . insupportable stupidity, in short! Nothing but a sense of duty could carry any European through the Koran!' (Ruthven, 1984, p. 102).

Theodor Nöldeke (d. 1930), a great German scholar of Arabic who wrote at length about the stylistic shortcomings of the Koran, stated that, if it were not for the flexibility of the Arab tongue itself, 'it would scarcely be bearable to read the later portions of the Koran a second time'.

7.12 Obscurity of the Koran

The deficiencies of the early forms of Arabic writing, the multiple meanings of many Arabic words and the often ambiguous language in which the Koran was written led to many grammatical and semantic problems, adding to the contradictions that arose in the interpretation of the sacred book and the confusion that often prevailed among the commentators.

Besides the difficulties inherent in the text itself, large parts of the Koran are obscure and sometimes incomprehensible without a knowledge of the 'occasion of the revelation' (*sabab al-nuzul*) – that is, the event or circumstance that prompted it, and the particular person or group to whom it referred. Traditions are full of guesses on such matters.

In attempting to provide clarification for an obscure verse, the biographers and interpreters of the Koran analyse the allusion and annotate the passage, each in their own way. They relate an anecdote leading up to the verse in question to give it authenticity and local colour, providing names, times and circumstances, some of which are known to be fanciful or plainly mistaken.

For example, the Koran says, 'Woe to every backbiter and defamer' (104:1). This might have been a simple admonition against calumny, but the commentators had to find a reason why the Prophet uttered these words. To explain the text, therefore, the commentators – most of whom lived long after Muhammad's day – provide a story, sometimes with dialogue, about the individual who slandered the Prophet and thus elicited the verses, along with the circumstances and the name of the culprit. In one account the offender is Akhnas ibn Shoraykh, in another it is Walid ibn Moghayra, and in yet another it is Omayya ibn Khalf.

The result is that several accounts and varying interpretations are often given of the same verse, and these may be contradictory and mutually irreconcilable. There may be a dozen different authorities for a single phrase, each giving his or her own preferred view. In consequence there are many variant scholastic opinions – some of long standing – about the reading and meaning of the verses, and Koranic commentary (*tafsir*) has been far from unanimous about their interpretation (see Section 8.2). The true meaning, as the Arabs say, is known only to God.

7.13 Alterations in the Koran

In the view of Muhammad's unbelieving opponents, the book dictated by him could not be regarded as a copy of an unalterable book in heaven, since changes were frequently made to it by the Prophet himself, who sometimes substituted one verse for another (16:103). The fact that the Koran states that Muhammad did not make changes on his own but only under guidance (10:16) did not weaken their contention.

The so-called satanic verses had been publicly revealed and publicly withdrawn. It is also known that many verses that had previously been dictated by Muhammad were later found to be missing (see Section 7.14). One scribe, Abdulla ibn Masud, who was a famous companion of the Prophet, took down a verse at his dictation, but the next morning he found the leaf on which he had written it missing. On reporting the matter to Muhammad, he was informed that the verse had been revoked during the night.

As the cynics pointed out, Muhammad would often command something in his book and then repeal it, commanding something else. In more than one instance he had added material to his revelations, making changes in the text prompted by suggestions from those present around him.

Once in the course of his dictation he said, 'Those believers who sit at home are not to be held equal to those who fight in the cause of God.' A blind man named Abdulla ibn Umm Maktum on hearing this raised a complaint, saying that if he were as other men he would certainly fight, whereupon the Prophet, after falling into a kind of trance, altered the verse to read, 'Those believers who sit at home, not having any impediment, are not to be held equal to those who fight in the cause of God' (4:97).

Another amanuensis, named Abdulla ibn Saad – foster-brother of Othman, later the third caliph – used to make changes in the text (Ameer Ali, 1965, p. 295), and on one occasion he added a concluding phrase to complete a verse that Muhammad was composing (23:14), and this phrase was embodied in the Koran. Later Abdulla abjured Islam and fled to Mecca, where he boasted about being the author of one of the sentences in the book said to be inspired by God to the final syllable and the last letter. According to him the revelations were a hoax (Glubb, 1979, p. 308): Muhammad simply dictated what came into his head (Thaalibi, 1968,

p. 69), and he himself had often induced the Prophet to alter the wording of his revelations.

It was also claimed that Abu Bakr was able through his daughter Ayesha – the Prophet's favourite wife – to influence the prophetic utterances, and indeed that some revelations occurred to Muhammad only when he was in the company of Ayesha. Other revelations were said to have been granted in response to suggestions from Omar. On a number of occasions Muhammad hesitated to make up his mind and asked advice before the revelation came. Omar too used to boast, perhaps innocently, of having more than once given advice which then miraculously turned out to correspond to what was sent down from heaven (Rodinson, 1976, p. 219).

Muslim theologians admit that alterations were made in more than 220 verses of the Koran, but explain these amendments by the doctrine of abrogation (nasikh). According to this, certain matters were inspired for a specific occasion and had only a temporary application; the verses relating to them could be altered or deleted when circumstances changed.

This of course did not satisfy the unbelievers, since it is stated in the Koran, 'No one may alter the word of Allah's scripture' (18:26). Any alteration of the text would imply that the unchangeable archetypal Koran in heaven – of which Muhammad's revelation was a true copy – must itself have only temporary relevance, and be subject to alteration.

The changes made to the Koran by the Prophet are a separate issue from the lesser changes that might have been slipped into the text, inadvertently or otherwise by the amanuenses, rememberers, scribes, copyists and compilers, and from the more extensive changes more deliberately made by Abu Bakr, Omar, Othman and the early Omayyads, about which another theory has been advanced (see Section 7.17).

7.14 The Koran Incomplete

There were dissidents who believed the Koran was far from complete. The revealed Koran, it was said, was not a full transcript of the heavenly book, nor was it claimed to be. It is inconceivable that what God had to reveal about this world and the next could possibly be contained within the covers of a single book. This is confirmed by the Koran itself (18:109).

The Koran made it clear that not all that was known about other apostles had been revealed to Muhammad (4:162). Again, the Koran was not a compendium of morals, nor was it a legal code, and Muslim law could scarcely be said to be based on it, except on certain broad principles enunciated in it, which are common to many other religious systems.

The Koran does not even contain all that Muhammad delivered. The Mutazilis were among those who held that neither amanuenses nor rememberers were always ready to hand when Muhammad first started receiving his revelations, and what he said could not have been recorded in its entirety. Much was lost, therefore. It is possible that Muhammad himself did not regard some of the early messages as part of the Koran (Watt, 1953, p. 47). Even when the material began to be taken down, its recording remained for some time a rather haphazard affair. Muhammad was not yet an important personality, and no one thought it worth preserving all his utterances in any great detail.

The possibility that Muhammad himself could not recall or might have forgotten parts of what had been revealed to him is likewise suggested in the Koran (2:100). Again, some of the suras and many scattered verses were carried 'in the breasts of men' – that is, memorized. Forgetfulness on the part of the rememberers, and death by natural causes or in war, as in the Battle of Yamama, could have further contributed to the loss, mutilation, distortion or corruption of material.

According to a tradition attributed to the Prophet's wife, Ayesha, a certain chapter now containing seventy-three verses once contained no less than two hundred, but when Othman's recension was being assembled the missing verses could not be found (Guillaume, 1983, p. 191). A page believed to contain the Verse of Stoning, which prescribed stoning to death of the partners in an act of adultery, was also missing. Ayesha stated that the page in question was under her bed during Muhammad's last illness, but in the confusion that followed his death a stray goat entered the room and ate the piece of parchment (Rahman, 1966, p. 65). Her statement was later taken up by the Mutazilis, who asked how Allah could permit a goat to devour and cause to be lost forever a law sent down from heaven for the guidance of the faithful.

It was also pointed out that many verses privately held by Muslims were not surrendered when the scattered material was called for by Abu Bakr and Othman. This material therefore failed to be embodied in the final recension. One of Muhammad's amanuenses named Obayi ibn Kaab, who compiled his own codex of the Koran which was well received in Syria, had two suras included in his version that do not appear in the standard text.

The Shias (the party of Ali) accused the Sunnis of corruption (*tahrif*) of the text by deliberately perverting or suppressing sections of the Koran. They alleged that, under Othman's orders, whole suras in favour of Ali once forming part of the original Koranic revelation had been deliberately omitted and consigned to the flames. It was therefore false to claim that Othman's recension of the Koran was complete.

From time to time for decades after the text was fixed, the rememberers continued to recall brief phrases and even longer passages, some consisting of several verses, which do not appear in the Koran. Also, many quotations on coins and inscriptions, as well as citations in written works, all said to have been dictated by the Prophet during his inspired moods, may represent an unknown number of other omitted passages.

One old tradition states, 'Let no one say that he has learned the whole of the Koran. For how does anyone know what the whole of it is, when much of it has disappeared? Rather, let him say that he has learned what is now extant of it' (Sweetman, 1985, p. 37).

7.15 The Koran as Poetry

The Koran says, 'Those who go astray follow the poets' (26:224). One of the reproaches of Muhammad's opponents which he found most hateful was that the Koran represented the outpourings of a poet (69:41), a medley of dreams (21:5), a recapitulation of old wives' tales which he caused to be put in writing (25:6).

For fear of being identified with poets or being mistaken for one, Muhammad expressed his detestation of poets and their work. According to a hadith, Muhammad once said, 'No creature was more odious to me than a poet, and I could not even bear to look at one. I thought, Woe is me, am I a poet? Am I possessed?' At the same time, aware of the power and popular appeal of poets, Muhammad engaged poets of his own, notably Hasan ibn Thabit, to counter accusations against him.

Yet the comparison between Muhammad and the poets was not without some foundation. The earliest Koranic utterances did indeed consist of measured and occasionally rhymed prose (saj), with formulaic phrases delivered in brief exclamatory style, reminiscent of the ancient rhapsodists. They are full of assonance, alliteration, and internal and final rhymes, and the iteration of words in successive sentences is like a refrain that works its hypnotic spell by means of sound (81:1–13).

Like other poets, Muhammad was likened to a soothsayer (52:29), a being possessed (44:13), a man bewitched (25:9). As was the habit of soothsayers and poets of the time, Muhammad sometimes covered his head with a mantle (burda) during a revelation. Like the poets, he dictated his inspirations to his scribes. More than a score of the early suras (numbers 37, 68, 77, 85, etc.) start with an 'oathing formula' of the kind used by poets and soothsayers. Like the poets and sorcerers, Muhammad directs curses and maledictions against his enemies.

In the view of some commentators, the very strength of Muhammad's asseverations that he was not a poet, that he was not mad (37:35), that he was not possessed (52:29), that he was not deceived (21:5) might indicate his early doubts and uncertainties, as well as his anxiety that he might be shown to be the victim of delusion. But he was reassured, for the Koran makes a clear disclaimer: 'We [God] have not taught him [Muhammad] poetry, nor is it proper for him' (36:69).

7.16 The Authorship of the Koran

From the very beginning of Muhammad's mission in Mecca and subsequently in Medina, his contemporaries ridiculed his claim concerning the divine authorship of the Koran. They scorned his revelations as a series of his own self-induced inventions (11:16), by which he falsely provided sanction for his views and for all his deeds and misdeeds. They rejected the holy text as a lie which he had forged (25:5), and denounced him as a fabricator of the Koran (16:103).

It has been suggested that, in order to make God appear to say what he himself wanted to say, the Prophet adopted a simple device. A chapter or verse began with the word 'Say!' (*Kul!*), as if Muhammad were being commanded by Allah to say what followed. The command 'Say!' occurs more than 300 times in the Koran.

Concerning disputed matters, this device sometimes takes a dialectical form, where Muhammad presents the objections of opponents and then instructs himself to counter the objections. Thus, in order to explain why it was necessary to fight during the sacred month when fighting was forbidden, Muhammad received an inspiration in the following terms: 'They [your opponents] ask you [O Muhammad] about fighting in the sacred month. Say [to them], "Fighting in the sacred month is bad, but turning aside from the cause of Allah is worse"' (2:214).

Muhammad's enemies alleged that, while the bulk of the Koran represented his own work, many passages were plagiarized from other sources or taken down to the dictation of others. They asserted that he had more than one assistant in the composition of his revelation, including Jews and Christians (see Section 10.2), and that he incorporated material based on his knowledge of their scriptures.

In company with the Mutazilis, the Ikhwan al-Safa and other rationalist groups, Muslim critics throughout Islamic history continued to express similar judgements in one form or another. The Koran was treated as an extended hadith, expressing Muhammad's own views. In modern times the eminent author Syed Ameer Ali, who wrote a book on Islam widely read in both Muslim and non-Muslim countries, also regarded Muhammad as the author of the Koran (Guillaume, 1983, p. 160).

Western scholars too have concluded that the Koran is a very human document, reflecting many sides of Muhammad's own personality. Muhammad's authorship, they believe, is confirmed by internal evidence provided by the borrowings, the abrogations, the amendments, the contradictions, the stylistic flaws, the ad hoc nature of many passages, and other indications of Muhammad's personal opinions, his desires and demands, his preferences and prejudices. They have tended to dismiss the idea of divine authorship through the angel Gabriel or a similar agency. The Italian Arabist Leone Caetani spoke of the Koran as a kind of newspaper, publishing orders of the day, bulletins, judgements on domestic affairs, and similar matters of current topical interest. It has been variously spoken of as Muhammad's 'Day Book', 'Utterances', 'Diary', 'Table Talk', 'Sermons', 'Autobiographical Notes' or 'Discourses'. And quite definitely all his own work.

7.17 A Revised Koran

At least twenty-five years were to pass after the death of Muhammad before the Koran was put into the form it is known today. During this period changes had already been made to the text, and further changes were still to come.

Most of the slender Meccan suras which formed the spiritual nucleus of the new faith were regularly used in prayers and rituals, and, being too well known to be tampered with, were generally left untouched. But the Medinan suras, still widely diffused in many variants and not popularly known, offered scope for revision, and could if necessary even be supplemented with fresh material.

There is little reason to believe that the caliphs who authorized the Koranic compilation and those who actually took it in hand held the text, particularly the later suras, in such reverence as to be above making their own insertions and omissions.

The first unedited collection of the Koranic fragments made on Muhammad's death was left in the care of Abu Bakr for over a year. On Abu Bakr's death the second caliph, Omar, had charge of the collection for ten years. Abu Bakr and Omar – ambitious men both – had ample opportunity to alter or add to the text while it was in their keeping. When Omar died, a huge corpus of Koranic material came into the possession of the third caliph, Othman.

Othman personally chose commissioners to edit the text and make an authorized version of the Koran from the miscellany. This process took about ten years. As all this was done under the supervision of Othman, he was later charged with having destroyed whole suras – and, indeed, with having 'torn up the Book', meaning the Koran.

The first three caliphs had charge of the Koranic material for a quarter of a century before the authorized version of Othman came into existence, and there were Muslim sects who accused them of inserting material not obtained by transmission through the Prophet (Hourani, 1991, p. 21). The Shias believed that for doctrinal reasons the Koran was altered through the machinations of these early successors of the Prophet and that several passages had been forged for propagandist purposes; and some refused to accept them as divinely inspired.

Modern 'revisionist' scholars go even further. They suggest that the rapid territorial gains made by the Muslims from the time of Omar, followed by the fresh contacts with peoples in countries outside Arabia, especially during the Omayyad caliphate, and the polemical disputes with Jews and Christians in those places, led not only to the revised compilation of Othman but to yet another recension later still, with interpolations of fresh material.

The writer al-Kindi (d. 915) tells of wholesale tampering with the text of the Koran by rival Muslim groups (Abbott, 1939, p. 48) which went on till the rule of the Omayyad caliph Abdul Malik.

The Omayyad caliph Marwan I had destroyed the original text of the Koran that had been given into the custody of Muhammad's widow Hafsa. This opened the way for Marwan's son, the caliph Abdul Malik, to make further alterations, and this was accomplished through his governor in Iraq, the much-hated Hajaj ibn Yusuf. On the pretext of removing the discrepancies from the different versions of the Koran by introducing vowel signs and diacritical marks, Hajaj made substantial alterations and additions to the text itself, and introduced what was virtually another recension of the Koran (Abbott, 1939, p. 47).

The changes made to the text by the early caliphs Abu Bakr, Omar and Othman had been for personal or doctrinal reasons. The changes now made by the Omayyads, it is said, were for political, dynastic and imperialist ends. The changes became necessary to give a more distinctive identity to the Muslim faith, to lend support to a specifically Arab scripture, sponsor Arab nationalism, buttress up the claims of Arabism, establish and maintain the cultural and religious hegemony of the Arab people, and present Islam as a unique religion different from and superior to Judaism and Christianity.

The belief that the Arabs were the best people ever created (3:106), that Arabia was the holy land, Mecca the sacred city, the Kaaba the hub and navel of the earth, Islam the perfect religion, Arabic the sacred tongue, the Koran the crown of all revelation, and Muhammad the prophet without peer – all these could not fail to fire the spirit of Arab chauvinism and provide justification for conquest and domination.

The perfect, divinely sent, unalterable Koran became the manifesto of renascent Arabism, and Muhammad himself was transformed into an archetypal figure, to become the patriarch of the Arab people and to be raised by some enthusiasts to semi-divine status as the Logos (see Section 11.15).

8

THE HADITH

The notion commonly held that the Koran is the ultimate and only source of Muslim law is quite erroneous. The Koran is not an all-encompassing legal code, and is far from sufficient for most purposes. It presents some general principles, and occasionally gives specific directions, but even on matters relating to such topics as the creed, prayer and pilgrimage it is not always clear and often ambiguous and conflicting.

It was realized by the early theologians that the Koran was inadequate for the needs of the Muslim as the sole guide for all occasions. It could not serve as a primary source of community regulation, and a comprehensive system of law could not be built out of it. A new and more precise source of doctrine and practice was gradually evolved and brought into the legal system.

This was the *hadith* – a term of pre-Islamic usage, commonly translated as 'traditions' – which constitutes a documentation of the inherited customs (*sunna*) governing the life of a Muslim. The hadith furnished a more exact and comprehensive code of guidance, forming a supplement and providing, as it were, qualifications, footnotes and addenda to the Koranic text. It acquired an importance second only to that of the Koran.

8.1 Origins of the Hadith

Just as the Koran is regarded as recited revelation – that is, recited by the angel Gabriel to Muhammad – so the hadith represents unrecited revelation, based on the Prophet's own utterances and actions. Some parts of the hadith are attributed to the direct prompting of Muhammad by God himself, and are treated as sacred (*kudsi*), though there is no agreement about which parts are to be so regarded.

The hadith actually contains material from pre-Islamic times; much was added to it after Muhammad's death, and it was augmented with fresh material as the Islamic empire grew. But all of it was attributed to Muhammad, for he was the ultimate fount of all hadiths, which were believed to be established on the Prophet's precept and example. Muhammad's life had an exemplary value and was held to be the perfect model to be followed by the faithful. In the apostle of God, says the Koran, you have an 'excellent example' (*uswatan hasana*) (33:21). The imitation of the Prophet therefore became a worthy ideal.

The hadiths provide descriptions of the Prophet's mode of dress; his gestures; his manner of standing, sitting, walking and speaking; and the way he washed his hands, ate his food, used a toothpick and tied his turban. Where feasible, his example in these matters was regarded as a pattern to be followed, and was long copied by pious Muslims.

Muhammad's views on any subject were noted, and his personal opinions on community relationships, women, the family, society and warfare, and even his casual remarks about his preferences and prejudices on topics like poetry and music, all provided guiding precepts and were considered legally binding.

It was not only what the Prophet said and did but also what he omitted to do that assumed significance, and what he did not do was also avoided by the faithful. The famous Muslim jurist Ibn Hanbal (d. 855) would not eat a water melon for fear of doing what the Prophet had not done: although a hadith records that the Prophet ate melons, it was not explicitly stated whether he ate them with or without the rind, or whether he broke, bit or cut them.

Muhammad was aware that people were taking note of all his casually uttered remarks, and that stories of what he did were being passed around. He was conscious too of the dangers, and warned against the practice, but the trend once started could not be stopped, and was accelerated after his death. In the beginning these traditions were transmitted orally, but later they began to be written down.

The truth of a hadith supposedly faithfully recording Muhammad's words and deeds was difficult to verify. In order to establish the authenticity or 'backing' (isnad) of a hadith, it was necessary to trace the text (matn) to its source – that is, to Muhammad himself. As the Prophet was no longer alive, anecdotes began to be garnered from his immediate associates, who were now regarded as the authentic repositories of tradition. Ayesha, the Prophet's widow, was the source of scores of hadiths.

As the first generation of associates died, the compilers had to fall back on others. Men strained their memories to recall what they had heard about the Prophet through a companion (sahib) of the Prophet, or through a successor (tabi) of a companion, or even through someone who had conversed with an earlier successor. In some cases there were as many as a dozen such links in the chain, spanning several generations.

A hadith might be phrased to indicate the succession in this way: 'It was told to us by Muadh ibn Hasan, who got it from al-Masud, who received it from Abdulla ibn Ali, who heard it from Abdul Rahman, to whom it was related by Abu Hurayra [one of the companions of the Prophet], that Muhammad said, "The wearing of silk is unfitted for God-fearing men."'

Since each link in the chain had to be a 'trustworthy person', and since the probity, accuracy and dependability of the transmitter were virtually impossible to verify, not all links in a chain were accepted as trustworthy by all theologians or all sects. The veracity of any tradition was therefore not easily accomplished, even though efforts were made to obtain as much information as possible about each person named in the chain.

(It is thought that, like the study of early poetry, the research undertaken by Muslim scholars to establish the genuineness of a hadith, entailing as it did the tracing of the lives and times of those who passed it on, made an important contribution to the writing of biography and history, and produced among Muslims some of the finest chroniclers of their time.)

From the time of their first compilation, scholars began to object to the wild proliferation of hadiths, many of which were known to be spurious. The great Muslim jurisconsult Abu Salama (d. 710) was among the earliest to point out the danger of accepting a tradition without due verification. It soon became evident that hadiths were being not only 'recalled' but invented, and there were soon conflicting accounts of what the Prophet had said or done. Even what were regarded as genuine hadiths were being altered and distorted.

Before long, the fabrication of hadiths became a recognized religious and political weapon of which all parties availed themselves. Even men of the strictest integrity practised this kind of fraud (tadlis). Hadiths were being invented to serve the special interests of the Omayyads, the Abbasids and later dynasties of caliphs, and the handing down of traditions sank to the level of a business enterprise (Goldziher, 1971, p. 169) and a means of livelihood. The result was that many of the hadiths came to be regarded as so unreliable as to be virtually worthless.

Also, a great deal of extraneous material was incorporated into the hadith, as this was found to be a convenient means of Islamizing attractive ideas, some clearly taken from foreign sources. Thus a great deal of non-Islamic material was drawn into the net by the hadith compilers and was presented as utterances of the Prophet. Such material included aphorisms from Greek philosophy (Gibb, 1969, p. 51) and the Roman Stoics, ancient proverbs, maxims of Buddhist wisdom, verses from the Zoroastrian, Jewish and Christian scriptures (including the Ten Commandments and the Lord's Prayer), rabbinical sayings, passages from the apocryphal gospels, and legal precepts from the Roman and Byzantine codes and – as Islam spread further afield – from the social and customary traditions of the peoples of Central Asia, Africa, India and Indonesia (see Section 8.2).

The number of hadiths in circulation and still being invented for every occasion soon became unmanageable. In order to bring some order into the chaos, it became clear that the material would have to be collected, sifted and sorted. The earliest collections were started more than a century and a half after Muhammad's death. One collector, Yahya ibn Mayin (d. 848), who had amassed some 600,000 hadiths, stated that his helpers had written for him twice that number.

The best-known and most authoritative compilation is by Muhammad al-Bukhari (d. 870), a Persian who took seventeen years to complete his work. He collected some 200,000 hadiths, not counting about 400,000 others which he rejected as unfit even for consideration. He finally selected 7,300 hadiths, but since many of them were repeated there remained in fact only about 2,760 in all. Towards the end of his life, however, al-Bukhari fell into disgrace with the authorities on the ground of heterodoxy.

Second only to al-Bukhari's text is the work of another Persian, Muslim ibn al-Hajaj (d. 875), of Nishapur, which contains three thousand traditions. Al-Bukhari and Muslim are among the six writers whom the Sunnis treat as authoritative.

The Shias have five authorities of their own, their traditions being transmitted not by the 'companions' of the Prophet but by the imams or spiritual leaders. Other sectarian groups have their own hadiths. The Sufis, in addition to their separate compilations, speak of an unwritten tradition handed down in secret and known to Sufis alone.

Besides the compilers, there were commentators and expositors on the hadith who endeavoured to sift the genuine from the spurious and expose the fakes. Among the more famous of these scholars were at least seven women, the best-known being Karima bint Ahmad of Merv (d. 1070), who was highly esteemed for her knowledge and her scrupulous analyses of the traditions.

The codification of the hadiths in the various scholarly compilations did not end the problems connected with them, for faked hadiths continued to be produced, by theologians themselves among others. Tendentious hadiths, cleverly making use of archaic words and old grammatical constructions, with a chain of transmission painstakingly worked back to give them authenticity, were written to foster partisan or sectarian interests.

Religious, legal, political and other contentious issues were settled by tampering with an earlier hadith or forging a new one. Traditions were forged to support a tribal demand, a social practice, a school of thought. Each party, each proponent of a teaching, each person advancing a point of view had a hadith to support him. There is hardly a school of law, a theological doctrine, a political opinion, a religious sect, a ceremonial practice that could not justify its particular viewpoint by reference to a hadith claimed as authentic. A Muslim authority wrote, 'In nothing do we see pious men more given to falsehood than in the traditions' (Nicholson, 1969, p. 145).

Hadiths differed from place to place and from period to period, and often expressed confusing and conflicting doctrines. Hadiths accepted by one school were rejected by another. They were given different interpretations by different authorities, or discarded if found unsuitable. It began to be accepted as axiomatic by many authorities that the more complete the chain of intermediaries in a hadith, the greater the chance that it was false.

In view of the uncertainties surrounding the traditions relating to Muhammad, some scholars are inclined to dismiss almost the whole corpus of the hadith as a valid source of Islamic law. The historical basis of most of the hadiths is disputable. Even the genuineness of the so-called classical hadiths has been questioned, and in the light of modern criticism it is doubtful whether more than a very small number can be accepted as genuine.

Problems relating to the origins of the traditions, their authenticity, their value and indeed their necessity have been debated for centuries. Some Muslim scholars have taken the extreme view that the hadiths are purely anecdotal and of small consequence in matters of faith, doctrine and conduct. Hadiths should be given little weight, they say, and indeed it is safest to leave them out of account altogether.

8.2 Muslim Law

Every activity of the strict Muslim needs a religious sanction, and, in theory at least, everything a Muslim does, important or trivial, has the backing of a religious law. The totality of Muslim law is known as the *sharia* – another term of pre-Islamic usage – and this governs the life of a Muslim in all its aspects: moral, devotional, political, social and personal.

Even matters like homosexuality and unnatural acts with minors, animals and corpses, although clearly sinful and prohibited, are dealt with in the codes, and urinating, vomiting and breaking wind are all the object of detailed prescriptions (Ruthven, 1984, p. 163). But the saying 'The Prophet taught us everything, from prayers to defecation' needs considerable qualification, as Muhammad's contribution to Muslim law was slender. Some of the sharia existed before Muhammad, and the bulk of it was formulated after his death.

The roots (*usul*) of Muslim law, with its countless provisions, have been traced to a number of sources. The earliest was the inherited custom (*sunna*) of the pre-Islamic Arab tribes, much of which was accepted by Muhammad and embodied within the framework of Islam. The next source was the Koran, which incorporated and in part modified ideas common to earlier faiths like Judaism and Christianity. Yet another source was the hadith.

From the Koran and the early hadiths were codified the basic elements relating to Muslim faith and observance. The six principles, or articles of faith, are: belief in (1) one God and his unity, (2) the angels, (3) the scriptures, (4) the prophets, (5) the Day of Judgement and (6) predestination. The five required observances, also called the five pillars of practice, are: (1) the recitation of the creed, (2) prayers, (3) fasting, (4) almsgiving and (5) the pilgrimage.

Any interpretation of the Koran by way of commentary (*tafsir*) or exegesis was once forbidden. The holy book, it was said, would speak for itself. The only acceptable activity in relation to the Koran was the recitation of its verses, without any attempt at interpretation.

Muhammad had hoped that the Koran would be understood by all who read it, and that in cases of ambiguity or doubt Muslims of good faith would come together and determine its meaning. 'My people', he said, 'would never agree upon an error.' But this was not to be. The text of the Koran was not always easy to understand. It required elucidation, so that its prescriptions might be clearly comprehended and properly applied.

From the beginning, however, because of textual and semantic difficulties, interpretations differed from place to place. Agreement was not always forthcoming and dissensions were frequent, leading to scholastic divisions and the proliferation of sects. There is therefore not one sharia, but the sharia of different denominations.

Not long after Muhammad's death there were founded among the Sunnis four major schools (set up by Abu Hanifa of Kufa, a scholar of Afghan or Aramaean stock; Malik ibn Anas, of Medina; Muhammad al-Shafi, of Askalon in Palestine; and Ibn Hanbal, of Baghdad) and several minor schools. The Shia, or party of Ali, held that their imams or religious leaders had authority at all times to make their own pronouncements on legal and religious matters.

Koranic interpretation inevitably became subject to the considered judgement (*ijtihad*) of a learned jurist, or the collective decision (*ijma*) of a council of divines (*mujtahid*). To clarify a doubtful point and arrive at a decision on any issue, the jurists had recourse to a number of methods, chief among them being personal opinion, reason, and analogy – all of which were soon found to have their own drawbacks.

Muhammad had warned, 'Whoever talks about the Koran on the basis of his personal opinion [*rayi*] or from ignorance, will surely occupy a place near hell-fire.' And Abu Bakr later said, 'What earth could bear me up, and what heaven protect me, were I to speak of the book of God what I know not?'

The application of reason (*akl*) was likewise condemned. On his deathbed the famous scholar Malik ibn Anas repented for the many decisions he had taken on the promptings of mere reason.

Analogy (*kiyas*) was used in a situation where no law existed and a new law had to be formulated from an analogous or parallel situation, as when drugs were prohibited because wine was. Analogy, it was found, was open to widespread abuse and to wild interpretations of the law that could lead to serious anomalies.

There were other problems as well. The consequences of strict application of legal precepts based on the sharia often forced the jurists to resort to legalistic shifts. To get around any difficulties encountered by too literal an interpretation of the law, one or another questionable device (*hiyal*) was contrived and adopted. Thus, usury, or lending money at interest, being prohibited in the Koran (2:276), the subterfuge was employed of regarding the borrower and the lender as partners and treating the interest charged as a gift. Such stratagems were widely used to circumvent inconvenient sharia requirements in other matters too, such as dowry, inheritance, punishment, divorce and almsgiving.

Another inconvenience of the sharia in practice was the requirement of having to treat every infringement of the personal or social code as a religious concern, and to deal with it in the religious courts, which were not always qualified to adjudicate on the matters concerned. The lawmakers had perforce to distinguish between what was to be rendered to Caesar and what to God, between revealed (religious) law and what might be termed the lay body of the law, which is called *kanun*, derived from the Greek word 'canon' but meaning secular law, the exact opposite of canon or church law in Western usage. A dualism thus arose in the administration of justice: a religious court dealt with strictly religious issues, and a secular court, separate from and independent of the sharia courts, dealt with non-religious cases on the basis of equity, common sense and traditional custom.

The spread of Islam outward led to a large influx of additional foreign elements into the legal system, and Muslim law was inevitably influenced as a result of early contacts with the highly civilized non-Muslim peoples of Mesopotamia, Persia, Syria, Palestine and Egypt. Certain aspects of the religious and legal codes of the Jews, Christians and Zoroastrians, once widely current in these regions, were incorporated without serious opposition into the evolving structure of Muslim law.

Hellenistic, Roman and Byzantine laws made their contribution as well. Goldziher states that the influence of Roman law on the legal system of Islam is 'unmistakable' (1981, p. 4). It is established too that the Institutes, Codes and Digest of the Byzantine ruler Justinian (d. 565) greatly influenced Muslim jurisprudence.

In time the sharia was adapted to suit the established ways of peoples living in countries some distance away from Arabia and its immediate borders. It became the view of these converted peoples that, since Muhammad himself had not interfered with the ancient practices of his own country – except on such grave issues as polytheism and idolatry, and abhorrent customs like female infanticide – so, on the principle of analogy, it should not be part of Islam's mission to overturn local laws long prevailing elsewhere.

These people felt that their own ancient customs were not in conflict with their dedication to Islam, and that such customs should be allowed to continue. Even practices like infibulation and clitoridectomy, which were prevalent in certain parts of the Sudan and Nigeria and so deep-rooted as not to be amenable to easy eradication, were assimilated into the sharia by way of a hadith.

In other Muslim states of Africa, among the Berbers, and among the peoples of Central Asia, India and Indonesia, the indigenous laws relating to matters governing the family, women, divorce, land tenure, property and inheritance, as well as many political, social and cultural traditions, including class and caste structure, were retained. Where necessary, adjustments were made in the orthodox system to accommodate them.

Often, old beliefs and practices that had disappeared with the advent of Islam reappeared in time, and the people gradually reverted to their ancestral ways, so that Buddhist, Hindu, shamanist and animist customs coexisted within an Islamic framework. As Gibb says, the popular forms of Islam differed between almost all Muslim countries, in strong contrast to the rigid orthodox system (1969, p. 104).

Finally, the legal system of the modern Europeans has, of course, had a considerable impact on the laws prevailing in all Islamic countries today. The sharia law has been abolished or considerably modified in Turkey, Egypt, Syria, Jordan, Iraq and other states, where the law codes are generally based on legal systems established on the Western model.

The sharia itself, considered in its entirety, represents a systematized patchwork of a multiplicity of legal codes and traditional practices, which have taken account of peoples of widely different cultures. It has slowly evolved over the centuries, and is still in the process of development.

9

THE JEWS AND MUHAMMAD

During the formative years of his religious career Muhammad had been in close contact with Jews and Christians. He knew something of their scriptures, if only through hearsay, and knew more directly of the basic doctrines that governed their lives. There were rumours, even in his own lifetime, that he had been coached by them.

He is reported to have said, 'He who wrongs a Jew or Christian will have me as his accuser on the Day of Judgement.' When he sought to establish a religion for the Arab people, he hoped at first it would form part of a common faith with that of the Jews and Christians (see Section 11.2).

For long Islam was regarded in the West as an outgrowth of the Judaeo-Christian tradition, and it still is in some quarters. It was said to be an eclectic religion, based principally on Jewish and Christian concepts, which Muhammad altered and reformulated into an Arab mould, to create a synthesis suitable for the purpose he had in mind. The evidence for this contention will have to be considered in somewhat greater detail.

Long before the advent of Islam, scattered Jewish populations were to be found in many parts of Arabia. In fact several Arab clans were classed as Jewish (see Section 2.2). Medina and its environs had thriving and influential Jewish communities, and the Ansars, the Medinan helpers of Muhammad, included Jews.

Also, there was a tradition that the two chief tribes of Medina, the Aus and the Khazraj, were of Jewish descent. More specifically, another tradition indicates that the Jews of Medina were considered as part of the Najjar clan – of the Khazraj tribe – to which the Prophet's own maternal relations belonged.

At first Muhammad maintained good relations with the Jews, and they in turn found little to object to in his endeavours to extirpate idolatry. He regarded them favourably as the recipients of a special revelation. The Koran mentions Jews as 'privileged above all peoples' (45:15).

Ibn Ishak preserves a document – some scholars deny its authenticity – which is headed 'The Covenant Between the Muslims and the Jews'. Drawn up in Medina shortly after the Hegira, this states, among other things, 'To the Jew who is well-disposed towards us belong help and equality. He shall not be wronged nor his enemies aided.' The rules of conduct issued by the Prophet to one of his generals about to march to the Yemen included the clause 'No Jew is to be troubled in the practice of Judaism.'

More than once the Koran refers to Palestine as the 'blessed land'. In the beginning Muhammad looked upon Jerusalem as the centre of his own faith, and as such it had priority over Mecca. It was to Jerusalem and not Mecca that he turned to pray (Lewis, 1966, p. 42), and he advised his followers to do likewise. And this rule was observed for twelve years, even after he had built the first mosque in Medina. It is known that the *kibla* (prayer-direction) of certain early mosques in Iraq built after the death of Muhammad continued to be Jerusalem and not Mecca.

The Koran states that the Torah (Pentateuch) enshrines the behests of God (5:47), and is 'a perfect code for the righteous' (6:155). Muhammad never regarded the Jewish scriptures as having been cancelled. He used many Old Testament stories in the Koran, though he may not have had access to the texts, nor been able to read them if he had. He probably heard them from the lips of Jews, some perhaps with no great book learning, since certain stories were incorrectly rendered and remembered in this form by Muhammad.

The Koran includes accounts of the creation of the world, the story of Adam and Eve in paradise, and their 'slip' (*zalla*) or Fall through eating of the forbidden tree (7:18), after which they became conscious of their nakedness and covered themselves with leaves (20:119). It also includes the stories of Cain and Abel, Noah and the Flood, the resting of the Ark on Al-Judi (11:46) – known to the ancient Greeks as Mount Gordyene in Armenia – Abraham and Ishmael, Lot and the 'overturned cities' (Sodom and Gomorrah), Isaac and Jacob, Joseph and Potiphar's wife, Moses and Pharaoh, Elijah and Elisha, David and Solomon, the Queen of Sheba, Job, Jonah and various other prophets and biblical personalities.

In the Koran, though, there are several unscriptural versions, for Muhammad's version was often different from the original. Where the material used by Muhammad does not correspond with the canonical books of the Old Testament it can often be traced to the Talmud, the Apocrypha and related writings. Some of the stories are given an Arab setting, as when Abraham and Ishmael come to the Hejaz to build the Kaaba.

Parts of the Koran are said to have been received by Muhammad through the inspiration of what is known as the Sakina. Zayid ibn Thabit, Muhammad's amanuensis who had charge of arranging the Koran after Muhammad's death, reported, 'I was at Muhammad's side when the Sakina came upon him. When he recovered he said, "Write down," and I wrote.' The Sakina concept comes from the Hebrew Shekina, which in the Jewish (cabbalist) tradition is the feminine aspect of the spirit of God.

It appears from a passage in Ibn Hisham that on at least one occasion Muhammad visited the Beth ha-Midrash, a house for the study of the Midrash (biblical commentary). Al-Baydawi relates that certain Jews used to repeat passages of ancient history to Muhammad, who would then discuss them and make observations. Occasionally, he even attended the synagogue (Hughes, 1977, p. 193).

While living in Mecca, Muhammad had been friendly with a learned rabbi named Abdias ben Salom who, it is said, recited the Jewish scriptures to Muhammad, described Jewish traditions, and gave him other information that was of use to him in the composition of the Koran. According to the commentators Abbasi and Jalalain, this rabbi became a Muslim himself, as Abdulla ibn Salam, and is believed to be the 'witness' mentioned in the Koran (46:9) who confirms the agreement between the Koran and the Jewish scriptures (Tisdall, 1911, p. 134).

It is also worthy of note that among Muhammad's Koranic amanuenses was a Jew, and that till about the middle of 625 Muhammad used Jewish secretaries for any dispatches to be written in Hebrew or Syriac. After his Muslim secretary Zayid ibn Thabit had learned these languages Muhammad ceased to employ Jews.

It has been suggested that Muhammad adopted certain basic doctrines and practices and several features of worship from the Jews – so much so that the French writer Ernest Renan (d. 1892) described Islam as 'petrified Judaism'.

Belief that God is one (Hebrew *ehad*) is emphasized in Judaism and forms part of the Jewish confession of faith (Deut. 6:4). In Islam likewise, the belief that God is one (Arabic *ahad*) is implicit in the Muslim creed and forms the first article of the Islamic faith. It is thought that the Muslim concept is modelled on the Jewish.

During these early days Muhammad used for himself the Jewish term for prophet (*nabi*). From the Jews he took over the notion of a chosen people – in his case the Arabs – with a great mission. Based on the Jewish custom of making contributions to charity, Muhammad instituted the practice of donating alms as an obligatory religious levy, giving it the same Aramaic name (*zakat*), and making it one of the five pillars of Islam.

Also following Jewish example, Muhammad placed a taboo on pig's flesh, introduced ceremonial ablutions and purifications, established the 'sabbath' observance on a Saturday, and introduced the midday prayer in addition to morning and evening prayers.

Again, in accord with Jewish practice, he favoured circumcision. The rite is not mentioned in the Koran, but Muhammad made it obligatory as a common custom of the past. There is no authentic record of Muhammad himself being circumcised, but to lend authority to the rite a late tradition said that Muhammad was one of the prophets born circumcised, like Adam, Noah, Joseph, Moses, Solomon and Jesus.

Then, on the analogy of the custom of self-denial observed by Jews during the first nine days of the first Jewish month of Tishri, culminating in a strict fast on Ashor, the tenth day (Yom Kippur), the Jewish Day of Atonement (Lev. 23:27), Muhammad instituted in July 623 a period of abstinence during the first nine days of the first Arabic month of Moharram, culminating in a fast on the tenth day, Ashura. This fast was to last from daybreak to sunset. Daybreak for this purpose was determined as 'when a white thread can be distinguished from a black thread' (2:183). This too was taken from the Jewish practice mentioned in the Talmud, which defines daybreak for the purpose of prayer as the time 'when one can distinguish between a blue and a white thread' (Rodwell, 1915, p. 357).

9.1 The Breach with the Jews

Discord between Muhammad and the Jews began to set in as his power increased and his claims became bolder, both on his own behalf and on that of the Arabs.

Muhammad claimed that Islam was the original faith of Abraham, who was the founder of monotheism in its pure and undefiled form. Abraham was a hanif and an early Muslim (3:60), and his own precursor. The religion of Abraham (*millat Ibrahim*) was the true religion, and he, Muhammad, was now restoring this ancient faith to its pure form (2:129). Abraham came before Moses, and his religion was older than Judaism. The Arabs, he observed, were descended from Ishmael, the first-born son of Abraham, and had a claim on his faith prior to that of the Jews.

The rabbinical response to this was that Ishmael was the illegitimate son of Abraham by an Egyptian concubine not of the Semitic race, and as such was outside God's covenant with Abraham. Besides, he was a person uncouth and violent, described in the Bible as 'a wild man; his hand will be against every man' (Gen. 16:12).

It was pointed out that, according to the Koran itself, the prophetic title was bestowed on the children of Israel (45:15) – specifically upon the family of Isaac and Jacob (29:27). The Jews were therefore not disposed to accept Muhammad as one of the prophets. He could not perform miracles, which was one of the credentials of prophethood. In any event, the last prophet had already appeared in Israel, though the Messiah was still to come.

When some of Muhammad's followers, though not Muhammad himself, stated that Muhammad was the Messiah they were expecting, the Jews replied that Muhammad was not of the line of David, did not possess the tokens of messiahship, and therefore could not possibly be the Messiah.

Muhammad claimed (7:157) that his coming had been foretold in the Torah. Although the precise verses confirming this foretelling are not cited, Muslim scholars since then have sifted through the Pentateuch and the rest of the Old Testament to find evidence of biblical predictions concerning the advent of the Prophet. All these are rejected by the Jews.

To the claim of the Muslims that the Koran was a book sent down from God, the Jews replied that, if it were indeed a divine book, it would have been sent down in one of the sacred tongues, like Hebrew or Syriac (Jeffery, 1938, p. 9), and not in Arabic, the language of poets and drunkards.

The Jews also rejected Muhammad's version of the events related in the Old Testament, which they said was garbled, fallacious and at times unintelligible. They taunted him with ignorance of the scripture he claimed to confirm. For example, he wrongly accused them of saying that Ezra (Ozayr) was the son of God (9:30), which they easily refuted. Several other errors were pointed out (Geiger, 1970).

Muhammad was constantly worsted in his long and bitter arguments with the Jews. The more they refused to acknowledge his prophetic claims, the stronger his antagonism grew.

The rift with the Jews came to a head in about October 623, shortly before the Battle of Badr. Smarting at being rebuffed and conscious of the damaging effect of the criticism to which he had exposed himself, and realizing too that there was no longer any hope of reconciling his message with the Jewish faith, Muhammad's attitude hardened.

He turned on his tormentors, accusing them of being his enemies. 'You will surely find', says the Koran, 'that those who show the most hostility to believers are the Jews' (5:85). The Jews, he said, had perverted the spiritual revelation they had received from Moses (2:70).

Instead of the Hebrew term for prophet (*nabi*), Muhammad now began to use the Arabic term for apostle or messenger (*rasul*). He also decided to do away, as far as he could, with the practices he had instructed on Jewish lines, in order to make clear the distinction between Islam and Judaism.

On 11 February 624 he received a revelation (2:144) and changed the direction of prayer from Jerusalem to Mecca. This also avoided turning to the east, as some of the early Christians did. The Jews immediately charged him with fickleness of mind and with worshipping towards a piece of black rock in an idolatrous temple.

He next abandoned Saturday as the sabbath, and named Friday as the special day of the Muslim week and the day of public worship, thus also avoiding Sunday, which the Christians observed. He did not impose on his followers the burden of a full day of rest: after the afternoon prayers and sermon, normal activity was not prohibited, and the Muslim was free to work, trade and if necessary fight. Here too the Jews accused him of indecisiveness, and of reverting to the ways of the pagan Arabs, who held Friday as a special day.

The taboo on pig's flesh remained, but the other strict dietary rules of the Jews were simplified (see Section 11.4), for, as the Koran says, the food prohibitions of the Jews were laid down as a punishment for their iniquity (6:147).

When Muhammad had earlier consulted his companions about a method of calling the faithful to prayer, someone had suggested using a trumpet (*buk*) as the Jews did. Muhammad, having first ordered a trumpet to be made, later decided against it, as by then he had turned against the Jews.

Late in February 624 the ten-day period of self-denial, ending with

Ashura, was declared to be no longer obligatory. Instead, all able Muslims were to fast during the sacred Arab month of Ramadan, following the observances of the hanifs. This was now to last the whole month, thus making it longer than, and different from, the Jewish ten-day fast ending with the Day of Atonement. At the same time, since Muhammad wished to make his community a 'middle people' (see Section 11.3), following neither Jews nor Christians, he made the fast shorter than the Christian forty-day Lenten period, for, as the Koran says, 'God wishes to make it easier for you' (2:181).

9.2 The Extermination of the Jews

Muhammad was now on a course of active persecution of the Jews, on the grounds of their alleged treachery in his struggle against his Arab opponents. Their economic supremacy was of course a 'standing irritant' (Guillaume, 1983, p. 43).

In April 624, on the excuse of a market brawl, he besieged the settlements of the Kaynuka tribe, the wealthiest of the Jewish communities in the region, comprising metalworkers, armourers, jewellers and goldsmiths. After fifteen days the Jews were forced to surrender. The men were bound, and preparations were made for their execution.

At this point a chief of the Khazraj clan named Abdulla ibn Obayi energetically intervened. Besides disliking bloodshed, he mistrusted Muhammad's position of leadership and had warned the Medinans about his ambition and growing powers. He had once checked Muhammad's attempt to convert him by saying, 'Refrain from troubling those with preaching they dislike.' He remained indifferent to Islam, never became a true believer, and was classed among the 'hypocrites'. But as long as he lived Muhammad treated him with caution because of his standing in the Medinan community.

When Muhammad now turned his back on him, Abdulla ibn Obayi caught hold of the Prophet's cloak. Muhammad's face, reports Ibn Ishak, became almost black with rage, but Abdulla held on. 'By God,' he said, 'would you cut down these seven hundred men in one morning?', adding ominously, 'I am a man that circumstances may change.' Muhammad, prudent as always, decided not to proceed with the slaughter. Instead, the whole Kaynuka tribe were exiled to Syria. They were given three days to leave, and forbidden from taking any implements of their trade with them, these and their houses being distributed among the faithful.

According to Ibn Ishak, Muhammad had earlier accorded permission to his followers to slay any Jew they encountered. This general order was carried out forthwith in July 624, resulting in the murder of at least one prominent Jew named Ibn Sunayna. But the large-scale killing of Jews was still to come.

In August 625 Muhammad sent an ultimatum to the Jews of Nadhir, three miles from Medina, to evacuate their homes and proceed to Syria on pain of death. They had had commercial dealings with Abu Sofyan in Mecca before the Battle of Ohod, but the reason given for their expulsion was that they had broken a treaty made with Muhammad, and a revelation was received by him in justification (Sura 59). Abdulla ibn Obayi denounced the charge of treason as being without foundation.

To speed up the Jews' departure, Muhammad proceeded to cut down and burn their date palms. The Jews complained that this was a violation of the law of Moses (Deut. 20:19) as well as the laws of Arab warfare, but in vain. Having condemned them to banishment, Muhammad confiscated their swords, cuirasses and helmets, and took possession of their houses and lands.

In April 627, following what became known as the Battle of the Ditch, Muhammad captured the stronghold of the Jewish tribe of Korayza, after a siege lasting twenty-five days. The Jews offered to depart on the same conditions as the Nadhir tribe, but Muhammad refused. Their lives would be spared, he said, if they accepted Islam. Only one Jew agreed.

In order to mitigate Muhammad's culpability in the atrocity that followed, tradition relates that the fate of the people was left by the Prophet to be decided by Saad ibn Muad, chief of the Aus tribe and one of Muhammad's most fanatical followers. He was known to be hostile to the Jews, and had been seriously wounded in the siege. Saad decided that the men of Korayza should be slain, the women and children sold as slaves, and their palm-groves and other property distributed in the usual manner.

In spite of protests raised by some Arabs against the harsh decision, Muhammad commended it as a judgement inspired by Allah from the seventh heaven. The Koran (33:26) refers to this incident. Saad ibn Muad died shortly after passing this sentence, and it was said that he was such a holy man that his death shook the throne of Allah in heaven (Rodinson, 1976, p. 213).

A trench was dug in the market-place and in Muhammad's presence more than eight hundred captives with their hands tied behind them were led to the brink in groups of five and there beheaded; their bodies were then pushed into the trench. This ghastly massacre – which even a writer sympathetic to Islam has described as impossible to dissociate from the Nazi atrocities (Armstrong, 1991, p. 207) – went on all through the day and continued by torchlight into the night.

One unnamed Jewish woman, whose husband had been among those beheaded, loudly demanded that she share her husband's fate. Her wish was granted, and she met her death with a smiling countenance. Ayesha, Muhammad's wife, who witnessed the massacre, was later to say that this heroine's smile as she stepped fearlessly to her death haunted her ever after.

An old Jew named Zabir, who had saved the lives of some Muslims, was offered a pardon, but he declined, saying his life was of no further use to him as his people had all gone, and he wished to join them. When Muhammad was told about it, he is said to have shouted, 'Yes, you will join them – in the fire of hell!' and ordered his execution.

The lands, chattels, weapons and cattle of the Korayza were apportioned as booty among the Muslims. After making certain presents of concubines and slaves to his friends, Muhammad kept a concubine for himself. She was a young and lovely captive named Rihana, whose husband had died in the massacre. She could have become a full-fledged wife of Muhammad, but feared it would have meant abandoning her faith, and this she was not prepared to do.

Muhammad sold the remaining women and children, about thirteen hundred in all, to the neighbouring tribes, thus bringing a large accession of wealth to the Muslims.

In May 628 Muhammad led an expedition to the rich and prosperous oasis of Khaybar, some seventy miles north of Medina on the way to Syria. The name of the place is a variant of the Hebrew word for 'companion' (*khebar*), signifying the close community of Jews living there.

Muhammad captured the oasis and then, according to al-Wakidi, Ibn Hisham and Ibn Saad, subjected Kinana, the chief of the tribe, to torture – fire was placed on his chest until his breath almost departed – to discover where his treasure was hidden, after which he was beheaded.

Kinana's wife was the seventeen-year-old Safiya, daughter of Hayi ben Akhtab (who had been beheaded at Korayza), and in the ensuing division of spoils she was assigned to one of Muhammad's followers. Muhammad, however, threw his mantle over her and claimed her for himself, and that same night he married the young widow.

Muhammad was enamoured of his newest bride, and when she mounted her camel for the return journey to Medina the Prophet went down on one knee so that she might use the other as a step (Rodinson, 1976, p. 254). Later, taunted by the jealous other wives about being a Jewess (she had retained her faith), Safiya haughtily retorted that Moses was her uncle and Aaron her high priest. Pleased when he heard her spirited response, Muhammad was prompted to recite a Koranic verse which hinted that she 'might be better than those who mock her' (49:11).

Among the other Jewish captives was a young woman named Zaynab, who prepared a dish of goat's meat for Muhammad and his close companions. One of those who partook of the meat suddenly changed colour, fell over and died within minutes. Muhammad, who had eaten a small piece, was also seized with griping pains, and immediately had himself and his guests treated for poison.

Asked why she had wanted to kill Muhammad, the woman replied that he had been responsible for the death of her father, uncle, husband and brothers, and had inflicted serious injury on her people. If he were indeed a prophet he would have known the meat was poisoned and refused it, but it was clear he did not know and so could not be a prophet. She was immediately put to death.

From time to time thereafter, to the end of his life about three years later, the poison appears to have caused Muhammad excruciating pains. It was later claimed that when Muhammad raised the poisoned morsel to his mouth it had warned him it was poisoned, but even so he partook of it, and could thus rightly be given the title of 'martyr', for he had suffered and been killed for the faith at the hands of an unbeliever, like other martyrs.

The plunder from the Khaybar oasis was greater than any Muhammad had gained in his previous expeditions. There were vast stores of dates, oil, honey, barley; flocks of sheep and herds of camels; and huge amounts of gold and other treasures, as well as lands and villages. Ibn Hisham records that from the time of Khaybar slaves became very plentiful among the Muslims.

A little later the remaining Jewish strongholds of Fadak, Kamus, Watih, Solalim, Wadi al-Kora and others were forced to submit. No important Jewish settlements remained within the areas around Medina. The expulsion of the Jews from the Hejaz by the caliph Omar a few years after Muhammad's death marks the virtual end of the Jews in the Arabian peninsula.

10

THE CHRISTIANS AND MUHAMMAD

From earliest times many Christians regarded Muhammad, if not as a Christian in the orthodox sense, or as a prophet in the Semitic or biblical sense, then as a Christian who had gone astray in his teachings.

The Christian theologian John of Damascus (d. 749), who was of Arab stock, defined Muhammad's religion as an errant form of Christianity. Muhammad, he wrote, 'having happened upon the Old and New Testament, in all likelihood through association with an Arian monk, organized his own sect' (Bethmann, 1953, p. 17).

Medieval ecclesiastics also regarded 'Muhammadans' not as members of an alien or non-Christian faith, but as dissenters, heretics and apostates from the Christian religion.

Dante (d. 1321), under the same belief, and in accordance with the medieval vogue of consigning men to either the celestial or the nether regions, placed Muhammad in the hell reserved for schismatics, rather than that for pagans. He described Muhammad as tearing his breast for having sponsored false teachings. For this blasphemy, Muslims in Italy have threatened to blow up his tomb in Ravenna.

The German philosopher Nicholas of Cusa (d. 1464), in his analysis of the Koran, found in it a strand of Nestorianism, a form of Christianity widely diffused in the Middle East during the early Christian centuries.

Some modern authorities also tend to the view that Islam is fundamentally an offshoot of Christianity, being based on Christian principles, but evolving differently because of the circumstances in which Muhammad found himself. Indeed, they say, if during the Medinan period he had not swerved so far from the basic Christian teachings, he might have been accepted by the Christian community and laid the foundations of an Arabian church (Muir, 1912, p. xcviii).

10.1 Early Christian Influence

The first nurse of the child Muhammad, Umm Ayman, was a Christian from Abyssinia, and, although it is not known precisely how long Muhammad remained in her care, this does indicate a Christian presence in the environment in which he was born and raised. Christians, it may be assumed, were among those from whom the future prophet must have received, in lesser or larger measure, his earliest spiritual awakening.

When he was twelve years old Muhammad met the monk Bahira in Syria, and, according to the chroniclers, as he grew older he regularly visited northern Arabia, Palestine and Syria on business journeys, continuing to meet and converse with Christians, named and unnamed. Among the persons named are the monks Sarjis (Sergius or Sarkis) of the tribe of Abdul Kayis, Jirjis (Georgius), and Nastur (Nestor).

According to an early account, one of these monks is said to have communicated certain doctrines and religious laws to Muhammad, and recited certain inspired passages, which Muhammad was to embody in the Koran, so that the Arabs might become acquainted with the one true God. Whatever the truth may be, it can be said with some assurance that Muhammad, with his deep religious curiosity and strong spiritual leanings, must have listened attentively to what these Christians had to say, and discussed their beliefs with them.

As a result of such encounters Muhammad became acquainted with religious practices and beliefs both within and outside the Arabian peninsula, and, although he did not approve of monasticism, he thought highly of Christian monks, and adapted the prayer ritual used by them.

Before Muhammad's mission began, Christian communities were to be found in most of the Arabian towns (see Section 3.5). Christian merchants who operated in the Hejaz attended the local fairs and took part in many of the local activities.

Some tribes maintained commercial depots in Mecca and had their own representatives there. Such were the Christian tribes of Ijl, affiliated by pact to the Koraysh clan of Sahm, and the Ghassan, affiliated to the Koraysh clan of Zuhra and having a privileged establishment in the vicinity of the Kaaba itself.

Mecca had a small but influential Christian population, both Arab and foreign, slave and free, from Abyssinia, Syria, Iraq and Palestine. Its members worked as artisans, masons, traders, physicians and scribes. Azraki (d. 858) writes of a Christian cemetery in Mecca (Trimingham, 1979, 260).

Itinerant Christian preachers often passed through the Hejaz, and the sermon of one of them, Koss ibn Sayda, left a lasting impression on Muhammad before his own mission began.

Khadija, Muhammad's first wife and companion during the twenty-four formative years of his life, had strong Christian links. Her cousin Waraka, who encouraged Muhammad in his resolve to reform the religion of the pagan Arabs, was a Christian himself.

As already mentioned, those of Muhammad's followers who went into exile in Christian Abyssinia in 615 included three of his cousins – Jaafar, Obaydulla and Zubayr – three women who later became Muhammad's wives – Sauda, Umm Habiba and Umm Salama (Sauda and Umm Habiba were both widows of Christians) – Muhammad's brother-in-law Malik ibn Zamaa, Muhammad's daughter Rokaya, and Othman, who was to become the third caliph of Islam.

Several of the exiles became Christians and remained in that country, notably Muhammad's cousin Obaydulla and Sakran, a Korayshi. The three wives of Muhammad who had been to Abyssinia would often recall pleasant memories of their visit there.

Muhammad's adopted son, Zayid ibn Haritha, and Salman the Persian, who saved the day for Muhammad when Medina was under attack in April 627, had both first been Christians. Harith ibn Kalda, Muhammad's friend and physician, was a Nestorian Christian. Bilal, the Abyssinian slave who was appointed the first muezzin, and ended his days in Christian Tarsus, and Hasan ibn Thabit, Muhammad's personal poet, both had strong Christian ties. Muhammad's favourite concubine, Mary the Copt, was a Christian slave from Egypt.

10.2 Christian Teachers

Besides the persons from whom Muhammad might have received indirect influences, there were a few by whom he seems to have been more directly influenced and to whom he owed much for the formulation of his doctrines.

Muhammad's enemies, aware that he used to visit the homes of Christians to inform himself about their teachings, accused him of artfully contriving the Koran out of material taken partly from earlier scriptures and partly picked up from various extraneous sources. He was rebuked for being 'all ear' (9:61), eager to listen and give gullible credence to all the stories he heard. They charged him with being instructed by others (44:13) who helped him, dictating tales of the ancients to him morning and evening (25:6). Besides, among his teachers was a certain foreigner (16:105).

To counter the charge of borrowings, Muhammad protested that he had not read any book before this, nor transcribed one (29:47). And, as for a foreigner teaching him, the language of the person they were hinting at was a foreign language, whereas the Koran was written in clear Arabic (16:105). From the writings of Yahya, al-Baydawi, al-Zamakshari, Abbasi, Jalalain and other Muslim commentators, scholars have attempted to identify the men – Arabs and foreigners – who might have been involved, but details are scarce and the matter remains uncertain.

Muhammad may have gleaned some information from learned Jews, but in most accounts his mentors appear to have been Christians. The commentator Husayn said the Prophet was in the habit of going every evening to a certain Christian and hearing the Torah (Pentateuch) and the Injil (Gospel). Several Muslim writers have alluded to other individuals with whom Muhammad was known to associate, and who were said by the Korayshis to have instructed the Prophet. Among those named the following deserve notice.

Kayis, of the tribe of Abdul Kayis, was a Christian whose house Muhammad frequented.

Jabra, a young Greek Christian, was a sword-cutter by profession, and servant of a family from Hadramaut who had settled in Mecca. He was well read in the Mosaic law, the prophets and the teachings of Jesus, and would read from these books in the presence of Muhammad, who frequented his house.

Abu Takbiha was also a Greek, and Muhammad would attend his discourses.

Sohayb, son of Sinan, was a Greek slave, nephew of the Persian governor of Obola in southern Mesopotamia, who had been carried off to Syria by a band of robbers who raided Obola. A Byzantine by education, Sohayb escaped to Mecca, acquired great wealth, and eventually embraced Islam.

Aysh, another slave, a man of some learning, also became a follower of Muhammad.

Abu Rokaya, of the Christian Tamim tribe, was known for the purity of his life. His devotions and selfless service earned him the title of 'monk of the people' (Archer, 1924, p. 60). He later embraced the Muslim faith and became one of Muhammad's close companions.

Tamim al-Dari, a Christian, was said to have influenced Muhammad's eschatological ideas (see Section 10.16). He too later became a proselyte of Islam. He is sometimes identified with Abu Rokaya.

Addas was a Christian monk from Nineveh who settled in Mecca. Khadija brought Muhammad to him, and he explained the significance of the angel Gabriel as the bringer of divine revelation. Muhammad had long conversations with him. He is not to be confused with the Addas who helped Muhammad in 619 when he sought refuge in Tayif.

Yunus of Nineveh, mentioned by Ibn Hisham, was the brother of the above-mentioned Addas of Nineveh, and was said to have attained prophetic powers through ascetic disciplines.

Yasra, or Abu Fukayha, was a learned Christian who worked as a servant in a Meccan household which Muhammad used to visit. It was related that Yasra would read from the Gospels while Muhammad listened attentively. Yasra's daughter Fukayha married Hattab, who took part in the Abyssinian exile.

Kayin, a Christian mentioned by the commentator Abbasi, is said to have imparted to Muhammad some of the stories included in the Koran.

Rahman of Yamama was believed by Muhammad's contemporaries to have given the Prophet certain of his ideas. Ibn Ishak confirms that Muhammad had contacts with a Christian of Yamama named Abdul Rahman. Scholars identify him with Musaylima (see Section 10.19).

10.3 Tolerance towards Christians

In the beginning of his prophetic career in Mecca and during the early days in Medina, Muhammad inclined very strongly to the Christian view with regard to Jesus as the Messiah, the Word made flesh and the Spirit of God.

In the Koran, God says to Jesus, 'I will place those who follow thee above those who believe not, until the day of resurrection' (3:48). The Koran records that Christians are free from pride and most inclined to entertain feelings of friendship for Muslims (5:85).

Muhammad accommodated in his own house the leaders of a Christian deputation who visited him in Medina in 628, allowing them to say their prayers in his mosque, which they did facing east as was the Christian custom.

In one of the treaties he concluded with the Christians of Najran in the same year, he gave them assurances in the following terms: they would have his protection and not be oppressed; their lives, religion and property would be secure; no Christian would be forced to renounce his faith, and no pilgrim would be obstructed in his pilgrimage; taxes would not be levied on Christians, nor would they be required to furnish provision for troops; Christian women married to Muslims were to enjoy the practice of their own religion; no church would be pulled down or converted into a mosque; help would be provided in repairing churches; no bishop would be removed from his see, nor monk from his monastery, nor priest from his residence; no image or cross would be destroyed; Christians could beat their wooden clappers at prayer times, and take out their crosses during festivals (Ameer Ali, 1965, p. 273). Muhammad's own pledge was given on these matters. He personally undertook and enjoined his followers to adhere to these commitments, and declared that any Muslim violating the terms would be regarded as having violated God's commandment.

As Muhammad had once thought of using the Jewish trumpet (buk) to summon the faithful to prayer, so for a time he also thought of using a bell or wooden clapper (nakus) such as the Christians used to assemble their congregations. However, the metallic sound of bells disturbed him, so he settled for the clapper. Ibn Hisham says Muhammad had given instructions for one to be made, and it had already been carved out, when he changed his mind in favour of the present method of having a man (muezzin) call out to the people that it is time to pray.

Following his triumphal entry into Mecca in January 630, Muhammad ordered the destruction of the Kaaba idols and the erasure of all the paintings from the walls and pillars. The effigies of Abraham and Ishmael were destroyed, as they were shown holding the divining arrows of the pagan soothsayers. But he himself, it was said, placed a protective hand over the picture of Mary and the infant Jesus (Esin, 1963, p. 109). The picture was said to have been painted by the artist Bakum (Pachomias) when the Kaaba was rebuilt after the accidental fire of 594. What happened to the picture is not stated, but no doubt it was disposed of in a suitable manner.

10.4 Parallel Passages

Scholars quoting chapter and verse from biblical and Koranic passages have shown that the Prophet drew extensively from Jewish and Christian sources, both canonical and apocryphal. Muhammad may have heard passages from the Old and New Testaments and then paraphrased them or produced his own versions from memory.

Some biblical texts quoted in the Koran are acknowledged as quotations. Thus 'the righteous shall inherit the earth' (21:105) is taken direct from the Old Testament (Ps. 37:29).

The Gospels are also cited. A verse from St Mark's Gospel reads, 'For the earth bringeth forth fruit of herself; first the blade, then the ear, and after that the full corn in the ear' (Mark 4:28). The Koran renders it thus: 'This is their picture in the Gospel: "They are as the seed which putteth forth its stalk, then strengtheneth it, and it groweth in the ear, and riseth upon its stem"' (48:29).

The Beatific Vision occurs in the New Testament and in the Koran: 'Now we see through a glass darkly; but then face to face' (1 Cor. 13:12). In the Koran, 'Faces on that day shall be bright, gazing at their Lord' (75:22).

Jesus said, 'He that loveth father or mother, son or daughter more than me is not worthy of me' (Matt. 10:37). In a hadith, Muhammad says, 'No man may be said to believe unless he believes that I am dearer to him than his father, child and all mankind' (Brandon, 1970, p. 277).

In the biblical parable of the wise and foolish virgins, 'The foolish said to the wise, "Give us of your oil; for our lamps are gone out." But the wise answered saying, "Not so, lest there be not enough for us and you. Go rather and buy for yourselves"' (Matt. 25:8–9). In the Koran, 'On that day the hypocrites, both men and women, shall say to those who believe, "Tarry with us that we may kindle our light at yours." It shall be said, "Return ye back and seek light for yourselves"' (57:13).

Jesus said, 'It is easier for a camel to pass through the eye of a needle, than for a rich man to enter the kingdom of heaven' (Matt. 19:24). According to the Koran, 'Heaven's gates shall not be opened to those who charge us with falsehood nor shall they enter paradise until a camel passeth through the eye of a needle' (7:38).

On the day of the Lord, says the Bible, 'the heavens shall be rolled together as a scroll' (Isa. 34:4). 'On that day will we roll up the heavens as one rolleth up written scrolls,' says the Koran (21:104).

St Paul writes, 'Eye hath not seen nor ear heard, neither have entered into the heart of man, the things which God hath prepared for them that love him' (1 Cor. 2:9). On one occasion Muhammad said to his friend Abu Hurayra, 'God has prepared for his good people what no eye hath seen, nor ear heard, nor hath it entered into the heart of anyone' (Ameer Ali, 1965,

p. 199). He then recited the following verse in the Koran: 'No soul knoweth what joy of the eyes is reserved as a reward for good works' (32:17).

The Bible says, 'Where two or three are gathered together in my name, there am I in the midst of them' (Matt. 18:20). The Koran: 'Three persons cannot meet secretly but God is the fourth' (58:8).

'There are many other things which Jesus did, which if they were to be written down, I suppose that even the world itself could not contain the books that should be written' (John 21:25). The Koran says, 'If the seas were ink it would be insufficient for the words of the Lord' (18:109).

Muhammad himself as well as his biographers sought to draw parallels between his life and that of Jesus. Thus, it was said that, like Jesus, Muhammad chose twelve disciples to carry the message of Islam. Like Jesus, Muhammad gave a Sermon on the Mount, which ended, 'This day have I perfected your religion.' Jesus announced in the synagogue in Nazareth, 'This day is this scripture fulfilled in your ears' (Luke 4:21). Jesus's last words on the cross, 'It is finished' (John 19:30), find an echo in the words with which Muhammad ended his last sermon: 'I have finished my work.'

After Muhammad's death his followers continued to find similarities between the two lives, as in Muhammad's performance of miracles, the idea of Muhammad's sinlessness, and his near-divine status (see Sections 11.13–15).

10.5 Terminology

It has been shown, not only by Western scholars (Jeffery, 1938; Sweetman, 1967; et al.) but by some early Muslim exegetes, that a number of basic religious terms used in the faith established by Muhammad originally belonged to the religious vocabulary of the Christian churches of Syria and Arabia, as found in Syriac (Christian Aramaic), and were adapted as convenient and ready-to-hand loanwords by Muhammad and his followers. A small selection of these is given below, and many others will be found scattered throughout the present work.

The term *islam*, from the Semitic root SLM, signifying completeness or safety, had acquired – some time before the birth of Muhammad – the more particular meaning of submission, resignation, acceptance or surrender. As a technical term in a religious sense, it was used by the Syrian Christians to signify 'devotion' – that is, to God (Jeffery, 1938, p. 63) – and it was used by them to describe their faith. A companion of Muhammad named Abbas ibn Mirdas wrote a poem in which he spoke of Islam as having existed before Muhammad, and of Muhammad having 'repaired' or reformed it (Bravmann, 1972, p. 26).

The term *muslim*, a formation from the same Semitic root, was also used by Christians before Muhammad, and meant a person who had devoted himself to God. The Koran speaks of Abraham as a Muslim (3:60), and the household of Lot as a Muslim household (51:36), and of Jews and Christians who were Muslims before the coming of Islam (28:53), and of the disciples of Christ calling themselves Muslims (3:45).

At first the term 'Muslim' was applied by Muhammad broadly, to include the disciples and followers of all the prophets from Abraham to Jesus. All such persons were regarded as Muslims, resigned to God and following the true religion of Islam (3:78). Later, the meanings were narrowed to signify specifically the religion and followers of the faith established by Muhammad.

The term *koran* for the sacred book revealed to Muhammad originated from a word (*kerana*) used by Syrian Christians for their lectionary or 'readings' of Bible texts used at their church services.

The word *sura*, used for a chapter of the Koran, comes from the Syrian Christian word (*surta*) for 'portion of scripture'; the word *aya*, 'sign', for a Koranic verse, was likewise taken over from Syrian Christian usage.

The term *furkan* is used in the Koran to mean 'revelation' (both pre-Islamic and Islamic) and also 'salvation'. It is also the title of the twenty-fifth sura of the Koran, and was employed to signify the means of distinguishing between truth and error. The term was derived from a word (*porkan*) of the Aramaic-speaking Christians, meaning 'salvation' (Dawood, 1990, p. 358).

The divine service of the church was called in Syriac *salat*, and this term of Christian usage was adopted for the Muslim form of prayer. The word *sajda*, used for the deep prostrations of the Muslim prayer ritual, was taken from the Syrian Christians (see Section 3.4). The word *zikr*, for the 'remembrance' of God by the repetition of God's name, was also based on a Syrian Christian term (*zurkrana*) with the same technical application.

The words *din*, 'religion', *shahid*, 'martyr', and several others as well have their origin in the vocabulary of the Syrian Christians. The obligatory alms tax (*zakat*) and the voluntary giving of alms in charity (*sadaka*) were both taken from Christian and Jewish practice (see Section 13.2).

The common Semitic background and the many common roots of the Syriac and Arabic languages might account for the shared usage of the religious terminology of the Syrian Christians and Muslims. But the fact that the borrowed words did not exist in Arabic, and that the concepts and practices to which they applied antedated Muhammad's mission by more than two centuries, leaves no room for doubt that they were taken over direct and virtually unaltered from Christian usage.

10.6 Rahman

The term *rahman*, 'merciful', appears in the early pagan inscriptions of the southern Arabs as a descriptive appellation for the divine being in heaven. Before the rise of Islam the name 'Rahman' was also used by the Christians of southern Arabia to signify God. The name occurs in the poetry of the early Christian poets, and is known to have been used by Christianized prophets like Musaylima of Yamama and Ayhala ibn Kaab.

Related to the word 'rahman', having the same root, is *rahim*, meaning 'compassionate'. 'Rahim' has feminine connotations of nurturing and protecting, and as a noun it means 'womb' (Ruthven, 1984, p. 115). Rahim was invoked as a divinity by Arabs of the Syrian desert from the fourth century AD.

Both the designations 'Rahman' and 'Rahim' were known to the Nabataeans, and both occur in the most famous of all Muslim formulas, the *tasmiya*, taught by Omayya of Tayif and adopted by Muhammad.

The Prophet recognized mercy and compassion as foremost among the divine qualities. Among the ninety-nine illustrious names bestowed upon God by the Muslims, Rahman and Rahim receive special honour. Muhammad regarded mercy as a characteristically Christian quality. The Koran states that God sent Jesus as a sign of God's mercy for mankind (19:21), and had planted mercy in the hearts of those who follow Jesus (57:27).

Muhammad was conscious of the pagan associations of 'Allah', and for a time during the Meccan period he made a persistent, if unsuccessful, attempt to introduce 'Rahman', along with 'Allah', both as a title of God (20:4) and as a personal name of the divinity. 'Rahman' is the only adjectival name of God frequently used in the Koran as a substantive name of God besides 'Allah'. It is Rahman who sits in majesty upon the heavenly throne, and it is before Rahman that we must prostrate ourselves. 'Rahman' is also a title given to one of the early suras (number 55).

The Meccans were unfamiliar with the name 'Rahman', as it did not figure in the Meccan pantheon, and they disliked it (25:61) – probably because of its constant use by Muhammad. They insisted on its deletion during the drafting of the Hodebiya treaty.

In one of the Koranic suras we are told, 'Call upon Allah, or call upon Rahman, by whichsoever name you will invoke him, his names are most beautiful' (17:110). Later, fearing that Allah and Rahman might be supposed to be two gods, Muhammad abandoned the use of 'Rahman'.

10.7 The Gospel

The Koran speaks in the singular of the Gospel (*Injil*, from Evangel, a word of Greek derivation signifying 'Good News') as a book of divine authority which was given to Jesus (57:27). The word for Gospel occurs twelve times in the Koran, but there are several other references to it. The hadith uses the Arabic equivalent of Gospel for the Koranic message, also meaning 'good news': *bushra*.

According to the Koran, the Gospel is inspired by God, and those who accept it are classed among the 'people of the book' (see Section 11.7). The Koran confirms the Gospel as the guide of mankind (3:2). The Gospel contains the truth (9:112) and gives guidance and light (5:50). If people follow the precepts of the Gospel they will enjoy abundance from above and from below (5:70).

At no time did Muhammad ever express a doubt about the authority or genuineness of the Gospel, nor did he ever say that the Christian scriptures had been cancelled. He never regarded the message as having been corrupted, but only as misunderstood or forgotten (5:17). The charges of modification (tabdil) or corruption (tahrif) of the words or meaning of the Christian scriptures were only made by later Muslim theologians.

10.8 The Trinity

In view of Muhammad's belief that God is one, the notion of the Trinity is rejected in Islam. The Koran asserts, 'They surely are infidels who say that God is the third of three' (5:77). Muhammad seems to have confused the Trinity of Christianity with tritheism, a belief in three gods: 'Believe in one God, and say not there are three gods' (4:169).

Again, Muhammad mistakenly implies that the Trinity is made up of God, Mary and Jesus. 'In the last day Allah will ask Jesus whether he had said to the people, "Take me and my mother as two Gods, beside God." And Jesus will reply, "Praise be unto you. It is not for me to say that which is not true"' (5:116).

While belief in the Trinity as God, Jesus and Mary is rejected in Islam, the concept of a threefold aspect of the Godhead may inadvertently have left its mark on the Muslim faith.

The 'In Nomine' formula of the Christian reads, 'In the name of the Father, and of the Son, and of the Holy Spirit'. This may be found reflected in the famous Islamic formula, the tasmiya, which reads, 'In the name of God [Bismillah], the Merciful [al-Rahman], the Compassionate [al-Rahim]'. Allah is God the Father; Rahman is the merciful Son; and Rahim, with its feminine connotations, could be interpreted as the Holy Spirit or, in the Muslim misconception, Mary. Indeed, from the third century after the Hegira, Christians themselves, seeing no difference between them, often used the Bismillah formula, instead of the Christian 'In the name of the Father . . .' (Abbott, 1939, p. 21).

10.9 The Holy Spirit

The Koran states that only a little information about the Holy Spirit (Ruh al-Kudus) has been vouchsafed to Muhammad (17:87). The Holy Spirit, which comes from God, strengthened Christ (2:81) and inspired the Koran (16:104).

Muhammad thought the Holy Spirit in the Christian Trinity was to be identified with Mary, an idea he may have received from certain apocryphal traditions prevalent in his day.

In Christian symbolism the Holy Spirit is represented by a dove, which in pagan times was believed to be a bird of the Great Goddess. The Hebrew word for spirit (*ruah*) is feminine, and the Holy Spirit has sometimes been equated with the Shekina, who, like the Sophia of the Gnostics (Walker, 1989, p. 41), was regarded as the feminine counterpart of the Godhead. In the apocryphal *Gospel of the Hebrews*, Jesus speaks of 'My Mother the Holy Spirit'.

10.10 Mary

The Virgin Mary (Maryam) was held in high esteem by Muhammad as an example of the perfect woman, and she continued to be so regarded by Muslim saints and mystics (see Section 13.16). J. Abdel-Jalil, a Moroccan Muslim by birth who became a Franciscan friar, has described (1950) the special status accorded to her in the Koran.

Muhammad believed in the immaculate conception of Mary, meaning that she was conceived without sin (Gibb, 1969, p. 31), and in her continued sinlessness (3:37). In the hadith, Muhammad said that every newborn child is touched by Satan, except Mary and her son (3:31). Having been chosen for her destiny above all the women of the world, she was purified by God (3:37), maintained in purity (66:12), and given as a sign to all creatures (21:91).

The Koran contains an angelic annunciation: 'Mary, verily God gives you glad tidings of a word from himself, whose name shall be Messiah Jesus' (3:40). God breathed his spirit into her womb, so the birth of Jesus was a creative act of God upon an immaculate virgin (19:20) who kept her maidenhood (21:19) and was a pure receptacle of the divine spirit.

10.11 Jesus

Muhammad once said that no one could love Jesus (Isa) more than he did (Esin, 1963, p. 109). Of no other prophet does the Koran speak in more numinous and exalted terms than it does of Jesus, who is shown to be as near to divinity as any mortal could be.

Jesus is an example of divine power. He had no human father but was conceived by the spirit of God and breathed by God into the womb of the Virgin Mary (66:12). He was strengthened by the Holy Spirit (2:254), which proceeds from God himself (4:169), and is without sin.

Jesus is the Messiah (*masih*) (3:40) – a word borrowed from Syriac – whom God has made blessed (19:32). He is the Word of Truth (*Kawl al-Hak*) (19:35). He is the Word of God (*Kalimat Allah*) (3:40) – a reflection of the

Logos doctrine – and the spirit proceeding from God (*Ruh Allah*) (4:169).

Jesus is the messenger of the Almighty (*Rasul Allah*) (4:169), has near-access to God, and is illustrious in this world and the next (3:40). He is appointed as a sign (*aya*, 'miracle') to mankind, bestows great blessings on the human race, and is a mercy (*rahman*) from God (19:21). Before death, says the Koran, all the people of the book (i.e. Jews, Christians and Muslims) will believe in Jesus (4:157).

10.12 The Son of God

Strongly opposed to polytheism, and with the moral support of the Jews, Muhammad denied the divinity of Jesus and his incarnation. Jesus was not the son of God, for 'God begetteth not' (112:3). God is one, and nothing can be brought into association with him: 'It is not proper for God that he should have a son' (19:36). 'It would be far from the glory of God to have a son' (4:169).

Ibn Ishak relates the story of Muhammad rebuking two Christian divines about their belief that God has a son. Since the Koran itself states that Jesus was the son of an immaculate virgin, they asked him, 'But who was his father, Muhammad?' The Prophet, it is related, remained silent, and did not answer them (Guillaume, 1955, p. 272). God later sent down a few verses which now form part of one of the longer suras, but these do not shed light on the problem posed by the divines, except to say, 'God can create what he will. When he decrees a thing, he only says, "Be!" [*Kun!*], and it is' (3:42). Such things, as the Koran says elsewhere, are 'easy for God' (19:21).

Muhammad's objection to Christian belief in the sonship of Jesus may have arisen from a concern that such ideas might once again open the door to polytheism among the Arabs. He had got into difficulties in this area when he had made an attempt to compromise with the pagans of Mecca over the daughters of God (see Section 5.21).

According to some scholars, certain polemical verses strongly repudiating the divine sonship of Jesus were added to the Koran as a result of Muhammad's growing antagonism to the Christians because of their rejection of his claims. Such, for example, were the verses added to Sura 19 (see Section 5.20).

The Koran calls down God's curse on all who say Christ is the son of God (9:30). Another passage reads, 'Those who say that the Lord of Mercy had begotten a son preach a monstrous doctrine at which the very heavens might be rent, the earth cleave asunder, and the mountains fall down in fragments' (19:91).

On the other hand, the fact that Muhammad is instructed quite unequivocally 'Say: If the Lord of Mercy had a son, I would be the first to worship him' (43:81) would seem to indicate that the idea was not as unthinkable as the verses quoted above might suggest.

10.13 The Miracles of Jesus

The Koran mentions several miracles performed by Jesus which are not recorded in the Gospels. He spoke while still an infant in his cradle (3:41). While a child, he spoke in vindication of his mother (19:28–31). He made birds of clay and breathed life into them (3:43). Some Gospel miracles are also cited. Thus he gave sight to the blind, cleansed lepers, and raised the dead (5:110).

Another miracle recorded in the Koran was performed when the disciples asked Jesus to send down a table from heaven for them to eat from. God sent down a table as a recurring feast to nourish them, for God is the 'best of nourishers' (5:112–15). The sura in which this passage occurs is called 'Maida', 'manna', the term *maida* being a technical term used by the Abyssinian Christians for the Table of the Lord (Parrinder, 1979, p. 88). The passage is clearly a mixture of texts relating to the provision of manna to the children of Israel in the wilderness (Exod. 16:35), the Lord's Supper (Matt. 26:20), the feeding of the multitudes (Matt. 14:20), and Peter's vision of the descent of a great sheet filled with things to be eaten (Acts 10:11).

10.14 Death and Resurrection

The Koran rejects the idea of the Messiah dying on the cross. Jesus was not crucified, but another person (unnamed) was made to appear in his likeness and was crucified instead. During this apparent crucifixion (*salab*) God took Jesus up to himself (4:156). In one Muslim tradition the person crucified in Jesus's place was Judas.

According to al-Wakidi, Muhammad came to abhor the cross (*salib*) and broke everything brought into his house that resembled one. Ibn Hurayra relates that Muhammad said, 'When Jesus will descend from heaven [see Section 10.16] he will break the crosses and kill the swine.'

Although the Koran rejects the crucifixion, it does accept the death, resurrection and ascension of Christ. While still an infant in his cradle Jesus said, 'The peace of God was on me the day I was born, and will be the day I shall die, and the day I shall be raised to life' (19:34).

In the Koran, God says to Jesus, 'Truly I shall cause you to die, and raise you up to myself' (3:48), though the actual time and place of Jesus's death and the place of his burial are not stated. Another text in the Koran says, God has prepared for Jesus and Mary, 'an abode in a lofty place, quiet and watered with springs' (23:52). These verses were interpreted by Muslim divines to mean that both Jesus and Mary were taken up bodily to heaven.

10.15 The Paraclete

According to the Gospels, Jesus told his disciples that, after he had gone, God would send a Comforter who would abide with them for ever (John 14:16). The Greek word for Comforter, *Paraklētos*, was probably rendered in some garbled versions as *Periklytos*, meaning 'Renowned', and translated into Arabic as *Ahmad*, 'praised'.

Since the names 'Ahmad' and 'Muhammad' are derived from the same root, Muhammad claimed to be the Paraclete. The Koranic reference to the above Gospel passage reads as follows: 'Remember when Jesus said, "Verily I am an apostle of God, giving good tidings of a prophet that shall come after me whose name will be Ahmad"' (61:6).

It is to be noted that Mani, or Manes (d. AD 276), the Persian founder of an influential semi-Christian sect active in Arabia long before Muhammad's birth, also declared that he was the last and greatest of the prophets, and the Paraclete. On the basis of his name, he claimed he had come to provide a refuge (Hebrew: *manos*) for mankind (Ps. 59:16); and that, as Jesus was the bread of life (John 6:35), so he, Mani, was the promised manna from heaven to nourish the people.

Christians refuted Muhammad's claim to be the Paraclete, and not only on the grounds of textual distortion. In the same chapter of the Bible (John 14:26) Jesus distinctly speaks of the Comforter as the Holy Spirit. Muhammad never claimed to be the Holy Spirit and therefore could not be the Paraclete. Again, the Koran speaks of Jesus as the Messiah (4:169), and no prophet can follow the Messiah. Finally, according to the Christians the Comforter descended on the day of Pentecost, ten days after Christ's ascension; they did not believe that he waited for over six centuries to come in the form of Muhammad.

A related claim made on behalf of Muhammad as the Paraclete, and the foretelling of his advent by name, appears in the *Gospel of Barnabas*, an apocryphal work written centuries after Muhammad's death by a Jewish or Christian convert to Islam. In this pseudo-gospel it is said that Judas was crucified in place of Jesus, which is in accord with Muslim belief. In the same work Jesus denies that he is the Messiah, whereas the Koran asserts more than once that he is. Instead, the book acknowledges Muhammad as the Messiah – a title Muhammad never claimed for himself.

Zealous Muslim scholars have scoured the Old and New Testaments for any verse that might be construed as alluding to Muhammad. References to a prophet to come – as in Deut. 18:18 – are claimed as pointing to the Arabian prophet. Where the context seems appropriate, the Hebrew word *mahmad*, meaning 'goodly', 'beloved' or 'lovely' that occurs more than a dozen times in the Old Testament – as in Song of Sol. 5:16 – is held to refer to Muhammad.

It need hardly be said that serious Muslim authorities dismiss these claims, along with the Barnabas forgery, perhaps because the case for Muhammad does not need to be supported from such an untenable position.

10.16 The Second Coming

The important part played by Jesus in Muslim thought is further shown in the Islamic traditions concerning the last days and the signs presaging the end of the world. Some of Muhammad's ideas on this subject were clearly derived from Christian sources.

Goldziher writes that the traditionalist Ibn Hajar agrees with more ancient authorities in acknowledging the significant part that Tamim al-Dari (fl. c. 628) played in shaping Muslim concepts about the last days. Tamim al-Dari was a Christian – a monk in some accounts – and a contemporary of Muhammad who later converted to Islam and became a companion of the Prophet.

Jesus, says the Koran, is a sign of the last days (43:61). It is written in a hadith that Muhammad once rhetorically asked, 'How can a people of which I am the beginning and Jesus the end, perish?' (McAuliffe, 1991, p. 132). According to the Khabitiya sect – followers of Ahmad ibn Khabit – Christ's second coming is also indicated in the Koranic verse reading, 'Your Lord shall come with angels, rank on rank' (89:23). It is Christ who will call mankind to a reckoning in the next life (Kazi and Flynn, 1984, p. 53).

Belief in the second coming gave rise to the idea of the Mahdi, a powerful personage who will appear during the last days to lead the people and establish a reign of peace and righteousness. Some believe the Mahdi will be of the line of Muhammad, but according to most traditions this is not so. Many would lay claim to the title of Mahdi, but they would all be impostors, for Muhammad has declared, 'There is no Mahdi except Jesus son of Mary' (D. B. Macdonald, in SEI, 1974, p. 174).

Also in the Muslim tradition is the notion that the second advent would be marked by the appearance of the Antichrist, the great deceiver known as Dajjal – an Aramaean loanword. A mighty battle will be fought between Jesus and the Antichrist, in which Jesus will finally overcome his adversary.

After this victory, Islam will pass into the hands of Jesus, who will reign on earth for forty years, bringing peace to all the lands (see Section 14.15). At the end of this period Jesus will die a natural death and be buried in Medina, where a place has been reserved for him between the tombs of Muhammad and Abu Bakr.

Then, after an interval of unspecified duration, an angel will sound three blasts on a trumpet announcing the Last Judgement of the human race.

10.17 The Apocryphal Gospels

Muhammad's views on the birth, life and death of the Virgin Mary and Jesus suggest that he may have been familiar with the material found in the apocryphal gospels and with popular Christian traditions, many of which were widely diffused and well known in the Middle East in his day. Some of these stories may have been accepted by him as true, for he used them in the Koran, adapting them in consonance with his own teachings.

The Trinity of God, Mary and Jesus, which according to the Koran was the accepted Christian doctrine, was held by certain schismatic sects such as the Mariamites. There was an Arabian sect known as the Collyridians who would offer small sacralized cakes (kollyra) to Mary.

The details relating to the birth of Mary as recorded in the Koran (3:31) are found in the apocryphal Nativity of Mary. The story about Mary being brought up in the Temple in Jerusalem, where she was fed by angels (3:32), appears in the Protevangelium of James the Less and in the Coptic History of the Virgin. The incident of Mary and the palm tree (19:23) comes from the History of the Nativity of Mary and The Infancy of the Saviour.

That Jesus spoke in his cradle (19:31) – a Coptic legend – is found in the Gospel of the Infancy. That he formed birds of clay and gave them life (3:43) in the Gospel of Thomas the Israelite. That Jesus was not crucified but only his likeness (4:156) is found in the Journeys of the Apostles, and was held by the Gnostic sect of the Docetists. That God is one, and that Jesus was a man chosen by God and filled in exceptional measure with the divine spirit, was held by sects like the Monarchists led by Paul of Samosata (d. 272), bishop of Antioch.

Several other works of varying date, including Narratives, Journeys, Acts, Infancy Gospels and miscellaneous apocrypha in Syriac, Coptic, Greek, Arabic and Armenian, were also circulating in the Middle East and were accessible to those who might be interested.

During the Medinan period Muhammad received a divine revelation about seven youths and their dog who remained asleep in a cave for many years (18:8–21). This is a variation of the story of the seven Christian youths of Ephesus walled up in a cave in Mount Celion during the persecution of Decius in AD 250 and miraculously kept alive through a long sleep lasting 200 years. The story is taken from the Syriac Homilies by the Christian writer Jacob of Sarug (d. 520) and is also found in a work by Gregory of Tours (d. 594), and is mentioned by Gibbon in his Decline and Fall of the Roman Empire (1776).

10.18 Hostility to Christians

Some time after Muhammad's migration to Medina a change took place in his attitude to Christians. He had been accused by the Meccans of having acquired certain of his doctrines from Christian teachers. Now the Christians themselves had rejected him, criticizing his teachings and his interpretation of Christianity.

Just as the Jews had pronounced the Koranic stories regarding the patriarchs inaccurate, so the Christians found his version of the life and teachings of Jesus to be a misrepresentation of the facts recorded in the Gospels, and they showed no intention of acknowledging Muhammad as a prophet.

Not one to take criticism lightly, Muhammad turned against them. Christianity was a rival religion. It too was a revealed teaching, and claimed to be the true and final doctrine. It was an international faith, with a burning sense of mission for all mankind, and, far from being eager for conversion, Christians were zealous to make converts themselves. Christians could therefore no longer be regarded as allies.

It was the Christians, Muhammad said in reply to their criticism, who had misunderstood the message of Jesus, just as the Jews had corrupted the message of Moses. The Koran states that Christians had forgotten part of what they had been taught (5:17). They had changed their prophet Jesus into a God, and then made one God into three.

The goodwill and friendliness he had hitherto shown towards Christians suffered a radical change as his own sense of mission grew. This change is found reflected in the Koran: 'O believers, do not take Jews and Christians as friends. If you take them as friends you are surely one of them' (5:56). Again, 'Do not take as allies those who received the scriptures before you, or who treat your religion as a joke and a game' (5:62).

The Koran speaks of Christians as infidels (5:19), because they are guilty of believing that Christ is the son of God, and it prays, 'May God do battle with them' (9:30). Muhammad not only rebukes Jews and Christians but denies them paradise, consigning them to hell (5:76), where, along with the polytheists, they will abide for ever (98:5). His bitter opposition continued to the end of his life. Among the last words he uttered as he lay dying were 'The Lord destroy Jews and Christians.'

With greater fighting powers now at his disposal, Muhammad was able to express more actively his hostility towards the Christians, especially to their presence in Arabia. This policy was to be carried to its ultimate conclusion by his immediate successors, Abu Bakr and Omar.

10.19 Expeditions Against the Christians

We find several conflicting versions, all written by late commentators, about the conversion of the Arab Christian tribes, both during Muhammad's lifetime and after his death. In some accounts the tribes were struck by the truth of the new revelation and willingly embraced Islam; in others there was considerable resistance to the new religion, and to the methods used to enforce it, and many submitted to Islam only for fear of extermination.

In February 630 Muhammad sent a detachment under Amr ibn al-As (later conqueror of Egypt) to the Christian tribes of Oman, summoning the rulers to accept the new religion and pay the contributions prescribed under Islam. After some negotiation, a few tribes agreed to accept conversion. One tribe, the Mazuna, wished to retain their faith and were allowed to remain Christian on surrendering half their lands and property to the conquerors.

In the same month, February 630, a delegation was dispatched to the Christian princes of Himyar, in the south, carrying letters in which Muhammad confirmed his belief in Moses and Jesus but denied the Trinity of the Godhead and the divinity of Jesus. The letters stated that there was only one God and that Muhammad was his prophet, and called upon the people to accept the new faith. Those who spoke the Himyar tongue were to use Arabic instead. They were to submit to Islam and pay the required tithes, taxes and tributes. Those who refused would be regarded as enemies of Muhammad. Rather than lose their lives, the princes sent back replies accepting the new religion.

Christians living in and around the Hejaz were likewise soon reduced to submission for fear of suffering the fate of others who had tried to resist. In July 630 Ali was sent to destroy the idol of the god Fuls, still being worshipped by one clan of the Tayi tribe. Having razed the shrine of Fuls and terrorized the people into accepting Islam, Ali turned his attention to the Christian clans of Tayi. The Tayi chief Adi, son of the famous Hatim Tayi, fled to Syria, but later, on the solicitation of his sister, returned and embraced Islam. Another Tayi chief, Zarr ibn Sardus, also left the country, travelling first to Christian Syria and thence to Constantinople.

In October 630 Muhammad, at the head of the largest force ever before assembled in Arabia, set out on an expedition to the north-west and halted at Tabuk, about 250 miles from Medina. Here Yohana (John) ibn Ruba, the Christian prince of Ayla (the modern port of Akaba), received the Prophet and made a treaty with him, agreeing to pay a tax and tribute in exchange for protection from attack. Muhammad halted in Tabuk for twenty days and then returned to Medina. Because of the growing disaffection of his tribal allies, the expedition to Tabuk was the last one personally undertaken by the Prophet.

While at Tabuk, Muhammad sent his general Khalid ibn Walid to the oasis of Duma, which was ruled by the Christian Arab prince Okaydir ibn Abdul Malik, of the Kalb tribe. (Okaydir's elder brother Bishr, who had died about twenty years earlier, is said to have taught the Meccans to write – see Section 4.2). Okaydir was out hunting with another brother when Khalid waylaid them, slew the brother, and brought Okaydir back to Muhammad in Medina as a prisoner. Muhammad concluded an agreement with him, granting him protection in exchange for conversion and the payment of the customary taxes, and the prince was allowed to go home. After Muhammad's death Okaydir revolted, and Khalid returned to Duma, killed the prince, and sacked the oasis settlement.

When Muhammad first came to Medina he had a long discussion with a highly individualistic character, a Christian of the Aus tribe living near Medina named Abu Amir. He was nicknamed al-Rahib, 'the monk', because of his ascetic habits, and is sometimes numbered among the hanifs.

Abu Amir had censured Muhammad for having taken his doctrines from the 'faith of Abraham', dismissed his claim to prophethood, and rebuked him for corrupting monotheism by interposing himself as a necessary element in the divine dispensation. He later came to oppose Muhammad on political, social and moral grounds. He regarded Muhammad's raids on merchant caravans as undisguised brigandage, and believed he was dangerously ambitious.

In order to escape Muhammad's known vendettas, Abu Amir went to live in Mecca; later, accompanied by some fifty followers, he migrated to Syria, where he died in about 628, in the Christian faith. The Koran refers to him as one who warred against God and his apostle (9:108).

Abu Amir's adherents among the Ganim clan in the Medinan oasis had built a place of worship not far from the Prophet's first mosque in Koba. It was also used as a refuge for the sick and needy, and was drawing away the congregation from the Prophet's mosque. When Muhammad was on his way to Tabuk, the people of Ganim had invited him to visit the refuge and pray there with them. He had agreed, but on his return he decided he could not attend a house of prayer that had not been approved by him. He declared that the supporters of Abu Amir, who had rejected his leadership, had built it to create infidelity and hurt the faithful. The Koran refers to this incident (9:108). Muhammad ordered the 'mosque of dissension' to be burned down, and this was done, after which it was converted into a dunghill (Sale, 1886, p. 152).

The general manner of dealing with Christian groups is demonstrated by Muhammad's handling of two tribes, one from the south and one from the north. In about February 631 an embassy from the important southern Christian tribe of Hanifa came to visit Muhammad in Medina. What transpired is not clear, but on their departure Muhammad gave the envoys a vessel with some water in it left over from his ablutions, and bade them on returning to their country to tear down their church, sprinkle the site with the water, and build a mosque in its place (Muir, 1912, p. 458). This command they were obliged to carry out. A month later, in April 631, another embassy, made up partly of Christians from the tribe of Taghlib wearing crosses of gold, paid Muhammad a visit. The Prophet made an agreement with them, allowing them to continue in the profession of their religion on condition they did not baptize their children into the Christian faith.

On a number of other occasions, about which there are confused accounts, Christian delegations from Najran came to see Muhammad in Medina. One notable visit by fourteen persons took place in 631. They were led by Abdul Masih, of the Kinda tribe; Abu Haritha, bishop of the Bakr tribe; and a representative of the noble Dayan family.

They listened as Muhammad recited passages from the Koran, and they concluded that he had a message for his people. On being invited to accept Islam, however, they declined. A long discussion on religious matters ensued, and the disagreement betwen them deepened. Then Muhammad suggested, 'Let us summon our families, and curse one another, so that the curse of God will fall on the families of those who are lying' (3:54). The Christians refused to participate in this strange test of reciprocal cursing (Rodinson, 1976, p. 271).

Before leaving, the Christians were assured by the Prophet that they would not be molested in the practice of their religion and would be allowed to retain possession of all their lands and rights. But later in the same year Muhammad sent an expedition under Khalid ibn Walid to call again on the tribes of Najran to embrace Islam, for their own safety. Knowing Khalid's reputation, some of them did so. As it happened, however, more pressing problems drew Khalid's attention elsewhere, and most of the tribes remained Christian until the death of Muhammad.

According to al-Baladhuri, the Najran Christians were numerous, influential and powerful, and Omar, the second caliph, saw them as posing a danger to the new religion. Under a fresh threat of attack and possible decimation, most of the tribes went over to Islam, and in 635 Omar exiled large numbers of their most prominent citizens, so as to deprive them of their best leaders and spokesmen. Many of the exiles settled in Kufa, to make their contribution to the cultural life of that town. Scattered communities in Najran continued clandestinely in their Christian faith for some two hundred years more.

Najran and Nejd produced several strong personalities who for a time wielded considerable influence in southern and central Arabia during Muhammad's own lifetime. Details of their careers are available only by piecing together references scattered in the early Muslim texts. Christian elements are traceable in their teachings, though in large measure they are found intermixed with local cultic beliefs and practices.

One such was a reformer called Tolayha, a contemptuous diminutive of his real name, Talha. Chief of the powerful Christian tribe of Asad and a confederate of the Meccan Koraysh, he remained hostile to Muhammad, whom he called a pretender. Muhammad retaliated by calling him a false prophet. In his teachings Tolayha advocated sexual restraint, abstinence from wine and regular prayers. He forbade prostrations as heathenish and undignified.

In 632 Tolayha claimed to have received a divine commission from the angel Gabriel, and went on to preach a kind of Christianity with some success in central Arabia. He marched northwards to meet the advancing army of Khalid ibn Walid, which had been sent against him. He was defeated and fled to Syria. Many of his followers, including his mother, refusing Islam, were burned alive; those who were left converted. Tolayha himself was said to have submitted to Islam some time later, though not with good grace. A verse in the Koran (49:14) is thought to record the lukewarm allegiance of Tolayha and his clan.

Another strange rebel was Ayhala ibn Kaab, of the tribe of Aus, otherwise known as 'the Veiled One', or 'the Black One' (al-Aswad), or, more curiously, 'the Master of the Ass'. A man of great eloquence, he too announced that he was the recipient of revelations – from two angels who brought divine messages from Rahman. He was hailed as a prophet, gathered many disciples, and for a time made himself virtual master of the largely Christian region of Najran, extending his influence as far as Bahrain, Tayif and Yemen.

Muhammad dubbed him a charlatan and arranged for his disposal by a party of assassins. Earlier, Ayhala had been responsible for killing Shahr, son of Badhan, the last governor of Himyar, and had forcibly married the widow. With the connivance of the aggrieved woman, the assassins gained access to the house at night and cut off Ayhala's head. This deed was said to have been perpetrated on the night before Muhammad's own death.

After Muhammad's death most of the Arab tribes who had pledged themselves to Islam broke away and had to be forced back into the fold by Abu Bakr. And, among the Christian tribes, those of Yamama had remained resolute in their faith throughout. Their ruler, the Christian king Hauda ibn Ali, had been among the first Arab princes to whom Muhammad sent one of his missives inviting him to embrace Islam.

On Hauda's death the rulership passed to Musaylima, a member of the Christian Hanifa tribe and probably the most extraordinary of the central-Arabian reformers. His real name was Maslama, but the Muslims used the derisory epithet 'Musaylima', signifying 'petty Muslim', by which he is better known. Musaylima started his reforming mission on the lines of the hanifs in about 608, and seems to have acquired renown as a prophet even before Muhammad. He gathered a large following, entirely by peaceful means, and claimed that half of Arabia 'belonged to him'.

Some time around 625 he joined forces with the prophetess Sajaz (or Sajah), of the Tamim tribe. She was brought up as a Christian in Mesopotamia and began preaching with great popular success among her own tribal people, north-east of Musaylima's Hanifa territory. The lives of these two reformers are briefly sketched in Muslim records, which dwell in particular on their allegedly obscene relations in order to discredit them. Fragments of their revelations are also quoted by Arab historians in a manner calculated to bring them into ridicule. Sajaz returned to Mesopotamia in about 632, and nothing more is heard of her.

Musaylima's religious doctrines predated those of Muhammad, and at the time it was suggested that Muhammad had been inspired by him. Professor Margoliouth of Oxford, one of the foremost Arabists of his day, offered the theory that the term 'Muslim' originally meant an adherent of Musaylima (Bravmann, 1972. p. 8). This extreme conjecture, as might be expected, was not received with favour.

Musaylima set down his revelations in rhymed prose (saj) in a style resembling the Koranic revelations that were to come to Muhammad in Mecca. He warned of the Day of Judgement, had strong ascetic tendencies, and advocated fasting and abstinence from wine, as well as sexual restraint, especially after the birth of the first son. He initiated a regime of prayers which involved kneeling, but without any 'degrading prostrations': God, he said, did not demand humiliating prostrations from his worshippers. He spoke of God as al-Rahman, 'the Merciful', and called himself Abdul Rahman, the 'servant of Rahman'.

Muhammad's opponents in Mecca maintained that he had derived some of his precepts from a certain Rahman of Yamama, which appears to be a clear pointer to Musaylima. Whether he borrowed from him or not, Muhammad did not fail to realize his rising influence as a rival reformer. He denounced Musaylima as a lying impostor and false prophet who deceived the people, pretended to perform miracles, and counterfeited the language of the Koran. On his deathbed Muhammad is said to have expressed a wish for Musaylima to be done away with.

When Muhammad died, the Muslim armies set out to convert the whole of Arabia by force of arms, and soon turned their attention to the Christian tribes of central Arabia. In the first encounter their troops were defeated by Musaylima's followers. In the second Battle of Yamama (634) the Muslims suffered an even more massive defeat: it is said that there was hardly a house in Medina where the sound of wailing was not heard.

But there was another reason why the second Battle of Yamama was so serious in Muslim history, for among the dead were thirty-nine of the 'chief companions of the Prophet', including the best Koranic 'rememberers'. This was more than twenty years before the caliph Othman began putting together the text of the Koran.

In the same year (634) but a few months later, the caliph Abu Bakr sent out his ablest general, Khalid ibn Walid, with a large army to dispose of Musaylima once and for all. A fierce battle was waged at Akraba, in the area that became known as the Garden of Death. Here Musaylima was slain, ten thousand of his followers were massacred, and the rest of the population was reduced to subjection and forcibly converted.

The teachings of Musaylima continued to be disseminated in secret by his supporters in Nejd. Known as the Nejdiya of the Hanifa tribe, they tried in 693 to preach more openly but were quickly crushed. No significant Christian presence remained in Arabia thereafter.

11

THE CULT OF MUHAMMAD

The evolution of the mystical tradition in Islam may be traced in terms of what has been called (Arberry, 1964, p. 63) the cult of Muhammad (*millat Muhammad*), in the same sense as the Koran speaks of the cult of Abraham (Yusuf Ali, 1991, p. 406), founded on the doctrine preached by that patriarch. The word *millat*, of Hebrew origin, is cognate with the Aramaic *memra*, both having the same significance as the Greek *logos*, 'word' (Hughes, 1977, p. 349).

The cult of Muhammad took firm root after the Prophet's death. Certain sects fastened on to the mystical aspects of his doctrines, and before long Muhammad's personality as charismatic leader began to assume almost supernatural dimensions, leading ultimately to his virtual apotheosis.

We shall trace briefly this development from its modest beginnings to the extravagant forms it assumed in some quarters.

11.1 Belief in One God

A belief in one God (*tauhid*) was preached among the tribes by Arab reformers long before Islam, and the idea was implicit in the invocation of the pagan Arabs when making the pilgrimage to the Kaaba: 'There is no partner with thee, O Allah!' Despite this, polytheism and idolatry remained deeply entrenched, and Muhammad's single aim in the Meccan suras was to convert the people, by means of persuasion, from faith in their false gods to the worship of the one true God.

The teaching of the Koran was simple and unequivocal. God is unique, absolutely and unconditionally one, and nothing can be brought into association with him. He exists alone, and can be conceived of only in terms of his oneness. To link anything with God constitutes in Muslim theology the heresy of *shirk* (see Section 14.9).

God is awesome, ineffably holy and inaccessible to mortal man, and perfect knowledge of him is unattainable. 'He takes in all vision, but no vision takes him in' (6:103). Even Moses only heard the voice of God, and never saw him (7:139).

Neither Muhammad nor any of his companions ever claimed that Muhammad had any direct relationship with God, or had ever seen or heard him. The Koran was communicated through the angel Gabriel, and even he stood some distance away from Muhammad. When the Prophet ascended to heaven he was separated from God by a thousand impenetrable veils. In a hadith, Ayesha says, 'It is a serious lie to think that Muhammad has seen God' (Goldziher, 1971, p. 257).

11.2 An Arab Religion

In the early Meccan days Muhammad spoke highly of the Jews and Christians. He was said to have predicted that 'the Muslim community would follow a path identical with that of the Children of Israel and of the Christians' (Kister, 1980, XIV, p. 232). In the view of some scholars, Muhammad's original intention was to make his followers part of one integrated Jewish-Christian-Muslim fellowship, for he felt the three religions were all variants of one fundamental faith which should not be divided (42:11).

The Jews and Christians had a form of worship suited to their own people. They had their own prophets, and their own scriptures written in their own language. The Arabs too needed a religion adapted to their own requirements. Now it had pleased God to send Muhammad with a faith for the Arabs comparable to those of the Jews and Christians.

At the outset, it would seem, Muhammad had no universal mission. Islam was to be an ethnic faith, designed specifically for the people of Arabia, and it is by no means certain that Muhammad intended it to carry any message except for them. His wife Khadija, his cousin Waraka, and Muhammad himself during the Meccan period believed he was founding a religion exclusively for the Arabs.

11.3 A Middle People

There was never any aggressiveness in the Prophet's early declarations. A modern authority speaks of the 'mild reasonableness' of Muhammad's rule (Guillaume, 1983, p. 98). The Prophet did not impose strict laws on his followers, but hoped by his example to make them a just and tolerant community. As the Koran says, 'We have made you a middle [intermediate, balanced, central, moderate] people' (2:137).

Muhammad held to the doctrine of the golden mean, of doing nothing in excess. One is warned against superfluity (israf, 'wasting') or extravagance in religious duties. Excess leads to outward observance and sanctimoniousness. There must be a proper balance between all extremes: between spirituality and sensuality, between self-denial and selfishness, between sentimentality and callous want of feeling, between the pursuit of pleasure and tormenting self-renunciation, and between rigid adherence to religious formalities and the complete abandonment of all required observance. This is the 'right path' (sirat al-mustakim) of the first chapter of the Koran.

Ibn Abbas, a cousin of the Prophet and an authority on Islamic law and tradition, said the Prophet simplified many observances in order to ease the demands on his followers. He did not wish to expose them to the dangers of sinning by overburdening them with strict and solemn prescriptions, or loading them with a host of legal obligations 'like an ass beneath a load of books they would be unable to bear' (62:5).

Muhammad rarely insisted on the precise order or details of the various rites, and he was liberal in the interpretation of what had been revealed. In one recorded instance, when some people were dismayed because they had not performed a ritual correctly, he said to them, 'No harm' (la haraja). 'Allah', says the Koran, 'has not laid any hardship on you in religion' (22:77).

Asked about certain sacrifices, he said, 'He who wants to sacrifice the firstlings of his flock may do so. He who does not may refrain.' The rules relating to such matters as prayer, the pilgrimage, diet, fasting and observing the sabbath were seldom precisely laid down, or if laid down they were leniently applied and sometimes abrogated, so as to indicate that the Koran was to be read in the spirit underlying it, rather than be taken in its inflexible, literal sense.

In fact Muhammad expressed no objection to variety, and said, 'Diversity in my community is a mercy from Allah' (Swartz, 1981, p. 126). It was a freedom permitted to the faithful by the Almighty so that they might not be hampered by fixed and unalterable regulations.

The unbending code that became the preoccupation of the legalists after his death was opposed to the whole tenor of Muhammad's early mission and way of thinking. He would have regarded the meticulous attention to ritualistic detail as thoroughly Pharisaical, and would not have given his approval to most of the laws laid down with such precision and authority by the jurists.

11.4 Diet and Fasting

In the matter of food and drink Muhammad showed great laxity. He did at first impose certain dietary rules, some based on Jewish practice, but later relaxed almost all of them.

The food of the peoples of the book (meaning the Jews and Christians), says the Koran, is allowed (halal) and may be eaten (5:7). Some flesh is forbidden (haram) – including pig's flesh (2:168) – but in case of hunger (5:5) or necessity (2:168) or under constraint (6:119) it is not a sin to eat what is thus forbidden. Finally, in one of the last suras, it is stated that no blame is attached to those who have eaten any food if they fear God and do good works (5:95).

The consumption of alcohol, says Fazlur Rahman, 'was apparently unreservedly permitted in the early years' (1966, p. 38). When some of Muhammad's companions held drinking parties which made them forget their religious duties and come drunk to public worship, Muhammad reminded them that, although it has its merits, wine is also a sin, and its sinfulness can outweigh its advantages (2:216). Wine was Satan's work, and was to be avoided if it turned one aside from the remembrance of God (5:91–2).

'From the fruit of the date-palm and the vine', says the Koran, 'you obtain wine and healthful nourishment' (16:69). Some theologians make a distinction between grape-wine (khamr), which is forbidden, and date-juice (nabidh), which is lawful and which Muhammad himself used to take. One hadith reports, on the authority of Ayesha, that the Prophet said, 'You may drink, but do not get drunk' (Goldziher, 1981, p. 60).

Otherwise, wine is praised as healthy, and is mentioned in a context implying that it is a sign of Allah's grace to mankind (16:69). Wine is also mentioned more than once as being among the delights of paradise (56:18).

The punishment of eighty stripes prescribed for drinking was imposed only later, and is not found in the Koran. The caliph Mutawakil (d. 861), a relentless enforcer of orthodox dogma, was himself an immoderate drinker. Another caliph, Kahir (d. 934), who took equally stern measures against drinkers, was hardly ever found sober. And throughout Muslim history numberless leaders, both religious and secular, were known to revel clandestinely in this forbidden indulgence.

Although drugs like opium are not specifically forbidden in the Koran, they are prohibited in Islamic law on the basis of analogy (kiyas). It is argued that wine (khamr) is forbidden because it intoxicates. Opium and related drugs are intoxicants, therefore they are forbidden.

Regular periods of abstinence from all food and drink were observed by both the Jews and the Christians, and when Muhammad instituted the thirty-day fast in the month of Ramadan he declared it was in accordance with earlier practice – or, as the Koran says, 'The fast is prescribed for you as it was for those before you' (2:179). Here too a certain laxity was permitted. According to the Koran, 'Those who can keep the fast and do not must redeem the neglect by the feeding of one poor person' (2:180).

11.5 Prayer

Prayer is not described or precisely regulated in the Koran. Neither Muhammad himself nor his associates observed the strict formalities enjoined by the later theologians. In formulating his prayer ritual Muhammad was undoubtedly influenced in many ways by the devotional routine of the Christian monks in the Middle East: prayers at regular intervals, kneeling, prostrations, and so on.

The Koran refers to monasteries, churches, synagogues and mosques as all true places of worship (22:40). According to a hadith referring to synagogues and churches, Muslims are told, 'Perform your prayers in them.

There is no harm in it.' Muhammad himself is said to have visited a synagogue occasionally. He also allowed a Christian delegation on a visit from Najran in 628 to pray in the Medina mosque.

Muhammad regarded public prayers as a communal, almost social, occasion, and he was casual about the observances. He did not pray in bare or stockinged feet, as is now demanded by the orthodox. On the contrary, he was in the habit of praying with his shoes on, only wiping them or stamping to remove the dust from them. Shahdad ibn Aus relates that Muhammad said, 'Act the reverse of the Jews, for they do not pray in boots and shoes' (Hughes, 1977, p. 470).

A hadith records that believers used to talk freely with one another during prayers. The Prophet himself sometimes carried his favourite granddaughter, Umama, on his shoulder during public prayers, setting her down only when he bowed or prostrated himself, then hoisting her on his shoulder once again. Another hadith records Hasan and Husayn, the sons of his cousin Ali, jumping on his back during prayers.

Nowhere in the Koran is there an explicit command to worship five times a day, and there is no good evidence that the five prescribed prayer periods of later orthodox Islam had been definitely fixed during Muhammad's lifetime (Torrey, 1967, p. 135). Nor does an analysis of the scattered Koranic verses on the subject lead to any conclusive statement about the number of times or the hours of the day when prayers are to be said.

The number of times a Muslim is required to pray could hardly be deduced from the practice of Muhammad himself. The Prophet was a prayerful man. He prayed at various times, occasionally more than five times a day, and not always at the same fixed times. And it is known that, like the Christian monks, he and some of his followers used to pray 'almost two-thirds, or half, or a third part of the night' (73:20).

Ibn Ishak records a story that when Muhammad stood before the heavenly curtains during his Night Journey he enquired how many times a Muslim should pray. A voice replied, 'Fifty times a day.' On the way down, Moses told Muhammad to return and get the number reduced, as it was unlikely that any Muslim would pray with such frequency. Moses kept sending the Prophet back again and again, and the number was progressively reduced to thirty, then to twenty, ten and finally five. Moses felt even this was excessive, but Muhammad, who had been back so often, felt ashamed to ask for a further reduction, and so it has remained.

The implication of this story is not that a Muslim should pray fifty times or five times a day, but that he should 'think of God frequently' (33:41). As the Koran has it, 'Remember God standing, sitting and reclining' (3:188), and also 'on foot or riding' (2:240).

In order not to put too great a burden on the faithful, Muhammad cut down on the devotions that the Muslims, following his example, had felt constrained to perform: before dawn, after dawn, before midday, after midday, before sunset, after sunset, at night and again after midnight, as well as various periods of an indeterminate 'middle prayer' (2:239). He combined the morning and afternoon prayers, and the sunset and night prayers, and so reduced the prayers to twice a day, which some Muslims regard as standard. This is based on the Koranic injunction, 'Observe prayers at sunset and daybreak' (17:80).

The direction faced during prayers has also been a matter of some doubt. The Mutazilis believed the requirement to turn towards Mecca must have been suggested by the Prophet to test the common sense of his followers, for the Koran explicitly says, 'There is no piety in turning your face to the east or the west' (2:172). And, again, 'The east and west are God's, therefore whichever way you turn there is the face of God' (2:109).

Muhammad did not insist on prayers being said in Arabic, but allowed his followers to say their prayers in their own native tongue, the first to be granted that permission being Salman the Persian (Ameer Ali, 1965, p. 186).

There were Muslims, such as the Sufis, who viewed the whole idea of scheduled prayers, in the direction of Mecca, intoned a fixed number of times, several times a day, in a language (Arabic) foreign to the vast majority of the faithful, with the rigid requirements of ablutions, genuflexions and prostrations, as a form of mechanical observance at variance with their convictions, and even sanctimonious and hypocritical.

11.6 The Pilgrimage

Muhammad is known to have visited the Kaaba in his youthful pagan days, but after his first revelation in AD 610 and during the rest of the Meccan period which ended in 622 there is no record of his ever having undertaken the great pilgrimage or *hajj*.

In February 629, on his three-day visit from Medina, he performed the lesser pilgrimage (*omra*), making the circuit of the Kaaba not reverently on foot but riding on a camel from which he never dismounted. He asked the muezzin Bilal to call the people to prayer from the roof of the Kaaba, so that the shrine, held in such reverence by the Meccans, was under the feet of an Abyssinian ex-slave. On the same occasion, while a pilgrim under taboo and still in a state of holiness (*ihram*), he was said to have consummated his marriage with Maymuna, contrary to long-established usage which forbade intercourse at such a time.

When he visited Mecca in January 630 he made the customary circuits of the Kaaba once again riding on a camel, touching the sacred Black Stone casually with his stick each time he passed it. This visit to the Kaaba took place in the eighth year of the Hegira, after Muhammad's conquest of Mecca, when he had the opportunity of celebrating the hajj publicly. But he did not do so. He took no part in the pilgrimage in 631 either, sending Abu Bakr instead. Although now lord of Mecca, he abstained from participating in the pilgrimage for two more seasons.

On 9 March 632 Muhammad performed what came to be known as the Farewell Pilgrimage. This was the only hajj in which he took part as head of the Muslim community. The Prophet's example at this final pilgrimage was supposed to have set the pattern for the various rites that have since become obligatory on all Muslims, yet the details of what he did on this occasion are not consistently reported in the different accounts but vary in several particulars. Nor are the regulations governing the pilgrimage explicitly recorded in the Koran. It has been noted that the diverse sects and schools, including the Shias, differ from one another in almost all details concerning the hajj (A. J. Wensinck, in SEI, 1974, p. 123).

Muhammad made the pilgrimage incumbent on all his Arab followers, to link them together in a common traditional ceremony. He destroyed the Kaaba idols but kept the Black Stone and retained most of the earlier rites. But how important he personally considered them is unclear.

The pilgrimage was to be performed once in their lifetime by all adult Muslims in good health, provided they were financially able to bear the expenses for the journey and for the support of their families during their absence.

When Muhammad first established the pilgrimage, a certain zealous believer named Soraka ibn Malik asked the Prophet whether it was to be performed every year. To this the Prophet was said to have turned a deaf ear, but being pressed a second and third time he replied, 'No, but if I had said "Yes" it would have become a duty, and if it were a duty you would be unable to fulfil it. Therefore give me no trouble on matters about which I give you none.'

It has been said that the Prophet did not lay any great emphasis on the ceremonies and attached little significance to many of them. One tradition, preserved by al-Wakidi, makes Muhammad declare them to be irrelevant. The stone-throwing at Mina is not among the observances directly prescribed in the Koran; as for the run between Safa and Marwa, Muhammad seemed indifferent to it, and the Koran says ambiguously, 'there would be no harm in it' (2:153).

Through the centuries many freethinking Muslims have raised objections to the pilgrimage. Several famous Sufis have virtually rejected it altogether. Rabia of Basra (d. 801) when she visited the Kaaba exclaimed, 'I see only bricks and a house! What do they profit me?' Bayazid of Bistam (d. 874) while about to set out on the hajj met an old man who said, 'Circle around me seven times. It is the same as going around the Kaaba and will save you time and trouble.' Bayazid did so and returned home.

Even the orthodox al-Ghazali (d. 1111) during a visit to Mecca spoke of watching with growing consternation the paganism of the rites associated with the Kaaba pilgrimage and the idolatrous regard the pilgrims had for the Black Stone, which he found incompatible with the uncompromising monotheism of Islam.

In recent times some have objected to the animal sacrifices that bring the greater pilgrimage to an end, when camels, cows, goats and sheep are sacrificed in the name of Allah and offered up to him in enormous numbers. Hundreds of thousands are killed in the course of a few hours and their carcasses are thrown into a lime-pit. This is considered an unnecessary and cruel holocaust, and a scandalous waste of what might better be used as food.

Those who feel strongly about the whole subject express the hope for the early fulfilment of a prophecy attributed to the Prophet himself (see Section 14.15): namely, that one day the Ethiopians would utterly raze the Kaaba and it would never be rebuilt, so that Islam might be freed from the incubus of a heathenish ceremony.

11.7 The Scriptures

To every age, says the Koran, God has given a revealed book (13:38), and belief in the revealed 'books of God' is one of the six basic principles of the Islamic faith. The people receiving a divinely inspired scripture are spoken of as the 'people of the book' (*ahl al-kitab*), and in the final reckoning on the Day of Judgement every nation will be judged according to its own book (45:27).

The Koran calls for the acceptance of the scriptures 'that have been revealed in earlier times' (4:135). More specifically, the will of God is contained in the revelations given to Moses in the Pentateuch (*Taurat*), to David in the Psalms (*Zabur*), and to Jesus in the Gospel (*Injil*). There are more than 130 passages in the Koran in which the Pentateuch, the Psalms and the Gospels are named, always with respect and frequently in terms of their having been 'sent down' by God (Tisdall, 1911, p. 115).

Before Muhammad, the Arabs had been unable to study deeply or to understand the sacred books of others (6:157), and thus lacked their own version of the common faith of Abraham. Through Muhammad, God had now provided them with their own book, an Arabic Koran (12:2) by which their faith and observances are to be guided. (At the same time Muhammad allowed the people to read the Koran in their own dialects – see Section 7.10.) The Koran reproduces for the Arabs what has already been revealed to others. This made the Arabs a 'people of the book', and put them on an equal footing with Jews and Christians.

Muhammad said, 'Believe in the Koran, the Zabur [Psalms], the Taurat [Torah] and the Injil [Gospel], but the Koran should suffice you.' There is a passage that Guillaume calls 'one of the most significant verses in the Koran' (1983, p. 30) where Muhammad is advised, if he is in doubt about what he has received, to 'ask those who have read the scriptures before you' (10:94), meaning Jews and Christians.

This advice has sometimes been followed. It is said that during his expedition against Daghestan the conqueror Nadir Shah (d. 1747) was present at a dispute in Kazvin between the Sunnis and the Shias about a verse in the Koran (48:29). Since the verse in question referred to the Torah and the Gospels, Nadir Shah ordered the prelate Mirza Mohammed of Isfahan to ask the Jews and Christians for information about its correct interpretation. With their aid, a decision was made in favour of the Sunnis. Again, in order to find confirmation for their views, the Druses also consulted not only the Koran but also the Bible (Goldziher, 1971, p. 111).

The Koran says, 'Do not dispute with the people of the book except kindly, and in discussing with them one should say, "We believe in what has been revealed to us and in what has been revealed to you"' (29:45–6). And another passage states that the scriptures sent down by God to Muslims and non-Muslims are equally valid, and 'we make no distinction between them' (3:78).

11.8 The Prophets

Belief in the prophets is another of the six central principles of the Muslim faith. The Koran states that a messenger has been sent to every people (10:48), and according to a common tradition Muhammad himself spoke of 124,000 prophets and 313 messengers sent to the peoples of the world.

The Koran names twenty-seven prophets (not counting Muhammad), out of whom twenty-two are found in the Old Testament (Adam, Noah, Abraham and Moses being the chief) and three in the New Testament (Zacharias, his son John the Baptist, and Jesus); the two others, Dhul Karnayn and Lukman, have not been identified but are thought to be Alexander the Great and Aesop, the latter being regarded as the vizier of King David. There are also other apostles, but about them Muhammad has not been informed (4:162).

God, says the Koran, has sent down no prophet who did not use the language of the people (14:4). Unlike the Jews and Christians, the Arabs for long had no prophet, till Allah sent Muhammad to be the prophet of the Arab people for the guidance of the faithful (17:9), to create an Arab faith and announce it in the Arabic tongue (12:2).

It is to be remembered that in the early Meccan period it was the message that was important, not the bearer (see Section 11.10). He was only an announcer (bashir), a plain-spoken warner (nadhir) (29:49), a reformer and purifier, admonishing and persuading. His mission was essentially that of a messenger (rasul) (3:138), appointed to deliver the word of God to the Arab people and call them to the service of the Almighty.

Muhammad did not at first claim to be exceptional among the prophets.

He emphasized that he was 'no apostle of new doctrines' (46:8), nor did he claim there was anything new in his revelations. In the words of the Koran, 'Nothing is said to you that was not said to the prophets before you' (41:43), and 'we make no distinction between any of the prophets' (2:285).

11.9 Religious Tolerance

In the beginning Muhammad showed great magnanimity to other faiths, and spoke of them without animosity or malice. In a hadith, he said that to dismiss other religions 'showed bad manners to God'.

God had made different peoples and different tribes, and 'if God had wanted he would surely have made you all one people' (5:53). There is not one inflexible law for all mankind. God has given to each community its own lawgiver, and there are different laws for different peoples.

'To every people', says the Koran, 'God has given a right way [*sharia*]' (5:52), sent the observances to be followed (22:66), and assigned the rites by which they may commemorate the name of God (22:35). And by what he has given to each, God will test each of them (5:53), and people should be free to follow their own faith. One verse explicitly declares, 'There is no compulsion in religion' (2:257).

To the faithful God has prescribed the same faith he revealed to Noah, Abraham, Moses and Jesus (42:11). All those who believe in God and the last day and do right, though they be Jews, Christians or Sabians, shall have their reward (2:59). Like similar Koranic verses supporting tolerance for other faiths, this verse has long been laboured over by the orthodox, as it puts all religions on an equal footing.

Although he repudiated idolatry, Muhammad did not in the early period advocate the persecution of idolators. To the pagans of Mecca he merely said, 'I shall never worship that which you worship. Neither will you worship what I worship. To you be your religion; to me my religion' (109:6).

At this period of his mission Muhammad was a man of peace, and early Islam was a religion of reconciliation and concord, which was expressed in a salutation of 'peace' (*salaam*). In his dealings with opponents Muhammad used to practise gentle persuasion rather than coercion. Violence was never to be resorted to, even in self-defence.

Later, in order to preserve the infant community from persecution and pillage, he enjoined his followers to fight for the protection of their lives, for if God did not permit men to repel the tyranny of others their churches, mosques and synagogues would all be destroyed (22:41).

No mention is made in the Meccan suras about the duty of taking up arms for the spread of the faith. Indeed violence in any form is repudiated. Contrary to the deeply engrained tradition of the pagan Arabs, whereby an injury must be repaid by an injury so as not to bring shame on the family or tribe, Muhammad ordained that people should pardon and overlook the offence of those who have wronged them (24:22), and should 'requite evil with good' (23:98). Paradise is promised to those who master their anger and forgive others (3:128). In a verse not frequently quoted, the Koran says, 'Twice shall be the reward of those who have endured with fortitude, returning evil with good' (28:54).

11.10 Muhammad the Man

In the Koran, Muhammad declares, 'In truth, I am only a man, like you' (18:110). 'I am not your guardian' (10:108), 'not your keeper' (17:56), 'not here to watch over you' (6:104).

He did not claim to possess the treasures of heaven, or to know anything secret (6:50), for only God has the key to all secret things (6:59), and God alone knows the unseen (27:66). There were mysteries about which he was not informed. He did not know when the hour of judgement would come, for that is known to God alone (7:186), 'neither know I what will be done with me or you' (46:8).

He did not claim the power to perform miracles. To those who insisted on a supernatural sign (aya), he stated that such signs are in the power of God alone (29:49). It is sufficient that the Koran has been sent down (29:50). The Koran is a sign such that, if it had been revealed on a mountain, the mountain would have been split asunder (59:21).

On one occasion, according to an old tradition, the Meccans demanded that Muhammad prove his divine mission by making a mountain move. Muhammad replied that only God had the power to do that, as when he raised Mount Sinai at the time when the Law was being given to the Israelites (2:60). Yet even if a Koran were revealed by which mountains could be moved, it would be a vain thing (13:30). Then, turning in the direction of Mount Safa, Muhammad commanded it to come to him, and when nothing happened he exclaimed, 'Allah is compassionate. Had it come it would have caused an earthquake or fallen upon us to our destruction. I will therefore go to the mountain instead, and thank God for his mercy.'

Although Muslim theologians state that after his first call Muhammad remained without sin, both the Koran and the hadith tell a different story. No one is free from guilt, and if God were to punish men for their misdeeds not a creature would be left alive on earth (35:45).

Muhammad too was not without sin, for the Koran speaks of God forgiving his 'earlier and later sins' (48:2). What these earlier and later sins were has been the subject of some speculation. It is thought the earlier sins may have been those committed in the days of his idolatry, but after his call his sinning was believed to have ceased. As the Koran says, 'Did we not find thee in error and guide thee?' (93:7). Yet even after guidance men have sinned, and the later sins may have been any misdeeds, unknown and unrecorded, he might have committed and about which he felt guilty.

Muhammad was very conscious of his human failings. In numerous hadiths he is said to have prayed for forgiveness: 'My Lord, accept my penitence, wash away my guilt [*haubati*] and remove ill-will from my heart.' In another prayer attributed to him he says, 'Thou art my Lord. I am thy servant and confess my sins.' This consciousness of sin continued to weigh upon him, and one hadith records him as saying, 'I ask God's forgiveness seventy times a day' (Schimmel, 1985, p. 54).

11.11 The Transformation

Several scholars have drawn attention to the two distinct personalities of the Prophet. One is revealed during his life in Mecca; the other gradually emerges as he moves from Mecca to Medina, and is confirmed from the nature of the revelations received there (see Section 7.5).

By the time he has established himself in Medina, Muhammad is seen in a less favourable light. The character of the Prophet suffers a change which, in the view of some authorities, is not one for the better. Sir William Muir (d. 1905), the author of a biography of Muhammad well known to a previous generation, expressed an earlier and harsher view when he wrote, 'The student of history will trace for himself how the pure and lofty aspirations of Mohammed were first tinged and then debased by half-unconscious self-deception.'

Two likely reasons for this change have been advanced. To begin with, in Medina Muhammad no longer had the restraining hand of his wife Khadija to guide him. She had died a little over two years before the Hegira, and with her death, says Sprenger, 'Islam lost in purity and the Koran in dignity.' It has further been suggested that Muhammad's seizures, which had apparently remained untreated, had caused a slow but progressive impairment of his state of mind, which continued to worsen during his ten remaining years in Medina.

Hitherto restricting himself to one wife, Muhammad soon became polygamous. His increasing preoccupation with women during the Medinan period became painfully evident. At the same time, his ambition soared. He was now desirous of worldly success, and indulged in political opportunism. His personal conduct and his religious teachings declined in quality as his influence increased.

The persecuted reformer who lacked all temporal authority in Mecca had become in Medina an administrator and statesman, general and warlord, judge and legislator, tribal ruler and worldly prince, sovereign potentate and patriarch of the people. He attained a completely new status, achieving absolute authority, with the power of life and death over individuals, families and entire tribes. He was free to exercise this authority without restraint, and often succumbed to the temptations of power.

He moved from tolerance to bigotry. The man of peace who once bore opposition with fortitude now emerged as overbearing and autocratic, bent on vengeance against his enemies. He recalled with bitterness the rejection of his prophethood by Jews and Christians, and dealt with them accordingly. He could not forget his treatment by the Meccans, and led his followers on raids on their peaceful merchant caravans. He ordered the assassination of those who opposed or ridiculed him. He directed several military campaigns, ending in a command for the mass killing of unbelievers and the waging of war for the propagation of Islam.

Muhammad had once asserted that God had 'appointed peoples and tribes that you might have knowledge of one another' (49:13), and that it was one of the signs of God that he had 'created a diversity of languages and complexions among people' (30:21). Now, in Medina, Arabic was held up as the language of God and the angels. Now, on the day of resurrection, all sinners will become black-faced, and the faces of those who believe will shine white (3:102). Now, the Arabs are portrayed as a superior race, and the best nation ever brought forth unto mankind (3:106).

During the last years of Muhammad's life some of his more zealous followers accorded him reverential honour, amounting almost to deification (Glubb, 1979, p. 268). Everything associated with him was regarded as being endowed with a special blessed virtue (*baraka*). Some drank the water in which he had washed his hands. Ibn Ishak records that when Muhammad spat his companions ran to collect the spittle and then smeared their bodies with it (Andrae, 1960, p. 158). Some of the women close to him were said to have collected his perspiration to use as a perfume. Ayesha was told that the earth swallowed up his excrement so that it was not visible.

Muhammad's assumption of superior status over all other prophets, and his claim to a unique revelation and special favour with God, were amplified by his followers when he had gone. As in the case of saints and holy men of other religions, the objects and places associated with Muhammad were honoured after his death. The areas frequented by him were visited as shrines, and prayers were said there. The stones and sand in and around the traces of his footprints were collected for the magical power they possessed. His relics were preserved, including his sandals and cloak, locks of his cut hair and beard, and his teeth and nail parings.

Muhammad's physical appearance and his features are described in great detail in the hadith, and in Persia, Turkey and to a lesser extent Syria, Egypt and North Africa there exist some paintings and illustrated manuscripts showing the Prophet's face, usually bearded, with piercing eyes and a halo around his turbanned head. But such depictions are not common, for, besides a general prohibition against making images of animals and men, drawings of the Prophet are regarded as particularly sacrilegious.

Normally, if the Prophet is portrayed at all, he is shown veiled, or with his face blanked out. No picture, it is felt, could possibly show the beauty of his countenance. Besides which, any representation would take away from his numinous power and august personality.

Muhammad's name is held in the highest reverence. There is a taboo on its utterance unless it is followed by the formula 'Peace and blessings of Allah be upon him' (often abbreviated in English texts to 'pbuh'). The names of other prophets may be uttered without the formula, though sometimes a lesser formula is used: 'On whom be peace'.

Nothing must be said that might tarnish the lustre of Muhammad's personality. To speak of him other than in terms of the greatest respect is regarded as highly offensive. To criticize or defame him is an even greater offence than to deny or defame God. The Indian poet Muhammad Iqbal (d. 1938) said, 'You may deny God, but you cannot deny Muhammad.' In some parts of the Muslim world, especially the Indian subcontinent, attacks on God will go unchallenged, but one can criticize Muhammad only at the risk of one's life.

11.12 The Seal of the Prophets

The preacher and warner of Mecca became in Medina a religious pontiff and divine oracle. Where he had once made no distinction between his own message and the prophets and the holy scriptures of other peoples, he now asserted that all earlier revelations were incomplete and flawed, and that Islam, sent down through him, was the only perfect faith, to be 'exalted above every religion' (48:28).

All the prophets before him were only his forerunners. He was the last and greatest among those to whom divine revelations had been vouchsafed. He was the seal of the prophets. With him the succession of prophets had ended, the gates of prophecy were shut, the tongue of prophecy was silenced.

In the Meccan suras Allah is mighty indeed, and there is none beside him. His name alone must be glorified. He alone must be obeyed. In the Medinan chapters the stress is on Muhammad as the leader of the new community and founder of a new religion. Muhammad the messenger becomes as important as the message he is elected to bring, and almost as important as Allah from whom the message is brought. In seals and talismans the names of Muhammad and Allah are linked and intertwined.

Muhammad begins to be mentioned in the same breath as the Almighty, and almost invariably it is Allah and his prophet to whom allegiance is due. In one hadith Muhammad says, 'He who does not believe in me does not believe in God' (Kazi and Flynn, 1984, p. 123). Since Muhammad now bears the authority of God, he is the one to whom obedience is due. As the Koran says, 'Who obeys the prophet obeys God' (4:82).

In the verse of one sura the Koran states, 'There is no God but Allah'

(47:21). This simple and unexceptionable declaration was at first the essence of Islam. Among the final suras of the Koran we find another verse: 'Muhammad is the apostle of God' (48:29). These two separate verses, which are nowhere found conjointly in the Koran, were brought together to form the two parts of the Muslim creed (*kalima*): 'There is no God but Allah. Muhammad is the apostle of Allah.'

The utterance of this formula with faith and understanding constitutes a form of witness (*shahada*), and is obligatory once in every Muslim's lifetime. It is one of the five required observances of the Islamic faith. It was now required to affirm not only that there was one God but also that Muhammad was his apostle and the sole arbiter in all matters, temporal and spiritual.

Muhammad's long-time opponent Abu Sofyan regarded the second part of the creed as unacceptable. He could not bring himself to utter it, and eventually did so only reluctantly and under duress. There have been mystics and contemplatives in Islam who used only the first part of the creed, without acknowledging the special rank of Muhammad.

A similar development took place in the call to prayer. At first it was a simple call, in no set form, shouted out by a crier walking the main streets and summoning the people: 'Come to public prayer. Allah is great. There is no God but Allah.' Then Muhammad, accepting as God-sent an alleged dream-inspiration of a zealous follower, introduced his own name into a new formula summoning his people to their devotions: 'Allah is great . . . I testify that Muhammad is the apostle of Allah . . . Come to prayer.'

Muslims who had objected to the inclusion of the Prophet's name in the creed further deprecated the linking of Muhammad's name with that of God in the call to prayer (Schimmel, 1975, p. 214). It was, they felt, contrary to the spirit of Islam, and a form of the heresy of associationism (*shirk*) that Muhammad himself had often condemned.

11.13 The Sinlessness of Muhammad

An important phase in the development of the cult of Muhammad was the notion held by an increasing number of Muslims that Muhammad was a man of blameless conduct, free of all the moral defects and evil desires that afflict mankind: that he was indeed infallible and sinless (*isma*).

It was related that while Muhammad was still an infant the angel Gabriel came to his crib as he slept, withdrew his heart from his body, squeezed from it the black drop of original sin that resides in all human beings as a result of the Fall of Adam, and then returned the organ to its proper place.

Questioned about it later, Muhammad replied that two men in white appeared to him when he was a child, threw him on the ground, ripped open his chest and belly from throat to navel, took out his heart, washed it, and replaced it. In another account, he fell to the ground while out walking as a lad of four years. In yet another version, this cleansing happened when he was a grown man and praying in the Kaaba.

Some theologians discern a reference to this incident in the Koran: 'Have we not opened your heart and removed your burden?' (94:1). The term for 'your burden' (*wizraka*) is interpreted by many authorities as meaning 'your sin' (Birkeland, 1956, p. 41).

During his lifetime the sinlessness of Muhammad could not possibly have been advanced – the Meccans and most of his followers would have derided the idea – but later it was universally accepted, and it is now virtually official doctrine.

11.14 The Miracles of Muhammad

Muhammad was convinced of divine and angelic intervention in his life, and his followers attributed many miracles to him. Some of his ancestors were said to have borne special bodily marks, indicating that they were the progenitors of a great prophet to come. There was an angelic annunciation to his mother, Amina: 'Thou bearest the Lord of this people.' Amina suffered none of the pangs of childbirth, and the infant was born already circumcised.

He bore on his back a token or 'seal' which the monk Bahira recognized as signifying his status as supreme among the prophets. When the first revelation was about to be made in the cave of Hira, the hills, stones and trees saluted him as the apostle of God, and an ox and an ass spoke in confirmation of his great destiny. He conversed with spirit beings, and the Koran records that he converted some of the jinn (72:1).

Shortly before the Hegira he was miraculously transported from Mecca to Jerusalem and back. At the Battle of Badr three thousand angels were sent from heaven to assist him. He fed multitudes with a small portion of meat and a few barley loaves. He miraculously healed the sick, and cured a maniacal boy by commanding the Devil to leave him. A number of the other miracles of Jesus mentioned in the Gospels and apocryphal works were also said to have been performed by Muhammad, and accounts of them appear in the hadith.

Jesus walked upon the water, and told his disciples that with faith they could move mountains (Matt. 17:20). Muhammad told his disciples, 'If you knew God as he ought to be known, you would walk on the seas and the mountains would move at your command'. This was taken to imply that Muhammad himself was in possession of this interior knowledge and secret power. Although one story has it that Muhammad did not move Mount Safa when asked to do so, it was believed that this miracle too was well within his power.

According to another hadith, when certain unbelievers asked for a sign, Muhammad split the moon in two with a movement of his finger and then joined the parts together again. This legend grew out of the Koranic verse 'The moon has been cleft' (54:1). The text continues, as if to confirm the miracle, 'Whenever people see a miracle they say it is only a well-devised illusion' (54:2).

11.15 Muhammad the Logos

All manner of esoteric concepts that taught or encouraged the notion that Muhammad was free from every human blemish and pre-eminent among mortals began to take hold of the imagination of the pious some time after his death. Once started, the tendency to glorify the Prophet could not be resisted.

In this development, Christian influences are unmistakable. The theologian Ibn Taymiya (d. 1328) was only one of several Muslim scholars who noted that many threads in mystical and popular Islam were influenced by Christian thought and practice. This was true in particular of the Muslim perception of Muhammad. The tendency was to draw a picture of the Prophet 'that should not be inferior to the Christian picture of Jesus' (Goldziher, 1971, p. 346).

Like the person of Christ in Christianity, so the person of Muhammad became central to what might rightly be called Muhammadanism. Like Jesus, the Prophet increasingly began to be regarded as a person of sublime wisdom (cf. 1 Cor. 1:24), all-knowing, sinless, pure (1 John 3:3), miracle-working, more than mortal, in special relationship with God, and finally as a transcendent power almost equated with the Almighty. According to Professor Qamaruddin Khan, there was a strong tendency in popular Islamic thinking to portray the Prophet as an 'incarnation of God' and possessing 'a higher divinity than Christ' (Schimmel, 1985, p. 311). The professor himself deplored this tendency.

Such un-Islamic notions are also repudiated by other scholars and strongly resisted by them as impious blasphemy. But they remain at the core of certain aspects of Muslim theological speculation and have found many eminent exponents; despite the continuing protests of Muslims, they continue to be held in parts of the Muslim world.

The scholar Annemarie Schimmel in her erudite work (1985) has amassed a great quantity of material about the evolution of Islamic piety, occasionally in its more extreme manifestations, having garnered this from original sources in many languages of the Islamic world, from theologians, mystics, philosophers and poets.

Although the exact date of Muhammad's birth is not known, a date was worked out for it, and, from the eleventh century on, the birthday (*maulid*) of the Prophet began to be celebrated, sometimes with singing, dancing, candlelight processions and banners. In 1714 the Ottomans issued an edict ordering the celebration of the Prophet's birthday in the Kaaba itself.

Poems began to be written similar to Christian carols, and Muhammad began to be honoured in hymns (*naat*) whose words of eulogy and devotion can hardly be distinguished from the hymns of Christian devotion in praise of Christ. Indeed, some Muslims today tend to ascribe this development to 'clearly jealous emulation of what the Christians say about Jesus' (Schimmel, 1985, p. 146).

God, says the Koran, sent Jesus as a sign of mercy for mankind (19:21). So also God sent Muhammad as a sign of mercy for all creatures (21:107). God is merciful, and the Prophet is a manifestation of the divine name 'Rahman', 'Merciful'.

Mystics began to uncover other hidden meanings that lay concealed in Muhammad's name. Thus the Koran refers to the Prophet by the name 'Ahmad', 'Praised' (61:6), and, according to a hadith, Muhammad is alleged to have said, 'I am Ahmad without the *m*.' The remaining letters spell *Ahad*, 'the One', which is a title of God. Also, since the letter *m* is the first letter of the word for death (*maut*), the omission of that letter also signifies the immortality of Muhammad, for he is exempt from death as we know it. The Prophet further declared, 'I am an Arab without the A', which leaves the word 'Rabb', 'Lord', a name for the Almighty. Altogether, mystics have bestowed upon Muhammad, as upon God, ninety-nine honorific titles, some of which are the same as those bestowed upon the Almighty (Danner, 1988, p. 248).

God, it is said, is inaccessible to mortal beings. Now he becomes accessible to Muhammad, through whom alone knowledge of God is attained and divine grace is mediated. In Muhammad the divine power is enshrined, and through him the divine law has been made manifest. Neither scholar nor priest, neither theologian nor saint can do aught without the Prophet.

Muhammad's presence lit the fire of Moses; his name enabled Solomon to subdue the jinn; his lips taught Jesus to quicken the dead. 'Truly [Arabic *inna* – 'certainly', 'verily'], says the Koran, 'God and the angels bless the Prophet' (33:56). Muhammad is God's beloved. Men swear in God's name, but God himself swears in the name of the Prophet, as when he said, 'By your life [*la umrik*]' (15:72).

Muhammad has been granted free access to the divine realms, and the power to admit souls into paradise is in his hands. In the Bible, Jesus says to his disciples, 'I will give unto thee the keys of the kingdom of heaven' (Matt. 16:19). The Koran says, 'To God belong the keys of heaven and earth' (39:63), and these keys, say the mystics, have been delivered to Muhammad. The Syriac term used for keys in the Koran (*mikalid*) is derived from the Greek word for key (*kleis*), the same word used in the Bible (Jeffery, 1938, p. 269).

The doctrine of the eternality of the Prophet also became part of his evolving cult. It was said that Muhammad existed before his earthly appearance (Bethmann, 1953, p. 40). According to a tradition, Muhammad declared, 'I was in existence when Adam was still clay.' The Egyptian poet and mystic Ibn al-Farid (d. 1235) wrote that Muhammad was the First Epiphany (manifestation) of the Godhead (Arberry, 1964, p. 63). Through Muhammad, Allah stepped forth from the concealment of Non-Being on to the plane of phenomenal existence.

Once begun, this developed in some sects into the notion that, by divine descent (*hulul*), Allah became incarnate in the form of Muhammad and acted and spoke through him. The pre-existent form of Muhammad embodied the Word (*kalam*) which was made flesh, and this in the mystical teaching of Islam acquired a significance similar to the Logos of the Gospels (John 1:14).

Muhammad embodied the Reality (*Hakika*), the Reason (*Akl*) and the Spirit (*Ruh*) of the Almighty. These three facets of the divine unity were made explicit in an archetypal being, conceived in the likeness of God and known, in terms of an earlier Hellenistic concept, as the Perfect Man (*Insan Kamil*) who was the primordial Muhammad, clothed in beauty (*jamal*), majesty (*jalal*) and perfection (*kamal*), through whom the light (*nur*) of God is revealed.

Jesus said, 'I am the light of the world' (John 8:12). In commenting on the Light Verse (*ayat al-nur*) in the Koran, where the light of God is likened to a niche in which there is a lamp (24:35), mystics explained that the lamp mentioned is the Light of Muhammad (*Nur Muhammadi*). 'The first light which Allah created', said Muhammad, 'was my light' (Rodinson, 1976, p. 304), and from this light came all things.

As it is said of the Logos in the Bible, 'Without him was not any thing made that was made' (John 1:3), so it was said of the archetypal Muhammad that the world was created through him and because of him. Again, in a hadith God tells Muhammad, 'If you had not been [*laulaka*], I would not have created the world' (Schimmel, 1985, p. 131).

From the light of the archetypal Muhammad there rayed out, or 'emanated', all that is above and all that is below: the heavens, the angels, matter, the earth, mankind, the jinn, and all the animal and plant species. This concept of emanation (*faiz*) was derived from Gnosticism and Neoplatonism.

A Muslim poet has written, 'If you want to reach God, know Muhammad as God' (Schimmel, 1985, p. 140). And Muhammad himself says in a hadith, 'He who sees me, sees God' (Hughes, 1977, p. 613). Although the aim of the Sufi mystic is union with the divine light, some mystics state that the last phase of mystical experience is union or annihilation (*fana*) of self not in the light of God but in the light of Muhammad.

According to the Bible, Christ sits at the throne of God making intercession for us (Rom. 8:34). In the Koran we read that the angels intercede on behalf of mankind (42:3). But in the mystical belief it is Muhammad, seated beside the throne of God – for there God himself has placed him (Hughes, 1977, p. 188) – who pleads for the faithful who have sinned, so that the punishment they deserve might be remitted. Without Muhammad's intercession (*shafaat*) men cannot obtain God's grace or receive God's forgiveness.

Jesus said, 'Lo, I am with you alway, even unto the end of the world' (Matt. 28:20). Like him, the archetypal Muhammad is ever 'present and watching' (*hazir va nazir*). Muhammad is seen as a cosmic power who is both transcendent and immanent. To him God has assigned, as his representative, the ordering, preserving and rulership of the universe.

Muhammad's great mission was preordained from the beginning and will continue to the end of time. As Christ is Alpha and Omega, the first and the last (Rev. 21:6), so Muhammad is the First (*Awwal*) and Last (*Akhir*) in terms of the divine names of Allah. As he existed before the beginning, so he will endure after all things have passed away.

12

THE SPREAD OF ISLAM

According to the biographer al-Wakidi, Muhammad is reported to have said, 'Two religions cannot exist in Arabia. Let there not remain throughout this land any faith except Islam.'

After the Prophet's death the process of religious 'cleansing' that had been set in train by Muhammad began to gain momentum. The Jews and Christians were dealt with first, and then the remaining unconquered and apostate Arab tribes. That accomplished, the frontiers of Islam were extended into foreign territories, the combined process being achieved during the reigns of the first four caliphs – Abu Bakr, Omar, Othman and Ali – and the early Omayyads.

12.1 The Medina Caliphate (632–661)

Abu Bakr (r. 632–4) is commonly regarded as having been elected the first caliph or successor (that is, of Muhammad). Following his election, his main objective became the unification of the Arabs under the banner of Islam. Many of the Arab tribes who had embraced Islam while Muhammad was alive had done so for what it could bring them in terms of the material benefits that came in the wake of Muhammad's forays: a share of the plunder (see Section 14.5). Others had joined so that they might be spared the attentions of the Prophet's raiding expeditions.

When Abu Bakr assumed the mantle of Muslim leadership many of these tribes felt there was nothing more to fear or to expect from the religion they had adopted, and the alliances they made with Muhammad were immediately forsworn. Ibn Ishak writes, 'When the Apostle was dead most of the Muslims thought of withdrawing from Islam and made up their minds to do so.' Casting off the yoke of Islam, the majority either reverted to their previous beliefs or turned to new prophets. Some chose to reject all authority except that of their own tribal leaders, and refused to pay taxes. On all sides the Arabs were rising in rebellion, and desertions and disaffection were spreading. (Al-Baydawi and others give lists of the apostate tribes.)

Many of the renegades were primitive bedouin tribesmen, a difficult and intractable class, regarded from earliest times as treacherous and untrustworthy, fierce desert nomads who were compared by the settled Arabs to wild beasts. Writing about them, Ammianus Marcellinus had said, 'I would not wish to have them either as friends or as enemies.' The Koran refers to them as 'stout in disbelief and dissimulation' (9:98).

Stern measures were resorted to by Abu Bakr for the reconversion of the dissenters in what came to be known as the wars of the apostasy (ridda). After bitter fighting, the revolts were suppressed and the recalcitrant tribes were brought into submission. Abu Bakr's commander in most of these operations was the redoubtable Khalid ibn Walid.

Large parts of the peninsula had never become Muslim in Muhammad's day, but remained pagan, Jewish or Christian. Now most of these too were compelled to accept Islam, following aggressive and sanguinary expeditions, notably at Yamama (634). The Jews had been virtually eliminated in Muhammad's lifetime. The Christians had also been expelled in large numbers, and the remainder were now forced into accepting Islam under threat of extermination. Within two years of such 'pacification' almost the whole of Arabia was converted into a Muslim state and Muhammad's vision of a country purged of all other religions had been realized.

Ruling at a difficult period of Islam's history, Abu Bakr at times appeared cruel, as when he had a freebooter named Alfujaa cast alive into a fire. And, as an example – in a vain attempt to put a stop to certain practices – he ordered a sodomist named Habar ibn Aswad to be burned alive as well.

In one account Abu Bakr died a natural death, but there is also a tradition that his end was hastened by poisoning, perhaps to mark him out as a martyr. He was buried beside Muhammad.

Omar (r. 634–44) succeeded Abu Bakr as the second caliph. Within four years of Muhammad's death the victorious Muslim armies had taken from the Sassanians the imperial winter capital of Ctesiphon following the Sassanian defeat at the Battle of Kadisiya (636). That same year they won the Battle of Yarmuk (Hieromax) against the Christian emperor Heraclius, and acquired from the Byzantines the major part of their provinces of Palestine and Syria.

At first, the guiding motive of Omar was religious integration: the taking of places with Arab populations for conversion to Islam, as well as the conquest of Palestine, the land promised to Abraham. He was especially desirous of capturing Jerusalem, and this he did in 637, riding in triumph through the main street seated on a white camel.

The conquest of Jerusalem provided the Muslims with the confirmation they needed that their religion was now comparable to the two earlier Abrahamic faiths, Judaism and Christianity. It also placed them in direct touch with the great centre of their common origins.

Having taken Jerusalem, Omar for a time restrained his forces from further conquest, as if the extent of Muslim interest had now been demarcated. It was only because the overthrow of foreign armies had been so easily achieved that the lure of still more victories became irresistible, and prompted the Arabs to embark in real earnest upon their career of aggrandizement.

They invaded the rest of Iraq and Syria, and by 642 they had annexed what was left of the Persian empire. The capture of Alexandria in 641 was followed by the conquest of the rest of Egypt under Amr ibn al-As, who afterwards became governor of Egypt and founded the city of Fustat, the forerunner of Cairo.

In 644, while leading prayers in the Medina mosque, Omar was assassinated by Abu Lulua, a Persian slave and by profession a maker of windmills, who had embraced Christianity. For long the day of Omar's death was celebrated as a day of rejoicing by Persians.

The third caliph, Othman (r. 644–56), of the Omayyad clan, was a cousin of Abu Sofyan. Muhammad, anxious to seal an alliance with the Omayyads – for long his traditional enemies – had sanctioned the marriage of his two divorced daughters Rokaya and Umm Kulthum to Othman. The Prophet declared he loved Othman so much that had he a third daughter free he would have given her to Othman too. There were no descendants of the two marriages. Othman then married a Christian woman named Nayla (see Section 13.3), who bore him a daughter.

Othman was among those who went into exile in Abyssinia. His indifference to Islam and his subsequent anti-Muhammad activities have been quoted against him. It was observed at the time that he did not offer to help Muhammad in the construction of the first mosque at Koba, but 'turned away out of the dust'. He did not fight at the Battle of Badr, but stayed at home on the excuse that his wife was ill. His opponents spoke of him as a runaway (*farrar*).

On his accession to the caliphate he made changes in the hajj ceremonies. He arranged for the final revision of the Koran, and was reputed to have made substantial alterations in the process. He had – not quite accidentally, it was said – dropped into the well of Aris the Prophet's signet ring that had been handed down to him by his predecessors, thus irrecoverably losing one of the few remaining personal tokens of Muhammad.

He annulled the exile order placed by Muhammad on Hakam (father of the Omayyad caliph-to-be Marwan I), allowing him to return to Medina.

He gave his patronage to Kaab al-Ahbar, a Yemenite Jew who had arrived in Mecca during the reign of Omar and was converted to Islam. Kaab subsequently wrote certain hadiths through which he was alleged to have introduced Jewish doctrines into Islam.

He exiled the ascetic Abu Dhar, who had been a friend of the Prophet, ostensibly for his criticism of the caliph and for having assaulted and flogged the above-mentioned Kaab al-Ahbar.

He gave refuge to his apostate foster-brother Abdulla ibn Saad (see Section 7.13), and appointed him governor of Egypt.

He installed his uterine brother Walid ibn Okba as governor of Kufa. Walid's father, Okba, had ill-treated Muhammad and once nearly strangled him (Ameer Ali, 1965, p. 295).

He appointed as governor of Syria his cousin, the ambitious Muawiya, son of Abu Sofyan, with unhappy consequences for the peace of Islam.

Othman's reign saw the beginning of an internecine war which led to a schism that put an end to any semblance of unity among the Muslims. In the twelfth year of his rule, in 656, the caliph was set upon and hacked to pieces by a group of Muslims at his home in Medina as he sat reading the Koran, so that his blood flowed over and stained the pages of the holy book. Among his assassins was the son of the first caliph and half-brother of Ayesha (Muhammad's widow) named Muhammad ibn Abu Bakr.

Ali (r. 656–61), Muhammad's cousin and son-in-law, succeeded Othman and moved his capital to Kufa (formerly the Christian town of Akula). Among his opponents was Ayesha, whose troops he defeated in a skirmish known as the Battle of the Camel (656), because she watched it seated on a camel.

Another and more formidable opponent was Muawiya, governor of Syria, who rebelled against him, accusing him of complicity in the murder of Caliph Othman. This time Ali was defeated, at the Battle of Siffin (657) – a place not precisely identified but known to be on the right bank of the upper Euphrates – and his claim to the caliphate was set aside by arbitration, though he continued to rule.

Because Ali had accepted arbitration and not God's guidance, a dissident branch of Islam came into being. Known as the Kharijites or 'seceders', they themselves were to split up into several factions over doctrinal matters, and for years they caused dissension among the theologians and remained a thorn in the side of the caliphate.

In 661, while praying in a mosque in Kufa, Ali was stabbed with a poisoned dagger by a man called Abdul Rahman ibn Muljam, and died three days later. His burial-place is not known, although tradition says he was laid to rest not far from Kufa. In 850 the Abbasid caliph Mutawakil had the mausoleum of Ali and his sons demolished.

The Shias, the 'party' of Ali, look upon Ali as their first imam or leader, and as the first and only true caliph, regarding his three predecessors as impostors. The Shia branch of Islam differs radically from the main Sunni branch of the Muslim faith, and the two are irreconcilable in most areas of doctrine, Koranic exegesis, law and practice. Certain Shia sects give Ali exalted status, equal to and sometimes greater than that accorded to Muhammad. Indeed, some sects believe in the divinity of Ali (C. Huart, in SEI, 1974, p. 32).

Ali's son Hasan (r. 661) reigned as the fifth caliph. But he had more interesting occupations, having contracted a hundred marriages and being known as 'the great divorcer'. Weak and unfitted to govern, he abdicated after only six months, having agreed to sell his rights and accept a large pension from Muawiya, who then assumed power as the first Omayyad caliph.

Eight years later Hasan was poisoned by one of his wives, a woman called Jaada. Ali's second son, Husayn, was slain at Karbala in 680 during the caliphate of Yazid I (see below).

The first four caliphs – Abu Bakr, Omar, Othman and Ali – are honoured by the Sunnis, or mainstream Muslims, as the 'patriarchal', 'orthodox' or 'rightly-minded' (*rashidun*) caliphs. Muslims of later genera-tions portrayed the rule of these four as an idyllic time and wrote nostalgic-ally of the simplicity, purity and piety of the ancients or ancestors (*salaf*). In more recent times several *salafiya* movements sprang up in Egypt, Syria and India, calling for a return to the good old days of the ancestors, when the religion of Muhammad was practised in its pristine form and Muslims lived like brothers.

But in fact all the four patriarchal caliphs (and the fifth caliph too) came to an untimely end, either by assassination or by poisoning, and the period of their rule was marked by internal division, clan and family rivalries, and almost constant strife; it saw the beginnings of the great rift in Islam between Sunnis and Shias that has never been resolved.

12.2 The Omayyads (661–750)

After the assassination of Ali, the Omayyads established themselves in Damascus, supported by the Syrian Arabs. This dynasty of caliphs – named after Omayya, son of Abid Shams and grandfather of Abu Sofyan – had a tradition of rivalry with the family of Hashim, to which Muhammad belonged.

All through the Omayyad period the Muslim conquests proceeded apace, both to the east and to the west. Eastwards the Muslim armies annexed Afghanistan (661) and Transoxiana (709), as well as Sind in western India (712). Westwards they took Libya (643) and spread swiftly across North Africa. During the reign of Walid I (d. 715) the conquest of North Africa was completed and that of Spain began.

Although the greatest territorial expansion of Islam – stretching from the Pamirs to the Pyrenees – took place under the Omayyad caliphate, the Omayyads were the most un-Islamic of the caliphs. Descended from or related to Abu Sofyan, they still carried the scars of the bitter feud between Muhammad and their notable kinsman, and often appeared to act as if in retaliation for the insults and humiliation to which their family had been subjected by Muhammad and the early Muslims.

The Omayyad caliphs were mostly lay rulers. With the single exception of Omar II (d. 720), they were Arabs first and Muslims afterwards. Some Muslim historians were at pains to establish their orthodoxy, but many others held them responsible for secularizing Islam and separating religion from the state. They attempted, it was said, to alter the direction of Islam and to steer it along new paths, and thus betrayed the faith.

In general they laid little stress on Muhammad's revelation, and had scant regard for its precepts. They were accused of having deepened the division between Shias and Sunnis. They introduced the custom, which continued to be practised by certain of the early Omayyads, of cursing Ali from the pulpit at Friday prayers, and encouraged the congregation to follow suit.

They persecuted and caused the death of many members of Ali's family, including his son – the Prophet's grandson – Husayn.

To play down the religious importance of Mecca and Medina, the Omayyads glorified Jerusalem (see Section 13.6). They even sought to remove the pulpit and staff of the Prophet from Medina to Damascus, but strong protests checked the impious project.

The Prophet had demarcated a market-place in Medina and set it aside for the people to use, decreeing that no building was to be raised there and no taxes were to be levied on the land. In defiance of this decree the caliph Muawiya deliberately built two houses on the site, to which the caliph Hisham (d. 743) added a third and larger building, besides levying taxes.

The Omayyads held Muhammad's first wife, Khadija, in high esteem. Her house in Mecca, long neglected and in need of repair, was bought, restored and turned into a place of prayer. The house where Muhammad was born, on the other hand, was used as an ordinary dwelling-place. They carried out other major changes in Mecca and Medina, almost obliterating the ancient landmarks linking them with Muhammad, and ruthlessly crushed the uprisings that followed. Large numbers of Byzantine architects, masons, carpenters and labourers were brought in and employed in the reconstruction of these two cities, and many of them later settled there.

The first Omayyad caliph abolished the practice – instituted by Omar – of determining a successor through consultation (*shura*), in favour of appointing one personally, and so made the caliphate hereditary. This innovation, too useful to be scrapped, was adhered to by all subsequent Muslim rulers.

Contrary to Muhammad's custom of delivering the Friday sermon (*khutba*) from the mosque pulpit while standing, the early Omayyads used to deliver it while seated, which was seen as a sign of their arrogance.

Furthermore, the designation of the caliph as an Agent of the Prophet (*Khalifat Rasul Allah*) was also dropped by the Omayyads, who preferred to call themselves the Agents of God (*Khalifat Allah*). They delighted in assuming other pompous honorifics, which the pious found offensive, such as Pontiff of God, Viceregent of the Almighty, Sultan of the Merciful upon the Earth, Shadow of Allah (*Zillu Allah*). This practice too was sometimes followed by the later caliphs, down to the time of the Ottoman Turks.

The lifestyle of the Omayyad caliphs was like that of the Byzantine emperors. They established a pattern of sumptuous living that the other Muslim rulers – the sultans, shahs and emirs of Iraq, Egypt, Morocco, Persia, Turkey, India and elsewhere – were to emulate through the centuries. It was the worldliness of the Omayyads that first raised questions about 'rulership', 'government' and 'state', all of which in the minds of the orthodox became equated with infidelity, if not with evil.

The Omayyads made no attempt to coerce their subjects into conversion. Islam meant submission to the ruler rather than acceptance of the faith. Centred in Syria, where the presence of Christianity was strong among the Syrian Arabs, they showed a certain bias in favour of that religion. Christian tribes like the Kalb and Kayis – though they were often mutually at loggerheads – were their chief supporters.

Many Omayyad caliphs had Christian advisers and gave their patronage to Christian poets. Some introduced innovations in imitation of church practice into mosque services. They permitted the use of music in the holy places. Incense too became one of the regular features of the mosque, and for some time after the Omayyads ceased to rule these practices continued.

Muawiya (r. 661–80), the first of the Omayyad caliphs, was the son of Abu Sofyan and Hind, and cousin of the caliph Othman. He had been one of Muhammad's amanuenses and had taken down parts of the Koran to Muhammad's dictation. As already stated, he served under Othman as governor of Syria and led the revolt against Ali during the latter's caliphate.

Knowing the reverence in which pious Muslims held the Koran, he ordered his men to stick pages of the holy book to the points of their lances at the Battle of Siffin (657). As a result the troops of Ali refused to attack Muawiya's troops and so lost the battle, and Ali lost the caliphate.

Muawiya had himself proclaimed caliph in Jerusalem, and on that occasion offered prayers at Gethsemane, where Jesus had prayed after the Last Supper. He also offered prayers at the grave of the Virgin Mary, and at Golgotha, the site of the Crucifixion (F. Buhl, in SEI, 1974, p. 270).

He called up Syrian Christians to administer the cultivated lands destroyed by the 'savage' bedouin conquerors. He protected Christians, respected their monks, and made gifts to churches and convents. He rebuilt the cathedral of Edessa, which had been ruined in an earthquake.

Muawiya was succeeded by his son Yazid I (r. 680–83), whose reign is principally associated with the tragedy that occurred at Karbala. In the autumn of 680, Husayn, the second son of Ali, who had refused to swear allegiance to Yazid, was on his way with family and retainers from Mecca to Kufa in response to a call from the faithful of that city to become their leader. Apprised of the plan, Obaydulla ibn Ziyad, the Omayyad governor of Basra, sent a detachment to intercept them and call on them to surrender.

Declining to do so, they encamped at a little village called Karbala, and here they were surrounded by Obaydulla's troops, whose commander, Omar ibn Saad – following the example of the Prophet at the Battle of Badr – cut off their access to the waters of the Euphrates, thereby increasing their suffering. Here six days later, on the tenth day of Moharram, the massacre of Husayn and his party took place, which is described in the Shia annals in terms, says the historian Edward Gibbon (d. 1794), that 'will awaken the sympathy of the coldest reader'. The seventy trunkless heads of men, women and children were taken to the governor in Basra. The head of Husayn was sent to Damascus, where it was publicly exhibited.

The fifth Omayyad caliph, Abdul Malik (r. 684–705), faced with uprisings in Mecca and Medina, sent Hajaj ibn Yusuf, his trusted governor of

Iraq, to deal with them. Hajaj was a scholar greatly detested by the orthodox (see Section 7.17), as well as a member of the Thakif tribe, which held a long-standing grudge against the Prophet, and he quelled the rebellion with a heavy hand (see Section 13.6).

In 702 Hajaj established the new town of Wasit, 'Medial', on the west bank of the Tigris, halfway between Basra and Kufa – its exact location is now lost – in order to keep a sharper watch on these two trouble spots, notorious as centres of unrest and insurrection. The two cities, often praised, received their share of opprobrious epithets as well: Kufa was likened to a costive gut, and Basra to a bladder filled with noxious fluid.

Abdul Malik was succeeded by his son Walid I (r. 705–15), who never bothered to learn Arabic, and spoke it incorrectly. He retained the hated Hajaj as governor of Iraq and controller of the holy cities. Walid had a passion for building, and took over and in part reconstructed a Christian church in Damascus to build a great mosque there (see Section 13.5). In Mecca he ordered a new well to be dug near the Kaaba and urged pilgrims to drink from its sweet waters, irreverently calling the hallowed well of Zamzam – whose water was bitter, salty and unpleasant – 'the mother of blackbeetles'.

Hisham (r. 724–43), the tenth Omayyad caliph, took as his adviser one of his close friends, a monk named Stephanus, for whom he obtained the patriarchate of Antioch. As his governor of Iraq he appointed a man named Khalid al-Kasri, the son of a captive Greek woman who never embraced Islam. Khalid had a convent and church built for her in Kufa, which made him unpopular with the Muslims. Both these were destroyed on his death.

Devoted to his master, Khalid declared his willingness to dismantle the Kaaba and remove it to Jerusalem if the caliph so desired. But that he retained a strong attachment to the religion of his mother is indicated by a remark he once made implying that in his view Christianity ranked above Islam in many ways.

Hisham's successor, Walid II (r. 743–4), had Khalid executed, under pressure from his advisers. Walid himself, objecting to the verse 'Every rebellious and obstinate person shall perish' (14:18), tore out the offending page of the Koran, stuck it on a lance, and shot it to pieces with arrows, saying, 'Do you rebuke every opponent? Behold, I am that obstinate opponent! When you appear before your Lord on the day of resurrection, say that Walid has torn you in this manner' (Sale, 1886, p. 52). Like his ancestor the caliph Othman, Walid II was murdered some time later as he sat reading the Koran.

The Omayyad dynasty came to an end with Marwan II (r. 744–9), who was defeated by the leaders of the succeeding Abbasids, pursued to Egypt, and slain on the banks of the Nile. He was the fourteenth of the Omayyad caliphs, out of whom two were deposed, two poisoned and two assassinated.

12.3 The Abbasids (750–1258)

The consolidation of the Muslim empire that had grown with such speed under the Omayyads was achieved during the Abbasid caliphate, named after Abbas, paternal uncle of the Prophet.

The first of the Abbasid caliphs, Abul Abbas (r. 750–54), gloried in the title of 'As-Saffah' – 'the Blood-Shedder'. He started his reign by rounding up all the members of the deposed Omayyad family, promising them an amnesty. He then invited them to a banquet, and at a given signal they were set upon and butchered.

In other places the surviving relations of the Omayyads were pursued and slain and their corpses left out on the streets for dogs to eat. Finally, the tombs of the Omayyad caliphs in Syria – with the exception of the pious Omar II – were opened, the bodies were exhumed, whipped and burned, and the ashes scattered to the winds.

During their initial struggle for ascendancy the Abbasids received strong support from the Persians. In fact, many of the caliphs had Persian mothers (see Section 13.3), and they were known to be proud of being Persian rather than mere Arabs. Persian became the language of the cultured élite, and many features of Sassanian imperial practice were adopted by them. Some caliphs took on the title of 'Shah-in-Shah' – 'King of Kings', on the Sassanian pattern.

Unlike the Omayyads, the Abbasids were not generally well disposed towards Christians. At the start of the Abbasid caliphate there were no less than ninety monastic establishments and eleven thousand churches within the eastern provinces of their empire, in Mesopotamia, southern Persia and Syria. Not many survived the policies of the new regime.

In 762, during the reign of the second Abbasid caliph, Mansur (r. 754–75), the capital of the dynasty was moved from Damascus to Baghdad, newly built near the ruins of the old Persian capital of Ctesiphon. The new city had been planned by the caliph's adviser Mashaallah, a Jewish mathematician and architect of great learning, and its location and orientation were determined on cosmological and geomantic principles by the caliph's minister Khalid ibn Barmak.

This minister belonged to the Barmak (Barmecide) family, descended from a line of Buddhist high priests of an ancient monastery in Balkh, near the Oxus river, who became converts to Islam when Balkh was captured by the Arabs in 663. They served under four caliphs, and were known for their generosity, their public works, their dedication to literature and the arts, and their devotion to science and philosophy.

The third Abbasid caliph, Mahdi (r. 775–85), waged successful wars against the Byzantines and for a while exacted tribute from them in exchange for peace. He forcibly converted the Tanukh tribe, one of the last great Christian tribes of Syria, because of their links with Constantinople.

The fifth Abbasid caliph, Harun al-Rashid (r. 786–809) – of *Arabian Nights* fame – was helped in his rise to power by his tutor Yahya (John) ibn Khalid, the son of Khalid ibn Barmak mentioned above. The end of the Barmak family in 803 was as sudden as their rise. Yahya was sent to prison, where he died, and his son Jaafar, the caliph's favourite, was executed. Their fall was said to have been due to their tolerance towards Christians and Zoroastrians, and despite their ostensible conversion to Islam they were thought to be crypto-Buddhists. In 807 the caliph passed discriminatory laws against Jews and Christians and decreed that they wear distinctive dress (see Section 14.8).

Harun's reign marks the apogee of Abbasid power. The Frankish chronicler Eginhard (d. 840) mentions an exchange of embassies in 798 between Charlemagne and Harun al-Rashid. This is not mentioned in the early Muslim chronicles, though an exchange of gifts is referred to in later accounts.

Harun's son Mamun (r. 813–33), a great patron of learning, built libraries and colleges, including a famous House of Wisdom in Baghdad. He encouraged the sciences, especially astronomy and mathematics, made the Mutazili doctrine the state creed, ushered in the 'Augustan Age' of Arabian letters, set up teams of scholars to translate Greek works into Arabic, and 'made the Muslims the spiritual heirs of Hellenism' (J. H. Kramers, in Arnold and Guillaume, 1965, p. 84).

The caliph Mutasim (r. 833–41), younger brother of Mamun, moved the capital sixty miles south of Baghdad to Samarra on the Tigris, a city built by the pagan Turks belonging to the caliph's retinue, and this remained the Abbasid capital from 836 to 876. Like Mamun, Mutasim championed the Mutazili heresy. It is said that when he lay on his deathbed Mutasim asked for prayers to be said over him with candles and incense, exactly after the fashion of the Christians (J. Pedersen, in SEI, 1974, p. 346).

Mamun's nephew, the caliph Mutawakil (r. 847–61), rescinded his uncle's pro-Mutazili decree. He revived the policies of Harun al-Rashid against Christians, adding ever harsher regulations to discriminate against them, and had the synagogues and churches in Baghdad torn down. Hostile also to the Shias, he had Husayn's shrine in Karbala razed. The caliph was murdered.

From the tenth century the unity of the overstretched empire began to be weakened by growing unrest in North Africa and other places where movements of discontent were fomented. These were mainly economic and social in origin, though many had a nationalist colouring, which forced the caliphs to give their outlying frontier provinces an increasing measure of autonomy.

By now large parts of the Arabian peninsula itself had come under the sway of the Karmathians, a quasi-Ismaili sect with close links with the Mandaeans and Manichaeans. They possessed a book in which it was written that Christ had appeared to one of their leaders and had given him a special commission as a 'demonstration' for the people. The Karmathians drew their support and leadership mainly from once-Christian tribes like the Kalb of

Duma and the Kayis of Bahrain, and they opposed most of the teachings of Muhammad and the Islamic institutions.

In 930 Karmathian troops invaded Mecca during the pilgrim season, stormed the Kaaba, and spilled wine over the monument. They jeered at those who took refuge inside the sanctuary in the belief that it would preserve them from harm, and went on to massacre some two thousand pilgrims and townspeople. They then proceeded to prise out the Black Stone from the Kaaba and carried it into the desert, where they were said to have pounded it to pieces and scattered the fragments to the winds.

In 951, some twenty-one years later, having been offered a great price for the return of the stone, they brought back a small mass of pebbles glued together with pitch. After the conglomerate had been restored to its rightful place, they mocked the Meccans by saying it was not the original relic, though the pious later assured the people that it was the genuine stone (Sale, 1886, p. 91).

Several of the later Abbasid caliphs were either murdered or blinded. By the end of the eleventh century the role of the caliph had been virtually reduced to that of a figurehead, and his jurisdiction was confined to the province of Baghdad, most of their conquered areas, from Spain to Persia, now being ruled by independent Muslim dynasties, each with its own separate history.

The nominal suzerainty of the Abbasids was finally brought to an end when Hulagu the Mongol, after capturing Alamut in north-west Persia, the mountain fortress and capital of the Ismaili sect of the Assassins, in 1256 descended on Baghdad in 1258 and, in the space of one fateful month full of sad memories for Islam, abolished the caliphate, put to death Mustasim, the thirty-seventh and last caliph of the house of Abbas, and killed every living thing in sight in the course of a massacre that went on for four weeks.

The splendid palaces, mosques, mausoleums and places of learning were sacked and set on fire and the ground was levelled. The literary and artistic treasures that had made Baghdad the Athens of her day and the 'centre of the world' were destroyed and burned. The Muslim province of Baghdad and its environs was incorporated into the heathen empire of the Mongols.

There is some uncertainty about the title to the caliphate thereafter. According to one account, the last Abbasid ruler bestowed the title on his uncle, who escaped to Cairo, and in 1517 this man's descendant transferred the title to the Ottoman sultan Selim I (see Section 12.7).

12.4 The Fatimids (908–1171)

In 908 Abu Muhammad Obaydulla, a religious leader of the Ismaili branch of the Shia sect, incurred the displeasure of the reigning Abbasid caliph and escaped to safety in Tunisia. Here by a series of fortunate circumstances he was raised to sovereign power and founded the Fatimid dynasty, with its capital at Mahadi, a hundred miles south of Tunis. This dynasty was so named because Obaydulla claimed direct descent from Fatima, daughter of the Prophet and wife of Ali.

Obaydulla's Abbasid opponents revealed that he was actually the grandson of a Jew, and had magian (Zoroastrian) antecedents too. His physician and personal adviser was an Egyptian Jew, known to the West as Isaac Judaeus, whose writings had much influence on Islamic and Western medicine up to the seventeenth century.

Obaydulla's grandson Muizz (r. 953–75) conquered Egypt in 972, and then Palestine and Syria. He was well served by two remarkable men. One, Yakub ibn Killis, was an Islamized Jew of Baghdad, a financial genius who organized the taxation and civil-service systems which endured to the end of Fatimid rule. The administration itself, right up to the highest levels of the bureaucracy, was almost entirely run by Christians. The other was his general, Jowhar, an ex-slave of Greek origin who was the real conqueror of Egypt. Jowhar built the new city of Cairo (Al-Kahira, 'the Victorious') as the new Fatimid capital, a few miles from the old town of Fustat. As a result of his successful sponsoring of trade with the Byzantines, Egypt prospered exceedingly.

More than a brilliant statesman, Jowhar was also keen on education. He built a House of Wisdom in Cairo, and in 970 he erected the school and mosque of Al-Azhar – named after a title of the Prophet's daughter Fatima, 'Al-Zahra': 'the Resplendent' – which was to grow into a great centre of Shia studies. Centuries later Al-Azhar was converted to orthodox use, and it has remained to the present day one of the main universities of Sunni religious life.

Aziz (r. 976–96), the son and successor of Muizz, married a Christian woman and installed her brothers as patriarchs of Alexandria and Jerusalem. His vizier or chief minister, another Christian, named Isa ibn Nasturis, was responsible for extending the House of Wisdom established under Muizz.

Aziz was succeeded by his son Hakim (r. 996–1021), the sixth Fatimid caliph, an eccentric and contradictory character, at once a good administrator and a cruel despot. His chief secretary was a Christian named Fahd ibn Ibrahim, and his military adviser was Husayn, the son of Jowhar mentioned above. On the advice of Fahd, the caliph made further additions to the House of Wisdom, with a library of forty rooms full of books.

In one of his unpredictable swings of mood, Hakim abruptly ordered the execution of Husayn and embarked on a campaign of repression against the Christians, ordering the demolition of their churches, including the Church of the Holy Sepulchre in Jerusalem in 1009. This prompted the Christians to appeal to their fellow Christians in the West (see Section 12.5).

Hakim next introduced the public cursing of the first caliphs, proclaimed himself the express image of God, and tried to found a new religion. He was eventually assassinated by his incensed subjects, though it was popularly rumoured that he had mysteriously disappeared while out walking. The Druse sect of Lebanon is founded on his claims.

During the reign of the eighth caliph, Mustansir (r. 1037–94), the great-grandson of Obaydulla, the Fatimid empire encompassed the whole of North Africa, Sicily, Syria and western Arabia. Towards the end of Mustansir's reign, however, the Turks invaded Syria and Palestine, capturing Damascus and Jerusalem, and the Sudanese, Berbers and other rebel factions within his domain began to create problems nearer home.

The caliph appealed to his governor in Acre, an Armenian named Badr al-Jamali, who hastened to Egypt with his Armenian troops and restored order. As commonly occurs when foreign assistance is sought, actual power soon passed into the hands of the deliverer – in this case Badr, whose daughter married the son of the caliph. Badr's son Malik al-Afdal succeeded him as the caliph's next adviser, and even chose the caliph's successor.

In such circumstances the grip of the caliphs could not be maintained, and the rule of the remaining Fatimids saw the gradual decline of the dynasty. It was marked by the ever-deepening rift between the Shias and Sunnis, and by ethnic rivalries between the easterners (*mashrika*, mainly Turks, Palestinians and Iraqis) and the westerners (*maghriba*, mainly Berbers, Moors and Sudanese).

The downfall of the dynasty was accelerated by the growing power of the viziers, whom the caliphs could not control and dared not remove. Rivalries amongst the viziers themselves led ultimately to the triumph of a Kurdish general called Salahuddin (known to the West as Saladin), who in 1171 deposed the last of the Fatimids and constituted himself sovereign of Egypt, founding the Ayubid dynasty (1171–1254).

This in turn was followed by the Mameluke ('Slave') dynasty (1254–1517), descended from former Turkish and Circassian slaves purchased to create a military bodyguard for the caliphs, who in time came to exercise praetorian authority and finally usurped power.

The greatest of the Mameluke sultans was Baybars, who in 1260 defeated the Mongols at Ayn Jalut (the Spring of Goliath) near Nazareth, thus halting the westward expansion of the Mongols. The Mamelukes ruled till 1517, when Egypt was captured by the Ottoman Turks, after which Egypt sank into obscurity. (The Mamelukes remained an independent and interfering military caste in Egypt until 1811, when they were massacred by the Egyptian pasha Mehemet Ali.)

12.5 The Crusades (1095–1291)

The large scattered communities of Christians in the Holy Land lived in comparative peace with their Jewish and pagan neighbours until the coming of Islam.

When the patriarch Sophronius was forced to surrender Jerusalem to the caliph Omar in 637, he was informed that the Christians were free to worship in their churches, but no new churches were to be built in Jerusalem. The Christians were to make no converts, exhibit no crosses over churches, nor make any public demonstration of their faith (see Section 14.8).

These prohibitions continued to be imposed off and on under Omar's successors. Christians who sought the right of access to their holy places, like Jerusalem and Bethlehem, were often granted this only on payment of exorbitant fees. They had no recourse to the law, which was not in their favour. Repression and discrimination, attacks on pilgrims, the ransacking of monasteries, and the destruction of places of Christian worship were common throughout the period of Muslim domination of those areas.

From the tenth century the situation began to worsen and persecution increased. In 943 the Muslims demolished the churches of Ramleh, Caesarea and Ascalon. In 969 the Fatimid caliph Muizz burned part of the Church of the Holy Sepulchre in Jerusalem. In 975 the patriarch of Jerusalem was burned alive on the charge of being a Byzantine spy. In 1009 the Fatimid caliph Hakim launched a violent persecution of non-Muslims, stopped pilgrimages to the Holy Land, and destroyed the Church of the Holy Sepulchre. (Its rebuilding was begun in 1027 by the Byzantine emperor Constantine VIII.)

The defeat in 1071 of the Byzantine emperor Romanus IV by the Seljuk sultan Alp Arslan, in Manzikert in Armenia, was a severe blow to the Christian cause. With Constantinople weakened, the Christians could look to no other security and source of protection for themselves than the West, and it was to the West that they appealed.

The Western response came in the form of the Crusades, a series of eight wars between Christian and 'Paynim', the Cross and the Crescent, East and West, representing a conflict between different races, religions, cultures, social systems and civilizations.

The Crusades came in a series of waves, mostly ill-organized, ill-equipped and poorly armed, and often disunited. The motley Christian armies were quite unprepared for the arduous trek that took them two thousand miles from their homelands and for the hazardous conditions they had to face on arrival; not surprisingly, they often got out of hand.

The tides of the conflict ebbed and flowed along an uneven Levantine coastline, with possession of Jerusalem remaining the chief objective. In 1076 the Seljuk Turks took Jerusalem from the Fatimids and sacked the city. Their atrocious cruelty to the Christians aroused much indignation in the West. In 1098 the Fatimids retook Jerusalem from the Turks. Their victory was of short duration, for in the following year the Crusaders captured Jerusalem and established a series of Christian principalities along the Syrian coast. In 1187 Saladin of Egypt occupied Jerusalem. In 1244 the city fell once more to the Turkish army.

And so it went on, with beleaguered cities from Acre to Aleppo being captured and recaptured alternately by one side or the other, until in 1291 the Crusaders were finally driven from the Holy Land.

The conflict throughout was further complicated by the shifting alliances made on either side. The two principal antagonists in the struggle, the Christians and the Muslims, were opposed because of religious differences. But equally, because of sectarian differences, both sides fell out among themselves, and sometimes sought alliances across the religious divide.

During the two centuries that the Crusades lasted, the various rival factions on the Muslim side included the Fatimid caliphate of Cairo, the Abbasid caliphate of Baghdad, the Seljuk sultanate of Iconium (Konya), and the emirates of Damascus, Antioch, Aleppo, Edessa and Tripoli. Certain regions of the Holy Land were controlled by Baghdad, sometimes by Cairo, and at times no one's authority extended beyond the gates of the fortified towns. Some of the subordinate Muslim chiefs hated the ruling caliphates as much as they hated the Crusaders, and on occasion they allied themselves or gave help to the Christian princes.

The Crusaders were equally divided. Those from the West, known as the Franks, belonged to the (Latin) Church of Rome; while their Eastern allies in Byzantium belonged to the (Greek) Orthodox Church. Despite their temporary coalition there was long-standing rivalry between them, and in 1204, during what was known as the Fourth Crusade – originally directed against Egypt – the Crusaders turned aside and attacked Christian Constantinople instead (see Section 13.1).

In 1260 the Mongol leader Hulagu, having sacked Baghdad, captured Damascus, but he was called away to settle dynastic problems in his own country. He left behind his chief general, Kitboga, who, along with many of the Mongol officers and men, was a Nestorian Christian. But the Crusaders regarded the Nestorians as heretics and had no wish to seek the Mongols' assistance, preferring rather to find allies among the Moors and Turks, and even with the sect of Assassins.

Throughout this period the great merchant houses of Venice, Genoa, Naples, Siena and Pisa both supplied the Crusaders with weapons and at the same time sold essential commodities to the Syrians and Egyptians in exchange for their luxury goods and other 'meretricious merchandise'.

The period of the Crusades was one of intense religious propaganda in Europe, and for the only time in history the whole continent seemed united, at least temporarily, in a common purpose. All classes of the population participated, directly or indirectly, in this endeavour: popes and peasants, rich prelates and paupers, noblemen and serfs, the devout and the romantic, the adventurous and the ambitious, and, in one misguided case, children. (In the Children's Crusade of 1212 the children reached Alexandria, only to be sold into slavery.)

Among the Crusading kings were Richard I, 'the Lion Heart' (d. 1199) – known to the Saracens as Malik Rik – and Edward I (d. 1307) of England;

Louis VIII (d. 1226) and St Louis IX (d. 1270) of France (the latter was seized by the Saracens and spent four years in captivity); Conrad III (d. 1152), the Hohenstaufen monarch; Frederick I, 'Barbarossa' (d. 1190), the Holy Roman Emperor, who was drowned in a river in Asia Minor; and Frederick II (d. 1250), Holy Roman Emperor, who undertook a Crusade though under papal excommunication and in 1229 temporarily recovered Jerusalem by treaty, without fighting.

So deeply did the notion of the Crusades become etched into the conscious-ness of medieval Christendom that even King Arthur of England (fl. c. 600) and Charlemagne of France (fl. c. 800), who lived long before the Crusades, were said to have participated in this great Christian enterprise.

The Crusades reflect little glory on either side. Intrigue, treachery, betray-als and broken promises were common to both Christian and Muham-madan. And, as the English reformer John Wyclif (d. 1384) remarked, both the Christians and their opponents were subject to the same vices. The Christians like the Saracens made use of slaves, and several Crusader princes maintained harems. There were prodigies of valour and savage barbarities on both sides. Both were guilty of rapine and plunder and the wholesale massacre of civilian populations, including women and children.

The haze of romantic glamour surrounding the names of Saladin and Richard the Lion Heart was hardly well deserved, but they were the best of an unscrupulous lot, exhibiting at times good faith and largesse of spirit, and at other times cruelty and ruthlessness. Unflattering portraits have been drawn of both.

The overall effects of the Crusades were enormous. They brought the feudal system of Europe to an end, and saw the emergence of a free peasantry and the creation of guilds of artisans and craftsmen. They brought great economic benefits to the merchant cities of Europe and to the rich bank-ing and credit houses, and stimulated trade with the East.

In spite of the considerable advances achieved in the Muslim world in many areas of knowledge, however, not much of this learning passed to the West in the course of the encounter. As Max Meyerhof writes, 'The influ-ence of the Crusades on the transmission of the Islamic sciences to Europe was surprisingly little' (Arnold and Guillaume, 1965, p. 349).

Both Crusaders and Muslims learned a great deal about military architecture and siege tactics from the Byzantines (see Section 13.1), and employed this knowledge against each other. But the conflict had mortally weakened the Byzantine empire, which for centuries had provided the moral bulwark for Christians living in Muslim countries. The Church of Rome fared no better, for in the long run the conflict served to impair the power of the papacy.

As a lesser, if more picturesque gain, the Crusades gave birth to the great chivalric orders of the Knights Templars, the Knights Hospitallers and the Teutonic Order. Flowing from this came the art of heraldry and the wider use of coats of arms and other heraldic devices which were originally designed to distinguish friend from foe.

The Crusades did little to heal the wide division between Christian and Christian, or between Muslim and Muslim, and left the two religions as divided internally as before. Nor did they do anything to bring the Christians and Saracens together. Attempts at reconciliation with Muslim rulers proved unsuccessful. St Francis of Assisi was politely received by the sultan when he visited Egypt in 1223, but five Franciscan missionaries sent by him to Morocco were killed, as was the theologian Raymond Lully, the 'Enlightened Doctor', who was stoned to death by a mob in Bejaia, Algeria, in 1315.

Above all, the centuries of bloody confrontation during the Crusades left an unhappy legacy of mistrust and suspicion that still endures between Islam and the West.

12.6 The Occupation of Spain (712–1492)

In 710 a Berber chieftain named Tarif, with the aid of a renegade Visigoth called Julian, led a raiding expedition across the narrow straits separating Africa from Europe. Where he landed in Spain, Tarifa, still bears his name.

Emboldened by this venture, Musa ibn Nosayr, Muslim governor of the province of North Africa (Ifrikiya) under the Omayyad caliphate of Damascus, prepared a larger expedition. In the spring of 711 he sent a freed Berber slave, Tarik ibn Ziyad, with a body of seven thousand Berbers reinforced by two thousand Arabs and the help of Julian's ships, across the same straits.

Tarik landed at the rock named after him, Jebel Tarik, 'the Mountain of Tarik' (Gibraltar), and went on to defeat and slay the occupying Visigoth king Roderick, taking possession first of Cordoba – which became the Arab capital – and then Toledo. The region to the north of Gibraltar was known to the Arabs as Andalus (Andalusia), the country of the Vandals.

Another Muslim army, now joined by large numbers of troops from the once-Christian Arab tribes of Kalb and Kayis, proceeded north, crossed the Pyrenees and raided the southern coast of France, where the Côte de Maures (Moorish Coast) is a reminder of their presence. Moorish armies penetrated deep into France, but in 732 met with disaster between Poitiers and Tours, about two hundred miles from Paris, being defeated there by Charles Martel.

The Battle of Poitiers, one of the most decisive in world history, is mentioned in Muslim annals, if at all, as a minor episode. But this defeat, exactly 100 years after the death of Muhammad, marked the limit of Muslim westward expansion and of any further aggrandizement on the same scale in this direction.

Victory for the Arabs would have changed the history of western Europe and of the world. Gibbon speculates on Arab fleets on the Thames and Rhine and the Koran being interpreted in the Muslim universities of Oxford, where 'her pulpits might demonstrate to a circumcised people the sanctity and truth of the revelation of Mahomet'.

Driven from France, the Muslims set about establishing themselves in Spain, though tribal rivalry between Berbers and Arabs long remained a source of bitter discord. This situation prevailed till an Omayyad prince, Abdul Rahman I (d. 788), grandson of the caliph Hisham, fleeing from the downfall of his clan in Damascus, founded in Cordoba an Omayyad dynasty which, like Omayyad rule in Damascus, was generally a model of tolerance and wise government. The dynasty (756–1031) reached its zenith in the reign of Abdul Rahman III (d. 961), whose minister and court physician was a Jew named Hasday ben Shaprut, a patron of music and the sciences.

By the beginning of the eleventh century Andalusia or Muslim Spain had become fragmented into a number of petty states, each state (or *taifa*) governed by a ruler of Berber, Arab, Vandal or Slav origin. There were more than a score of such principalities, most Moorish, a few Christian, each forming fleeting alliances of convenience, to get the better of their rivals.

Indigenous people who chose to remain Christian during the Moorish occupation of Spain were known as Mozarabs (Arabized, Arab-like or would-be Arabs) and were often of mixed blood. These Spanish Christians dressed and lived like Arabs and served as an important link between the native Spaniards and the Muslims. They were bilingual, as were most of the Spanish Muslims. They spoke and wrote Arabic, which was the official language, but they also used a Romance patois – mainly derived from Low Latin – which was to develop into the Spanish language. The Mozarabs contributed greatly to the culture and administration of Muslim Spain, as well as to the diffusion of Arabian science and learning after the Moors had left. By this time, too, some of the Spanish noble houses were part Arab.

Another invasion of Spain, by African Berbers from Marrakesh, set up the Almoravid dynasty (1085–1147), and this was followed by yet another invasion by Berbers from the Atlas region, who established the Almohad dynasty (1133–1270). They combined to abolish the *taifa* states, to form a more unified kingdom. Both these dynasties tended to be orthodox and were generally intolerant of non-Muslims, including the Mozarabs. In 1143 the Almohad caliph Abdul Mumin ordered the expulsion of all Jews and Christians who refused to accept Islam, but confusion soon followed and the move was abandoned.

By now the cultural development of Spain had come virtually to a halt. There were also growing ethnic conflicts between the occupying powers: Berber soldiers opposed an Arab political and social élite. The dispossessed Christian nobility, with Frankish assistance, took advantage of the situation and began regaining their annexed territories one by one.

The reconquest of their homeland by the Spaniards was a long and faltering process. The capture of Toledo in 1085 by the Christians had been a crushing setback to Spanish Islam, and the first great step in the Iberian crusade. Then a freebooting condottiere named Ruy Diaz de Bivar, popularly known as the Cid (Arabic *Sayyid*, 'Lord'), who alternately served both Moorish sultans and Christian princes, finally opted for Spain and in 1094 captured Valencia, which remained for a time in Christian hands. Although probably a Mozarab, the Cid was given a noble Castilian lineage, and became the subject of innumerable romantic ballads and chronicles.

Much more still remained to be done to restore Spain to Christian suzerainty. But then came the fall of Saragossa (1118), followed by that of Cordoba (1236) and Seville (1248). On 2 January 1492 the city of Granada, ruled by Abu Abdulla Mohammed XI (known as Boabdil), was taken, and all non-Catholics were expelled from the peninsula.

The loss of their Spanish territories and the thought of the Cross on the Alhambra palace in Granada were a bitter blow to the Muslims. The memory of once-Muslim Spain is kept alive to the present day among the 'exiles' in North Africa, many of whose descendants still hang on their walls in Marrakesh and Casablanca the keys to the houses their forbears had once owned in Cordoba or Seville.

There are two schools of thought about the Muslim occupation of Spain. Some scholars see it as a period of enlightenment, a time when in all areas great advances were made that put Moorish Spain ahead of the rest of Europe. Others regard the influence of the alien occupation as short-lived and superficial, and point to there being relatively little to show today for nearly seven centuries of Moorish suzerainty, apart from a few examples of Moorish architecture, like the Alhambra, and the addition of a few hundred foreign words to the lexicon of the Spanish language.

On the whole, it has been said, the progress of Spain as part of the European community of peoples – with the democratic and cultural institutions that characterize the nations of the West – was held in abeyance during the period of Moorish thraldom, which led eventually to stagnation. Had the occupation been allowed to continue, Spain today might well have been in the same cultural and economic condition as the other Muslim states of North Africa.

12.7 The Turks

The Arabs first came in contact with the Turks – a 'Turanian' people – in central Asia. Because of the superior military skill of the Turks as mounted horsemen and the speed of their cavalry, they were widely imported as mercenaries by the caliphs.

By about 1040 a large migration of Turkish tribes known as the Seljuks crossed into the territories of the caliphate and began to accept Islam. In time they went on to conquer the greater part of Persia, then Iraq, and finally they wrested Syria and Palestine from the local Muslim rulers, as well as Iconium (Konya), the eastern part of Anatolia (Asia Minor), from Byzantium.

The Seljuks were supplanted by a new rising power closely related to them, the Ottoman Turks, who themselves had been driven westward by Mongol incursions. In 1299 they founded the Ottoman empire in eastern Anatolia, and continued a policy of ruthless aggrandizement. Their ferocity and cruelty were matched only by those of the Mongols.

In 1362 the Ottoman sultan Murat I (r. 1362–89) established a corps of youthful Christian captives, seized as tribute from his Greek vassals in the Balkans. He named them the New Troop – Yeni Sheri, or Janissaries – and they were to become an élite corps of the Turkish army. (Like the Ottoman Turks, the Safavid kings of Persia also recruited large numbers of slave troops – Ghulams – mainly Christians, from the Caucasus, including Georgians and Armenians.)

In about 1420, because of their acquaintance with Christian customs, the reigning sultan Mehmet I (r. 1413–21) appointed the Bektashi order of dervishes to serve as 'chaplains' to the Janissaries. (Over the centuries the Janissaries grew powerful enough to engage in palace coups and resisted any reorganization or reformation of their order, until in 1826 their leaders were assassinated and the order was abolished.)

Mehmet II (r. 1451–81) was the son of his predecessor, Murat II, by a slave girl. In 1453, equipped with cannon larger than any used anywhere else hitherto, specially cast for him by a Hungarian master gunsmith named Urban, Mehmet II captured Constantinople, which by this time was an easy prey for any determined predator. The outer walls were first breached and the ramparts and inner defences scaled by the Janissaries. The last Byzantine emperor, Constantine XI Dragases, was killed during the attack, and the victorious sultan passed his lifeless body as he rode into the city. The Conqueror ('Fatih') proceeded straight to the church of St Sophia – the glory of Constantinople – and ordered the mullahs to proclaim its conversion into a mosque.

Mehmet, desiring to be remembered as a universal ruler and not wishing to lose the services of the Christians and Jews in his kingdom, restored the patriarchate of the Greek Orthodox Church for the benefit of his Christian subjects and authorized the installation of a grand rabbi for his Jewish subjects.

Proud of having gained possession of the Queen City, with its long historic associations, he regarded himself as being in the line of the Roman emperors and assumed the title of Kayser-i-Rum (Caesar of Rome). He invited Italian humanists and Greek scholars to his court, collected Greek and Latin works for his library, and sent to Venice for Gentile Bellini to paint his portrait and decorate the walls of his palace with frescos.

He married Gulbahar, said to be a daughter of 'the king of France' who had been sent as a bride for Constantine XI Dragases. She became the mother of Mehmet's son and successor Bayazit II (r. 1481–1512). She never embraced Islam and died a Christian. Mehmet was said to have died by poisoning.

Selim I (r. 1512–20), known as Selim the Grim, was the grandson of Mehmet II. He came to the throne after having his father (Bayazit II) poisoned, and his brothers, nephews and all other likely candidates to succession put to death. He beheaded his grand viziers at the rate of one every year. Realizing that the Turks lacked the ability to create a prosperous economy on their own, he speeded up the policy of his predecessors and repopulated the capital city with Greeks, Armenians and Jews, and as a result of their industry and enterprise Constantinople (Istanbul) once again became a rich and flourishing metropolis.

In 1517 Selim I conquered Egypt and the Hejaz, including Mecca and Medina, and received, so it was claimed, the title to the caliphate from a descendant of the last Abbasid caliph in Cairo. Thus Muslim power and the authority of the prestigious caliphate had passed in the course of its history from the Arabs (Medina caliphs), to the Syrians (Omayyads), Persians (Abbasids) and Egyptians (Fatimids), and finally to the Turanians (Turks).

The Ottoman empire reached the pinnacle of its glory during the reign of Suleiman I 'the Magnificent' (r. 1520–66), the great-grandson of Mehmet II and son of Selim I. His grand vizier Ibrahim Pasha, a Greek convert to Islam, was strangled in his sleep by the sultan's chief wife, Roxelana, who was jealous of his power. The sultan's favourite concubine was Khurrem, a Russian slave girl.

Suleiman invaded Hungary, captured Budapest and besieged Vienna but failed to take it. Khayruddin (Khair-ed-din) 'Barbarossa', a renegade Greek corsair who had been terrorizing the Mediterranean, was recruited as an Ottoman admiral, and with his help Suleiman conquered all of North Africa except Morocco. In 1565 the sultan's fleet trying to reduce Malta was heavily defeated. In the following year, while laying siege to Szigetvár in Hungary, Suleiman died. In accordance with ancient custom, the 'heart and inside parts' of the body were removed and buried where he died. Later, a Christian church was raised on the site.

At its zenith the Ottoman empire embraced Asia Minor, the Balkans, Mesopotamia, the Hejaz – including the holy cities – Egypt and Syria, and North Africa as far as the frontiers of Morocco, so that virtually the whole Arab-speaking world was under Ottoman suzerainty. The Ottomans adopted a policy of transplanting hundreds of thousands of their poorer subjects from the arid provinces of Anatolia to the richer Balkan lands, populating the region with Turks to form Rumelia, an extension, as it were, of Anatolia into Europe. This was to have a bloody consequence in our own day.

The death of Suleiman marked the end of Ottoman greatness, and was a turning-point in its steady decline. The drunkenness and debauchery of the later sultans led eventually to the Rule of the Women, harem intrigues and hostility between the chief wife and the mother of the ruling sultan and between the grand vizier and the chief eunuch of the palace. Court and palace murders became commonplace, such as when Nur Banu, chief wife of the dissolute Selim II (r. 1566–74), had all the sultan's sons by his other wives strangled so that her own son should survive to rule.

This son was Murat III, whose chief wife was a Venetian girl named Safiya. When Murat died she too had rival brothers strangled – nineteen of them – so that her own son might become sultan, which he did, as Mehmet III. In time Safiya suffered the same fate, being strangled by one of her own rivals. The favourite wife of Ahmet I (r. 1603–17) was a Greek girl named Kosem, whose sway was cut short when she was strangled on the orders of the sultan's brother.

The power of the sultans remained absolute and they could do as they pleased. Thus, on the orders of the sultan Ibrahim (r. 1640–48) – a man of whimsical and eccentric temperament – all the concubines in his harem, nearly three hundred in number, were trussed up in weighted sacks and flung into the Bosporus. The sultan gave no reason for his barbarous command, and none dared question him.

Throughout the seventeenth and eighteenth centuries, all departments of the administration, from those of the Sublime Porte (the seat of government in Constantinople) to the distant provinces, were ridden with venality and mismanagement. Never in the history of any of the subject peoples was the weight of oppression, misrule, despotism and spiritual decay more heavily felt than during the rule of the Ottomans.

In confrontations with the West the Turks were now increasingly the vanquished. They had not yet acquired the skills of modern diplomacy, and their chief ministers had religious scruples about the use of non-Muslim languages in their dealings with the Western nations. In about 1670 the Porte engaged a Greek named Panayotis Nikosiya to act as chief dragoman (interpreter) to conduct negotiations with Western diplomats, and thereafter the chief dragoman was always a Greek, serving as a buffer between the Muslim Porte and the infidel Europeans.

When in 1789 the exigencies of the international situation necessitated an agreement with the Western powers against Russia, the head of the Turkish military judiciary denounced the move because it involved an alliance with Christian peoples, contrary to the principle clearly set forth in the Koran (60:1 and 5:56). But he was overruled by a sharia expert with a verse from the hadith.

By the middle of the nineteenth century Turkey, so long in decline, had become 'the Sick Man of Europe'. And by this time too the subject nations began thinking of regaining their national freedom. How Turkey dealt with nationalist – especially Christian – movements of emancipation might be illustrated by the cases of Bulgaria and Armenia.

Bulgaria was occupied by the Turks in the fourteenth century, and for the next five hundred years the name of Bulgaria was virtually blotted out. But Bulgarian nationalism was never quite extinguished and remained dormant, with sporadic attempts at freedom being made from time to time. The struggle for Bulgarian independence came to a head in 1876 in a series of popular uprisings that were put down by massacres of atrocious cruelty which raised strong protests throughout Europe and prompted William Gladstone's stirring denunciation in his famous pamphlet on the Bulgarian atrocities.

Armenian uprisings in 1897 were put down in similar fashion by the sultan Abdul Hamid II, when hundreds of thousands of Armenians were killed and their villages burned. These Armenian atrocities aroused equally strong revulsion in Europe and earned Abdul Hamid the title of 'the Great Assassin', or 'Abdul the Damned'.

In 1915 the Ottoman government under Mehmet V, fearful of possible Armenian sympathies towards the enemy powers fighting against Turkey in the First World War, ordered a fresh campaign of genocide against the Armenians. As a result of this, over one and a half million Armenians were killed by being shot, burned alive, drowned, or forcibly deported into the north Syrian Desert, where they were massacred by the Kurds or died of thirst or starvation in their thousands.

By the end of the First World War Turkey had lost all its possessions outside Anatolia. In 1922 the sultanate of Turkey was ended and the last sultan, Mehmet VI, fled to Malta on a British battleship. The repatriation of the European inmates of the sultan's harem was left to a British naval officer. Among the women was an English girl who was sent back on the Orient Express to her home in Leamington Spa in Warwickshire.

When Mehmet VI died in poverty in San Remo, Italy, in 1926, his body was conveyed in a coffin borrowed from a charitable institution and buried in a nameless grave in Damascus (Esin, 1963, p. 193). His brother and successor Abdul Mecid II was allowed to hold the title of caliph, but not of sultan. When in October 1923 Turkey was proclaimed a republic he too was forced to flee. He sought refuge in Switzerland, and after a short delay on the grounds that polygamists were not admitted he was allowed to enter the country.

Then in March 1924 even the pretence of religious leadership was abandoned when Mustafa Kemal – the later Kemal Ataturk, the Turkish general of Macedonian and Albanian stock who had assumed charge of the government – announced that Islam was no more the state religion and declared Turkey a secular state. He abolished the caliphate, until then the central directorate of most branches of Islam.

A dedicated modernizer and reformer, Ataturk held Islam responsible for the deplorable state of Muslim countries at the time. He denounced the religion and its observances as 'the rules and theories of an immoral Arab sheikh' (Laffin, 1981, p. 131). He regarded Islam and civilization as incompatible, and in a moment of cynicism he said of the Turks, 'If only we could make them Christians!' (Kinross, 1964, p. 437).

He changed the day of rest from Friday to Sunday, replaced the Islamic calendar for the Western one, adopted the civil codes of Europe in place of the sharia, and converted the great mosque of Constantinople – once the church of St Sophia – into a museum.

He instituted the use of the Latin alphabet in place of the Arabic script, which for centuries, he said, 'has held our minds in an iron vice', and urged the substitution, as far as was feasible, of Old Turkish – 'Turanian' – words to replace Arabic. He discouraged the wearing of distinctive attire by religious teachers, forbad the wearing of the fez (which itself had replaced the turban in 1826 by order of the reforming sultan Mahmut II) – calling it the badge of ignorance, backwardness and hostility to civilization – and encouraged European dress – because it would make the Turks think like Westerners. He also encouraged the adoption of Western-style last names or surnames, and civil marriage in place of religious ones. Finally, he abolished polygamy and the veiling of women and extended civil rights to women, including the right to vote.

12.8 The Mughals (1526–1857)

Meanwhile, on the Indian subcontinent, civil strife, caste division and sectarian conflict among the Hindus made the conquest of the country a comparatively easy task for successive waves of Muslim invaders. The Arabs conquered Sind as early as AD 712, and were followed by other Muslim colonizers of Afghan, Turkish, Persian and Central Asian stock, each of whom set up independent dynasties of their own: Ghazni, Ghor, Khilji, Tughluk, Lodi. The most notable of these Muslim dynasties was that of the Mughals, who built upon and consolidated the work of their co-religionist predecessors.

The founder of the Mughal empire was Babur (r. 1526–30), a brilliant military strategist, descended from the Mongol emperor Timur (Tamerlane) on his father's side and Genghis Khan on his mother's side. He won the battle of Panipat (1526), defeating the Afghan emperor of Delhi by the use – for the first time in India – of European field artillery.

He was succeedeed by his son Humayun (r. 1530–56), who had a frequently broken reign and was in turn succeeded by his son Akbar the Great (r. 1556–1605), a ruler of exceptional competence who governed with wisdom, vigour and humanity. Elsewhere abroad, his royal contemporaries were Shah Abbas ('the Grand Sophy') of Persia; Suleiman the Magnificent of Turkey; Ivan IV, 'the Terrible', of Russia; and Charles V, the Holy Roman emperor. Another celebrated contemporary was Elizabeth I of England, who in 1600 granted a trading charter to the East India Company. By the eighteenth century the Company was to rule over large parts of India, until in 1858 its powers were assumed by the Crown.

Among his other attempts at reform, Akbar sought to combine Islam with the other great faiths to form one universal 'religion of God', calling for a policy of tolerance and mutual understanding that endeared him to his non-Muslim subjects. The Parsi (Zoroastrian) high priest in Delhi had an honoured place among the savants at the imperial court, and Akbar himself wore the sacred shirt and girdle of the Zoroastrians.

Equally interested in Christianity, the emperor held long talks with the Jesuits, appointing one of them to be the tutor of his son Murad. After his conquest of the Deccan in southern India, Akbar erected a magnificent triumphal arch in Fatehpur Sikri and, as a *memento mori* in his hour of victory, adorned it with the inscription 'Jesus son of Mary (upon whom be peace) said, "This world is a bridge; pass over, but build no house upon it."'

Akbar's eldest son, by a Hindu princess, was Jehangir (r. 1605–27). Intemperate, self-indulgent and pleasure-loving, he beguiled his leisure hours between wars in his extensive harem. He was addicted to drink, as were most of the emperors of the Mughal court before and after his time.

A ruler of ferocious cruelty, Jehangir introduced many refinements to the techniques of torture. When his son Khosro rebelled, he ordered three hundred of Khosro's followers to be impaled alive on stakes, and as an object lesson he forced the prince – loaded with chains, trembling and weeping – to watch them die a slow agonizing death, after which he had him blinded.

Paradoxically, there was a strong religious streak in the emperor's nature. He favoured the Jesuits, and Catholic processions became a frequent sight on the streets of Agra. Christian paintings were hung on the palace walls, and in the emperor's private prayer-room was an engraving on stone of the Virgin Mary and Jesus. He encouraged open discussions between the Jesuits and Muslim theologians, even though the outcome was not always to the advantage of the mullahs. For a time it was thought that he himself might become a Christian (Rawlinson, 1954, p. 322).

Jehangir was followed by Shah Jehan (r. 1627–58), his son by a Rajput princess, whose first act on assuming the reins of empire was to have one brother garrotted, another blinded, and all the other male relatives massacred. A devout Muslim, Shah Jehan ordered the demolition of all Hindu temples recently built or in the course of construction and the razing of all Christian churches in Agra and Lahore.

Shah Jehan reigned for thirty years, until seized and imprisoned by his son Aurungzeb, impatient to rule (r. 1658–1707). He was then allowed to spend the remaining eight years of his life – he died in 1666 – in luxury and sensuality, gazing from his confines in the Agra fort at the distant Taj Mahal, which he had had built as a mausoleum for his favourite wife, Mumtaz Mahal, who had died in 1631 at the birth of their fourteenth child.

During his last few months the ailing ex-emperor was looked after by his daughter, the devout and highly talented Jehanara, who for eighteen years of his reign had been the official keeper of the imperial seal. Describing herself as 'a disciple of the holy men of Christ', Jehanara wished to have only a simple tomb for herself, and when she died her grave, at her own request, had only grass above it.

Having deposed his father, Aurungzeb went on to secure the throne by ordering the murder of the rightful heir, his elder brother Dara Shikoh. Among other reasons for this was Dara Shikoh's sympathy towards Hinduism: he had had a Persian translation made of the Upanishads and declared it to be a revelation older than the Koran. In the summer of 1659 the prince was caught in his apartment and held down by three men while a fourth cut his throat. When the blood-soaked head was brought to him, Aurungzeb had the face washed to ensure that it was indeed his brother's, before ordering it to be buried.

The depredations wrought during the fifty-year rule of this religious bigot may be judged from the fact that he pursued a policy of large-scale conversions by the sword, combined with the demolition of Hindu places of worship. In a single year, 1679, he reduced to rubble almost two hundred temples, and in Benares, holy city of the Hindus, he razed to the ground a shrine of special sacrosanctity and built on the site a Muslim mosque.

Aurungzeb was the sixth and last of the so-called Great Mughals. He had brought the country to such a pass and rendered the situation so dire that civil wars and insurrections followed his death, and continued unchecked to the end of the dynasty. He was succeeded by nonentities, a procession of phantom emperors who fell victims to moral corruption, intrigue and fratricidal strife.

Aurungzeb's eldest son, Bahadur Shah I (d. 1712), killed two brothers to gain the throne, and by the time he died conditions had deteriorated to such an extent that his corpse lay around for ten weeks before it was finally buried.

The break-up of the Mughal empire had already begun, and its decline is pitiful to trace. The emperors, and the lesser Mughal nobility – the nawabs, khans and sheikhs – spent their days watching cockfights and training falcons for the chase. Many were sodden with drink, glutted with drugs and infected with venereal dissease. They patronized mountebanks and charlatans, palmists and astrologers, and their courts were filled with buffoons and nautch-girls, transvestites and catamites, out-at-heel European adventurers and other hangers-on.

The reign of Bahadur Shah's successor, Jahandar Shah (d. 1713), ushered in a period of unmitigated debauchery and violence. When the emperor died, say the chroniclers, he became the victim of indignities that do not bear recital (Sharma, 1947, p. 172).

Farukh-siyar (d. 1719) on his own downfall was dragged from the throne bareheaded and barefooted, then abused, beaten, imprisoned, fed on poisoned food and finally strangled to death.

He was followed by Rafi-ud-Darajat, Neku-siyar and Rafi-ud-Daula (Shah Jehan II), whose combined reigns lasted from February to September of 1719.

During the reign of Muhammad Shah (d. 1748) the process of disintegration intensified, and it was further accelerated during the reign of Ahmad Shah (d. 1754). The latter had a seraglio covering four square miles, where he used to retire for weeks at a time. He was finally deposed, blinded and imprisoned.

His successor, Alamgir II, ruled for five years before being stabbed to death. His body was thrown out of the window and dragged naked along the banks of the Jumna, and only later was picked up and hurriedly interred.

His son and successor, Shah Alam II (d. 1806), was imprisoned, flogged and blinded, and eventually had to seek the help of the English East India Company and live as its pensioner. The affairs of his son Akbar II (d. 1837) were in like manner controlled by the English, who, out of sentiment, continued the charade of treating him as an emperor.

The last titular Mughal emperor, Bahadur Shah II (d. 1862), was deposed in 1857, ruling only as king of Delhi, and remained for his own safety a stipendiary détenu in the Delhi fort under English protection. He spent his days writing poetry, listening to musical recitations and practising calligraphy, and knew little of what was happening around him. He was constantly short of funds and kept writing complaints to the English authorities, dunning them for more money. Following the Indian Mutiny of 1857, in which he was distantly involved, he was deported to Rangoon, where he died.

The lesser Mughals were quite unable to deal with the problems of civil insurrection and the wars against the Marathas, Jats, Rohillas, Sikhs and Rajputs, and cared little for the cultural inheritance bequeathed to them. Maratha insurgents felt free to stable their horses in the imperial palaces, break up and carry off whatever was valuable, strip the silver ornaments from the ceilings, and turn the Taj Mahal into a dwelling-place.

The English authorities, as their power increased, did what they could to arrest these depredations, but planned action on a national scale was taken only when Lord Curzon, viceroy of India from 1898 to 1905, promulgated an act for the preservation of ancient monuments, issuing special orders for the restoration of the Taj Mahal, which by then was in a state of sad decay through neglect and vandalism.

12.9 Causes of Decline

Historians, both Muslim and non-Muslim, have sought to provide reasons for the decline of almost all Muslim states along a fairly consistent downward path that is not generally in evidence to quite the same degree in the history of other nations.

Within a Muslim dynasty, once established, power was often achieved – somewhere along the line of succession – by usurpation or a palace coup, in which all likely rivals were either blinded and thus rendered unfit to rule, or were put to death by knife, poison or garrotting. The successful candidate in this contest had next to secure his own position, which he usually did by the traditional method of assassination, until he had attained the status of absolute ruler, with autocratic, unfettered authority.

The caliph was the successor of the Prophet, and as such saw himself as being above the law, and most of the lesser rulers believed that they too governed by a kind of divine right. There was no established clergy to check them, and obsequious theologians were always ready to sanction their excesses. Held back by few constraints, they had a free hand in virtually all matters.

According to the political doctrine formulated quite early in Muslim history, obedience was due to the one who held the reins of power and was able effectively to maintain that hold against all conspiracies against him. Muslim states were thus often governed by tyrants, who were seldom respected because they were loved but always because they were feared.

Almost invariably, the ruler was surrounded by fawning courtiers who served him with sycophantic deference and flattered him to advance their own careers – if not to save their necks – not daring to object or suggest a course of action that might be at variance with the one he favoured.

Large numbers of idle, sometimes clever and often ambitious women in the harem and the plots of scheming eunuchs, favourites and – usually foreign – royal guards led to intrigues and palace machinations behind the scenes that frequently determined the course of events.

In the absence of democratic institutions of any kind, the common people could do little to influence their own destinies. An excellent system of espionage ferreted out dissent, and opposition was effectively silenced by political repression, with imprisonment, torture and execution – without trial and with no avenues of appeal. Long years of experience had inured the populace to the oppressive rule of despots. They had neither the will nor the wherewithal to resist. And their faith had conditioned them to a fatalistic acquiescence in their lot.

Again, a religion that sanctioned polygamy, and concubinage without limit, and that held out the prospect of an afterlife of unending sensual pleasures (see Section 14.17), fostered a view of existence in terms of unrestrained self-indulgence. With few exceptions, sybaritic luxury and moral decadence characterized the lifestyles of the caliphs, sultans, pashas and emirs all over the Muslim world. The Islamic prohibition against alcohol rarely served to check the intemperate habits of Muslim rulers.

Widespread official corruption, combined with administrative breakdown and economic decline, led to political instability, which facilitated the intervention and finally the control taken by foreign powers – and in recent times by the Europeans – over their affairs.

13
FOREIGN INFLUENCES

The Muslims had burst upon the larger world before their fundamental doctrines had been formulated in detail or their legal system had taken on precise form. Neither culturally did the Arabs nor doctrinally did Islam come fully armed from Arabia. Nor did they have the experience to organize or the experts to administer the regions they had so easily acquired.

The rapid progress made by their armies brought the desert Arabs face to face with other cultures, and they found themselves suddenly exposed to the dazzling glare blazing in from more advanced civilizations. What they felt when first confronted with the grandeur of these ancient nations is well illustrated in their dazed reaction on capturing the Persian city of Ctesiphon (see Section 14.5).

Every one of the countries they took over – Mesopotamia, Persia, Syria, Palestine, Egypt – had been the cradle of an earlier civilization, and each had a history going back thousands of years before the birth of Muhammad. Their contemporary heirs – the Sassanians, Seleucids, Ptolemies and Byzantines – had long-established social and administrative institutions and deep-rooted religious traditions, with astonishing achievements in every field of endeavour.

The traditional models the Arabs brought with them were unable to withstand the impact of the mature cultures they encountered, and presented problems that could never hope to be solved by a simple affirmation that God is one and Muhammad his prophet and a few outward observances of prayer, pilgrimage and fasting. In contrast to what was now spread out before them, the Arabs seemed to have made slender contributions indeed, and they were to seize in full measure the rich treasures that now lay at their feet.

The tendency to regard all the cultural features of the post-Muhammad period in the Middle East as 'Islamic' is greatly overdone and needs to be more closely examined and reassessed. This misplaced emphasis does grave injustice to the many earlier cultures on which the Muslim cultural seedlings were nourished and grew to efflorescence.

It is useful to remember that there is little that is 'Islamic' about most of the so-called Islamic studies. Muslim theology and jurisprudence may legitimately be termed Islamic, but when we speak of Islamic science, astronomy or medicine we mean by these terms simply the pursuit of these studies – all made up of intricate strands from many diverse traditions – in the Muslim world in the post-Islamic period.

Few Muslim achievements were truly original, and most were built around a pre-existing core, as will be seen. Islam provided a flimsy if colourful mantle beneath which still streamed the powerful currents of old. The arrival of Islam did not bring much that was new, and indeed the effect was often lessened where the religious element was stressed. As Guillaume says, the legacy of Islam 'has proved least valuable where religion has exercised the strongest influence' (Arnold and Guillaume, 1965, p. v). In view of the prohibitions imposed by Muhammad and the Koran, it would be true to say that the development of architecture, literature, music and the arts in the Muslim world must have developed from impulses given from sources other than the religion of Islam.

Converts learned Arabic to read the Koran, and, as Islam spread, Arabic became the medium of communication in many parts of the Islamic world. Scholars, non-Arabs and non-Muslims, wrote in Arabic and introduced into the language of their adoption many words from their own native tongue that are now regarded as Arabic in origin, and many ideas that are now thought to be Islamic.

A number of races and creeds made their distinctive contributions to the Islamic order, and each modified the order in its own way. There is no such thing as a uniform 'Islamic culture': different regions evolved different institutions. The diversity of creative expression found in such fields as literature and the arts, and even in Muslim sectarian differences and religious practices, shows variations representing native elements that characterize not the religion of Islam but the bias of the national, racial or communal groups in particular regions.

The material splendour of Omayyad Damascus, Abbasid Baghdad, Fatimid Cairo, Safavid Isfahan, Mughal Delhi and Ottoman Istanbul comes not from the Arabs or the Islamic faith but reflects the millennia-old cultures of Syria, Mesopotamia, Egypt, India and Byzantium.

As these regions came within the ambit of Islamic suzerainty, problems of adjustment arose that the newcomers soon realized could not be settled by tools fashioned in the Hejaz. Contact led first to conflict and then to compromise. The entirely different milieu the desert Arabs had to face led to a long process of interaction which in an expanding empire called for adaptation in all spheres of life. This involved the assimilation of cosmopolitan ideas which were eventually to work subtle changes in Islam that in time were to transform its basic concepts and soften its rigid orthodoxies.

The inherited conventions and native instincts of the conquered peoples could not be blotted out, and none of the subject peoples entirely abandoned its own social patterns, political institutions, cultural traditions and customary laws. Often the Arabs were as much victims as victors of the peoples they conquered. Having taken their territories, they were now to fight a long and in some cases a losing battle with the cultural sophistication and intellectual subtlety of their vanquished subjects.

The early Arabs had little skill in the professions, and disdained the arts and sciences. In general, they believed that ability in the professions was hereditarily preserved in certain peoples: that the Jews were proficient in finance; the Greeks skilled in engineering, architecture and the arts; and that the long tradition of learning among the Christians fitted them for law, medicine, education and administration. As far as was expedient, the Arab conquerors left these people to continue the work in which they were better skilled than themselves.

Islam has been shown to be a syncretic religion based principally on Judaism and Christianity. Islamic culture is likewise a synthetic phenomenon that emerged from the pluralistic societies that arose in the countries of Muslim conquest. The Muslims entered upon a rich inheritance with ready-to-hand institutions and ready-to-use cultural tools.

The majority of great men who have contributed to Islamic civilization were not Arabs by birth. As the Tunisian historian Ibn Khaldun (d. 1406) was later to confirm, the greatest scholars and pioneers in all fields of knowledge – religious and secular – were for the most part non-Arabs. Indeed, some of the most eminent were not even Muslims. From the beginning Islam was nurtured by foreigners. This fact is so frequently forgotten – where it is not deliberately overlooked – that it needs to be given greater emphasis.

There is no single aspect of Islamic life or cultural activity in which a strong foreign element is not discernible: in language, grammar, lexicography, logic, philosophy, theology, jurisprudence, administration, history, biography, geography, natural history, chemistry, physics, optics, medicine, surgery, mathematics, astronomy, architecture, music, literature and the arts. If one removed from any of these disciplines the work contributed by foreigners the best part would be gone.

The far-flung areas of the vast and heterogeneous empire whose outside influences were brought to bear on Islam are too numerous to mention in detail, and here one can attempt only a brief and unadorned outline of the contributions made to some of the features of what we call Islamic civilization.

13.1 Warfare

The ancient Arabs had domesticated the camel, and could use the bow and fight while mounted, but their great ally and defensive advantage against outside aggression was the desert.

The Greek geographer Strabo, who described the expedition of Aelius Gallus through Arabia, wrote, 'The Arabians, being mostly engaged in traffic and commerce, are not a warlike people, even on land, much less at sea. They do not make skilful use of their weapons, which are bows, spears,

swords and slings, but the greater part of them wield the double-edged axe.'
Abdul Muttalib, grandfather of Muhammad, admitted to Abraha, the Abyssinian viceroy of Himyar, that the Arabs were not skilled in warfare.

They were expert in swift raiding forays, and their own local battles, like
the famous battles of Badr and Ohod, were more in the nature of skirmishes.
But, as Islam gained ground within the Arabian peninsula, the Muslims
gradually improved their skills. Salman the Persian showed the people of
Medina the Persian method of trench fortification, for the defence of their
city, and the use of the war catapult, which Muhammad employed in the
campaign against Tayif.

Little is known about the military history of the early Arab conquests,
since the details of these victories – like those over Byzantine Syria and
Persian Iraq – were preserved orally. None of the annals was written in the
years immediately after the event (see Section 13.12), and today most are
regarded as thoroughly unreliable.

Some historians believe it unlikely that the Arabs at this time would
have had the leadership, the manpower or the equipment to achieve their
conquests unaided. They had no decisive military superiority over their
opponents, no experience of fighting in large formations, no skill in offensive
or defensive strategy, and no knowledge of the weapons of siegecraft. They
could blockade but not besiege cities.

The first foreign territories taken by the Arabs during the Medinan
caliphate were the outlying provinces of the Persian and Byzantine empires
adjacent to the Arabs' own borders, which would have constituted the main
obstacles in their path to expansion. And although both Persia and
Byzantium were already exhausted by long wars against each other, this
would not have prevented either side from now joining the Muslims to
defeat their bitter rival.

Besides, the autocratic regimes of Zoroastrian Persia and Christian
Byzantium had to a great extent lost touch with the people, in addition to
which the disaffected local populations struggled against economic hardships and social oppression. This would have left them indifferent to the
fate of their rulers and open to the lure of a new dispensation and the
egalitarian social system that appeared to go with it. They did not help to
resist and may even have welcomed their conquerors.

It has also been suggested that the initial successes of the Arabs were
due in large measure to the element of surprise caused by the suddenness of
the Arab onslaught. Often the early Muslim victories resulted from simple
swift attacks on unresisting provincial towns. Frequently the inhabitants
put up no defence, as they were quite unprepared for this new brand of
fierce and fanatical aggrandizement. Persian Iraq and then Persia itself succumbed, and the southern Byzantine provinces capitulated. Otherwise the
Byzantine empire remained virtually intact.

The Byzantine and Persian armies had been hamstrung by military hierarchies whose rigid cadres offered little scope for the emergence of military leaders outside their ranks. The Arabs, on the other hand, were not at first held back by the restraints of family background, race or caste, and were able to recruit good commanders wherever they could be found. Many Muslim conquests of this period were due to the employment of non-Arab generals, trained in foreign military establishments, who brought with them the newest military techniques.

Increasingly, too, the fighting men were hired from among non-Arab soldiers. Hordes of freebooters also joined the Muslim forces as auxiliaries, attracted by the prospect of riches and plunder. Because of their better fighting qualities, foreigners soon replaced Arabs in the ranks. According to the historian Makrizi (d. 1442), in 835 the Abbasid caliph Mutasim had the names of his Arab soldiers struck off the payrolls, and recruited Turkish mercenaries to replace them. In the long run, however, mercenaries turned out to be a blight for many Muslim states.

As the Muslim conquests progressed, the conquering armies had fewer and fewer generals and fighting men of Arabia and more and more men of Persian, Greek, Turkish, Armenian, Egyptian, Mongol, Berber, Visigoth and other foreign stock. It was indeed these races that eventually created some of the great ruling dynasties of the Muslim world.

The Muslims also built up their naval forces from the seafaring populations of Syria and Egypt, but they were never good at sea and in the course of their empire-building their fleets suffered several major reverses.

Although the Muslims had overrun most of the Persian empire in a matter of months, and within a century their territories stretched from India to the Atlantic, they were unable to take Byzantium. It remained the cynosure of covetous Muslim rulers, and over the years fresh attempts continued to be made, sometimes in small formations and sometimes with large land and naval forces, to gain that glittering prize, the Queen City of Byzantium.

In 670 the Omayyad caliph Muawiya tried to besiege Constantinople through the Dardanelles, and maintained pressure for seven years, but failed in his objective and had to retire after severe losses.

In 716 another Omayyad caliph, Suleiman led an army of eighty thousand men and eighteen hundred ships and laid siege to the capital for a full year during the reign of the emperor Leo III, 'the Isaurian'. The Byzantines had a powerful incendiary substance called Greek fire, developed in AD 668 by Callincus of Heliopolis, and this caused devastation and immense losses of men, ships and equipment. The caliph was said to have died of frustration, grief and shame.

In the meantime Byzantium was also engaged in lengthy wars with the Avars, Slavs, Serbs, Bulgars, Magyars, Seljuks and others, often involving onslaughts against the capital, which increasingly eroded its capacity to resist. In 1204, during the Fourth Crusade, the Crusaders themselves – mainly French and Venetians – invaded and looted Constantinople and set fire to part of the city, leaving it in smouldering ruins, thus dealing a mortal wound to the last great Christian empire in the East, though it survived, if feebly, for two and a half centuries more.

Throughout this period the Muslim armies never desisted from their attacks on the capital. It was not till well over seven hundred years had passed since the first attempt had been made by Muawiya, when Byzantium had lost all her outlying provinces and the once huge empire had virtually ceased to exist, having miserably shrunk to little more than the area immediately surrounding the shell of Constantinople, that the city was finally taken in 1453 by the Ottomans.

13.2 Nationalism

Muhammad spoke of the Arabs as the best nation in all mankind (3:106), and as the Arabs gained more territory the caliph Omar proudly declared, 'The Lord hath given us of Arab blood victories and great conquests.'

Islam was regarded essentially as the religion of the conquering Arabs, intended principally for those who were of Arab race, living in and around the Arabian peninsula and speaking the Arabic language. For long, Muslims of Arab origin tended to regard themselves as the aristocrats of the Muslim world. They formed a class apart, dominant over all others. Islam to them meant an Arab hegemony in which the Arabs ruled supreme. A non-Arab convert could not be considered a full Muslim, nor a non-Muslim a full Arab.

Full status was accorded only to those who were free (not slave), male (not female), Arab (not non-Arab) and Muslim (not non-Muslim). During some of the early internecine hostilities in the peninsula, prisoners of Arab blood were freed and those of foreign blood slain. Even slaves, if of Arab descent, were given their liberty on payment of a small token ransom, a privilege denied to non-Arabs. Distinctions were made between Arab Muslims, Arab non-Muslims, non-Arab Muslims and non-Arab infidels.

Sometimes the better classes among the conquered converts who were influential in their own lands were permitted to secure an honorary quasi-Arab status by affiliating themselves as 'clients' (mawali; singular mawla) to some Arab patron, if they could find one. But even the mawali, including the foreign mercenary generals who fought Arabs' wars, were denied the full privileges of Arab Muslims.

The conversion of non-Arab populations was part of the Arab endeavour, but certain problems arose for the conquerors as the Arab empire spread, since conversion frequently became a means of avoiding the burden of extra taxation exacted from the unconverted. The Arabs did not care to share the prerogatives of conquest, or be deprived of the substantial tax revenues payable by 'outsiders'. A special tax system was therefore evolved.

All Muslims, Arab and non-Arab alike, were required to pay an income or property tax (*zakat*); this was a form of mandatory almsgiving, and one of the five basic duties of the Islamic faith (23:4). The term 'zakat' occurs in one Koranic passage in relation to the Mosaic covenant (2:77) and is said to have no satisfactory etymology. It is of Aramaic origin, and was used before Islam for the obligatory contributions made for charitable purposes in Jewish and Christian communities (Jeffery, 1938, p. 153).

This tax is to be distinguished from the voluntary alms (*sadaka*) given to the poor by all Muslims, which is considered very meritorious. This word too is of Aramaic origin, and was used by Jews and Christians for donations to charity. There was also an additional land tax (*kharaj* – again a word of Aramaic origin), which had to be paid by non-Arabs, both Muslims and non-Muslims.

Finally, there was the extra poll tax (*jizya*) imposed on all infidels and bitterly resented as a levy of servitude. The large-scale conversion of non-Arab communities, however, resulted in massive tax losses, seriously affecting the state revenue, so non-Arab Muslims were sometimes obliged to pay the poll tax required of non-Muslims.

Inevitably, the disadvantages suffered by the barbarian (*ajam*) or non-Arab converts under such a policy of racial exclusiveness created bitter disaffection in their ranks. Popular resentment at being deprived of the equal status that had been promised them under a Muslim dispensation gave rise to a number of people's (*shuubiya*) movements in various parts of the Muslim world, some ending in armed rebellion.

From demanding equality (*taswiya*) with the Arabs, the subject nations went on to the 'vaunting' (*tafdil*) of their own national heritage, asserting their right to go their own way as dictated by the imperatives of their race, history and culture. The dissidents further strengthened their position by publicly deriding the pretensions of the Arab 'tent-dwellers', their cultural shortcomings, their dependence on non-Arabs for their conquests and the administration of their territories.

The champions of the various traditionalist causes were of diverse origin, including Bactrians and Greeks. One of the most formidable, a Koranic exegete and philologist named Abu Obayda (d. 875) was of Nabataean – some say Jewish – stock. The shuubiya polemicists of Iraq, Palestine and Egypt boasted of their nations' great achievements, as compared with the paltry accomplishments of the Arabs of the peninsula.

The most strident exponents of the shuubiya cause were the anti-Arab chauvinists of Persia, who declared they had more reason than the Arabs to be proud of their ancestry and to glory in their history, their literature and their learning. The conquests of their forbears were more extensive and against greater adversaries than those of the Arabs. They claimed for themselves the credit for everything of value in Muslim culture.

They alleged that the tribal genealogies of the Arabs were fabricated and when scrutinized revealed links through dubious marriages or the taint of slave blood. From their own records the proud bedouin aristocrats were seen to be of mixed descent and of partly Jewish stock.

They portrayed the Arabs as sheep-herders, camel-drivers, 'desert-squatters' (Persian *sahara-nishin*, whence 'Saracen') and lizard-eaters, and denounced the 'sodomites and pathics' among the Koraysh (Thaalibi, 1968, p. 25). The Arabs, they said, were a wild, uncouth and uncivilized people, and it was from the Persians that they had acquired what they knew of manners (*adab*).

The shuubiya movement clearly demonstrates that the various Islamic nations have never represented one unified community (*umma*: Aramaic, 'nation'). The Koran, the fast of Ramadan and the pilgrimage serve as the most tenuous of bonds. The Muslims are separated by many factors at least as powerful as the religion that holds them loosely together. Ethnic differences, regional histories and the compelling attraction of indigenous social, linguistic and cultural ties militate against the emergence of any enduring pan-Islamic union.

The vast majority of Muslims are not Arabs, and have their own distinctive traditions and way of life. The people of the Maghrib (Libya, Tunis, Algeria and Morocco) are not of Arab stock, and the Berbers have a long history of resistance to Arab attempts at domination. The Negroes and other Hamitic peoples of Africa represent strongly nationalist non-Arab elements. The same applies to the Egyptians, Persians, Afghans and Turks, as well as the Uzbek, Tadzhik and other races of Central Asia. The Kurds of Iraq, Syria, Turkey and Iran are said to be descended from the ancient Medes. The Muslims of the Indian subcontinent and Indonesia – mainly converts once having Hindu, Buddhist or animist beliefs – are of widely mixed ethnic stock.

Finally, the presence of influential non-Muslim minorities within Muslim countries adds another item to the complex problems faced by Islam. Almost 10 per cent of the Egyptian population are Copts, who are Christians. In the Lebanon more than half the population are Christians. In Syria and Jordan, too, Christians still form rich and influential minorities.

In the view of some scholars these anomalies do not constitute an Arab problem. Throughout their history the Arabs have tended to go their own way. They have, with few exceptions, always been and continue to be more deeply race-proud than religion-orientated. Religious extremism has generally been shown to characterize the non-Arab states of the Islamic world. For their part, the Arabs feel they are a distinct people with a great history and a rich heritage of their own, and quite a few see the Arab past as Arab rather than Islamic.

Just as a European might write a plausible history of Europe without reference to Christianity, so, it is said, a history of the Arab people could be written that is independent of the Muslim religion. Indeed, a project on these lines was launched in Baghdad in 1989 (Akhtar, 1989, p. 84).

13.3 Miscegenation

The intermarriage of Muslims – Arab and non-Arab – with women belonging to other faiths and races was an important factor contributing to the dilution of religious dogmatism and the assimilation of alien elements into the structure of Islamic civilization.

Such intermarriages had started from the very inception of Islam, with the Prophet himself taking into his household women of assorted pagan tribes, as well as a Jewish wife and Christian and Jewish concubines.

As the Islamic empire spread further into Persian and Byzantine territories, the practice of Muslims marrying Christians, Jews, Zoroastrians and Buddhists became more widespread, because of the generally higher standard of education and culture and perhaps the relatively exotic physical appeal of non-Arab women. Many of the Muslim upper classes – including the caliphs, administrators and theologians – had very involved genealogies, being the product of a miscegenative process, through both wives and concubines, that was constantly going on. Because of the secrecy with which the harem archives were maintained, and the change of names undergone by the new female entrants, whether as wives or concubines, it is not always easy to trace the genealogy of children born within the seraglio.

The conversion of the non-Muslim woman was not always a precondition of such unions, and even when conversion did occur it did not necessarily mean the complete abandonment by the woman of her original faith, so a strong undercurrent of non-Muslim beliefs, traditions and cultural influences was carried over and can be presumed in such households.

Nayla bint al-Furafisa, a Christian of the Kalb tribe, was the wife of the third caliph, Othman, and was said to have lost three fingers in trying to defend her husband against his assassins.

Husayn, son of the caliph Ali, married one of the daughters of Yazdagird III, the last Sassanian (Zoroastrian) king of Persia. Their son was Zaynul Abedin, the fourth imam of the Shias. The linkage of old Persian families with the Shia imams and with leaders of the Shia community became customary from the start, and continued for some time.

The intermarriage of members of the Omayyad dynasty of Damascus with Christian women of the Syrian and at times Byzantine nobility met with some opposition from the pious in Medina.

The wife of Muawiya, the first Omayyad caliph, was Maysun bint Bahdal, a Christian from the tribe of Kalb. She and her father and family remained Christians, and she was gifted by her husband with a church in Damascus. She became the mother of the notorious caliph Yazid I whose drunken habits were in large measure attributed by the orthodox to the Christian background of his mother's family.

The Omayyads did not disclaim their mixed antecedents. The twelfth caliph, Yazid III, boasting about his lineage used to say, 'I am descended from the Persian emperor; and both the emperors of Byzantium and the khans of the Turks were my ancestors.' (The Byzantine line itself was often linked with other royal dynasties, from Sicily to Inner Asia. It was believed, for instance, that the Byzantine emperor Nicephorus I (d. 811) was of Arab extraction.)

Few of the Abbasid caliphs were of pure Arab blood. In tracing their ethnic origins the Baghdad scholar Ibn Habib (d. 860) showed that almost all had non-Arab – mostly Persian, often Zoroastrian – mothers. Many were born of slave women of foreign blood. Only three Abbasid caliphs were born of free mothers. Mansur (d. 775) was the son of a Persian slave, Mamun (d. 833) of a Berber woman; Wathik (d. 847) and Muktadir (d. 932) had Greek mothers. The mother of Muntasir (d. 862) was a Turkish maidservant.

Obaydulla, the founder of the Fatimid dynasty, was said to have had both Jewish and Zoroastrian antecedents, and the succeeding members of the dynasty were also very thoroughly mixed. Aziz, the fifth Fatimid caliph, married a Christian woman whose two brothers, Jeremiah and Arvenius, he made patriarchs of Jerusalem and Alexandria.

The high culture attained by the Muslims in Spain has been ascribed, among other things, to the frequent intermarriage between Muslims and Christians. The conqueror of Morocco and parts of southern Spain, Musa ibn Nosayr, was a descendant of a Christian from the Bali tribe of Palestine. Musa's son Abdul Aziz married Egilona, the widow of the Visigoth king Roderick.

The Berbers who accompanied Tarik across to Gibraltar and made their home in Spain were said to have 'intermarried freely' with the native population. And the early conquests of the Spanish mainland were achieved largely with troops from the once Christian tribes of Kalb, who became prominent in Cordoba and Granada, and of Kayis in Seville and Valencia.

Berbers, Arabs and Syrians mixed freely with the local populations of Slavs, Franks, Visigoths and Vandals, and from the beginning 'fair-haired ladies from the northern territories were highly regarded' (Lalaguna, 1990, p. 25). By the tenth century miscegenation had inextricably mixed their blood.

Throughout the Iberian peninsula the Muslim ruling classes, nobility, scholars, theologians and men of letters and learning were almost all of mixed blood. The Mozarabs, or Arabized Christians, who played such a significant part in the spread of learning and artistic skills, were often of mixed origin.

The great Omayyad caliph of Cordoba Abdul Rahman IV (d. 961), who had red hair and blue eyes and was equally fluent in Arabic and the Romance language, was a typical hybrid of Andalusia, with a half-Arab father and a Frank mother. His grandmother Princess Iniga was the daughter of King Fortun Garces of Pamplona. Another Omayyad caliph of Cordoba, Hisham II (d. 1013), was the son of a Basque woman.

The Ottoman line of Turkey was so mixed with Greek, Armenian and Slav stock, not to mention Jewish and other 'blood', that there was hardly a pure-Turkish ruler, vizier or nobleman left by the seventeenth century. The Ottoman chief Orkhan, the second sultan of the line, married a daughter of the Byzantine emperor John V. Palaeologus. In 1366 his successor, Murat I, married the sister of the Bulgarian king Shishman III. Murat's son and successor, Bayazit I – also known as Bajazet, who was to be defeated by the Mongol emperor Timur (Tamerlane) and allegedly carried about in a cage – married a Christian woman, Lady Despoina, sister of the ruler of Serbia. Greek, Armenian, Slav and other foreign wives and concubines filled the seraglios of all the succeeding sultans.

A similar process of miscegenation took place among the nobility. It was said that only seventy-eight of the 292 grand viziers of the Ottoman empire could claim Turkish parentage.

In India, Mongol, Turkish, Persian and above all Hindu lines were amalgamated to form the great dynasty of the Mughals. (The Muslim populations of the Indian subcontinent are virtually all of Hindu stock.) During the same period European and Eurasian women were often to be found in the harems of the Mughal rulers and the nobility (Dover, 1937, p. 121), being largely favoured because of their fair skin and delicate beauty.

The mother of Shah Ismail, founder of the most famous of the post-Islamic dynasties of Persia, the Safavid (1499–1736), was Princess Martha (Halima Alamshah Begum), descended from the Commeni emperors of Christian Trebizond (1204–1461).

From such material as is available it is clear that from North Africa to Central Asia the rulers of the Muslim dynasties and the scions of the great houses of the Muslim aristocracy married women of the native ruling families or took as wives women of the conquered territories, and often chose women of European origin to 'improve the colour' – that is, the complexion – of the dynastic line.

By this time miscegenation had become so ubiquitous as hardly to be worth the labour of noting. In any case, the instances already cited – which could be endlessly multiplied – may be accepted as illustrating a trend that went on throughout Muslim history, both during and after the period of Islamic colonial expansion.

Medieval legend has furnished several examples of the love between Christian and Muslim, one of the best known being the thirteenth-century romance of Count Aucassin and the beautiful Saracen captive Nicolette. The historical scene was also fictionalized to add its quota of tales about the mixed origins of some notable heroes. Thus Imaduddin Zangi, a Turkish officer of the Seljuk army who carved out a principality for himself in Mesopotamia and northern Syria, and captured Edessa from the Crusaders in 1144, was alleged to be of Christian birth, as was Killij Arslan (d. 1178), the Seljuk sultan who played a significant role in the affairs of the Turkoman dynasty of Danishmend in north-east Anatolia.

To account for his chivalry amongst a people regarded as notorious for their bigotry and barbarism, medieval Christendom gave the great Saladin a Christian mother – the Countess of Ponthieu – who had been shipwrecked on the Egyptian coast.

Thomas à Becket (d. 1170), archbishop of Canterbury, martyr and saint, was credited with having a Saracen mother, although he was known to have been of Norman parentage.

13.4 Administration

With little understanding of the complexities of state management on a multinational scale, the Arabs had perforce to fall back on the knowledge of trained men already in position, and these experts in their respective fields naturally carried on in the traditions with which they were familiar.

Omar I, the second caliph, appreciating the merits of a fully functioning administrative machinery already in place, instructed his provincial governors to continue with the Byzantine and Sassanian procedures and not to attempt any radical changes (Zakaria, 1989, p. 48).

Under the Omayyads, Hellenistic and Sassanian influences continued more energetically than ever to shape the governing institutions of the emergent Arab empire. In its administration, says Bernard Lewis, the Omayyad caliphate 'was not so much an Arab state, as a Persian and Byzantine succession state' (1966, p. 66).

The principal government offices and many key departments of the caliphate were headed by Christians and Jews from the once-Greek and Byzantine dominions. When Omar II – the only Omayyad caliph respected by the orthodox – later tried to remove all Jews and Christians from government service, because the Koran warned the faithful against them (5:56), so much confusion ensued that the order had to be rescinded.

Several caliphs employed Christian secretaries or counsellors. Sarjun (Sergius) ibn Mansur (d. 684) was the chief secretary and trusted adviser of Muawiya, and continued as secretary to three other Omayyad caliphs. Sarjun's son, the famous Syrian theologian John of Damascus, represented Christians at the court of the caliphs, who often sought his advice.

The members of the Christian family of Banu Wahab (some of whom became Muslim) served as secretaries to the Omayyads and went on to work under several Abbasid caliphs, to form the longest unbroken chain of succession in any family holding the same office. By the time the Abbasid dynasty took over, many Christian posts were secure even against some of the more fanatical rulers. Fazl ibn Marwan, secretary of the caliph Mutasim, was a Christian who also later embraced Islam. Stephanus (d. 935) became secretary to the Abbasid caliph Muktadir.

In general, the Abbasids favoured the Persians and brought in changes on Sassanian models, which were denounced by the orthodox as alien and anti-Islamic. On the model of the Persian *divan* or bureau, the caliph set up bureaux dealing with finance, taxes, the police and the navy.

Borrowing from the Sassanians, the Abbasids also introduced the office of vizier (Persian, 'helper') or prime minister. This term was once thought to be of Arabic origin, because it appears in the Koran for Aaron as the 'helper' of Moses (25:37), but it is now known to be of Pahlavi (Middle Persian) derivation. The most notable of the early Abbasid viziers came from the Barmecide family, mentioned in the *Arabian Nights*.

At first the language of government communication was dual, the local language being used side by side with Arabic. In Syria, official documents were issued bilingually, in Greek as well as Arabic; in Palestine, Aramaic and Arabic; in Egypt, Coptic and Arabic; in Persia, Pahlavi and Arabic. In AD 690, during the reign of Abdul Malik, the official language was declared to be Arabic, but for several decades thereafter Arabic and the local languages continued to be used together.

To bring their ever-expanding empire into the framework of a cohesive organization, for more efficient supervision and control, the Omayyads hired Byzantine engineers to map out and build a comprehensive highway system (*barid*). This involved the extension of an already existing network of roads and bridges in the former Byzantine territories to link together all points of the caliphate, which soon began to be dotted with imperial outposts. Here fresh horses stood ready to carry relays of messengers, so that rulers could be kept quickly informed of developments in the provinces. The existence of these depots also facilitated the assessment and collection of taxes.

In the pre-Islamic states of Mesopotamia, Syria and Persia, the management of state accounts was almost always left to the local Jews or Christians. The financial advisers to the later Sassanians were generally Christians, the most notable being Yazden (fl. c. 620), the high treasurer of Khosro II. When the Omayyad caliphs took over they again had to fall back on the existing financial structure and retained the services of this community.

Usury (*riba*), or all forms of gain or interest on loans, was forbidden in Islam. In the Koran, those who engaged in usury were said to be infected by the touch of Satan and were condemned to hell, where they would abide for ever (2:276). Because of this, farmers and traders who needed loans were forced to resort to non-Muslim moneylenders.

The result was that the financial houses were invariably in the hands of Jews and Christians, many of whom enjoyed a reputation for their efficiency in handling trading transactions across the empire. Often these banks had connections with financial establishments outside the caliphate as well, and thus helped in the international exchange of goods and the large-scale organization of commerce.

For many years the coinage circulating in the early Muslim countries remained Greek, Byzantine or Roman. Coins with the owl of Athens were current in southern Arabia till some time after the Arab conquest. The Alexandrian merchant and traveller, and later monk, Cosmas Indicopleustes (d. 560) wrote that the most excellent Roman coins in universal use in his day were regarded with admiration by men of all kingdoms, and with their aid 'trade is carried on from one extremity of the earth to the other'. Similarly, Byzantine currency was widely used in the areas once governed by the Byzantines and even beyond, and remained legal tender for many decades, circulating freely in the caliphate.

From about 690, during the reign of Abdul Malik, a new style of coinage began to be minted in Damascus, using the earlier models: the gold *dinar* from the Byzantine denarius; the silver *dirham* from the Byzantine drachma; and the copper *fuloos* or *fils* after the Byzantine *follis*.

13.5 Architecture

The Arabs of the Hejaz had a very meagre building tradition, and even the Kaaba, the most venerated of the Arab shrines, was a plain rectangular structure of simple design and construction. When it was destroyed by fire and flood in AD 594 it was rebuilt by a Coptic Christian workman.

Muhammad himself was opposed to building on a grand scale. He once said, 'Truly the most unprofitable thing that eats up the wealth of a believer is building' (Hughes, 1977, p. 178). He did not think that vast and costly structures were necessary. 'Every expense of the believer will be rewarded,' he said, 'except the expense of building.' Great edifices, however imposing and durable they might appear, were ephemeral creations and were not worth the money and time spent on raising them.

He disliked arches and similar elaborations and all forms of architectural embellishments. Both the mosque at Koba and the Prophet's mosque in Medina – the first and second mosques ever built – were primitive structures, made of rough stone, unbaked bricks and clay, with palm-stick roofs supported on trunks of date trees. Rain used to drip into the mosque in Medina, and the floor would be filled with muddy water. When asked whether the roof should be repaired the Prophet replied, 'No. A mosque should be simple and modest, a booth, like the booth of Moses.' The mosque was left in that state until his death.

Hardly anything we associate with the architecture of the mosque today – cupola, arches, minaret, pulpit, niche – is rooted in the time of Muhammad. The very word for mosque, *masjid*, is an Arabic rendering of the Aramaic *masgeda* (O'Leary, 1927, p. 200) used by Christians for their 'place of prayer'.

Muhammad used to preach or lead the services at the Medina mosque while leaning on a palm-tree post. When standing began to tire him, one of his followers suggested, 'Shall I make a pulpit [minbar] for you, such as I have seen in the churches in Syria?' Muhammad agreed, and a raised pulpit was built in the Prophet's mosque by a Byzantine carpenter. It consisted of two steps and a seat. A later hadith sought to forbid the use of the minbar, since it was based on the Christian pulpit and represented an inheritance from the church. The first pulpit built in Egypt provoked a scandal and was destroyed by order of the caliph.

In the Prophet's mosque in Medina a large black stone placed against the base of the northern wall, facing Jerusalem, indicated the direction (kibla) in which people had to turn during prayers, but when the direction was changed by the Prophet the stone was moved to the wall on the southern side, to face Mecca. During the reign of the Omayyad caliph Walid I an innovation was introduced in the shape of a niche cut into the wall of the mosque to indicate the approved direction. This too at first met with fierce opposition from the orthodox, since both the niche and the word for it (mihrab) were taken from Christian usage. In the early church the mihrab was a small alcove, made to hold the bust or small statue of a Christian saint.

In Muhammad's time the call to prayer used to be made by a caller walking the streets, or from the top of a building, such as the roof of the Kaaba. The Omayyads introduced the minaret (manara) for this purpose as an adjunct to the mosque on the analogy of the tower (manar, 'light turret') that once formed part of the Christian church. In this tower a lamp used to be kept constantly burning. The word manara is cognate with the Syriac menarta, and the Hebrew menorah, meaning candlestick.

The first minaret was erected in AD 705, again during the reign of Walid I, and was followed by others. In many places there was initial resistance to the idea of raising the minaret higher than the walls of the mosque, but before long many mosques had a minaret that towered even above the dome. This is now found to be almost universal.

Many other features typically associated with Muslim architecture came from outside the Muslim world. The dome originated in Asia Minor before being adopted by the Byzantines and then the Muslims (Strzygowski, 1923, p. 27). The vaulting system was derived from an ancient bricklaying technique in pre-Islamic Persia. From the Sassanian palace-builders the Arabs acquired the squinch, a structural device which made it possible to erect a dome over a square space. The capitals of Muslim columns were designed on models provided by the architects of classical antiquity.

The horseshoe arch was copied from the Buddhist architecture of Turkestan. The semicircular and pointed arches came from Sassanian Iran via Syria, into both Europe and the Arab dominions. The cusped arch originated in Buddhist India. The multiple niche, sometimes found on the inner curve of arches and the underside of domes, was also taken from the Buddhist architecture of Central Asia.

Much else of what we now associate with the Muslim city was already in existence in the Middle East before the Muslim era, and an abundance of architectural styles and techniques from pre-Islamic and non-Islamic traditions – Mesopotamian, Hellenistic, Roman, Sassanian, Central Asian and Byzantine – came into the Islamic inheritance. Great palaces and opulent villas, temples and churches, and public and private buildings of every variety and for every purpose, fully formed and with a multitude of details, served as prototypes to be copied or adapted by the conquerors.

These included imposing entrances and magnificent façades; complex interiors, cloistered ambulatories, colonnaded chambers, internal courtyards and audience rooms; vaulted halls leading out into open spaces; formal gardens; arcades to provide shade and shelter from the sun; lattice-work screens and windows to reduce glare; towers and pavilions, as well as dozens of lesser facilities for public use like hostelries, poorhouses, public squares, market enclosures (the *suk* or covered bazaar area was a commonplace in the Middle East from Babylonian times); wells, fountains and aqueducts; and public bathhouses, an inheritance from the Roman *thermae* or *balnaea* – all of which soon became part of the architectural scene of the Islamic world.

Elaborating on the vast wealth of material, both secular and religious, from the building traditions of the different regions of their empire, the Muslims wrought their architectural masterpieces from Granada to Delhi in what is broadly called the Saracenic style. The older exemplars before them were utilized in full measure – altered in the case of mosques only for specific ritual activities to suit the needs of the worshippers.

In the light of this it would be true to say that, apart from the modifications demanded by the exigencies of religious usage, many of the features that have contributed to the beauty of Islamic buildings are not intrinsically Islamic at all, and that the architecture of the Middle East – along with the colourful pageant of eastern life – would have evolved much along the lines it did whatever the political or religious history of the region might have been.

For long it was Byzantium, which itself owed much to its Hellenistic legacy and its pagan neighbours, that remained the focus of wonder and the chief source of inspiration to the caliphate. When Abdul Rahman II (d. 796) of Cordoba decided to build the finest mosque in the world he called in architects from distant Byzantium to superintend its construction.

It is known that certain elements of Byzantine architecture, in particular the dome-centred types of building like the church of St Sophia (AD 537) in Constantinople, left a lasting impact on Muslim building styles centuries before the capture of that city in 1453. One traveller, who visited

Constantinople in the fourteenth century, declared in an excess of enthusiasm that compared with that great metropolis Baghdad had nothing to recommend it but its bathhouses, bakeries and brothels.

The first to benefit from the rich legacy of the past were the Omayyads. They had come into possession of a great building tradition, and they set about beautifying their capital of Damascus and other cities in Syria and elsewhere with hundreds of structures in sumptuous style. The Dome of the Rock in Jerusalem was built with the help of Byzantine architects. Some Omayyad mosques, also built with the aid of Christian craftsmen, were adorned with silver and gold in an attempt to rival the splendours of Christian cathedrals in Constantinople.

The great mosque in Damascus was raised on the site of the basilica of St John the Baptist, parts of which were incorporated into the mosque. The basilica itself had stood on the site of an earlier Roman temple, which again was the last of a succession of pagan fanes built on the same spot down the ages. The interior of the Damascus mosque has aisles and transepts like a Christian church, and its decorations in marble mosaic were the handiwork of Byzantine artisans.

Under the Abbasids the Byzantine style was partly replaced by the Sassanian (Persian) style, and together these two great streams – the Byzantine and Sassanian – continued to nourish the Muslim creative endeavour. No fresh contributions seem to have been made to Islamic architecture at this stage, until further innovations began to be devised, first by the Mughals of India and then by the Ottoman Turks.

Mughal architecture was a mixture of styles ranging from Central Asian to Hindu. From Constantinople the emperor Babur (d. 1530) invited the pupils of a famous Albanian architect to work on his mosques and monuments. An Indian authority, Dr Kalikinkar Datta, is of the opinion that the mausoleum of Akbar (d. 1605) near Agra was influenced by the Khmer architects of Cambodia and that it was actually their work.

Mughal rulers filled the country with scores of costly monuments, few of any public utility, such as elaborate victory columns, showpiece forts in red sandstone, and lavish marble tombs. Even a town like Fatehpur Sikri, which was built complete with palaces, gateways, baths, mosques, and public and private residences, was abandoned after completion. These follies were raised at the expense of an overtaxed people and an underpaid labour force.

The experts and craftsmen responsible for the planning and building of the Taj Mahal came from Cairo, Baghdad, Shiraz, Samarkand, Balkh and Kandahar. It is thought that European architects may also have had a hand in its construction (Majumdar, 1948, p. 596). From the memoirs of European diplomats, artists, travellers, traders and savants – French, Dutch, English, Portuguese, Italian – who visited India at this time and wrote some of the finest accounts we have of that period, we know the Mughal emperors were kept up to date with the latest advances being made in Europe.

The story that a Venetian named Jerome Veroneo chose the marble of the Taj for its texture and sensitivity to light, and had a hand in designing the building, is rejected by some authorities (Rawlinson, 1954, p. 361) but is worth bearing in mind. Muslim pride in their own masterpiece would naturally suppress any hint of foreign intervention. Yet even in the Muslim records the principal designer and chief architect of the Taj Mahal – who came from Constantinople – was known as Ustad Isa, which in literal translation means Master Jesus.

It was not till the Ottoman Turks had reached the zenith of their power, in the sixteenth century, that a Christian-born builder created the Ottoman style of architecture. Of its several important innovations, many again derived from Central Asian and Byzantine models.

This prodigy, the greatest of Islamic architects, was Yusuf (Joseph) Mimar (Architect) Sinan, known as Sinan the Great, the son of Greek Orthodox parents. His father was a carpenter, stonemason and master-builder who taught the young Sinan the techniques of his craft. As a consequence of the Ottoman custom of taking talented Christian youths into state employment, Sinan's genius as a draughtsman and builder caught the attention of the Ottoman ruler, and at the age of twenty-four he was recruited and put to work.

Sinan was responsible for Ottoman 'classical architecture'. He completed over 250 projects, including palaces, royal lodges, colleges, *madrasahs* (religious schools), libraries, hospitals, mosques, aqueducts, public baths, tombs, caravanserais, hostels, almshouses, granaries and fountains. Many of them rank among the most exquisite in the Muslim world. His most important works were the mosque of Suleiman the Magnificent in Constantinople, based on the design of the St Sophia, and the mosque of Selim II, Suleiman's son, at Edirne (Adrianople), based on the model of a Byzantine church.

Sinan's building style inspired the Ottoman architects who came after him, and is seen reflected in all the major buildings built or reconstructed by the Ottoman Turks wherever they extended their huge empire, including the holy cities of Mecca and Medina.

13.6 The Holy Cities

The Medinan caliphs Omar and Othman called in Christian engineers to build dykes, canals and embankments to counteract the calamitous floods that periodically damaged the Kaaba. To encourage agricultural development in the Hejaz, the Omayyads also sent for Greek engineers to construct wells and reservoirs to conserve and provide water (O'Leary, 1927, p. 8).

In general, however, the Omayyads neglected the holy cities of Mecca and Medina (together known as the Haramayn). They referred to the tradition – recorded by the chronicler al-Zuhri – according to which

Muhammad had spoken of Mecca, Medina and Jerusalem as being of equal value but himself esteemed Jerusalem above the others.

Ruling from Damascus, away from the centre of Muhammad's ministry, they tried to give Jerusalem a status higher than that of the other two cities. Besides, Jerusalem was easier to reach and control than Mecca or Medina. Muawiya, the first Omayyad caliph, chose to have himself proclaimed ruler in Jerusalem, and the fifth Omayyad caliph, Abdul Malik, sought to promote Jerusalem as a new religious centre and a substitute place of pilgrimage.

It was contended that Jerusalem was the site of Mount Moriah, upon which lay the sacred rock (sakhra) – fifty-six feet long, forty-two feet wide and almost semicircular – where Abraham, tested by God, made ready to sacrifice his son Isaac. (In another Arab tradition this is supposed to have taken place not on Mount Moriah but on Mount Thabir, near Mecca.)

Further, it was on Mount Moriah that David had raised an altar, and here Solomon had levelled a great terrace to build his temple. Upon the summit of the same Noble Sanctuary (Haram al-Sharif) there also stood the 'more remote' (al-aksa) mosque marking Muhammad's famous ascent to heaven. After he conquered Jerusalem in 638, the caliph Omar had a small wooden mosque erected at the south end of the terrace, on the site of the Byzantine church of St Mary built by Justinian, believing it to have been the site of Muhammad's ascent, although no one is clear about the precise location. Again, Jerusalem and not Mecca was the kibla to which the early Muslims first turned to pray.

In 680 the caliph Abdul Malik commissioned Byzantine architects to build over the sacred rock an edifice known today as the Dome of the Rock (Kobat al-Sakhra), on the site traditionally regarded as that of Solomon's temple. He proclaimed that the circumambulation of the new shrine was just as meritorious as a circuit around the Kaaba. In contrast to the anticlockwise circuit of the Kaaba, the Dome was to be circumambulated in a clockwise direction, keeping the shrine on the right. At the same time the caliph also issued an edict forbidding pilgrims from visiting the sepulchre of the Prophet in Medina.

The rotunda of the edifice has an octagonal base, and is modelled on Byzantine examples, such as the Church of the Holy Sepulchre. The Dome itself is of timber, covered on the inside with stucco, gilded and ornamented, and on the outside with lead. This had originally itself been covered in gold leaf, but when this was stolen it was re-covered in a gleaming aluminium–gold alloy, making it a landmark of the holy city. Almost all the columns and capitals come from Byzantine and late Roman buildings, and some still have the original crosses on them. The diadems and breastplates in the mosaic decorations are Christian in conception.

The Dome of the Rock is believed to contain a footprint of Muhammad

(Christians claimed it was the footprint of Jesus), as well as a hair from the Prophet's beard. The Dome is not a mosque and is not intended to mark the site of Muhammad's miraculous experience.

Nor far from the Dome of the Rock stands the Dome of the Ascent (Kobat al-Miraj), and it is this lesser building that, according to some, marks the actual place from where the Prophet was translated to heaven.

In 712 the Omayyad caliph Walid had the first wooden mosque of Omar torn down, and commissioned Byzantine architects and master craftsmen to build another mosque in its stead. This was the Al-Aksa mosque, which is also said to stand on the exact spot whence Muhammad mounted heavenwards. Behind the pulpit of the mosque is a stone taken from the Church of the Ascension which is alleged to bear the footprint of the ascending Christ. Walid set over this mosque a dome of brass, removed from a Christian church in Baalbek (ancient Heliopolis, in Lebanon). After its destruction in an earthquake, the mosque was rebuilt in 780 with a silvered dome by the Abbasid caliph Mahdi.

While they were beautifying Damascus and Jerusalem, the Omayyads left the Arabian peninsula to revert to its primitive tribal ways, and within thirty years of the Prophet's death Arabia had become an outlying province of the Omayyad caliphate, a centre of pilgrimage and nothing more. By about 680 the religious life of Mecca had come virtually to an end. Vices of every kind were openly practised, and the moral environment of the pilgrimage had sunk to its lowest levels. Banquets were given and liquor was sold in the mosques.

Medina fared no better. In contrast to the honour in which Medina had been held by the Prophet, the Omayyads dubbed the town 'the stinking' (al-natna) and 'the filthy' (al-khabita). It soon became a place of notoriety, a sybaritic haven of pleasure and ease, with singing girls and slaves, courtesans and catamites, drinking and opium gardens and brothels. Among the patrons who frequented these places were to be found the sons of the companions of the Prophet.

The neglect of the holy cities and the sacrileges the Omayyads allowed to be committed there, as well as the excesses in Damascus at the court of the drunkard and profligate Yazid I, exasperated the pietists of Medina and Mecca, and between 682 and 690 a series of insurrections took place. The rebels in Medina were crushed by the caliph's Syrian soldiers, who massacred them, plundered the other townsfolk, and turned the mosque into a stable. For a time the holy city was the haunt of wild beasts (Ameer Ali, 1965, p. 303).

The uprisings in Mecca were put down with equal ferocity. The Omayyad's Syrian infantry brought in huge siege catapults to hurl missiles at the Kaaba, one of which broke the Black Stone into three pieces (Esin, 1983, p. 134). In a fire that swept through the enclosure, large parts of the Kaaba were destroyed. The shrine was in danger of collapse – so much so, it was said, that if the doves of the Kaaba flew over the place it would have brought the whole structure tumbling down.

Order was imposed with great severity by Hajaj ibn Yusuf, who was later promoted by the caliph Abdul Malik to become the viceroy of Iraq. For his part in the Mecca uprising the governor of Mecca, Abdulla ibn Zubayr – the son of Asma, daughter of Abu Bakr, the first caliph – was executed in 691 and his head was exhibited at the city gate.

When the Omayyads did eventually turn their attention to the work of restoring the holy cities, the first step was to carry out a scheme involving the demolition of the earlier buildings. And this they did with remorseless efficiency. It seemed as though they were trying to alter beyond recognition, if not completely obliterate, the original landmarks made sacrosanct by association with the Prophet.

The ensuing reconstruction was planned on new and alien lines, so that the character of both the cities underwent a radical transformation. The fact that the tribespeople of the Hejaz had no building tradition of their own provided an excuse for the Omayyads to import into the holy cities hundreds of workers from foreign, including Christian, countries.

In place of the old hallowed shrines, the Omayyads raised new structures in a style at variance with the spirit of Islam and deeply offensive to the people. Some of the columns around the Kaaba itself long bore the signs of Greek workmanship. Islam's first mosque in Koba, which Muhammad himself had had a hand in building, was enlarged, then razed and another and more ornate one built in its place. The opulence of the Omayyad innovations was such that the Arabs complained that their sacred places had been turned into churches.

The Prophet's mosque in Medina was pulled down for rebuilding by the caliph Walid I, regardless of popular protests. During the preliminary demolition work, the external walls of Muhammad's mausoleum collapsed, and the soil where Muhammad, Abu Bakr and Omar were buried was exposed to view. Omar's grave had crumbled and his feet were visible. The followers of Ali, as Muhammad's descendants, were directed to repair the mausoleum.

In order to clear a larger area for the redesigned Prophet's mosque, the dwelling-places of the Prophet and his family were levelled, Fatima's house was pulled down, the palm trees in her garden were uprooted, and the living descendants of the Prophet were dispossessed and unceremoniously evicted. For this new mosque the Greek emperor Justinian II sent a gift of gold bars, ornate silver lamps, and forty camel-loads of cut stone, along with a hundred Christian (Coptic and Greek) masons, decorators and engravers to work on the gilding and mosaics.

The reconstruction of Mecca presented a similar picture. Thus the house of Amina, where Muhammad was born, was enlarged and beautified and then turned over to the Omayyad governor for use as his residence. The planning and rebuilding of the great mosque at Mecca (Masjid al-Haram) with galleries, ornamental lamps and chandeliers were also ordered by the Omayyads, and here again Christian architects were imported from Syria and Egypt to carry out the work. At this time, too, the city witnessed a great influx of foreign dignitaries and representatives from Muslim countries in North Africa and Central Asia, who set up their own new establishments in Mecca.

Over the succeeding centuries violent rainstorms, lightning, fire and other natural disasters caused havoc to what little remained of the earlier monuments. In the course of reconstruction, fresh and extended foundations were laid, walls were demolished, columns were removed, arches and cupolas were substituted, and new gates were added. The present door of the Kaaba was brought from Istanbul in 1633.

In sectarian conflicts and raids by hostile tribes both Mecca and Medina were periodically ravaged, the holy places were devastated, and the treasures were rifled – the official custodians of the shrines often taking part in the looting. In general this type of vandalism by avaricious rulers and officials continued off and on for centuries. In 1020 Hakim, the sixth Fatimid caliph of Egypt, sent his agents to steal the bodies of Muhammad, Abu Bakr and Omar and transport them back to Egypt, but the attempt failed (Hughes, 1977, p. 345).

In 1256 the Prophet's mosque in Medina was once again severely damaged by an earthquake, followed by a fire started from lighted lamps falling into the debris. Every memento that had so far survived from the time of Muhammad and the first successor-caliphs of Medina, including the Prophet's bench, was reduced to rubble and rapidly consumed.

In 1490 the walls of the Prophet's mausoleum were so badly damaged that they had to be demolished. The burial mounds over the graves of Muhammad, Abu Bakr and Omar had subsided and no signs remained of their location, so the precise spot of Muhammad's grave is lost. From tradition it was known that the graves were close to the southern wall, and here three new mounds were put up on the approximate site of the original graves (Esin, 1963, p. 160). And while this devout work was in progress the area had to be patrolled by armed guards to protect it from attack by bandits and foraging bedouin.

When the Wahabis – a puritanical Arabian sect founded in 1735 – captured the holy cities in 1803 they destroyed many of the shrines or removed the decorations and votive gifts from them, because, they said, all acts of adoration performed by visiting pilgrims constituted a form of idolatry. Since minarets were unknown in early Islam, minarets were toppled wherever the Wahabis went (Hughes, 1977, p. 662).

In Mecca the Wahabis demolished a small shrine of special sacrosanctity on Mount Hira, marking the cave where Muhammad received his first revelation. In Medina they stripped the Prophet's tomb of its ornaments, burned the trappings, and demolished the dome. The Baki cemetery outside Medina, where Muhammad used to go when he wanted solitude and where so many of his companions were buried, was levelled.

In 1850 the Ottoman Turks had further alterations and additions made to the Prophet's mosque in Medina, much to the annoyance of the local inhabitants. During the First World War the sherif (chief magistrate) of Mecca protested about the hardships which the people of Mecca were undergoing because of Turkey's entry into the conflict. The Turkish garrison promptly bombarded the sherif's palace, and one of the shells landed near the Kaaba, setting fire to the curtain and damaging the building.

As a result of periodical calamities, both natural and man-made, and the constant despoilation and reconstruction of the ancient monuments, hardly a single stone or even the outline of the groundwork of any of the original buildings in Mecca and Medina has been preserved. As they stand today, the sacred shrines represent entirely new structures from the foundations up, raised first by the Omayyads and Abbasids and reconstructed by the Ottoman Turks and the Saudis.

13.7 Art

The Prophet disapproved of music and poetry and generally tended to discourage all forms of art as frivolous pursuits. He also condemned luxuries of any kind, and specifically deplored the use of gold and silver ornaments and the wearing of silk and other showy garments, thus leaving a strong puritanical legacy for Islam. In a way 'Islamic art' might almost be regarded as a contradiction in terms.

The Koran (14:38) forbids the worship of images (*asnam*; singular *sanam*), a prohibition which was extended in meaning to include all iconographical or sculptural portrayals or the representation of living beings in any form. Muhammad puts a curse on those who paint or draw men and animals. The progress of Islam in many places was marked by mutilated idols, despoiled paintings and defaced image-bearing coins. Dolls for children were prohibited, and if found were broken.

Muslim theologians held that anything that tended to turn people's minds away from religion was to be viewed with suspicion. The beauty of Persian art which created rapture among the Arabs who first beheld it (see Section 14.5), was regarded by the orthodox as a heathen abomination and a snare of Satan.

The term 'Islamic art', as commonly understood, needs to be employed with some qualifications. European or Chinese art may be conceived of without any necessary Christian or Buddhist connotations. But, because of the ambiguity of terminology, we tend to think of the post-Islamic art of the Middle East as if it were exclusively Islamic, when in fact the bulk of it, in concept, design and technique, was long anterior to the Muslim period.

The names of several textiles survive in the European languages in their Arabicized form. Thus in English we have muslin (from Mosul), satin (ultimately a Chinese word), damask (from Damascus), baldachin (from Baghdad), fustian (from Fustat, or Old Cairo), taffeta and shawl (both ultimately Persian) and tabby (both the cloth and the colour, from Persian). These Arabic derivations have led some scholars to conclude, erroneously, that the fabrics themselves originated in the Muslim world.

The manufacture of fine textiles in Persia (the shawls of Rayy in particular), Syria, Egypt and Central Asia was already highly developed before the Arab ascendancy. From the Byzantine weaving centres – also before the birth of Muhammad – came sumptuous fabrics in many varieties, brightly hued from plant and mineral dyes and embroidered in gold and silver thread.

The same applies to words for furniture, like sofa, mattress, divan (ultimately Persian) and ottoman (despite its name, ultimately Byzantine); for buildings, like magazine (meaning storehouse), arsenal and barbican; for aspects of trade, like tariff and cheque; and for foodstuffs and drinks, like sherbet, coffee, yogurt, halva, kebab and pilau.

On the basis of names alone, it would be no more valid to attempt to link these items with the Muslims than to treat flowers, plants and fruit with Arabic-derived names – like damson (from Damascus), artichoke, lemon, rice and sugar (both the latter ultimately Sanskrit), apricot (ultimately Greek), sultana, tulip and lilac (ultimately Turkish) – as having some connection with Islam because their names came into the language via Arabic. These words were either introduced by non-Arab converts to Islam, or are simply the relics of borrowings that came in the wake of international contacts the world over.

Indeed, far from bestowing, the Arabs borrowed extensively, and nothing more clearly illustrates the extent of such borrowings than the arts and crafts. With few of their own artefacts to begin with, they took over almost *in toto* the artists and artefacts, motifs and the methods of the developed nations with whom they came in contact. Detailed evidence for this is conclusively presented in technical books and journals on the subject.

Throughout the period of Islamic empire there was a brisk interchange of crafts and skills between countries that helped to further the diffusion of foreign art forms in the Islamic world. Coptic and Abyssinian workers were employed in Mecca and Medina, Byzantine craftsmen did considerable work for the Omayyads, Armenian masons were employed in Moorish Spain, and architects from Central Asia went everywhere, from Morocco to Mughal India.

It is established that long before Islam such crafts as ceramics – including the art of making coloured tiles and lustre pottery – ivory-carving, inlaying, carpet-making, mosaic work, frescos, book-binding, miniature-painting, illuminating manuscripts, lacquering on wood, faceting and 'ouching' (setting) of jewels, and the more domestic arts and crafts had all been well-nigh perfected by the Egyptians, Mesopotamians, Sassanians and Byzantines. The two latter had already borrowed from every corner of their own vast domains, which covered virtually the whole of south-eastern Europe, North Africa, the Near East and Central Asia.

Work in metals of all kinds – copper, bronze, silver and gold, sometimes encrusted with precious stones of unsurpassed craftsmanship – was in a very advanced stage of development all over the Middle East by the sixth century BC. The famous metalwork of Mosul and the renowned damascene sword (a combination of wrought iron and cast iron named after Damascus) were known in the early Indian period about 200 BC. Enamelling, the applying of a metallic vitrified coating to metals, was known and practised from the Rhône to the Danube, and came to Byzantium in the third century AD, where it reached the peak of excellence.

Glass-making and glass-blowing passed from Ptolemaic Alexandria to Seleucid Damascus by the first century BC, the Syrian glass creations of astounding thinness and translucence being especially renowned.

The many designs commonly regarded as characteristically Islamic found on household accessories – on lamps, candlesticks, caskets, perfume-burners, vases, plates, writing-boxes, jewel-cases and drinking vessels – as well as these accessories themselves, can be traced without exception to the predecessors of the Muslims.

Byzantine artists produced excellent specimens of naturalistic art, and, despite the prohibition on the representation of living beings, the Omayyads sought the services of Byzantine artists for decorating their palaces and lodges, which was done with representations of human and animal forms. They painted landscapes as well as interiors, with stylized shapes of animals, serpents, birds and fishes. The absence of perspective that we find in Byzantine art is among the many legacies bequeathed to Islam, which for centuries produced work lacking in distance or depth.

Byzantine artists excelled in non-representational and non-figurative art too, employing patterns and designs consisting of circles, squares, angles, zigzags and other geometrical shapes, decoratively repeated to fill in all blank areas and leave no empty spaces.

The ornamental style called arabesque, formed by the interlacing of flowing lines, curves and scrolls, as well as floral, foliate and stellar patterns and delicate interweaving leaves and branches, is derived from the work of Byzantine craftsmen, mostly in Syria and Asia Minor.

The art historian A. H. Christie writes of the Arabic script as 'the sole Arab contribution to Islamic art' (Arnold and Guillaume, 1965, p. 113). Yet this again needs to be amended, for, as we have seen, the Arabic script was not solely of Arabic derivation, and Syriac Christian scholars had a hand in its creation and development. The beautiful calligraphic style, with decorative lettering, found in Muslim books and illustrated manuscripts, and on Muslim buildings and monuments, is often executed in the intricate and elaborate Kufic characters, a form of writing first developed by the Christian calligraphers of Akula, later named Kufa (see Section 4.2).

13.8 Music

The early Arabs, says Lyall, had virtually no indigenous system of music and the art was not cultivated among them till many years after the great conquests (1930, p. 87). They possessed only a few very primitive chants, which appear to have been intoned above and below a simple monotonic drone.

Muhammad himself did not approve of music. In a tradition attributed to Ibn Omar (fl. c. 660), the Prophet put his fingers in his ears when he heard the music of a pipe. In another tradition he is said to have instructed Ali, 'I send you, as God sent me, to break lutes and flutes.' Because it is held to be contrary to the teaching of the Prophet, music is banned from mosques, plays no part in religious services, and is regarded as 'the Devil's muezzin'.

But already before Muhammad's time more advanced musical forms were being introduced among the Arab tribes, and they came to play an important part in the life of the people, 'from the lullaby to the elegy'. In the immediate post-Islamic period the Arab kingdoms of Ghassan and Hira were influenced respectively by Byzantine (Greek) and Sassanian (Persian) musical theory and practice.

The Arabic word for music (*musika*) is derived from Greek. The female entertainers who sang at the feasts of the early Arabs were mainly Greeks from Syria or Persians from Mesopotamia. They sang the words in their own language, probably to their own native airs. By the Abbasid period Persian music and song had become more popular, but Greek performers long remained in great demand.

It is said that a visitor having presented himself to the Abbasid caliph Mamun (d. 833) on Palm Sunday found himself surrounded by twenty richly clad Greek girls dancing with gold crosses around their necks and olive branches in their hands. But the Islamic prohibition against music was still much in evidence. An Arab poet of the time writes nostalgically of the days of paganism when he heard Greek girls singing Greek airs to the accompaniment of the lyre.

The speculative theory of music, founded on the physical basis of sound, and the spiritual and philosophical assumptions arising from it were opened up to the Arabs from about the ninth century, when the classic Greek treatises on music began to be rendered into Arabic (see Section 13.10). These ranged from the work of Pythagoras (fl. c. 500 BC), to studies on rhythm, harmonics and the metaphysics of sound by Aristoxenus of Athens (d. AD 300), Themistius of Constantinople (d. AD 388), and Simplicius of Alexandria (d. AD 540).

Among the more notable Muslim writers were Masudi (d. 956), who wrote books on early Arab music and on the music of foreign lands, and the Persian authority Abul Faraj of Isfahan, better known as al-Isfahani (d. 967), the greatest of all writers on music in Arabic, who produced an encyclopaedic work in twenty-one volumes on composers, poets and musicians.

The names of some musical instruments derived from Arabic or Persian survive in the European languages, but the instruments themselves – such as the lute, rebec, guitar, tabor, bandore and sackbut – are known to have originated in ancient Egypt, Babylonia, Greece and Persia. The philosopher and polymath Alfarabi (d. 950) of Turkestan, who studied under Greek masters, was the most renowned of all music theorists in Arabic. He invented a simple pneumatic keyboard instrument, like a primitive harmonium, which he called *urghanum*, from the Greek *organon*.

Music entered with some considerable impact into the Islamic mystical tradition through the Sufis (see Section 13.16), who acquired it mostly from the Christian monks with whom they were associated from the beginning. They were aware of the spiritualizing potential of music and held it to be a means of revelation and religious enlightenment, often using song and dance as an intrinsic part of their ritual devotions. The Sufi mystic Dhul Nun (d. 859) wrote, 'Music is a divine influence and those who listen to it spiritually attain unto God.' The Persian philosopher and theologian al-Ghazali (d. 1111) wrote that singing was 'more potent in producing ecstasy than the Koran itself' (H. G. Farmer, in Arnold and Guillaume, 1965, p. 359).

13.9 Education

The ancient Persians held knowledge in high esteem, and the Zoroastrian sages, the magi, had a proverbial reputation for wisdom. When the Achaemenian capital of Persepolis was burned and partly destroyed by Alexander the Great, the contents of its famous library were among the treasures the conqueror sent back on five thousand camels and ten thousand mule carts to his own new capital of Alexandria, which he had founded in 332 BC.

These manuscripts formed the nucleus of the great library of Alexandria built by the Ptolemies, and by the fourth century AD this renowned storehouse of learning – despite losses through occasional fires – was said to have contained 700,000 volumes and 200,000 parchment scrolls.

Academies of learning, with libraries attached, were set up in most of the countries occupied by the Ptolemies and Seleucids. Islamic scholars like Makrizi wrote that each of the great cities in pre-Islamic Egypt and other places in the Middle East had a House of Wisdom (*Dar al-Hikma*) or Hall of Learning (*Bayt al-Ilm*) where scholars would give instruction in various subjects – an obvious reference to the early Hellenistic academies.

Many such institutions survived, to become centres of Christian learning in places like Alexandria, Damascus, Antioch and Aleppo, and also in Armenia – largely Monophysite and under the political suzerainty of Byzantine Constantinople – where a university was founded in AD 425. Among the Christian Arab tribes of Syria, the Ghassan scholars also benefited from Byzantine patronage.

Several other towns were Nestorian centres, such as Edessa, Nisibis and Seleucia. Edessa (modern Urfa), the most important bishopric in Syria, had a famous Nestorian college which specialized in Syriac studies. Among the Arab tribes of Mesopotamia, the Lakhmids of Hira came under the sway and received the patronage of the Sassanian rulers.

Christian monastic communities of the time carried out extensive propaganda for their faith, and through their efforts all these centres in Syria and Mesopotamia enjoyed a reputation for learning years before the coming of Islam. Less only than the impression made on the Muslims by the piety, discipline and life of renunciation of the Christian monks was that made by the Christians' dedication to the pursuit of knowledge and its dissemination among the people. Wherever they settled the Christians sponsored education, promoted the study of philosophy, science, astronomy and related disciplines, and established schools for the translation of Greek works into Syriac, and these traditions continued to be fostered after the Muslims took over their domains.

Like the Ptolemies and Seleucids, the Sassanians too, continuing the tradition of their forebears, went on to found renowned institutions across the whole expanse of their empire – many on older Achaemenian foundations. One of the earliest colleges in the heart of Asia was established in Balkh (modern Wazirabad), the capital of the province of Bactria, once a satrapy of the Achaemenian empire. Balkh, known to the Arabs as the 'mother of cities' (*umm al-bilad*), was one of the oldest cities in the world. It was also the place where Zoroaster is said to have been murdered.

In 328 BC Bactria was conquered by Alexander the Great, to become after his death part of the Seleucid empire and eventually an independent multiracial state ruled by the Bactrian Greeks (290 BC–AD 90) – an outpost of Hellenistic civilization in the heart of Asia. By the middle of the third century AD the university of Balkh, famed now throughout the whole region, became the focus of Zoroastrian, Mithraic, Buddhist, Hindu, Greek and Nestorian studies. Its influence spread far and wide, from the Tadzhik, Uzbek and Turkmen regions across Khorasan to northern Persia and beyond. Balkh was captured by the Muslims in AD 663.

Among the famous towns, with colleges, that branched off from Balkh, or developed schools of their own, the following deserve mention. Samarkand, ancient Marakanda, capital of Sogdiana. Bukhara, which had been restored by the Sassanians in about AD 170. Khiva (Kharazm), on the highway leading into the Kazakh region. Merv, ancient Mouru, sacred city of the Zoroastrians mentioned in the Avesta. Tus, once the site of an ancient Zoroastrian temple. (The Shia holy city of Meshed grew up as an offshoot of Tus.) Nishapur, built on an earlier Achaemenian foundation by the Sassanian king Shahpur I (d. AD 272). (Nishapur is the burial-place of the astronomer-poet Omar Khayyam.) Rayy, another sacred city of the Zoroastrians, is also mentioned in the Avesta. (Tehran, a few miles north-east of Rayy, grew out of Rayy.) Qom, ninety-two miles south of Tehran, contained a great Zoroastrian tower for the disposal of the dead. In Islamic times the town became the burial-ground for kings and saints. Ecbatana (modern Hamadan), capital of Media from 650 BC, and later summer capital of the Achaemenian kings, is referred to in the Bible as Achmetha.

The Bible (Ezra 6:1) speaks of the 'house of the rolls' – meaning a store for archives, or a library – that existed in Ecbatana in the time of Darius I (d. 486 BC), and such libraries were doubtless to be found in other major Achaemenian towns.

All the places mentioned above were once within the satrapies of the Achaemenian empire, important as centres of commerce and crafts as well as seats of learning, and they came down as such to the Sassanians. All were taken over by the Muslims and served as models for their own scholastic institutions that sprang up in those places.

In Sassanian Persia, the Nestorian Christians were leaders in the field of education, as well as being active missionaries. They used Syriac in preference to Greek and were loyal to the Persian kings, whose patronage they received in return. Besides Seleucia (Ctesiphon) – which in the early sixth century contained a Christian college – the Nestorians established a number of educational and medical schools in various parts of the Persian empire. Their work became renowned throughout the Middle East and was later cited by Koranic traditionalists.

In the year 531, a century before the Muslim conquest, the Nestorians, at the invitation of the Sassanian king Khosro I, founded a great Nestorian university, with affiliated colleges, at Jundishapur in south-west Persia, near the Persian Gulf – not far from the ancient city of Susa, former capital of Darius and his successors. Attached to the university were a large library, a hospital and an observatory.

To this famous university came Zoroastrian magi, Buddhist monks, Christian theologians from Syria, and Greek philosophers, including those who had been exiled after the Byzantine emperor Justinian I closed the celebrated schools of Athens in AD 529. The language of instruction was Syriac, and the subjects taught included religion, logic, philosophy, mathematics, astronomy, medicine, grammar and languages.

Many scholars from Jundishapur later settled and taught in Basra, and their influence is discernible in the work of the famed grammarians and Koranic commentators of that city, as well as in the writings of the freethinking Ikhwan al-Safa. The Persian scholar Sibaway (d. 793), who wrote a systematic exposition of grammatical principles which became the foundation of Arabic linguistic studies, owed much to the work of the grammarians of Jundishapur.

A great step forward in every sphere of learning followed the dispersal of the Hellenistic library of Alexandria. Muslim scholars – with some reason – deny the truth of the oft-quoted story that in AD 641 the caliph Omar ordered the destruction of the library on the grounds that if it contained knowledge already in the Koran it was superfluous and if it contained information not in the Koran it was erroneous and would mislead the faithful. According to this story the books were burned, and were said to have supplied fuel for the public bathhouses of Alexandria for six months.

If the story is not true and the library was left intact, we have to conclude that this, the most extensive collection of books and manuscripts ever assembled till then, containing the accumulated wisdom of antiquity, was preserved and inherited by the Arabs. Some authorities think this was indeed the case, and that part of this immense store found its way by 720 to Damascus.

The Abbasid caliphs subsequently transferred the Damascus library, as well as most of the functions of the university of Jundishapur, to Baghdad, and here again Christian scholars continued to be widely recruited to organize and head the various faculties there. The director of education during the reign of Harun al-Rashid – who did not otherwise favour Christians – was Yohana (John) ibn Masua, a Nestorian Christian of Damascus.

In 820 the caliph Mamun founded in Baghdad a House of Wisdom containing lecture rooms, reading rooms, debating rooms and a library, where work on all aspects of scholastic research was coordinated, along with a large team of translators.

In 856 the caliph Mutawakil decided to extend the Baghdad library and translation rooms. Although an avowed persecutor of Jews and Christians the caliph, unable to find a Muslim scholar, organizer and administrator equal to the task, entrusted the direction of it to a Christian, Honayn ibn Ishak, the great translator.

It was on the model of the Baghdad school that the prestigious House of Wisdom was established in Cairo by the Fatimid caliph Muizz, with a library and reading room for scholars. Great emphasis was laid on Greek philosophy and the Greek sciences (Watt, 1990, p. 215). Still further additions were made to the college by his successors Aziz and Hakim.

When Saladin – a zealous Sunni – overthrew the Fatimid caliphate in 1171, he disposed of the stock in the famous library of Cairo – by then consisting of about a million books, manuscripts and scrolls – on the grounds that it was designed for the propagation of Shia teachings. Some items were sold, some burned, some cast into the Nile, and the rest were made into a pile to form a great 'hill of books' and covered over with sand and left to rot.

These Muslim institutions in the Middle East, and others like them in Muslim Spain, had been the principal centres of learning but they were now on the decline and there were signs of an eclipse. The European schools began to be set up from the tenth century, and Europe, having received a fillip from the Muslims, started to take a more serious interest in the advancement of knowledge.

All the early universities in southern Italy and Sicily had once been Byzantine centres of learning. Near Naples, for example, the earliest university in Europe, that of Salerno (famous for its medical studies) was founded in the ninth century; the university of Naples dated from the thirteenth century. Sicily, where liberal-minded rulers like Roger II (d. 1154) and Frederick II (d. 1250) held sway, had several colleges.

Universities were beginning to spring up in many other European cities: in Paris (1150), Bologna (1200), Padua (1222), Oxford (1249), Cambridge (1284) and Montpellier (1289). When in time the shackles of the church were cast aside, European scholarship began to take great strides in all secular fields.

13.10 The Translators

It is difficult to appreciate the enormous impact of the foreign influence on Islamic thought, or to put in perspective the vast strides made by the Muslims in philosophy, science, medicine and related fields, unless one is acquainted with the work of the scholars who translated into Arabic the writings in which the wisdom of the ancients had been immortalized, and thus gave the Muslim world access to those treasures.

In general, the works referred to, mostly written in Greek and to a lesser extent in Latin and Coptic, were first rendered into Syriac. This was because from about the third century AD Syriac (Neo-Aramaic or Christian Aramaic) had begun to replace Greek as the language of learning in western Asia (Arnold and Guillaume, 1965, p. 313) and the custodians of Hellenistic civilization were in the main Christians.

This task of translation was being undertaken – three centuries before the Arabic versions made their appearance – in the monasteries of Syria, Palestine, Egypt and Mesopotamia, and by the middle of the fifth century such translations represented a continuous tradition in the eastern churches. There was also a flourishing translation department in the Nestorian university at Jundishapur in southern Persia.

With the Muslim conquests came a demand for this material to be assembled and made available in Arabic. The work of collecting and translating the books was started under the Omayyads and greatly expanded and speeded up during the Abbasid caliphate.

The caliphs, it is related, sent Christian scholars to scour the empire and beyond in search of more and more books and manuscripts: to Alexandria in Egypt; to Harran in Mesopotamia; to Jerusalem and Bostra in Palestine; to Aleppo, Edessa, Antioch and other centres in Syria; even to Christian Byzantium and Greece (Grunebaum, 1961, p. 54). In a treaty with the Byzantine emperor Michael III (d. 867), the caliph Muntasir included a clause for the dispatch of a large collection of rare Greek manuscripts to Baghdad.

Cartloads and caravans of books in foreign languages were brought back to Damascus and Baghdad for the marvels of ancient learning to be rendered into the language of the Prophet. Hundreds of camels, it was said, might be seen entering the gates of Baghdad with no other freight than books and manuscripts. 'Every part of the empire is ransacked by the agents of the caliphs, for the hoarded wealth of antiquity,' writes Ameer Ali (1965, p. 371).

Most of the Arabic translations were made from the already available Syriac versions, and sometimes direct from Greek texts, and the subjects covered the whole gamut of learning. The titles of the works translated ran into hundreds (Arnold and Guillaume, 1965, p. 318), and a very considerable body of literature now became available to the Muslims.

As the treasures were being brought to light, the Arabs were amazed to think that so much wisdom was known to mankind before the coming of the Prophet. Certain caliphs, it is said, ordered the originals of the Greek and Latin manuscripts, where these had been used, to be cast into the flames after they had been translated. It was as if they wished to leave no evidence of past influence, so that certain branches of learning might be thought to have begun with the Muslim period. Indeed, scores of Greek and Latin texts mentioned in the ancient writings now survive only in their Arabic versions.

Over eighty classical authors – Greek, Roman, Alexandrian and Hellenistic, most represented by several works – and hundreds of treatises by lesser authors on a wide variety of subjects were translated into Arabic, including giants like Homer (d. 850 BC), Pythagoras (d. 500 BC), Empedocles (d. 425 BC), Hippocrates (d. 360 BC), Plato (d. 347 BC) and Aristotle (d. 322 BC).

Also translated were the works of the great mathematicians, like the *Elements* of Euclid (d. 283 BC, the *Conics* of Apollonius of Perge (d. 280 BC), the *Pneumatics* of Philo of Byzantium (d. 270 BC); the *Spherics* of Menelaus of Alexandria (d. AD 105) and the *Arithmetic* of the Neopythagorean mathematician and geometer Nichomachus (d. AD 120).

The great compendium of the Alexandrian astronomer Ptolemy

(d. AD 161) known by the Greek name of *Magiste*, and in its Arabic translation as the *Almagest*, had an immense influence on the development of
scientific thought throughout the Islamic world. So did the work of
Diophantus (d. AD 290), the Alexandrian who laid the foundations of
algebra.

Among the inventors whose writings appeared in Árabic versions was
Archimedes of Syracuse (d. 212 BC), with scores of mechanical and
engineering marvels to his credit: complex pulleys, cranks, gears, screws,
pumps, aerodynamic machines, missiles, war catapults and a whole range
of other military weapons. Also translated was Hero of Alexandria
(d. AD 70), a mathematician whose manuals on simple machines and
automata described the many ingenious devices he had invented, like walking images, dancing dolls, water-clocks (clepsydras), hydraulic pumps,
mechanical fountains, siphons, valves and other gadgets. Later, the
reproduction of some of these devices was to make the reputation of many
a Muslim artificer.

Among the translated writers on medical matters was Dioscorides
(d. AD 65), a physician and botanist who wrote on drugs and the medicinal
properties of plants. Another, who towered above the rest, was Galen
(d. AD 210), a Greek who attended several Roman emperors, wrote over
200 medical treatises, and was considered the greatest medical authority of
his time. His works were translated into Arabic by more than a dozen
scholars. Oribasius (d. AD 403), who had made a vast compilation of the
works of Greek and Roman medical writers, was also frequently rendered
into Arabic.

A Christian priest and physician named Ahron of Alexandria (d. AD 590)
wrote a treatise in Greek called *Pandects*, containing a full clinical description of various diseases including smallpox. Translated into Arabic, this
served as a model for Muslim books on diagnostics.

An Alexandrian surgeon, Paul of Aegina (d. AD 690), in his *Epitome* summarized almost everything known in medicine in his day. Arabic translations of this survey influenced the research work of Arab physicians for
centuries. A famous treatise on surgery and surgical instruments written by
the Muslim court physician of Cordoba named Abulcasis (d. 1013) was
based almost entirely on the work of Paul of Aegina.

The writings of the classical historians and geographers were of special
interest to Arab scholars. The *Commentaries* of the mathematician and
astronomer Hipparchus (d. 120 BC), with an accompanying map of the
world showing the coordinate axes of latitude and longitude intersecting at
Rhodes, and fixing the geographical position of places on the earth, inspired
many Arab imitators.

National and universal histories also appeared in Arabic versions, ranging from the chronicles of the early historians to the *Chronographia* of Sex-
tus Julius Africanus (d. AD 245) – five books tracing world history from the

Creation to AD 217. He in turn influenced Eusebius of Caesarea (d. AD 340), whose *Chronicon* was a history of the world to the year AD 325 and the source book of many larger works by Arab historians.

Countless translations of works by authorities less well known but no less significant were made on a wide variety of subjects: the arts and crafts, music, alchemy, metallurgy, mining, meteorology, optics, hygiene, diet, cattle-breeding, veterinary medicine, horticulture, agriculture. In particular, the translation of a book on husbandry written by the Byzantine scholar Cassianus Bassus (d. AD 565) had a great influence on Muslim dissertations on the subject. Partly from this book and partly from Babylonian and other ancient Semitic sources, the writer Ibn Wahshiya (d. 910) compiled a treatise called *Nabataean Agriculture*, containing curious lore on soils, crop-magic, grafting and plant poisons, along with much legendary material.

Scores of savants undertook the labour of translating the ancient masterpieces and lesser works into Arabic, and with very few exceptions they were all Christians (Walzer, 1962). Some were followers of the Orthodox Church; others were Nestorians, Jacobites (Monophysites) or Melchites (anti-Monophysites). There were also a few Jews and Sabians, the latter a pagan star-worshipping sect mainly from Harran in Mesopotamia. It is not recorded that any of the translators were Muslims.

One of the earliest workers in the field was the Monophysite Christian priest Sergius of Reshayna (d. 536), in Mesopotamia, who translated Greek medical works into Syriac; a number of these were later to be translated into Arabic as well. Others were Athanasius of Balad (d. 696), a Jacobite; Jacob of Edessa (d. 708), a Nestorian; and George of Kufa (d. 724), 'bishop of the Arabs', who translated Greek works on medicine, astronomy and philosophy.

Under the Omayyad caliph Omar II, a Persian Jew of Basra named Masarjaway (d. c. 725) translated several medical works. Theophilus of Edessa (d. 785), a celebrated astrologer and Christian scholar, and favourite of the Abbasid caliph Mahdi, translated large sections of Homer's *Iliad* and *Odyssey* into Syriac, from which Arabic translations were made. Another notable scholar was Balabakki (d. 835), a Nestorian Christian who translated several Greek works on geometry, mathematics, astronomy and engineering.

The most prolific and the greatest of all the translators – and a philosopher and scientist in his own right – was Honayn ibn Ishak ('Johannitius son of Isaac'; d. 874), of the Ibad tribe, a Nestorian Christian doctor of Jundishapur, who translated Hippocrates, Plato, Galen and many other medical and scientific works.

Among the more important of Honayn's school of almost 100 pupils and translators, some deserve special mention. Yahya ibn Bitrik ('John son of the Patriarch'), a Melchite scholar, translated Aristotle, Galen and others. Abdul Masih ibn Abdulla, a Jacobite, translated the Neoplatonic philosopher Plotinus, besides various works on logic. Ishak ibn Honayn, Honayn's son, translated some of the works of Aristotle and Euclid, and the *Almagest* of Ptolemy. Hubaysh, Honayn's nephew, translated a number of medical works.

Thabit ibn Kurra – a Sabian astronomer, mathematician and physician – made dozens of translations of scientific works. His son Sinan ibn Thabit ibn Kurra later became renowned as one of the greatest of Arab geometers.

Kusta ibn Luka ('Constantine, son of Luke'; d. 932), translated works by Greek and Alexandrian writers on science, including the treatises of the mathematician-inventor Hero of Alexandria.

Abu Yahya al-Marwazi (d. 920), a Nestorian philosopher and grammarian, founded another famous school of translators in Baghdad that endured for over a century. His pupil and successor, a Nestorian logician and grammarian named Abu Bishr Matta, friend of the philosopher Alfarabi; as well as his pupil and successor Yahya ibn Adi, a Jacobite philosopher and commentator on Aristotle; and in turn his pupil and successor Hasan ibn Suwar, a Nestorian philosopher and physician, were all well-known scholars with scores of translations to their credit.

A great scholastic zeal inspired the translators, and the Islamic world owes them a debt that is rarely acknowledged. They did more than give a literal rendering of the ancient books into the Arabic language: in order to make unfamiliar and often complex subjects comprehensible, they wrote in a lucid Arabic style which served as a model for the Arab writers who followed them.

The translators were linguists, proficient in at least three languages, and to aid them in their work they compiled word-books, dictionaries and technical lexicons. Because hundreds of foreign words had no Arabic equivalents, a new vocabulary – suitably Arabicized on philological principles, and making the transition from the Indo-European languages to the Semitic with great skill – was added to the Arabic language: scientific and philosophical terms from Greek; theological terms from Syriac, Hebrew and Coptic; administrative and political terms from Pahlavi (Middle Persian); medical and legal terms from Latin. In all branches of learning the translators built up a massive terminology that remained a light to the feet of Muslim scholars from Damascus to Toledo.

Without the painstaking labours of the translators, Arabic writing would not have evolved the way it did. The introduction of ancient works into Islam through their Arabic renderings opened up the wonders of philosophy, literature, medicine and science, and had a profound influence on the evolution of Islamic thought and religion. It provided a new, exciting and vastly extended outlook across a wider horizon that set up an intellectual ferment in the Muslim world and helped to usher in the Islamic renaissance.

13.11 Literature

The Prophet's dislike of poetry and, after his death, the aversion of the pious to secular writing not relevant to Islam did not create a climate favourable to the advancement of literature, which had to be cultivated without the endorsement of the orthodox.

We have noted how much the Arabic script and the Arabic language, including its vocabulary, grammar and philology, owed their early development to Christian writers, and how many words directly connected with writing were disseminated from the Christian town of Hira (see Chapter 4). Also, how the vocabulary of Muslim philosophy, science and even theology was augmented by the labours of mainly Christian translators who rendered Greek and Syriac works into Arabic.

In the field of poetical writing, the famous style of love poetry known as Udhrism was developed by the Banu Udhra, a Christian tribe of Syria. This type of verse became very popular among the Arabs and spread from Baghdad to Spain. Arab poets dwelt in detail on the lives of great lovers like Yusuf (Joseph) and Zulaykha (Potiphar's wife), Khosro II of Persia and a Christian girl of Syria named Shirin, the poet Antara (d. 590) and his mistress Abla, and the poet Jamil (d. 710) of the Udhra tribe and the lovely Buthayna.

The Omayyad caliph Muawiya, who admired fine poetry, ordered a collection of poems to be made for the education and edification of his son, Prince Yazid, as he believed it would help in the appreciation of literary skills, demonstrate the need for good manners (*adab*), and inspire deeds of bravery. This was the first anthology of the poems of ancient Arabia and included the famous odes of the Moallakat.

The caliph Abdul Malik commissioned a second and more comprehensive anthology of Arabic poetry, which long remained a source book of early Arabic writing. The caliph's resident poet, Akhtal (d. 710), was a Christian of the Taghlib tribe and used to go about the palace with a cross about his neck. The caliph offered Akhtal a large sum of money and a generous pension if he became a Muslim, and although he declined – on the excuse that he could not give up his love for wine – the caliph proclaimed him 'Poet of the Commander of the Faithful' and referred to him as 'the best poet of the Arabs' (Nicholson, 1969, p. 242).

Another well-known poet, Farazdak (d. 729), was of the Tamim tribe and also a Christian, grandson of the philanthropist Sasaa. He too was held in high repute, and served as court poet to the Damascus caliphs. His contemporary and rival the Muslim poet Jarir ibn Atiya, of the Kolayb tribe, enjoyed the powerful patronage of Hajaj, the governor of Iraq, and was famed for his poetic duels with Akhtal and Farazdak, in which none of them held back in attacking the poetic skills and personal conduct of the others.

When Greek verse appeared in Arabic translation, the impact of the Hellenistic tradition on Arabic prosody and poetical forms, including the love lyric, began to show itself. Grunebaum writes, 'It should be remembered that the dependence of Arabic on Greek love poetry is far reaching' (1961, p. 317).

Kodama ibn Jaafar (d. 922), a Christian convert to Islam and an expert on Aristotle's *Poetics*, was one of the first to introduce Greek methods into Arabic literary theory. He wrote on poetry and poetical forms and on rhyme, rhythm and metre, and was long quoted with admiration by authorities on Arabic style.

Greek influence on another important genre of Arabic writing has also been pointed out: namely, the collection of tales known as the *Arabian Nights*. These were originally written in the Pahlavi vernacular some time in the early Islamic centuries and began to be translated into Arabic in the eleventh century, until their virtual completion in the present form in about 1400. The tales show clear borrowings from Buddhist, Jewish and, above all, Hellenistic sources (Grunebaum, 1961, p. 294).

Creative writing and the spread of knowledge were greatly facilitated from the Abbasid period by the manufacture and use of paper. At first papyrus was commonly used for writing, but by the time the Koran was being written papyrus had been replaced in the Graeco-Roman world by parchment, prepared from animal skins. The word for parchment (*kirtas*) used in the Koran (6:7) comes from the Greek word (*chartēs*) meaning a sheet of parchment. Parchment was only one of the materials used by the amanuenses to take down the Koran.

In AD 751, during a chance encounter following a battle in Central Asia, the Arabs captured some Chinese paper-makers in Samarkand from whom they learned the techniques of paper-making. A paper-factory was set up in Baghdad in 794 followed by paper-mills in various other centres, and a new industry was born. The use of paper spread to Europe, replacing papyrus for good.

13.12 Historiography

Semi-historical material dating from a very early period is found in rock inscriptions in many parts of the Arabian peninsula, written in Mosnad, Thamudic, Safaitic and Nabataean characters (see Section 4.2). For centuries these inscriptions were subject to weathering and damage through neglect, or were vandalized by bedouin. It was not till the end of the nineteenth century that a number of distinguished European scholars began the task of deciphering them and piecing together fragments of a long-forgotten chapter in the history of pre-Islamic Arabia (Philby, 1947, p. 128).

This material is not history in the recognized sense, but a cryptic record of miscellaneous events inscribed *ad hoc* at different periods by the rulers of the states where they occurred. Otherwise, details about Arab history preceding and immediately succeeding the advent of Islam are obtained from the following sources: the early chronicles of neighbouring countries; the works of Jewish, Greek, Syrian and Roman writers; the pre-Islamic poetry of Arabia; and a tangled mass of oral traditions handed down by the professional storyteller (*kass*) from which a legendary and semi-historical account has been sifted.

Muslim writers themselves have dealt inadequately with the period before the Prophet. Scholars were discouraged from the pursuit of studies relating to those times, and Faris speaks of the determination of official Islam to 'stamp out' all that belonged to pagan Arabia (1952, p. vii). In a hadith, Muhammad is reported to have said, 'Islam demolishes all that preceded it.' The term 'historian' (*akhbari*) had a derogatory meaning, and men like Hisham al-Kalbi (d. 820) who wrote about Arabia before Muhammad were violently attacked by the pious. The result was that material not considered suitable by the orthodox was destroyed, or neglected and so lost, and the rest was retained only after appropriate alterations had first been made.

History and biography relating to the post-Islamic era first began to be chronicled by Muslim writers more than a century after the death of Muhammad. During most of this time, till well into the Omayyad period, the bulk of traditional evidence that made up the historical data was being haphazardly, unmethodically and uncritically collected, and consequently suffered from the drawbacks of any information that is received and transmitted orally before it is set down in writing.

Both at the time of oral transmission and at the time it was committed to writing, glosses were added, facts were omitted and tendentious interpolations were made in order to accord with the reciter's or the writer's own viewpoint, or to make the text acceptable to the sect or party for which it was intended. Those who in turn wrote later versions reformulated the work of their predecessors. Many details continue to be disputed, and there is ample room for conjecture in the different versions.

The early chronicles are thus frequently distorted by partisan tendencies depending on the tribal or sectarian bias of the writer. The historian generally exalts the deeds of his own faction and remains silent or uninformative about rivals or opponents, except to vilify, mock or discredit them. Setbacks and defeats of his own side, or anything that might show Islam in an unfavourable light, are seldom referred to. The contributions to Islam of non-Muslims frequently go unrecorded, and where such contributions do receive positive comment it may be taken as axiomatic that this reflects the truth.

The early chronicles are full of anecdotal material, and there is a strong tendency to exaggerate and ascribe doughty exploits to stalwarts of the faith and to drown facts in rhetorical verbiage. For example, the second caliph, Omar, pierced in more than six vital parts of his body, so that water spurts out of his wounds like little fountains when he drinks, nevertheless survives for days, giving advice and instruction to the people, ending with a lengthy farewell oration.

Again, the presentation is generally disconnected and lacking in uniformity. What emerges from an account is obscure and muddled, with contradictory data that cannot be reconciled. No precise details are given for many of the principal events, like some of the major battles, so that even the date of the taking of Jerusalem by Omar varies. Furthermore, the early histories lack chronological order, so even the precise sequence of events cannot always be determined.

This applies to most of the early material: to the biographies of Muhammad and the lives of the other important personalities, as well as the early companions. Thus, in different accounts of the conquests of Persia, Mesopotamia, Palestine, Syria and Egypt, there is considerable confusion about the facts – a confusion about which Arab historians themselves are aware.

It was only from about the ninth century that great Muslim historians emerged and serious historical works – many of them exemplars of their kind – began to be written. As in many other areas of intellectual activity so in the recording of history these writers continued a tradition that had been set by their Greek predecessors. Some wrote universal histories, beginning with the creation of the world and ending with the days in which the historian lived. Such universal histories are traceable to similar Greek and Alexandrian works available at the time in Arabic versions.

Books on geography too – many historians were also competent geographers – were likewise based on the examples of earlier Greek and Latin writers, describing towns and their inhabitants, flora and fauna, and the mountains, rivers and coastlines, sometimes furnishing maps giving latitude and longitude. Here again it should be noted that most of the great historians and geographers who wrote in Arabic were not Arabs by birth.

Much of the information relating to the history and traditions of Mecca and Medina was written by Muhammad al-Azraki (d. 858), 'the Blue-Eyed', who expanded material assembled and recorded by his grandfather, a descendant of a Christian prince of Ghassan.

Ahmad al-Yakubi (d. 897), of Armenian origin, was both a historian and a geographer. He wrote a history of the world from Adam to Jesus, with lists of the kings of Egypt, Nineveh, Babylon, India, China, Greece, Rome and pre-Islamic Arabia, and a history of Islam from the time of Muhammad to his own day.

Not much is known about the life of al-Masudi (d. 956), called 'the Pliny of the Arabians', who was a great globe-trotter, travelling as far as China for material. Like many other scholars who wrote in Arabic but about whom little has been recorded, he was probably not an Arab. Only two out of the thirty volumes of his encyclopaedic history, with some geographical and chronological material, have come down to us.

Among other non-Arab historians who wrote in Arabic were al-Tabari (d. 923), a Persian, called by Gibbon 'the Livy of the Arabians', and Biruni (d. 1050), a native of Armenia, famous for his account of India, written after a stay there of nearly forty years. Biruni, who was also an astronomer, invented an instrument for calculating dates in the Muslim calendar, but used the Byzantine months and was accused of being an infidel.

The eminent geographer Idrisi (d. 1140) worked at the court of the Norman king Roger II of Sicily, who commissioned him to write a descriptive account of the known world, which he completed with accompanying maps and a silver globe. The historian Yakut ibn Abdulla (d. 1229), the author of a dictionary of places and a gazetteer with valuable historical notes, was the greatest of the Muslim geographers, and an Anatolian Greek by birth.

Ibn Sayid (d. 1274), who wrote a survey of the West African coast from Senegal to Nigeria, was an Andalusian. Ibn Khalikan (d. 1282), author of a biographical dictionary filled also with useful historical notes, came from the famous Bactrian family of the Barmecides. Ibn Batuta (d. 1369), who travelled all over the Muslim lands, the interior of Africa, Ceylon and the Maldives, was a Moroccan. Ibn Khaldun (d. 1406), the greatest of the Muslim philosophers of history, who laid emphasis on its social and cultural aspects, was a Tunisian.

13.13 Medicine

Information derived from the pre-Islamic poets indicates that the early Arabs possessed an empirical knowledge of the healing properties of certain herbs and plants and were acquainted with some elementary surgical techniques, but that most of their scientific knowledge of medicine came from outside.

Christians in Arabia, as elsewhere, took an active part in the care and well-being of the sick and aged. They set up rest-houses for travellers and pilgrims, places of refuge providing free food and shelter for the poor, orphanages for the young and abandoned, and hospitals where the sick were looked after.

The large monastic establishments also had poorhouses, hospices and hospitals. The monastery of Hizkil (Ezekiel) built in the fifth century on the banks of the Tigris was known throughout the Middle East for its care of the insane, a group of unfortunates neglected in all early societies.

During the first centuries of Muslim expansion the Christians had a virtual monopoly in medicine. We hear of Christian, and to a lesser extent Jewish, physicians working in Islamic countries, and of medical books written by Nestorians being used in their dispensaries.

In 707, on the example of the Nestorian hospital at Jundishapur

(AD 531), the Omayyad caliph Walid I built the first Muslim hospital in the Islamic world. The Abbasid caliph Harun al-Rashid founded the first hospital in Baghdad in 800, on the initiative of one of the members of the Christian Bukht-Yishu family (see below), and this was followed by the founding of four other hospitals in the beginning of the tenth century.

By now, most of the physicians in the caliphate followed the methods set out by the Greek schools of Hippocrates (d. 350 BC) and Galen (d. AD 210). As late as the eleventh century, an Egyptian physician known to the West as Haly Rodoam was proud to assert that in his professional work he fulfilled the requirements of the Hippocratic oath.

In surgery, simple operations as well as trepanning for mental diseases and Caesarean section were routinely carried out. The taboo on dissection, widely prevalent in Islamic countries at the time, for long hampered any further advances in surgical techniques, until the translation of a manual on the subject written by Paul of Aegina.

Both the Omayyad and Abbasid caliphs depended almost entirely on Christian physicians for their medical care. When sick, the Abbasid caliph Mansur would send for his personal physician Jirgis (Georgius) ibn Gabriel (d. 760), whom he appointed head of the medical faculty in Baghdad. Educated in Jundishapur, Jirgis contributed a great deal to medical research, and in many respects it was mainly to him, it was said, that the Saracens were indebted for the study of medicine.

Jirgis ibn Gabriel belonged to the famous Christian family of Bukht-Yishu ('Jesus hath Redeemed') which produced seven generations of distinguished physicians from the eighth to the eleventh century. They acted as court physicians to Hadi (d. 788), Harun al-Rashid (d. 809) and several other caliphs, and were responsible for building free dispensaries to serve the needs of the poor.

Yohana (John) ibn Masaway (d. 859), a Nestorian Christian physician who also served at the Abbasid court, wrote medical treatises expanding on the legacy of Galen. His work directly influenced the Persian physician known to Europe as Haly Abbas (d. 928), whose encyclopaedic survey of medicine, translated into Latin, was consulted in the West until superseded by the celebrated Canon of Avicenna (d. 1037), the 'Galen of Islam'. Masaway was also the author of a pioneering dissertation on the eye, the first on the subject in Arabic, which inspired an equally famous treatise on optics written by the Muslim physicist known to the West as Alhazen (d. 1038).

The Christian physician, philosopher and theologian of Baghdad Ibn Butlan (d. 1066) wrote a controversial thesis criticizing Galen on certain fundamental principles of physiology. He left a valuable compendium listing his contemporaries who had excelled in the sciences, philosophy and literature. It is noteworthy that the famous theologian al-Ghazali based the classification of his authoritative disquisition on the religious sciences (Ihya) on the arrangement found in the medical works of Ibn Butlan.

A number of other scholars, knowledgeable in medicine, put together compilations of the works of earlier physicians so as to make the mass of information more readily accessible. One of the most influential of these compilations was a collection of medical lore, with emphasis on experimental medicine using the latest techniques, written by the Christian physician Ibn Tilmid (d. 1165) of Baghdad, which gave a great fillip to general medical practice as well as to surgery.

The writings of Gregorius Barhebraeus (d. 1286) – also known as Abul Faraj – a Jewish convert to (Jacobite) Christianity who rose to be a bishop, exerted an influence that continued well beyond his day. A master of Hebrew, Syriac, Arabic and Greek, this polymath wrote on philosophy, theology – with speculations on God, angels and demons – astronomy, the sciences and medicine, in addition to a universal history of the world.

The Christian oculist Ali ibn Isa (d. 1290) of Baghdad, known to the Latins as Jesu Haly, wrote a classic handbook on ophthalmology which remained the best treatise on eye diseases until the Western theses began to appear after 1750. He carried out extensive clinical research, and was said to have used anaesthetics during operations.

But the creative days were now over, although a spate of imitative works continued to pour out, as well as hundreds of lesser theses (called *Akrabadhin*, from the Greek *graphidion*: a small treatise) on all varieties of medical and pseudo-medical subjects, mostly copied or plagiarized from earlier sources.

13.14 Science

The French writer Ernest Renan said that the Arabs were above all the pupils of the Greeks, and that the so-called Arabian sciences were a continuation of Greek science. But the roots of many Arabian sciences in fact go back even earlier than Greece, to Mesopotamia, China and India.

Advanced mathematics and its applications in geometry and mensuration were known from the time of Hammurabi (d. 1750 BC). The ancient Babylonians had already made great advances in mechanics and hydraulics, were masters of irrigation techniques, canal engineering and flood control, made extraordinarily accurate land surveys, and, as the greatest astronomers of the ancient world, also studied the movements of the stars and planets. The stars known today by Arabic names like Aldebaran, Altair, Rigel and Betelgeuse were first charted by the Babylonians, and it is thought their names may stem from Babylonian originals.

Similarly, the famous observatories of the Islamic world had many earlier prototypes. The Babylonian ziggurat was said to have served both as temple and observatory. A well-known Greek observatory was built at Rhodes in about 150 BC by Hipparchus, who also made many outstanding discoveries in astronomy.

Among the earliest pre-Islamic observatories inherited by the Muslims was the one attached to the Nestorian university of Jundishapur in Persia. Modelled on this, a Jewish convert to Islam named Sind ibn Ali (d. 850) built another famous observatory, near one of the gates of Baghdad, which ranked next only to its Nestorian exemplar.

The illustrious Arab astronomer known to the West as Albategnius (d. 915), who is quoted by Copernicus in his *De Revolutionibus*, belonged to the star-worshipping Sabians of northern Mesopotamia. The astronomical tables of the Uzbek astronomer al-Kharazmi (d. 975) – after whom the number system called algorism was named – were based on Hindu astronomical tables computed in India, and his latitudes and longitudes go back for the greater part to Ptolemy.

The so-called Arabic numerals are now known to be of Indian origin, and the decimal system with its place-value structure – one of the greatest of all mathematical creations – is of Chinese derivation (Needham, 1959, p. 12). The Syrian bishop Severus (fl. *c.* 680) wrote in praise of the 'Indian system' and so brought it to the attention of the Arabs.

It is also to be noted that several of the inventions attributed to the Arabs of the Muslim period had prior origins. The mariner's compass, for example – one of the earliest of navigational aids – was familiar, in one form or another, to the early Chinese navigators, as well as to the Carthaginians and the Norsemen. The astrolabe, an instrument used for determining the altitude of the sun and other heavenly bodies, was known to the Greeks among others.

Dozens of ingenious mechanical toys and scientific gadgets, like the water-clock, had been invented at the beginning of the Christian era by the Ptolemaic artificers, of whom the most renowned was Hero of Alexandria, whose writings were known through Arabic translations made by Thabit ibn Kurra and others. According to the chroniclers, the Abbasid caliph Harun al-Rashid sent the gift of a water-clock to Charlemagne as a Muslim invention.

In the field of chemistry, a number of words used today survive only in their Arabicized form, though some may be of foreign, possibly Egyptian (Alexandrian), derivation. Such are alcohol, elixir, alembic, carboy, alkali, naphtha, natron, alchemy, borax, talc and benzene. Historically, the first of the Muslim alchemists was Khalid (d. 680), son of the Omayyad caliph Yazid I. Khalid became interested in the subject after reading a book by the philosopher-alchemist Stephanus of Alexandria (d. 641), and acquired a knowledge of alchemical processes from a Christian monk of Syria called Morienus Romanus, who himself had acquired the art at the fount of all alchemical studies, Alexandria in Egypt.

Several famous Arab philosophers were also alchemists, one of the best-known being Jabir ibn Hayyan (d. 815), a Sabian from Harran, who discovered sulphuric acid, nitric acid, and the combination of hydrochloric and nitric acids called aqua regia, 'royal water', because it could dissolve the royal metals, gold and platinum. Three notable Muslim alchemists of the time were Dhul Nun (d. 859), Rhazes (d. 930) and Alfarabi (d. 950).

The Arabs carried alchemy to Moorish Spain, where elements borrowed from North African magic mingled with Iberian necromancy to produce an amalgam of magic and goety that made certain of their universities notorious centres of occult studies. Such centres were said to have been established in Granada, Seville and Cordoba in the south, Toledo in the centre, Salamanca in the west, and Saragossa in the east.

A prolific writer on metallurgy, drugs, alchemy, astronomy and various other scientific and semi-scientific matters, quoting many Greek names, was Geber (d. 1290) – his name Latinized from Jabir (ibn Aflah) – a Christian author of Seville who either assumed or was given the name of Jabir ibn Hayyan, the Sabian alchemist mentioned above. A number of works on mathematics and astronomy by Jabir were ascribed to the later Geber, but the confusion between the two authors remains unresolved.

Another equally prolific writer on a wide variety of scientific and related subjects was Khazini (d. 1210), a Byzantine Greek who had once been a slave in Merv, Turkmenistan. He was fascinated with problems connected with the conflict of opposites and the harmonizing of stresses, and sought to work out how the tension between physical energies might be resolved and brought to equilibrium. He wrote on weights and measures, statics and dynamics, scales and balances, and specific gravity, besides a treatise on the steelyard, a weighing-machine of Greek origin.

13.15 Philosophy

From the Greek *philosophos* was formed the Arabic *filasuf*, 'philosopher', and along with the name much of Greek philosophy also passed to the Arabs. From Pythagoras and Plato to the Roman Stoics – perpetuated chiefly in the Hellenistic schools of the Ptolemies, Seleucids and Byzantines – the influence of the classical thinkers on the development of Islamic speculation has been considerable.

Various other factors also made their contribution to the evolution of Muslim philosophy. Confrontation in their own environment with faiths far older than theirs (like Buddhism, Zoroastrianism, Judaism and Christianity) forced a new outlook on the conquering Muslims – so much so that some Western scholars regard Arabian philosophy as a 'hotchpotch of the opinions of the ancients into which heterogeneous matter of all kinds has been thrown and left to seethe' (Arnold and Guillaume, 1965, p. 239).

Converts to Islam often retained many of their old beliefs, which in time infiltrated the faith of their adoption. Many features of Islam merged with and were thus modified by these outside contacts, and many new ideas were assimilated into the still growing religion. The result is that Islamization has never been complete in many of the areas where Islam exists today. By the time Islam had reached maturity it was no longer a pure product.

The non-Arab converts were among the keenest students of the Koran and the finest exponents of its religious philosophy. Inevitably they gave their own interpretations to what they studied, so that even religious law and the exposition of the sharia were modified by the local traditions in which Islam was being established. Among the more renowned Koranic commentators were Kaab al-Ahbar (d. 655), a Jew; Ikrima (d. 723), of Berber origin; Makhul (d. 731), of Afghan stock; Ata ibn Rahab (d. 732), of 'African' descent; and Yazid ibn Abu Rahib (d. 745), a Nubian.

In the beginning the Arabs possessed no clear-cut doctrine of religious jurisprudence, and the theologian (*mutakalim* or expounder of theology (*kalam*)) began to develop codes of religious law and dogma only after debate with foreigners – Christians among them. Thus the polemical writings directed against Muslims by Christians like the theologian and hymn writer John of Damascus (d. 749) and Theodorus Abucara (d. 850), Melchite bishop of Harran, contributed to the growth of philosophical tendencies among the Muslims themselves (Ameer Ali, 1965, p. 365).

It was as a result of such confrontations with non-Muslims that Muslim theologians acquired the dialectical weapons and the art of religious controversy, with all their attendant drawbacks. They adopted the weapons of the enemy in order the better to oppose them (Makdisi, 1981, p. 105).

As they settled down, the thinkers of Islam – of whom only a few were Arabs – had time to reflect on the many vexing issues that arose in considering the problems inherent in their own religious dogma, and they found themselves faced with similar situations and involved in disputes with other Muslims on similar points to those that had racked and plagued the Christians. And here again the intellectual tools they employed in dealing with their problems were the same as those the Church Fathers and schoolmen had inherited from their Greek and Hellenistic predecessors and sharpened and refined through use in controversy.

The history of Muslim thought abounds in the names of eminent scholars, many of whom were polymaths – versatile geniuses who wrote not only on philosophy, but on history, geography, mathematics, astronomy, physics, languages, music and religion. Under the compelling impact of Greek thought, with its strictly rational basis, they came to regard reason as superior to religious faith and mystical speculation, and in the course of their writings they – like their Christian counterparts – often took up positions that were at variance with the teachings of the orthodox theologians.

The father of Islamic philosophy, with whom the subject is said to have started, was known to the West as Alkindus (d. 868), after the once-Christian tribe of Kinda to which he belonged. He was the only pure-blooded Arab philosopher – Guillaume speaks of him as 'the first and last philosopher the Arabs produced' (Arnold and Guillaume, 1965, p. 251) –

and distinguished himself by his mastery of complex metaphysical problems. Alkindus attempted to integrate the various strands of Greek philosophy and Islamic doctrine, and in doing so he naturalized Greek philosophy in the Islamic world. He enjoyed the favour of the caliph Mamun, and was tutor to one of the sons of the caliph Mutasim.

The philosopher and physician known in the West as Rhazes (d. 925) was a Persian, born in Rayy and educated in Baghdad under a disciple of the Christian scholar Honayn ibn Ishak. In later years he was associated with the Greek school at Harran in north Mesopotamia, and was greatly influenced by Plato's *Timaeus*. He laid emphasis on reason as the sole guide, and dismissed revelation as false and religion as dangerous (Hourani, 1991, p. 78). Rhazes was the first scholar to classify substances as animal, vegetable or mineral.

Muslim philosophers were especially enamoured of the empirical outlook of Aristotle, and a few achieved renown for their exposition of his ideas. The Turkoman philosopher Alfarabi (d. 950), born in Farab across the Oxus (Amu Darya), came to Baghdad, where he studied music, philosophy and the Greek sciences, chiefly with Christian teachers. He was inspired by Platonism and Neoplatonism, but above all by Aristotle, and became known as 'the Second Aristotle'.

Another renowned Muslim philosopher, the Uzbek scholar Avicenna (d. 1037), was born in Bukhara and studied in Balkh, once a centre of Zoroastrian and Buddhist studies. He made enormous contributions to several fields of learning, notably medicine. He too was especially famed as an expounder of the Greek school of thought, paying particular attention to Aristotle, because of which he became known as 'the Third Aristotle'.

Al-Ghazali, or Algazel, was born in Tus, Persia, and taught in Baghdad until 1095, when for a time he abandoned academic life for that of the ascetic, to become a Sufi, though of rigid orthodoxy. He insisted on strict adherence to religious doctrine, criticized both Alfarabi and Avicenna, and held theology to be superior to philosophy. He was later accused by the poet Rumi of lacking the type of true spirituality manifested in the writings of his younger brother Ahmad al-Ghazali, who wrote a mystical treatise on the theme of love.

The result of the elder al-Ghazali's teaching was the triumph of anti-philosophical orthodoxy in the eastern schools of Islam, though philosophy continued to flourish for a time in Moorish Spain through the work of such writers as Avempace or Ibn Bajja (d. 1138), who, in addition to philosophy, wrote works on medicine, meteorology, mathematics and music, and the poet and philosopher Abubacer or Ibn Tufayl (d. 1185), author of works on mathematics and medicine, and of a philosophical romance in praise of the solitary and independent life.

The Andalusian philosopher Averroes (d. 1198) spoke of Aristotle as 'the Perfect Man', wrote lucid and original commentaries on the same Greek

master, and earned the title of 'The Commentator'. He expounded the
Koran in Aristotelian terms and founded a system of Muslim philosophy
which became the fount of many heresies. Averroes had been a judge in
Cordoba, but he was deprived of his post and banished following accusations of unorthodoxy, unbelief and, curiously, even apostasy to Judaism.
Ernest Renan called Averroes the absolute rationalist, and regarded him as
the father of freethought and dissent.

Alfarabi, Avicenna and Averroes followed Aristotle even in matters
which involved the virtual negation of the fundamental principles of Islam.
It is not surprising that with this record before them the orthodox
theologians tended to resist all forms of 'ancient learning' (ilm al-kadim),
derived from early and indeed any non-Muslim sources. They distrusted
books and secular wisdom, which they believed caused confusion and led
to schism.

In general all philosophers, Muslim or not, came to be seen as heretics.
The door was shut on all speculative inquiry and free debate. And, as in
Christendom, many of those who differed in their views from the orthodox
position suffered persecution for their temerity.

By about the end of the thirteenth century it was clear that the Muslim
initiative in almost every branch of learning, including science, medicine
and philosophy, had virtually come to an end, and was passing by slow
degrees to the West. This was due mainly to the increasing hold exerted on
all Islamic studies by religion, which discouraged such 'foreign' pursuits as
hostile to Islam, the study of science being regarded as particularly 'accursed'.

Al-Ghazali, the last of the great medieval Muslim scholars, expressed a
view that was beginning to gain ground by this time: namely, that all studies must be judged by their conformity to religious doctrine. Once it became
adopted in practice, this view put an end to further progress in the advancement of secular knowledge in the Islamic world. The initiative thus lost,
was taken up by the Europeans.

13.16 Sufism

A feature of Islam that has generally been viewed with considerable
understanding in the West is Sufism. It is seen as something approaching a
universal faith, with liberal teachings and a wide tolerance.

The Sufis represent a miscellaneous grouping of sects or orders embra-
cing mystical doctrines – from pantheism to antinomianism – that seem to
have arisen as a reaction against the rigidity and formalism of orthodox
Islam. They regarded adherence to the sharia and the observance of its
regulations as the lowest grade on the scale of a person's spiritual evolution. The life and disciplines of a Sufi are designed to lead one on a mystical journey through progressive stages from law to liberation, from

orthodoxy to illumination, from knowledge of self to the extinction (*fana*) of selfhood in the Godhead.

The origin of the term 'Sufi' has been traced by some authorities to the Greek word for wisdom (*sophia*), but it is more generally agreed that it is derived from the Arabic word for wool (*suf*), and was originally applied to those Muslim ascetics who, in imitation of Christian hermits, clad themselves in coarse undyed woollen garb as a sign of penitence and renunciation. The Sufis' patched cloak (*khirka*) was likewise taken from the mantle of the Syrian monks, which consisted of 'rags of many colours'.

Although puritanical in many ways, Muhammad was opposed to renunciation (*zuhd*) and the monastic life, and is reported to have said, 'No monasticism in Islam.' According to the Koran, the Christians invented monasticism seeking thereby to please God, but they failed to observe it properly (57:27). The Sufis, who favoured the monastic life, interpreted this to mean that monasticism was divinely ordained but had become corrupted.

Many Sufi orders were established on monastic principles, and eminent Sufis wrote in praise of poverty and extolled the ideal of the beggar (*fakir*) and the religious mendicant (*dervish*). A small number voluntarily embraced such a way of life, giving up the delights of the world – wealth, fame, feasts, women and companionship – and seeking instead penury, anonymity, hunger, celibacy and solitude – even welcoming abuse and disgrace as a means of strengthening the spirit by remaining indifferent to censure and ridicule.

Despite Muhammad's prohibitions, the Sufis made the widest possible use of music and musical instruments, and the development of Muslim poetry is also closely linked with the work of the Sufis.

Sufi adepts evolved a variety of techniques to enhance the religious experience so as to attain the supreme state of ecstasy (*hal*), and some orders were popularly known by the methods they used. Thus the Silent Dervishes (of the Nakshbandi order in Central Asia) conducted all their devotions in total silence; the Whirling Dervishes (of Turkey, founded by the poet Rumi) spun around in circles; the Howling Dervishes (the Rifai order of North Africa) called out the names of God in loud ululations; the Wandering Dervishes (the Kalandar order) never stayed in one place but travelled far and wide to free their souls in the process.

The Sufis picked up some of their practices in the course of foreign contacts. Thus the breathing techniques which were part of the devotional exercises of the Hesychast monks of eleventh-century Greece were adopted by the Sufis of Syria and Turkey in their rituals of remembering (*dhikr*), just as the breathing exercises and postures of yoga were adopted by the Muslim mystics of India.

Often only a thin line separates Islamic mysticism – best exemplified in Sufism – from Islamic heresy. Certain scholars, like A. C. Bouquet, hold that Sufism is not a natural outgrowth of Islam but a foreign element which has worked its way into it, and is really inconsistent with Muslim dogma. Another scholar, R. C. Zaehner, writes that Sufism represents so radical a distortion of orthodox doctrine as to constitute almost a separate religion. In spite of this, Sufism has made a permanent impact on Islamic thought, and its influence has continued to the present day.

Because certain individuals and groups among the mystics, while remaining ostensibly within the Islamic fold, chose to follow an unorthodox path, they were regarded as being 'outside the law' (bi-shar) or antinomian, and were known as Bishariya. The Bishariya thinkers were regarded by the theologians as un-Islamic, frivolous and pagan freethinkers who were attempting to subvert the laws of God. Daring and blasphemous, they were condemned as infidels, holding doctrines that were false (batil).

Essentially, the Bishariya believed that direct experience of God might be obtained by means other than those approved by the orthodox, and did not require the guidance of an official religion. If Muhammad was mentioned in their speculations, he was given no greater importance than the other prophets. According to some of their proponents, men need the candle (Muhammad, the Koran, the sharia, the ceremonies) in the darkness of night, but when the sun (the truth of Bishariya teachings) shines they should extinguish the candle and lay it aside.

The text of the Koran, when quoted, served the Bishariya as an excuse for their own expositions, which were often at variance with it. In their eyes, many of the prescriptions of Islamic law, such as the pilgrimage, the five daily prayers, the fasts – if one insisted on these rituals – could be more usefully performed interiorly. One could pray in private and perform the pilgrimage without stepping out of the house.

The Bishariya rebels were especially caustic about the Black Stone, a subject on which other Muslim writers have also been known to express some unease. Their contention was that Arabia is a sacred land only because of the city of Mecca, and Mecca was sacred long before Muhammad, who himself preferred Medina to Mecca and regarded Jerusalem as superior to both. Mecca is sacred only because of the Kaaba, which is simply a house that has been destroyed and rebuilt more than a score of times. So, what makes Arabia the sacred land, Mecca the sacred city and the Kaaba the sacred house is a black stone, and it is to this prehistoric pagan fetish that the faithful turn to pray and around which they circumambulate during the pilgrimage.

Islam is opposed to idolatry, but, the Bishariya argued, the real idolatry was slavish adherence to the law. The legal and ritual obligations that the theologians held up as the bulwarks of Islam were lifeless things, 'like lions painted on the walls of a latrine'. The Persian Sufi al-Hiri (d. 911) wrote, 'I have always had an aversion for the followers of formal religion.' 'Ritual acts', declared al-Wasiti (d. 932), 'are only impurities.' 'Know this,' God was said to have revealed to al-Nifari (d. 965), 'that I will not accept from you anything of the sunna.'

Throughout the history of Islam many Sufis, mystics, ascetics, free-thinkers – a few theologians and scholastics among them – have turned their backs on various elements of the sharia and adopted radical rules of their own. Some, indeed, have felt the need to free themselves entirely from the trammels of the law.

The appearance within Islam of rationalist groups like the Mutazilis, esoteric groups like the Batinis, antinomian groups like the Bishariya and mystical groups like the Sufis was stimulated by the growth and spread of similar trends throughout the Middle East before the Muslim era.

Sufis claimed that their teachings were known long before the mission of Muhammad. They believed these were received and handed down from antiquity through such exalted personages as Idris (either Enoch or Hermes Trismegistus, the source of hermetic philosophy), Ilyas (Elijah), Khizr (unidentified, but sometimes said to be either Joshua – Yusha – or a general of Alexander the Great), Dhul Kifl (either Ezekiel or Zacharias, the father of John the Baptist) and Jirjis. The last named is identified with St George, a figure now regarded in the West as legendary, but known in the East as a resurrected martyr whose exploits are traditionally linked with Palestine, Syria and Asia Minor.

Christological sects like the Gnostics and Manichaeans, and mystical groups like the Hermetics and Neoplatonists, all to a greater or lesser extent played a part in the evolution of the mystical systems of Islam, including Sufism. The writings or alleged writings of the Pythagorean wonder-worker Apollonius of Tyana (d. AD 80) – known to the Arabs as Balinus – were used as a source book in magical and alchemical operations.

We also learn from al-Masudi, Bagdadi and other Muslim scholars that the early Muslims were acquainted with the teachings of Marcion (d. AD 165), Valentinus (d. AD 175) and other Gnostics (Walker, 1989), and that the doctrines of some Shia sects like the Ismaili represent ideas prevalent in Gnosticism (Ameer Ali, 1965, p. 343).

Neoplatonic ideas gave an immense impetus to the upsurge of Muslim theological and philosophical speculation. Plotinus (d. 268) was honoured with the title of 'the Greek Master' (Sheikh al-Yunani), and his teachings, like the theory of the creation of the world through the emanations of the Godhead, were widely discussed in the writings of Muslim mystics.

The writer who took the name of St Paul's Athenian convert, Dionysius the Areopagite (Acts 17:34), but is better known as the Pseudo-Dionysius (fl. c. 500) was a Syrian monk, a disciple of the Neoplatonic philosopher Proclus. By about AD 850 his works were known from the Tigris to the Atlantic.

Christian ideas were also all too evident. Historically, Sufism originated in southern Iraq, and its earliest development took place in the region between Basra and Kufa, where Christian influence was particularly strong (Nicholson, 1969, p. 473). The influence of Christianity on Islamic mysticism as exemplified in the faith and practice of the Christian monks has been extensive and significant.

Among the early Muslims Jesus often occupied a place alongside and little if at all inferior to Muhammad. In some regions Jesus and his Virgin Mother became exalted symbolic figures, and the holy days dedicated to them were observed by Muslims. 'Well into the Middle Ages,' writes Gibb, 'the Christian festivals survived alongside the official feasts of Islam as the great public festivals of the Mohammedan world' (1969, p. 89).

Jesus, as a model of poverty, purity and virtue, was often praised by Muslim mystics as 'the seal of the saints'. The concept of Jesus as a person more than mortal, which even the Koran acknowledges, opened another avenue for Sufi mystics and devotional poets, leading ultimately to the wholly un-Islamic doctrine in which the Logos is made incarnate in Muhammad (see Section 11.15).

In the Islamic traditions, Sufi mystics frequented the monasteries and studied the devotional literature of the Christian monks, and consulted Christian hermits on religious questions. The meeting of a truth-seeking Sufi wayfarer and a Christian ascetic or sage who expounds mystical doctrines to him is a favourite theme in the lives of many Sufi teachers.

A catalogue of the various Sufi leaders is outside the scope of this book. What follows is a brief list of the principal Muslim mystics, some of whom showed the influence of Christian teachings.

Hasan of Basra (d. 728) was an ascetic, pietist, Arabic scholar, and staunch believer in free will. He spoke of Jesus as Lord of the Spirit and the Word (Arberry, 1964, p. 59), and had a high regard for his followers – especially for their dedication to learning. Much loved by his community, it was said that when he died the whole city of Basra attended his funeral.

Wasil ibn Ata (d. 749) was a pupil of Hasan of Basra, and used to frequent the house of a certain Buddhist (sumani), where Manichaean, Zoroastrian and Gnostic scholars would assemble to discuss matters of philosophical and religious interest. Wasil left the circle of Hasan of Basra to form the earliest of the rebel Mutazili schools, which took a rationalist and critical view of religious dogma.

Abdulla ibn Maymun (fl. c. 760), a Zoroastrian by birth, settled in Syria and came under the influence of the Gnostic Paulicans. His followers formed the Batini (esoteric) sect, which gave to the Koranic text a hidden meaning which allowed considerable latitude in its interpretation. Many of his doctrines were adopted by the Egyptian Fatimids.

Ibrahim ibn Adham (d. 777) – the Abou Ben Adhem of Leigh Hunt's poem (1814) – was a prince of Balkh who, during a journey to Syria, stayed with a Christian anchorite, Father Simeon, from whom he learned the art of meditation (murakaba) as a way to acquiring gnosis (maarifa).

Rabia of Basra (d. 801), the first and most famous of the women Sufis, was said to have been very beautiful, receiving many offers of marriage – all of which she refused, saying, 'I am wholly God's.' Asked if she loved the Prophet, she replied, 'My love for God leaves room for naught else.' She regarded all holy rites as meaningless, and on seeing the Kaaba she turned away, saying, 'I saw only a house of bricks and stones. What does it profit me?' One of her most celebrated prayers was, 'O God if I worship thee for love of paradise, exclude me from paradise. If I love thee for fear of hell, burn me in hell!'

Maaruf al-Kharki (d. 815), born in Basra of Christian parents, was converted to Islam, though many of his sayings reflect a fundamentally Christian spirit. When he died, Jews, Christians and Muslims all claimed him as one of themselves.

Ahmad ibn Khabit (d. 820), founder of the Khabitiya sect, believed that Allah cannot be known or even speculated about, for whatever we say of him will be wrong. The Supreme Being was made manifest through Masih (Messiah), or Christ the eternal Word made incarnate, who put on a body of flesh that he might reveal himself to humanity.

Harith al-Muhasibi (d. 857) in his treatise on religious observances drew largely on Jewish and Christian sources for the exposition of his ideas and for purposes of edification. His pupils included the famous mystic Junayd of Basra, and among the later mystics on whom he left a deep impression was the Persian philosopher al-Ghazali.

Dhul Nun (d. 859), an Egyptian ascetic, mystic and alchemist, was well versed in hermetic doctrine and Hellenistic science, and was said to have been able to read and understand the hieroglyphics of ancient Egypt. He was a propagator of speculations about gnosis, and came to be known as the father of Islamic theosophy.

Hallaj (d. 992), grandson of a Zoroastrian priest and son of a Zoroastrian convert to Islam, lived in a Christian settlement in Jerusalem and in a Mazdaean community in Wasit, and was suspected of dealings with the Karmathians. He held that the Kaaba should be destroyed and the pilgrimage performed in one's own room. He taught that Jesus was a person in whom deification had been perfectly realized. Hallaj's doctrines had a pronounced Christian bias, and some regarded him as a secret Christian. He was accused of heresy for preaching the primacy of saints over prophets, for degrading the status of Muhammad, and for announcing, 'I am the Truth.' His request to be crucified was denied and he was flogged to death.

Abu Sayid (d. 1049), a Persian Sufi, wrote, 'Our holy work will not be accomplished until every mosque lies in ruins and faith and infidelity are one.' He regarded religious observances as a bondage, the sharia as superfluous and the Kaaba as nothing but a stone house. He never performed the pilgrimage, saying that if he so desired the Kaaba would visit him and perform the circumambulation around his head. He encouraged his pupils to dance and sing, forbidding them to interrupt their dancing even when the muezzin made the call for prayer.

Omar Khayyam (d. 1123), a Persian mathematician, astronomer and author of freethinking quatrains – delightfully if rather loosely rendered into English by Edward Fitzgerald in 1859 – was born in Nishapur, spent his formative years in Balkh, and was buried in Nishapur. His frequent references to wine and women in his verses are given a mystical interpretation by some, but are thought by others to suggest less than spiritual inspiration.

Sanai (d. 1131), a Persian poet and moralist, was, like almost all the other great poets of Persia, deeply influenced by Sufism. He wrote an epic survey of ascetic and mystical thought and introduced Jesus into many of his illustrative anecdotes as a gentle yet firm being and a stern antagonist of Satan, whose stratagems he sets at naught at each of their many encounters.

Ibn Arabi (d. 1240), poet and Sufi, called the greatest theosophist of Islam, claimed descent from Hatim Tayi, a pre-Islamic prince of the Christian tribe of Tayi. He was influenced by hermeticism and Neoplatonism, and employed the designation *Kalima* (Logos) in regard to both Jesus and Muhammad. Extremely liberal in his attitude, he boasted that he was able to worship with the monk in his chapel, the Jew in his synagogue and the Muslim in his mosque – with equal devotion. He was execrated by the orthodox and his works were frequently burned.

Rumi (d. 1273), the greatest of the Persian Sufis, was born in Konya (ancient Iconium), where Greek and Christian traditions were very much alive in his time and where the population spoke partly in Greek. There were large monastic settlements not very far from the capital, and Christian teachings clearly influenced his thinking. His masterpiece, the *Mathnavi*, is highly venerated and is known as the Koran of the Persians.

Hafiz (d. 1389), most celebrated of the Persian lyric poets, was a Sufi. Like Omar Khayyam he uses a wine vocabulary that has been given a symbolic significance. Like most other Sufi poets he showed a great affinity with Christianity. One of his verses reads, 'Where the turbaned anchorite/ Chanteth Allah day and night,/Church bells ring the call to prayer/And the Cross of Christ is there' (Nicholson, 1963, p. 88).

14

THE CRITICS OF ISLAM

Islam has never wanted for critics, and it has had its detractors among the Arabs from the beginning of Muhammad's mission. Here, however, we are concerned with the critics in the West, of whom there has been no dearth either, starting with the churchmen of the Middle Ages, who were unremittingly hostile to Islam.

In recent times the climate of scholarly opinion has changed only in presentation and emphasis, and, if the words used are less intemperate than those used in the past, the general intention remains unaltered. A careful reading between the lines of those who have a good word to say about Islam often reveals a damning with faint praise, or a marked condescension, or a less than subtle undercurrent of censoriousness. Substantially, the implication is that what is good about Islam is what it shares with Judaism and Christianity. What is most typically Islamic is quite often seen as unacceptable to rational thinkers.

While Western critics are prepared to consider all forms of religion, from great faiths like Buddhism and Hinduism to primitive beliefs like paganism and animism, with tolerance and understanding, 'they are prone', says Watt, 'to see only the worst in Islam and its prophet'.

Muslims dismiss all attacks on their faith as anti-Islamic polemic, a calculated misrepresentation of their religion stemming from Christian prejudice and Zionist-instigated ill will. For almost thirteen hundred years the Muslim and Christian worlds have been in constant, sometimes sanguinary, conflict, with Islam making steady inroads into Christian domains and – from the Crusades onwards – successfully resisting Christian encroachments into its preserve. The West, in the view of Muslims, is motivated by jealousy at their successes in the past and chagrin at Islam's unassailable power today.

Western scholars would insist that neither the early successes of the Muslims nor the Crusades are relevant to the issue. The Western perception of Islam has little to do with those far-off and long-forgotten battles, or with the current wealth of the Muslim oil states, but reflects a deep-seated and instinctive distrust of what is seen as an alien, aggressive and fanatical faith. Even the most sympathetic scholars seem to have a genuine problem with writing about Muhammad as a prophet under divine guidance, or the Koran as the authentic word of a benevolent God.

Today there exists between Islam and the West not only a lack of understanding but often a lack of a desire to understand. Any rapprochement between the two has been described as being at best 'coexistence on a cold-war basis'. We shall consider some of the main targets towards which the barbed, and often envenomed, shafts of Western critics have been directed.

14.1 The False Prophet

The prime target of Western censure has been Muhammad himself. No great figure in history is so poorly appreciated and no great religious leader so maligned in Western writings as he.

Not that he has lacked his champions as well. Among those who came forward to pay tribute to the Prophet in the last century was Thomas Carlyle, who rejected the frequently held view that Muhammad was a charlatan and a fraud. He was, in Carlyle's opinion, a combination of poet, prophet and reformer. He could not have attracted so many high-minded adherents – mystics and philosophers among them – if he had not been sincere.

Other defenders have stated that from the record of his early mission in Mecca there can be little doubt about Muhammad's stature. He was imbued with a passionate desire to reform Arab society and was convinced he could provide the message and devise the means by which the reformation could be accomplished. Through divine inspiration he received the message and resolutely proclaimed it in the face of ridicule and fierce opposition.

He was a great leader of men, faithful to his friends and allies. He inspired unfaltering loyalty in his followers and showed concern for their welfare. He could be statesmanlike and forgiving, and was often magnanimous to his enemies. All in all, he was a powerful moral force who steered the Arabs from the path of idolatry into a simple monotheism, and imposed unity among a divided people.

It is foolish to dismiss him as an impostor. Too much can be made of his polygamy by the prudish. The significance of his raids and battles can be overstated. He should, it is said, be judged by the standards of his time. He was attempting to change a lawless and headstrong people and had to use guile and force to ensure the survival of the faith he was called upon to proclaim.

The case by the opposition is presented with equal conviction and has a long history in Christendom. In the medieval Christian tradition Muhammad was identified with the one mentioned in the Book of Daniel, who would arise after the empires of Babylon, Persia, Greece and Rome, and 'wear out the saints of the most High, and think to change times and laws' (Dan. 7:25). He was the Beast of the Apocalypse who would 'make war with the saints' and have authority over 'tribes, languages and nations' (Rev. 13:7). He was the False Prophet (Rev. 19:20), the man of sin

(2 Thess. 2:3), and the Spirit of the Abyss who would be cast into the bottomless pit (Rev. 9:11).

In the Christian view the gospel concerning Christ was final. Any other teaching was false and, as the Bible cautioned, even if an angel from heaven – here meaning Gabriel – came down to preach it, was not to be accepted (Gal. 1:8). Jesus specifically spoke of false prophets yet to come, and warned that if people report that such a one is in the desert – meaning Muhammad, some believe – 'do not go there' (Matt. 24:26).

It would be on the inspiration of the false teaching promulgated by such a prophet that the 'abomination of desolation' (Dan. 11:31) – meaning the Dome of the Rock in Jerusalem – would be raised upon the holy place of sacrifice where once stood the Temple of Solomon (see also Mango, 1988, p. 205). 'Whoso readeth', Jesus had said, 'let him understand' (Matt. 24:15).

The information compiled by Dr Norman Daniel for the 250-year period from AD 1100 to 1350 shows how strong was the feeling against Muhammad and his religion during the Middle Ages in Christian Europe. St Bernard of Clairvaux, who preached the Second Crusade, referred to the Arabian prophet as 'the prince of Darkness'. Pope Innocent III identified Muhammad with the Antichrist.

The denunciations went on through the succeeding centuries. Martin Luther (d. 1546) found it incredible that reasonable people could be induced to accept such a religion. To Blaise Pascal (d. 1662) Muhammad was without authority, his coming was not foretold, he worked no miracles and revealed no mysteries.

Voltaire (d. 1778), perhaps more than anyone, summed up the judgement of Enlightenment critics when he wrote what has since continued to be affirmed in different words by different critics: that there is nothing new in the religion of Islam except the claim that Muhammad is the prophet of Allah. All else is borrowed. Edward Gibbon summarized the religion as being made up of an eternal truth and a necessary fiction: that there is no God but God; and that Muhammad is the apostle of God. One may suspect, writes Gibbon, that the Prophet 'secretly smiled at the credulity of his proselytes'.

More recent critics, again not necessarily taking a Christian standpoint, also tend to question the idealized version of Muhammad's life. Few, even among the most sympathetic, have been drawn into an unqualified defence of the Prophet, and most find it difficult to accept, without considerable reserve, the view of Muslims who hold him in such high esteem. The yawning gulf between the Muhammad of faith and the Muhammad of fact cannot be bridged, they feel, except by the most credulous. The Prophet had his share of human foibles, and to attempt by silence or denial to suppress them is a wilful distortion of the truth.

The evidence on which these judgements are based is taken not, as might be supposed, from the writings of Jews and Christians, but represents the views of Arabs, mostly belonging to his own tribe and family, who lived in close contact with him in Mecca, supported by confirmatory verses from the Koran itself and by the records and traditions preserved and reported by Muhammad's Arab biographers.

Muhammad, it is said, possessed the quality of what the Arabs call *hilm*: a calculated guilefulness in the pursuit of his aim, a tireless cunning in the manipulation of men (Rodinson, 1976, p. 221). He was the great pretender, who put on an appearance of benignity when it suited him but was inspired by more ruthless instincts. When he showed magnanimity it was for shrewd political ends. He made a show of forgiveness when it was expedient to do so; otherwise he could be remorseless and vengeful, and pursued without mercy anyone who opposed him.

To the contention put forward by Muslim apologists that Muhammad should be judged by the standards of the time, the critics submit that the great religious leaders of the world – Buddha, Zoroaster, Confucius, Guru Nanak and indeed many others of lesser stature – may be judged by any standards. Muhammad has been described as an ambitious and designing Arab sheikh, full of worldly stratagems, who lured people to his banner by the prospect of loot and sensual indulgence.

Such harsh sentiments, it must be added, are a mild reflection of some of the more unflattering comments made on the Prophet by Western scholars and historians of modern times. In short, it is argued by his detractors, Muhammad's life in his later years does not bear close inspection, and his claim to be an apostle of God appears incompatible with his character, conduct and career.

With regard to the Koran, as we have seen, the almost unanimous view among non-Muslim Western scholars is that it was Muhammad's own composition, which he claimed to be divinely inspired to ensure its acceptance. This was also the view of several of Muhammad's contemporaries, in particular the Meccans, who believed that he was self-deluded, if not mendacious, pretending to revelations he knew were untrue. They spoke of both the Torah and the Koran as impostures (28:48). Scraps of such opinions survived among sceptical groups in the Near East for centuries. The saying attributed to Frederick II (d. 1250) that the world had seen three great impostors, Moses, Jesus and Muhammad, originated in the Muslim world.

It was perhaps inevitable that Western scholars should also attempt a psychological diagnosis of Muhammad's character and temperament. Their conclusions – mostly hostile – range over a wide gamut, from Muhammad as a neurotic personality with a severe mental disturbance to Aloys Sprenger's view that he was a psychopath (Schimmel, 1985, p. 248).

The Prophet's mental states during his early inspirational phases have likewise been explained in many ways. Gustav Weil sought to show that Muhammad suffered from epilepsy. Aloys Sprenger suggested he may in addition have been subject to attacks of a hysterical nature. The Arabist

Theodor Nöldeke believed the ecstasies were uncontrollable emotional fits. According to D. S. Margoliouth, however, Muhammad's seizures were artificially produced. D. B. Macdonald was also inclined to believe they were merely a device by which he secured sanction for his revelations.

14.2 Fanaticism

One of the grimmer judgements found scattered in Western writings on the Prophet is that he inspired in his followers a fanaticism to the death for the faith, and a fierce intolerance towards those who rejected the faith. He showed scant concern for treaties or alliances, professions of friendship or family obligations, if Islam and his own prophethood were at issue.

His followers therefore were not deterred by similar sanctities either. Some were prepared to murder their fathers and brothers if Muhammad so wished, or to gain his approval. Hisham al-Kalbi writes that the son of Abdulla ibn Obayi begged the Prophet to give him permission to kill his own father and bring him his head, but as Abdulla was an influential figure in Medina the Prophet did not think it expedient to give his sanction to the would-be patricide. Such fanaticism is also recorded of the murderer of the Jewish merchant Ibn Sunayna (see Section 14.3).

When Muhammad ordered the elimination of an enemy, his emissaries, having performed the deed, severed the head of the victim and brought the grisly trophy to the Prophet as proof of a mission accomplished. The severing of heads became common practice among Muslim assassins. As we have seen, in 680, during the reign of Yazid I, the same act of barbarous mutilation was carried out on Husayn, the grandson of the Prophet, and his whole family.

By precept and example, it is pointed out, the Prophet demonstrated to the people that violent and bloody methods were necessary to advance the cause. This cause was the enslavement of the world to the will of Allah as interpreted by Muhammad. He advocated jihad as an unflagging war against unbelievers; taught that the Muslim who kills an infidel goes to paradise; sanctioned the assassination of his critics and mockers; made raids on merchant caravans for booty; and attacked and plundered defenceless towns, prompting Margoliouth's blunt appraisal of him as 'a captain of banditti' (Glubb, 1979, p. 154).

Behaviour of this nature, say the critics, is beyond any excuse that might be put forward to justify it. Such conduct, wrote Voltaire, cannot be defended by any person, 'unless superstition has choked all the light of reason from him'.

Muhammad's repeated injunctions to kill continued to be carried out with ruthless zeal by his followers. Khalid ibn Walid, who had fought against Muhammad at Ohod but later embraced Islam, became one of the most bloodthirsty and brutal of conquerors, judged even by the standards of his day, yet his cruelty and rapacity were and still are greatly extolled among Muslims, who honoured him with the title of 'the Sword of Allah' (Sayif Allah).

In May 633, after Khalid defeated the Zoroastrian Persians at the Battle of Olayis in southern Iraq (between Hira and Basra), he issued orders that the captives should not be slain. For two days his soldiers rounded up a great multitude of prisoners and fugitives, who were then herded on to a dry river bed and there butchered until it became a crimson stream. The place thereafter proudly bore the title of 'the River of Blood'. Abu Bakr, the ruling caliph, was overjoyed when he received news of the victory and the massacre that followed it.

A wine-lover and debauchee, Khalid took a sadistic delight in beheading a defeated chieftain on the battlefield, selecting his wife (if young) or daughter, and celebrating his nuptials with her on the spot soaked with the victim's blood.

The example and command of the Prophet, critics believe, have left a terrible legacy for Islam and cast a lurid light on the history of that religion. Time and again we read accounts of how the enemies of Islam were slain without mercy. And often the victors first inflicted atrocious penalties – lopping off limbs, gouging out eyes, cutting off tongues, noses, ears, fingers, hands, feet, testicles; and disembowelling not only with the knife but with instruments first made red-hot over a fire.

The inflammatory fervour bred in the early Muslims created a supreme contempt for life. Incidents of massacres in the name of Allah and his Prophet are cited by Ibn Ishak, Ibn Hisham, al-Wakidi and other Muslim biographers and historians to demonstrate how dedication to Islam hardens all hearts and blots out all allegiances, all loyalties of kith and kin, as the Prophet had ordained.

In the Middle Ages in Europe the name 'Saracen' (Muslim) became a byword for fury, deception and brutality, and the bogey of Muhammad and his Saracenic followers was used to frighten little children (Armstrong, 1991, p. 11). Judged by the contemporary scene it would appear that violence for the advancement of the faith – once common enough in other religions too – is not an outmoded shibboleth, but remains a living reality with fundamentalists in Islam to the present day (Taheri, 1987, Ahmad, 1989).

In the extreme view of Western critics, everything that is thought to be wrong with the religion is to be ascribed to the Prophet. His influence created a climate of bigotry, intolerance and dogmatism across the lands that Islam conquered. The peoples in these countries, it is repeatedly urged, are not behind any others in forbearance and compassion, except when intoxicated by the fanaticism generated by the Prophet and his book. It has been said that the religious impulse of the Muslim world and the devotion it inspires show their noblest and best side not because of Muhammad but despite him.

14.3 Assassinations

Another feature of Muhammad's life that has drawn adverse comment from Western critics has been the number of killings carried out on his orders. From the records of the Muslim chroniclers we learn that, besides those slain during Muhammad's raiding sorties and those who fell victims to large-scale massacres, like the Jews killed at Korayza, Muhammad personally ordered the assassination of individuals, male and female, whom he regarded as his enemies. These included not only those who were actively hostile to him but those who rejected him and, above all, those who mocked his prophetic claims.

One such was the poetess Asma bint Marwan of Omayya, who had directed her satires against the citizens of Medina for being 'like gluttonous people looking towards the cooking-pot' – that is, to advancement under Islam. In January 624, on Muhammad's orders according to al-Wakidi, a purblind assassin named Omayr the Blind stabbed her to death as she slept with her suckling infant and four other children. On learning that the deed was done, Muhammad bestowed upon the murderer the title of 'Omayr the Seeing', and said to him, 'You have done a service to Allah and his messenger' (Rodinson, 1976, p. 171).

In February 624 an aged Jewish proselyte named Abu Afak, of the Amr tribe, becoming discontented with the direction Islam was taking, composed a number of stinging verses which annoyed the Muslims, who complained to Muhammad. According to Ibn Hisham, Muhammad expressed a wish to be rid of 'this pestilent fellow', and another Muslim convert from Abu Afak's own tribe soon dispatched the culprit with a sword as he lay sleeping.

In June 624, after Muhammad had gained power in Medina, a man and his wife were murdered, again at Muhammad's behest, because they had reputedly written insulting verses about him and the new religion he was preaching (Frieling, 1978, p. 33).

Another victim was Kaab ibn Ashraf, a poet of the Tayi tribe, whose mother was a Jewish woman of the Nadhir tribe. Being on good terms with the Meccans, Kaab had composed a lament on the Korayshis slain at Badr. According to Ibn Ishak, Muhammad exclaimed with annoyance that he hoped someone would dispose of Kaab. One of the Prophet's followers told Muhammad he was willing to do so, but would have to resort to cunning, trickery and lies. The Prophet had no objection to this (Rodinson, 1976, p. 176). So, in July 624, Kaab, who was with his newly married bride at the time, was thrown off guard by friendly words, lured out of doors, and set upon and killed, and his severed head was brought and placed at the feet of Muhammad.

Also according to Ibn Ishak, on the morning after the murder of Kaab, Muhammad, exasperated at the continued opposition of the Jews, said, 'Kill any Jew who falls into your power.' Thereupon a Muslim named Muhaysa, encountering a rich Jewish merchant called Ibn Sunayna, killed him even though he knew the Jew to be a confederate of his own tribe. When his brother upbraided Muhaysa for killing a confederate, the assassin replied, 'By Allah, if he who commanded me to kill him had ordered me to kill you also, I would have cut off your head' (Andrae, 1960, p. 149).

On another occasion a Meccan poet named Abu Azza had been taken prisoner while loitering after the Battle of Badr, but was released by the Prophet on promising not to bear arms against the Muslims. On his return to Mecca, however, he continued to write poems urging the desert tribes not to join Muhammad. When in March 625 he was captured again at the Battle of Ohod, he pleaded that he had kept his word and not taken up arms against the Muslims, but Muhammad motioned to a bystander who immediately decapitated the poet.

After the same battle, another Meccan, named Muawiya ibn Moghira, stayed behind when the Meccan army had left the scene of the conflict. In April 625 he secretly visited the Medina house of Othman, the Prophet's son-in-law, who was able to procure for him a three-day truce from Muhammad. But the Prophet was not disposed to forgive anyone who had fought against him, and when the man set out for Mecca Muhammad sent men to pursue and kill him.

Shortly thereafter Sofyan ibn Khalid, the chief of the Lihyan clan – now a branch of the Hodayl tribe – banded together with several other tribal leaders to follow up their victory at Ohod. When Muhammad came to hear of it he dispatched Abdulla ibn Onays with instructions to assassinate Sofyan ibn Khalid, giving him permission to say whatever he liked – even to abuse the Prophet if need be (Rodinson, 1974, p. 189) – in order to win the chief's confidence. Sofyan ibn Khalid fell for the ruse, invited the man into his tent, and was slain. The assassin returned to Medina with the chief's severed head and presented it to Muhammad while he was in the mosque. As a reward the Prophet presented him with his own staff (Muir, 1912, p. 276).

The biographers Ibn Ishak, Ibn Hisham and al-Wakidi relate that in the fourth year of the Hegira (AD 626) the Prophet sent a professional assassin named Amr ibn Omayya to Mecca to kill his arch-enemy Abu Sofyan (Glubb, 1979, p. 220). Amr failed in his mission, though he did kill three Meccans in the process and brought a fourth man captive to Muhammad, who praised his henchman for his devotion.

Al-Wakidi relates an incident about an aged Jew, Abu Rafi, chief of the Nadhir tribe, who had not migrated to Syria as directed by Muhammad but instead had taken refuge with the Jewish community in Khaybar. The Prophet ordered his execution, and in December 627 a party of five Muslims gained admittance to his house under false pretences and killed the old man as he slept. Muhammad commended the assassins when they returned to Medina.

But Muhammad continued to be worried about the Jews of Khaybar, who were now led by Osayr ibn Razin. So in January 628 he sent a delegation to Khaybar, headed by the warrior-poet Abdulla ibn Rawaha, ostensibly to invite Osayr and a party of thirty leading Jews to Medina on the assurance that Osayr would be formally declared Khaybar's ruler. The Medina delegation consisted of thirty picked killers, among them Abdulla ibn Onays. On the way, the escorting party of Muslims set upon and murdered Osayr and his entourage. The Muslims continued their journey to Medina and reported to Muhammad, who gave thanks to Allah for being delivered from an unrighteous people (Muir, 1912, p. 349).

When Muhammad returned to Mecca in triumph in January 630 he ordered the executions of certain persons whose names had been entered on a proscribed list. Members of influential families whom it was considered expedient to propitiate were pardoned, as were some of those who now accepted his mission as the prophet of Allah. The rest were executed.

Among the victims were two singing girls who had once taken part in a satirical performance ridiculing the Prophet. Ibn Ishak gives one girl's name as Furtana; the other one is not named. Also killed were a certain Huwayrith, who had once insulted the Prophet in his early Meccan days, and two men who had accepted Islam but then returned to Mecca and apostatized.

Such slayings were carried out on Muhammad's instructions till the very end of his life, as is seen in the case of a man called Ayhala ibn Kaab, whose murder was accomplished on the night before Muhammad's own death.

It has been suggested by certain Western scholars that it was such examples set by the Prophet that made political terrorism so prominent a feature of Islamic history through the centuries to the present day. The very word 'assassin' comes from the Muslim sect of Assassins who resorted to this device.

Assassination became a policy of ambitious rulers and the strategy of religious opponents. It provided a quick way to end disputes, silence troublesome rivals, shorten hostilities, end dissension, eliminate enemies, exact retribution and vengeance, and intimidate opposition.

14.4 Raids

For ten years after he had established himself in Medina, Muhammad was involved in unprovoked freebooting raids, when merchant caravans were repeatedly harassed and plundered by his raiding parties, many of which he led in person. This point figures prominently in Western appraisals of the Prophet's life.

Usually, after such a raiding expedition (*razya* or *ghazwa*), the captive women and children, along with the camels and other goods, were distributed among his followers; the men were forced either to accept Islam or to suffer enslavement, exile or death.

The early chroniclers describe the manner in which Muhammad dealt with his captives, and his response to their slaying sometimes surprised even his companions. Often the executions took place in the presence of the Prophet, who would call out exultantly that this was the punishment the victims deserved for rejecting God, his prophet and his book. The treatment of prisoners after his raid on the Meccan caravan in 624 at Badr (the so-called Battle of Badr) is taken as typifying the fate of those who fell into the hands of the early Muslims.

When the head of one of his enemies, Abu Jahal, who had lost his life in the encounter, was thrown at Muhammad's feet, the Prophet thanked Allah and exclaimed in triumph, 'This is more acceptable to me than the choicest camel in Arabia!' A prisoner named Nofal ibn Khuwaylid while being led away was spotted by Ali, who, recalling that he had overheard the Prophet praying for his death, fell upon the man and killed him. When Muhammad heard of it he cried, 'God is great! It is in answer to my prayer' (Muir, 1912, p. 227).

Another victim was the Korayshi balladeer Nadhir ibn Harith, who had once lived at the court of the Lakhmid king of Hira. Nadhir habitually boasted that his own stories were as good as any of the fictional narratives about the ancients and similar stories revealed in the Koran, and used to delight in drawing away Muhammad's Korayshi audiences with his tales of Persian heroes like Rustam and Isfendiar. Muhammad referred to him as a man 'for whom is prepared a shameful punishment' (31:5). He was brought before Muhammad and, as the Prophet's eye fell fiercely on him, Nadhir, knowing he could expect no mercy, murmured to a fellow captive, 'There is death in that glance.' On Muhammad's command he was instantly beheaded by Ali in Muhammad's presence.

When yet another captive, named Okba ibn Abu Muwayt – who was said to have acquired heterodoxy from the Christians of Hira – found himself also condemned to death, he asked in anguish who would take care of his little daughter, soon to be fatherless. Muhammad replied, 'The fires of hell' – adding, 'And I give thanks to Allah that he has brought comfort to my eyes by your death.'

Muhammad was said to have contemplated the execution of all the Meccans captured at Badr, but his more moderate followers – moved by compassion and anxious to avoid a butchery, and to forestall what would have created a bitter and long-lasting blood feud in which they would all be involved – prevailed on him to hold them up for ransom instead.

Historians record that, in addition to his numerous plundering forays,

Muhammad organized twenty-seven major raiding campaigns and eighty-five others on a smaller scale, most of which proved highly lucrative and all of which were invested with religious significance.

In time, the early raids evolved into larger battles which eventually began to take on the character of a religious war (*jihad*) against infidel or enemy populations.

14.5 The Spoils

The Muslims had been promised 'rich booty' in the Koran (48:20), and this promise began to be realized when Muhammad started his raids on merchant caravans after establishing himself in Medina.

It continued to be fulfilled when he fought against the other Arab tribes – pagan, Jewish and Christian – who resisted him, and whose lands and wealth he confiscated. All his followers had a share in the spoils, which included camels, goats and sheep, and often male and female slaves. One-fifth of all the booty went to Muhammad (8:42).

But the promise of wealth was fulfilled in full and overflowing measure as the conquest of foreign countries began to be undertaken after the Prophet's death.

It was said that when the Arabs captured the Persian winter capital of Ctesiphon (Madain) in March 637, and beheld in awe the famous dome that dominated the city gleaming in splendour across the Tigris, they gave thanks to Allah for having realized the promise made to Muhammad and shown them a glimpse of heaven on earth.

After the city was taken, the Arab soldiery wandered in a daze about the wonderful palaces and gardens beautiful as paradise. For centuries Arab writers were to dilate upon the marvels of that dream city. What the various treasures were they could not tell. The exquisite decorations seemed to them the work of celestial beings.

There were gold and silver ornaments, gorgeous vestments studded with jewels of prodigious size and brilliance; precious objects of untold variety and incalculable cost. Camphor, musk and rare spices lay around in sackfuls in the storehouses, and perfumed the surrounding chambers and corridors.

In all the rooms were carpets the like of which they had never seen. One in particular covered the wall opposite the entrance into the immense banqueting hall and represented a garden. The ground was wrought in gold thread, the walks in silver, the verges studded with emeralds, the rivulets made of pearls, the trees and flowers of rubies, amethysts and other precious stones of variegated colours. Since all the booty was dealt out in certain fixed proportions, this fabulous carpet was cut up into small pieces and distributed along with the rest of the plunder.

The ostensible purpose of the early conquests was the propagation of

Islam, but the victors soon succumbed to the belief that they had the God-given right to exploit the unlimited opportunities opening up on all sides for pillage and wealth. The conquerors began to feel that Allah had given them the free run of the world, and their primary objective became economic: to obtain territory, tribute, treasure and slaves.

After each victory there were always multitudes of captive women, young and beautiful, many of them cultured and of high birth, who remained at the free disposal of the conquerors. In 745 the caliph Marwan II in his engagements in the Caspian took a fancy to the beautiful Circassian girls, and simply ordered six hundred of them to be sent to grace his harem. The caliph Mutawakil had four thousand concubines. Down the chain of command the princes, generals and others made their several selections. The fighting men too were given a share of the human booty.

The Christian writer Alkindi (d. 915), in his *Apology*, inveighed with scathing denunciation against the conduct of his Muslim compatriots after a battle had been won.

Incredible fortunes were acquired in the process of empire-building. Arab chroniclers were at a loss for words to describe the wealth amassed by the caliphs and their subordinate chiefs, the army staff, the members of the administration and even minor officials. Every soldier garnered a rich harvest in loot. In some campaigns each rider received his reward of plunder in bags of gold and silver.

Accounts survive of men, once famed for their simple lives, ending their days as owners of hundreds of male and female slaves, vast acres, stables of the finest horses, herds of camels, cattle, sheep and goats, and treasuries stacked with leather bags filled with gold, silver and precious stones. 'Never in the history of the world', goes one account, 'has so much wealth been seen.'

Starting with the Omayyads, the caliphs and nobles lived in the grand manner. They built palatial residences for themselves, adorned with fine sculptures and paintings of plants and animals, and even of men and women. They spent weeks in their luxurious hunting lodges, where they held wine-drinking parties and were entertained by slaves and dancing girls. And this style of living prevailed not only in Damascus and Alexandria, Baghdad and Basra but in Mecca and Medina itself.

14.6 Conquest and Conversion

In the course of his early trade journeys to Palestine and Syria, Muhammad could not have failed to be impressed by Christianity's universalism. Although at first he thought of Islam as an essentially 'Arab religion' (see Section 11.2), he believed – as his influence spread – that there might be a larger sphere for its operation, and in the end went on to declare in one of the later suras of the Koran that God had sent him 'to make the religion of Islam victorious over every other religion' (9:33).

As we have seen, he had already demonstrated his growing intolerance towards Jews and Christians who refused to accept his apostleship, and – having disposed of his Meccan opponents – he started out on a career of persecution and extermination of both these religions in Arabia. The flourishing towns of the Jews – Kaynuka, Nadhir, Korayza and Khaybar – were captured one by one, their lands taken and their wealth and possessions confiscated. He then turned his attention to the Christians, and towards the end of his life he planned several incursions across the borders of Arabia, until a fever carried him off.

The programme initiated by Muhammad was maintained after his death by the caliphs Abu Bakr and Omar. By the end of the rule of the third caliph, Othman, all the remaining Jews and Christians in Arabia had been forcibly converted, expelled or slain, so that, as Muhammad had demanded on his deathbed, no second religion remained on the sacred soil.

The same general pattern prevailed during the conquests outside Arabia. In Palestine, Mesopotamia and Syria the Christian kingdoms of Ghassan, Lakhmid and Taghlib were brought to an end. The many thriving Christian communities in other parts of the Middle East were virtually blotted out.

The speed with which these Sassanian and Byzantine provinces fell to the sword of Islam convinced the Muslims that more extensive conquests could be accomplished with ease, and tempted the conquerors, elated by their success, to further aggressive ventures. The momentum once generated could not be arrested, and the expansion of Islam became assured.

Most Muslim historians insist that the Muslim conquests did not involve forcible conversions. The new religion was simple to understand and egalitarian in principle, and the conquered peoples realized that many practical advantages flowed from its acceptance. Conversion followed naturally and peacefully in the wake of conquest.

In the opinion of other scholars the facts are considerably at odds with this view. Conversions were seldom voluntary and in many cases were forced on the people by placing great obstacles in the way of those who chose not to change their faith (see Section 14.8).

It became a legitimate pursuit of Muslim rulers to invade peaceful communities and harass or persecute them into accepting Islam. The conversion applied only to the first generation and did not need to be repeated, for if a person became a Muslim by coercion, his descendants remained Muslim if not by conviction then from inertia.

In many cases the glorious conquests of the Muslim armies and the spread of the Islamic empire involved little more than the ruthless seizure of territories and the forcible proselytization of the subject populations. Large parts of North Africa, Central Asia and India were there for any strong aggressor to appropriate, and the process of religious 'cleansing' took place and Islamization proceeded apace wherever the Muslims went.

In Persia, the ancient religion of Zoroaster was obliterated. In Central Asia, where Buddhism, Christianity and the older indigenous faiths had lived side by side for centuries, Islam became dominant and the other religions were stamped out. Eastwards in Sind, and in time in parts of the rest of India, the people were converted to the new religion by methods that the Hindus today do not care to forget.

In North Africa the same process took place, though for more than two centuries the conquests were limited to the coastal cities and fortified towns. Alexandria after the Ptolemaic period was a predominantly Christian city notable for a number of remarkable, if at times choleric, teachers of theology and practitioners of the mystical life. In fact the whole region of North Africa from the shores of Egypt to Mauretania (Morocco) came under Byzantine suzerainty and was dotted with Christian churches.

Many towns in North Africa had Christian governors and large and influential Christian communities linked with the churches of Rome, Alexandria and Constantinople, and of crucial importance to the Christian world. Cyrenaica (Libya) was associated with Synesius (d. 413) bishop of Ptolemais. Carthage (in Tunisia) was known as 'the Little Rome', where both Tertullian (d. 230) and St Cyprian (d. 258) had lived and worked. Hippo in Numidia (Algeria) was associated with St Augustine (d. 430). Following the Muslim occupation the church of North Africa came to an abrupt end. Christianity was extinguished, the whole region was Islamized, and all evidence of the earlier faith was virtually effaced.

Asia Minor (modern Turkey) could boast of a long and brilliant chronicle of saints and theologians famous not only in the Eastern church but throughout Christendom. Such were St John the Divine (d. 100), associated with Patmos and Ephesus; Polycarp (d. 155), with Smyrna (Izmir); St George (fl. c. 300), with Paphlagonia; Theodore of Mopsuestia (d. 429), with Cilicia; and St Basil the Great (d. 379), Gregory of Nazianzus (d. 390) and Gregory of Nyssa (d. 395), with Cappadocia.

The region had ten archbishoprics, forty-five metropolitanates and more than 370 bishoprics, and a rich and colourful tapestry of Christian history continued to unroll through the successive centuries. Hardly a shred of that glorious fabric survived the Seljuk and Ottoman onslaughts.

14.7 Jihad

The term *jihad*, 'striving', in the cause of God (5:39), which is enjoined in several passages in the Koran, is commonly interpreted as signifying a holy war against the infidel. The 'striver' (*mujahid*) is one who participates in such a war, and his purpose is the conversion of unbelievers, the extermination of unbelief, and the spread of the faith.

The Prophet declared that Muslims should never cease from fighting in the cause of God. This confirmed the view in the minds of his followers that the sword, the symbolic weapon of the faith, must ever remain unsheathed for the glory of Islam, and for many centuries jihad in its most violent forms was seen as a religious duty incumbent upon all Muslims.

It was believed that a person who lost his life in a religious war became a martyr (shahid – from the Syriac sahada, 'witness'), and ascended immediately to paradise. This enticing prospect, it is thought, may have been one of the motives behind the almost continuous and unprovoked wars of aggression undertaken by the Muslims against non-Muslim countries.

In many quarters jihad was regarded as a constant and unending mission, leading ultimately to the conversion of the whole world. With the objective of universal Islamization in mind, modern exponents of the holy war have revived an earlier concept: that for the true Muslim the world must be considered as being divided into two great camps. One is the world of Islam (dar al-Islam), consisting of countries where Muslims are in the majority and where Muslim law prevails (see Section 14.8). The other is the non-Muslim world, called the land of conflict (dar al-Harb), where infidels predominate and non-Muslim laws prevail, such as Europe and America. Christendom is par excellence such a land of conflict (Schacht and Bosworth, 1974, p. 180). The land of conflict is potentially a seat of war until it is turned into the abode of Islam (D. B. Macdonald, in SEI, 1974, p. 69).

The Western democracies are seen as effete and without moral direction. In their blind dedication to the myths of freedom and tolerance, they will fall easy victims to the uncompromising authority of Islam. The West today is mammon-obsessed and clearly destined to lose its religious, cultural and social inheritance by default. The conversion of the West is thus the immediate objective of modern jihad.

Muslims have already gained a small but secure foothold in Europe and America, and propose to concentrate their best efforts in these regions. Once the West is Islamized, the other infidel countries will fall like ripe plums into the lap of Islam. With the West conquered, the writ of the Prophet will rapidly run like a flame through all the nations around the globe.

Muslims living in the infidel West today, it is said, have very clear obligations for the furtherance of their cause. By propaganda and personal contact, spread the message of the Prophet with ever-growing zeal. Claim special privileges as a minority community. Strive for positions of influence in government, business and the media, and in the legal, medical, scientific and teaching professions. By every available means, make the Muslim voice more distinctly heard and the Muslim presence more clearly visible.

Increase the Muslim population by methods already sanctioned in Islam, and by promoting – legally or clandestinely – the influx of Muslim immigrants into the Western countries. Campaign for more Muslim representatives in state institutions, at both central and local level, and strive for virtual autonomy within each of them. When the balance of power begins to shift, however slightly, in their favour, Muslims, although still in a minority, will be in a position to manipulate the policies of any government and dictate the changes they require. They can insist on the free and unhampered practice of Islamic fundamentalism, including time off for prayers in schools and places of work, and on the introduction of an Islamized curriculum in educational institutions and of the sharia into the legal code.

Muslims, it is said, must never forget that Islam and Christianity are incompatible. History has demonstrated that the two can never be reconciled. Integration in any form is not to be contemplated, nor is compromise. If any concessions are to be made, these must be made only by the host country.

The economic pressure that the Muslim oil states could bring to bear – at least as long as the oil continues to flow – would preclude any effective action being taken by the Western powers against the Muslims living in their midst. The ultimate triumph of Islamic jihad is assured, making the world one indivisible Islamic community.

Some regard the expectation of a wholly Muslim world as a pipedream, and point to the impracticality of extending in any appreciable measure the sphere of Muslim influence and control without provoking considerable resistance. It is difficult enough, they maintain, to find areas of reconciliation between the warring factions within Islam itself, like the Sunnis and Shias, or to arrest the growth of modern schismatic sects like the influential Ahmadiyas, and flourishing offshoots like the Bahais. It is unrealistic to believe that even a modest conversion of people from other world faiths, like the Buddhists, Hindus, Sikhs and Jews, and from non-religious groups like the atheists, humanists, agnostics and Marxists, is remotely feasible, far less the total engulfment of the Christian world within the Islamic fold.

Because the division of the world into the two hostile camps of Islam and the Infidel can no longer make sense, Muslim reformers have revived and modified the concept of an earlier school of canon law which recognizes a third category, called the world of reconciliation (*dar al-sulh*), based on truce or treaty, for the guidance of Muslims living in non-Muslim countries. Generally, they are advised to abide by the laws prevailing in the land of their adoption, live there as good citizens, and keep the peace.

The concept of jihad has also been given a more temperate interpretation. Jihad in its militant form may have been justified in the early days of Islam, when the religion was in the process of growth and was meeting with hostile opposition. Today, jihad should be taken to mean a fight against social evils and against one's own evil instincts. The concept of an everlasting militant jihad for the conversion of the world no longer applies, and the tendency to invoke jihad on every trifling occasion can only bring the idea into ridicule and should be resisted.

14.8 Pax Islamica

The Muslim attitude towards their non-Muslim subjects varied under different rulers. While the fairness of some was exemplary, it can hardly be said to have compensated for the bigotry of the majority of others. The harsh legislation against non-believers introduced by the Omayyad caliph Omar II was made even harsher by the Abbasid caliph Mutawakil, and this became standard policy in many areas of the caliphate. Under the Pax Islamica, only Muslims were accorded the privileges of full citizenship, and there is little evidence of the much-vaunted tolerance of Muslim rule.

In theory, idolators and atheists living in a Muslim country (*dar al-Islam*) were expected to convert or risk being sold into slavery or perishing by the sword. Although the actual extermination of such classes did not usually take place, they were not considered as being under the protection of the state, and they counted in law as virtual non-persons. Most people in this category accepted conversion in order to survive.

Non-Muslim 'people of the book', like Jews and Christians, though not forced to become Muslims, had to submit to various disabilities. Such non-Muslim minorities were classed as *dhimmi*, 'permitted', people to whom life and only restricted liberties were granted. They paid a special capitation tax (*jizya*) and were treated – as Jews were in Christian countries till recent times – as an inferior people, with the status of second-class citizens. Many were forced into conversion by this discriminatory policy.

Dhimmis were frequently confined to their own neighbourhood, and their religious, cultural and economic life given no scope for growth. They could not aspire to high office, and although many Jews and Christians were taken into official service, and some reached eminence in other spheres, it was only because their communities paid greater attention to education and they had made themselves useful and indispensable.

Dhimmis were expected to remain inconspicuous. They were not allowed to build grand houses or live in ostentatious style, even if they could afford to do so, as this would offend the Muslims. Under some rulers they were required to wear special clothing when venturing out of doors, so that they might be distinguished from Muslims. Unbelievers could not marry Muslim women (60:10), whereas Muslims were free to marry non-Muslim women. Often the sharia was applied to dhimmis to their disadvantage. The evidence of a non-Muslim was not accepted against that of a Muslim in a court of law.

Religious discrimination was particularly stringent. In the case of

Christians, although existing churches and religious schools were not as a rule destroyed, they could not be repaired, nor could new ones be built. Churches were sometimes turned into mosques. Religious observances such as church processions during the great festivals and the use of church bells or the public display of crosses were banned, as constituting the open demonstration of an alien faith in a Muslim country. Christians could not propagate their religion, print or distribute religious literature, or criticize Islam or the Prophet. It is known that in some instances, as with the Christians of Taghlib, they were not allowed to baptize their children.

In most Islamic countries the policy has been, and by various devices continues to be, to discriminate against non-Muslims, or to impose sharia regulations on all citizens, irrespective of their religion. The strict imposition of the Pax Islamica by Saudi Arabia, which refuses to allow the building of places of worship for its large populations of non-Muslim workers, has the tacit approval of the whole Muslim world. For its part, it appears to be the policy of the Saudi government to provide financial backing to make the minaret – the unmistakable symbol of Muslim triumphalism – dominate the skyline of every major city in the Christian West.

Proselytization by coercion proceeds apace in Islamic states today, as with the forcible conversion of thousands of non-Muslims in the Malaysian state of Sabah in northern Borneo in the 1970s, and the conversion by the governments of Pakistan and Indonesia of their animist and pagan subjects in the remoter regions of their respective states. The policy of calculated genocide of Christians and animists by the authorities of the Sudan has been going on for almost a decade. Yet not a whisper is ever heard from any Muslim organization about these covert or overt acts of state transgression against international law and human rights.

Muslim countries are making it increasingly difficult for Christians to live in their midst. This is in keeping with an overall and long-term policy, as was made clear at a number of Muslim conferences held first in Lahore, in 1985, and then in Germany, Switzerland, Australia and other places. The declared policy of these convocations was to ensure that the governments of the Middle East make no concessions to their non-Muslim subjects but progressively restrict the conditions under which they live, so that these aliens are forced out of their areas and the whole of the Middle East becomes totally Islamized. This would involve, besides the elimination of Israel, the forcible conversion or 'removal' of all Christian and non-Christian minorities. Their churches and places of worship would be bought out or taken over by force (Hiskett, 1993, p. 245).

14.9 Infidels

In the Koran (2:37) the non-believer is spoken of as a 'denier' (*kafir*), because he turns down the message brought by Muhammad and is consequently not of the true faith. The term 'kafir' embraces all categories of non-believers, false believers and doubters. Their sin is rejection and blasphemy (*kufr*); contact with them brings uncleanliness (*najasa*), and is to be avoided at all costs.

Among the infidels is the materialist (*dahri*), who stresses the eternity (*dahr*) and self-sufficiency of matter. It follows that the materialist is also an atheist, who maintains that God is not the First Cause and that belief in his existence is mistaken. The polytheist (*wasani*), who believes in more than one God, is likewise an infidel; he is so called because he worships images (*wasan*), and is therefore also an idolator, and like the atheist he is held in abhorrence.

The presence of such people should not be tolerated, and the Koran has specific directives against them: 'When you meet infidels strike off their heads till you have made a great slaughter among them' (47:4). Those who are troubled about having shed blood in dealing with the infidel hosts are assured, 'It is not you who slew them, but God slew them' (8:17). An additional exhortation is embodied in the celebrated Verse of the Sword, enjoining Muslims to 'seek out, ambush, besiege, seize and slay unbelievers wherever they may be found, unless they are converted to Islam' (9:5). Infidels of all these categories are destined for the lowest pits of hell-fire.

The 'people of the book', such as Zoroastrians, Jews and Christians, who do not accept Muhammad as the last and greatest of all the prophets and who repudiate the revelations embodied in the Koran, are also classed as kafirs.

The Zoroastrians, it is said, once possessed a true revelation, which they lost. They now follow the Zend religion (named from the Zend-Avesta, their 'corrupted' scriptures). They believe in two eternal principles, represented by darkness and light, and are thus guilty of the heresy of dualism (*zendik*). The Koran states quite clearly that it is God alone who brings into being both the darkness and the light (6:1, and cf. Isa. 45:7).

The Jews have failed to understand the religion of Abraham and have departed from his original teachings and gone their own way, ignoring the true doctrine that has been announced afresh by Muhammad and set forth in the Koran. A hard-hearted people, the Jews have refused to see the truth of the message and have rejected conversion to Islam; they must therefore also be counted among the infidels.

Christians believe that by direct descent (*hulul*) God became incarnate in Jesus. This constitutes the abominable heresy of associationism (*shirk*), or linking Jesus with the unitary God and giving him divine attributes. The Christian is thus an associationist (*mushrik*) and, like the Zoroastrian and the Jew, is destined for hell-fire. (The term 'mushrik', like the term 'kafir', is sometimes used for all classes of infidel.)

Infidels include not only the non-believers who lived during or after Muhammad's day and heard or learned about his message and rejected it, but everyone who had ever lived in the past and had no chance of knowing about the Koranic revelations. They too would be consigned to hell.

Various categories of Muslim were also drawn into the infidelity net. A close companion of the Prophet named Abdulla ibn Omar records that Muhammad once predicted that after his death the gate of Muslim dissension (*fitna*) would be opened, never to be shut again. And, just as the Jews were divided into seventy-one sects and the Christians into seventy-two sects, so, he prophesied, the community he had established would be split up into seventy-three sects, and all the Muslim sects would go to hell except the saved (*najiya*) who followed the true religion. When the people asked him which sect that would be, Muhammad replied, 'The one professed by me and my companions.'

To orthodox members of one Muslim sect, persons of all other Muslim sects not of their persuasion are to be treated as infidels. According to the Shias, for instance, all Sunnis are kafirs (H. M. T. Ahmad, 1989, p. 73). Many Muslims have a particular hatred for schismatic sects like the Ahmadiyas and quasi-Muslim sects like the Bahais, with their millions of converts and flourishing congregations.

Because of the complexity of the subject, infidelity is not always easy to determine. God is one (*wahid*) and the true Muslim is a believer in one God (*muwahid*). But the oneness of God must be clearly defined. Thus belief in the oneness of existence (*wahdat al-wujud*), if interpreted to mean that everything is God, constitutes pantheism and is a form of heresy. Many other pitfalls lie in wait for those who are not sufficiently versed in the subtleties of theological speculation.

Muslims who pretend to believe in Islam but who secretly oppose, ridicule or deny Muhammad and his message are classed as hypocrites (*munafik*) and are guilty of the offence of duplicity (*riya*) towards God; they will therefore receive their due deserts by shameful punishment in the everlasting fire.

An abhorrent species of infidel is the heretic (*mubtadi*, 'inventor'), the Muslim responsible for introducing innovation (*bida*) into Islamic doctrine or practice. Another is the deviator (*mulhid*), who shifts from the true teaching and presents his own interpretation of the Koranic message. All such misguided reformers who initiate novel ideas and opinions opposed to the settled and orthodox doctrine and so create doubt and dissension among the faithful will burn for ever.

The worst class of infidel is the apostate (*murtad*), a former Muslim who has renounced his religion and by his defection has dishonoured the faith. Apostasy (*irtidad*) is regarded as particularly reprehensible, because the culprit has abandoned Islam after having savoured its blessings. It is an insult to the Prophet and an affront to the whole community of Muslims, who, by the apostate's rejection of the faith, are treated as being in error.

In his collection of traditions, al-Bukhari relates an instance where

Muhammad had a group of camel-thieves and apostates punished by having their hands and feet cut off and their eyes pulled out, after which they were left to die in the desert (Hughes, 1977, p. 64). The third caliph, Ali, had several apostates burned alive.

There is no mention of death for apostasy in the Koran, but by inference it is argued that, since the Koran clearly prescribes death for those who are infidels, the same penalty is certainly due for apostasy, unless the culprit recants. Islamic rulers generally dealt (and in some countries still deal) very severely with apostates, the punishments ranging from loss of civil rights, exile or confiscation of property, to imprisonment, torture or death.

14.10 Inquisition

Muhammad spoke out very firmly against backsliders and hypocrites and was himself responsible for ordering the killing of those who took a stand against him.

In 783 the Abbasid caliph Mahdi ibn Mansur established a department of state headed by a minister whose duty it was, by means of interrogation, to search out and put down heresy and punish apostates and infidels. In the very first year, this inquisition (mihna, 'test') apprehended 'a great multitude' of heretics and put them to death.

In 833 the caliph Mamun, who favoured the Mutazili doctrine – that the Koran was not eternal, but created – had the powers of the inquisition extended to apprehend and discipline anyone whose opinions differed from the official Mutazili view in this matter. The famous theologian Ahmad ibn Hanbal was found to disagree with the Mutazili belief and was flogged and imprisoned on the orders of the caliph.

Action on these lines was halted in 850 by the caliph Mutawakil – a great persecutor of Jews and Christians – as it was regarded as superfluous. But the idea underlying the inquisition was too useful to be abandoned and was never quite relinquished. Throughout the caliphate unofficial inquisition courts came into operation, presided over by orthodox theologians, to silence dissent and censor unorthodox books and publications. Free-thinkers and heretics were apprehended and punished as a matter of course.

Over the centuries literally thousands of people were deprived of their rights, reviled, persecuted, punished – with tortures no less gruesome than those employed by the inquisitors of Christian Spain – because their speculations concerning the Prophet, the Koran and the religion of Islam were too bold, their ideas too unscriptural, or their conclusions too uncompromising.

The full story of the great Muslim dissenters is one of the still unwritten chapters of Islamic history, and here we can give only a representative list of a few of the individuals who fell victim to the inquisition, either official or unofficial, under Muslim rule.

The theologian Jaad ibn Dirham was executed in Wasit in 737 by order of the Omayyad caliph Hisham for having advanced the Mutazili doctrine of the created Koran. The philosopher Ghaylan of Damascus was executed in 743 by order of the same caliph for expressing belief in free will. The theologian Jahm ibn Safwan was executed in 746 for his theory that man was a puppet entirely manipulated by God, and for denying the eternity of paradise and hell, saying that both would pass away in time.

Ibn al-Mukaffa wrote a book criticizing Muhammad and claiming that he could imitate the style of the Koran. In 758 first his limbs were hacked off one by one and thrown into the flames, then his trunk followed. The blind poet Bashar ibn Burd, accused of introducing Zoroastrian dualism into Islam, was thrown into a swamp in Batiha in 784.

Fayad ibn Ali, head of the Mimiya or Muhammadiya sect, was executed in 895 for preaching the divinity of Muhammad, which was thought to resemble the Christian concept of Christ. Mansur al-Hallaj was executed in 922 for heresy, blasphemy and infidelity when he claimed spiritual union with God.

The Shia mystic Shalmaghani was executed in 934 for declaring that both Moses and Muhammad were impostors: Moses because he had behaved treacherously in the mission entrusted to him by Aaron (Harun), and Muhammad because he had behaved treacherously in the mission entrusted to him by Ali.

Shihabuddin Yahya Suhrawardi was executed in 1191 for apostasy, on the order of Saladin. He was later to be honoured as a martyr, with the title of 'al-Maktul' – 'the Slain'. He taught that all living things have their being in Truth, and based his proof of God on the symbolism of light. Abul Futuh, a voluminous and imaginative writer in Persian who tended to pantheism, was found guilty of heresy and executed in 1191.

Fazlulla of Asterabad in Khorasan, Persia, claimed that God had disclosed to Adam the secret of nine letters of the Arabic alphabet, to Abraham fourteen and to Muhammad twenty-eight; but to him God had revealed the meaning of all four orthographical signs as well, making thirty-two letters in all. He was executed in 1398. Imaduddin Nesimi, a Turkish poet who also claimed to have received a special revelation on letter mysticism, was flogged to death in Aleppo in 1417.

Muhammad Sayid Sarmad was a rabbi before he embraced Islam. A great Persian poet and idealist thinker, he denied the reality of matter. He was executed in 1661 in the reign of the Mughal emperor Aurungzeb. His tomb in Delhi attracts hundreds of Muslims.

Mirza Ali Muhammad, known as the 'Bab' (meaning Gate), founder of Babism, the predecessor of Bahaism, proclaimed his own prophethood and was executed in the public square of Tabriz in 1850 as a heretic. His followers – men, women and children – were hunted down for years and were put to death with atrocious cruelty.

Muhammad Mahmud Taha was executed in 1985 in the Sudan because he believed the Medinan part of the Koran was no longer applicable.

In India the persecution of the Ahmadiya sect started in the early years of this century, and continues unabated in Pakistan to this day. It has been suggested that the fervour of the Muslims in this region may represent the zeal of a community largely descended from Hindu converts to Islam, for intolerance of the same intensity is not generally found in many other Muslim countries. The Canadian scholar Dr W. C. Smith, who made a close study of the Muslims of the Indian subcontinent, said of them that they had 'a fanaticism of blazing vehemence' (Ahmed, 1989, p. 100).

In February 1989, some three months before his own death, the Iranian religious leader Ayatollah Khomeini (the appellation 'Hindi', or Indian, was sometimes attached to his family name, because his grandfather came from India) pronounced the death sentence on the novelist Salman Rushdie for blasphemy; it is still in force. It should be noted that several prominent Muslim clerics, including the imam of the Grand Mosque of Al-Azhar in Cairo, have discredited the ayatollah's edict.

14.11 Punishments

In pre-Islamic Arabia crimes and certain civil offences incurred retaliation (*kisas*). At the same time the punishment even for murder and adultery could be commuted for a fine (*diya*), which could be paid in camels, sheep, goats or money, or other agreed compensation.

In Islamic law the punishment for bodily harm was likewise retaliation in kind, on the Jewish principle (Exod. 21:24): 'Life for life, eye for eye, nose for nose, ear for ear, and tooth for tooth' (5:49). In the strict sharia law of Islam, punishment (*hadd*) tended to be very severe, often with Koranic backing, and was often rigorously enforced.

For drinking wine, a sentence of eighty lashes was prescribed, though this did not have Koranic backing (see Section 11.4).

For theft and simple robbery, whether the thief be man or woman, the right hand was to be cut off (5:42). It is said by the early traditionalists that Muhammad himself had a woman guilty of theft punished in this way. When one of his followers pleaded on her behalf, the Prophet said, 'Do you intercede in respect of a punishment prescribed by Allah? If Fatima my daughter were guilty of theft, I would certainly cut off her hand.'

Those guilty of highway robbery, or robbery with murder, were banished or were killed either by the sword or by crucifixion (*salab*) (5:37).

Religious offences ranged from disbelief to false belief. Those who made war against God and opposed Muhammad were punished by having their opposite hands and feet cut off, or were executed by decapitation or crucifixion. For apostasy the punishment was death.

The punishment for sexual transgressions varied. Abu Bakr had a sodomist cast alive into the fire, but the offence was too widespread to be regularly noted and dealt with.

Whores and whoremongers were given 100 lashes (24:2). Both men and women were given 100 lashes for fornication.

Adultery being a serious offence, a punishment of eighty lashes was imposed on anyone who falsely accused a person of adultery (24:4). This was introduced after the scandal against Ayesha.

Stoning to death for adultery was once prescribed in the Koran, and on more than one occasion Muhammad himself ordered the stoning to death of persons guilty of adultery. After the Prophet's death Ayesha stated that she knew about the existence of the Koranic Verse of Stoning (see Section 7:14). Later these verses were said to have been abrogated and the Verse of Whipping was substituted (24:2).

Despite the absence of Koranic confirmation, the caliph Omar himself instituted stoning for adulteresses. Stoning to death for both parties is prescribed in the hadith.

Upholders of the strict sharia still insist on the literal imposition of the Koranic or traditional penalties, and in a few Islamic countries punishments like lopping off the hand for theft and stoning to death for adultery are occasionally prescribed and carried out even today. The most noteworthy case of one such penalty being carried out in modern times was the execution of the Saudi princess Misha and of her lover in 1970.

14.12 Slavery

The capture of slaves and the trade in slaves were old traditions in Arabia. The Bible records that when a caravan of Midianites (from the northern Hejaz) rescued Joseph from the pit into which he had been cast by his brothers, they sold him as a slave to the Egyptians (Gen. 37:36).

Among the objectives of the Muslim conquests was the acquisition of slaves. The fact that some of those captured in war were willing to embrace Islam did not preclude their being sold as slaves, for the growing empire was in dire need of their services. Slaves were sent back from the conquered territories to the Muslim countries in great numbers. After one brief expedition in AD 712, some sixty thousand were dispatched to Kufa from Sind (western India, now Pakistan).

Some officials in the caliphate were known to have had as many as a thousand slaves, male and female. In some households the slaves' treatment was humane, but in general their lot was wretched. They were classed as property and were used as unpaid labour in town and country. Female captives of true believers 'whom their right hands possess' (23:5) were enslaved, and the owner could cohabit with them even if they were already married to someone else.

In later centuries the free descendants of some of the slaves rose to high rank, and slave (*mamluk*, 'owned') dynasties are known in Egypt and India. Such slaves were almost invariably of non-black racial origin, like Turks, Circassians and Georgians. They took as their exemplars the patriarch Joseph, who was a slave freed by Pharaoh, and Ishmael, who was the son of Abraham's concubine Hagar.

The appointment of the freed Abyssinian slave Bilal as the first muezzin is often quoted to show that Muhammad made no distinction between races of different colour. But colour prejudice was common in the Middle East. Black slaves were for the most part despised, being considered the height of personal unpleasantness (Thaalibi, 1968, p. 117). Each year thousands of black boys were castrated to provide eunuchs for the seraglios of the large polygamous establishments of the nobility and the wealthy in all parts of the Muslim world. In 917, during the reign of the Abbasid caliph Mukta-dir, an ambassador from the Byzantine emperor Constantine VII visiting Baghdad wrote of two thousand black eunuchs who served solely in the caliph's palace.

Till comparatively recent times tropical Africa remained a vast pool of potential slaves. The rounding up of slaves in West Africa and their sale to European slave-traders for transportation to America and other places abroad was largely an Arab monopoly. And for savage brutality in the slaves' treatment it is difficult to choose between the Muslim vendors and the Christian buyers of this human commodity.

Trade in the supply of slaves to certain eastern countries continued till well into the present century, though under pressure of reform movements – led by Great Britain – the flood of traffic was slowly reduced to a trickle. Already by the end of the nineteenth century the numbers who were being shipped every year to Egypt, Arabia and Turkey had fallen to about fifteen thousand slaves for domestic work and eight thousand eunuchs for the seraglios of the wealthy.

14.13 Women

The Muslim attitude to women is regarded by Western critics as being among the worst features of Islam. Through his example and his teachings Muhammad himself has been held responsible for what is seen as the low status of women in the society he founded, and by this disservice he imposed on Islam a burden that survives to this day.

Like certain rabbinical authorities, Muhammad permitted a man to have four wives, provided he treated them equitably, without strong preferences or favouritism. At the same time, human nature being what it is, the Koran states quite clearly, 'You will never be able to be fair and just between the wives no matter how much you desire to do so' (4:128). Therefore, if a man felt he could not treat his wives with equal affection he should marry 'only one' (4:3).

In the view of some scholars these verses put the case for monogamy in Islam on a very clear foundation. But Muslims have generally ignored the proviso, and it has remained the almost universal rule that a man can have four wives. Further, there were those who interpreted the Koranic sanction to mean that a man could have a multiplicity of wives provided he did not have more than four wives at any one time.

Muhammad himself was married at least eleven times, had more than four wives at a time, and was known to have had favourites among them. The practice of polygamy remains widely prevalent in Islam and has many defenders, for Muslims will not willingly surrender the indulgence that has been granted to them by the Prophet in this matter.

A change of wives was made possible by divorce (*talak*), although, according to a hadith, Muhammad had stated, 'Of all lawful things, the most hateful to Allah is divorce' (Guillaume, 1983, p. 175). Muhammad himself is said to have divorced two of his wives and threatened to divorce others. Hasan, the Prophet's grandson, marrying four wives at a time, was able by this means to marry more than a hundred women.

Divorce in Muslim law allows a husband to divorce his wife without any misbehaviour on her part and without assigning any cause. A divorce becomes effective by the husband simply pronouncing the words 'Thou art divorced' before witnesses. In most Muslim countries today the laws relating to divorce are being liberalized and women are equally free to institute divorce proceedings. Such proceedings are now more formal, and usually take place along lines prescribed in Western law courts.

Besides four legally married wives, a Muslim was allowed an unlimited number of kept women or concubines (*sarari*; singular *suriya*), who were slaves (4:3) obtained as prisoners of war, or purchased, or received as a gift, or the descendants of family slaves.

Polygamy on the scale practised by those who could afford a plurality of women made it impossible for the natural demands of all the women to be met by a single male, and the stratagems used by women to seek satisfaction elsewhere frequently formed the subject of popular tales, like the *Arabian Nights*. The caliph Mamun, son of Harun al-Rashid, had hundreds of concubines and, it is said, an equal number of old women and eunuchs to spy on them.

Muhammad's marriage when he was fifty-two years old to Ayesha when she was nine likewise provided an example to be followed, confirming the institution of child marriage. It must be said, however, that child marriage was widely practised in many parts of the world, East and West, centuries before and after Muhammad.

The Prophet is also said to have sanctioned temporary marriages to meet the demands of his army in AD 630 after the Battle of Autas. This arrangement received endorsement in the Koran, where it is stated, 'Give those women with whom you have cohabited their reward for the enjoyment you have had of them. This is the law. It will be no crime for you to make arrangements over and above the law' (4:28).

A temporary marriage (*muta*, 'pleasure'), contracted on payment, could last from a few days to a few months, and became common in some Islamic countries, though its Muslim critics condemned it as a form of legalized prostitution. In Iran the practice continued till the middle of the present century. Writing in 1956, Guillaume stated, 'In Shia Persia today men await travellers at popular halting places to offer them "wives" for the period of their sojourn there' (1983, p. 104).

Muhammad drastically curtailed the great freedom women had had in pre-Islamic Arabia. The seclusion and veiling of women became obligatory in Muslim society. References to these new restrictive measures occur in the later suras, and are believed to have been prompted by the ageing Prophet's concern over the behaviour of the young wives in his own grow-ing harem. Such rules became obligatory for all Muslim women.

Koranic regulations meant that women were required to stay in their homes, obey God and the Prophet, and observe prayer (33:33). No unauthorized person could speak to them unless they were properly concealed behind a veil (*hijab*) (33:53). Women were not to show themselves or speak unveiled to any males, even of their own household, except those in a listed category of close relations (33:55 and 24:31). They were not to be agreeable in speech to others, lest men with lecherous hearts lust after them (33:32).

When they ventured out of doors into public places, they were not to go decked out as in the days of idolatry before Islam, but were to cover themselves with their outer garments (33:59). This was variously interpreted by different schools to mean that the outer covering should conceal the hair and forehead only, or the eyes, or the face, or the head, or the entire body from head to foot.

Women were restricted to their special quarters, or the harem (*harim*, 'forbidden' to outsiders), and here the wives and concubines were confined. In the heyday of Islam the rulers, and others who could afford it, had enormous harems, with scores – sometimes hundreds – of women, and the numbers would be augmented with each fresh conquest.

In the Koran – as in the scriptures of many other faiths – men are regarded as superior to women and have authority over them (4:38). Women must obey their fathers, and after marriage their husbands, and those who do not obey should be admonished and beaten (4:38). A man may have intercourse with a woman in any manner, for as the Koran says, 'A man's wife is his pasture and he may enter his pasture in any way he pleases' (2:223). So grim were the lives of some women that a saying went, 'He who weds his daughter to the grave has found the best of bridegrooms.'

By reference to the Koran and hadith, religious jurists added other restraints to the lot of women. In the sharia courts a woman's testimony was worth only half that of a man. Women were not allowed to enter the medical or legal professions, or branch out on their own in business; where they were already known to be active in trade or other enterprise, all transactions were conducted behind the scenes and through a proxy. They were discouraged from praying in mosques, but if they did they could never – because of the postures of the prayer ritual – pray with or within sight of the men, lest their presence disturb them.

In defence of this, Muslim apologists point out that women in the West suffered many legal disabilities, especially with regard to property, which were unknown to Muslim women. Also, the emancipation of Western women is of very recent growth and not yet in full bloom, and there is no reason for the West to be self-righteous about it. Muhammad's sanction for polygamy and concubinage was intended primarily to bring about a natural increase in the Muslim population, so as to help in the growth of Islam.

The veil was part of female attire almost everywhere in the Middle East, and Islam merely legislated for its continuance, which was socially necessary at the time. Many parts of the Muslim world – such as Indonesia, black Africa, and Kurdistan – have never known the veil, and there has never been any demand to enforce it there.

Today, feminist movements for the emancipation of women are gaining ground in many Islamic countries, and, taking into account the evolving social environment, the women of Islam will adapt in their own way and at their own pace to changes in the modern world.

14.14 Predestination

All things, says the Koran (54:49), have been made in accordance with the fixed decree (kadar) of God. The interpretation of how inflexible this divine decree is led to centuries of hair-splitting debate and created two schools of thought in Muslim philosophy to determine whether man has free will or not.

One school, known as the Kadariya, argued that if a man had no free will then every one of his actions would be accomplished through the power of God. Man would therefore not be responsible for his actions, and God would have no right to judge or punish him. The Kadariya held that, in making his decrees, a just and merciful God in fact left ample scope for the operation of free will. All individuals have been endowed with the faculty to determine between good and evil, and with the power to choose between right and wrong.

This doctrine, first propounded by a Zoroastrian priest converted to Islam, named Mabad al-Johni (d. 670), was taken up by two Sufi mystics, Hasan of Basra (d. 728) and Wasil ibn Ata (d. 749), and from the latter it was adopted by the Mutazilis, the rationalists and freethinkers of Islam, and staunch advocates of free will.

The opposite doctrine was based on an ancient concept known in pre-Islamic Arabia as *manaya*, meaning the unassailable power of fate in directing the destinies of all things. It was held by the school of orthodox Muslim thinkers called the Jabariya, according to whom all things are under compulsion (*jabr*) to act in accord with God's foreordained decree, which is inflexible and predetermined for all time. The Jabariya concept of a preordained destiny constitutes the doctrine of predetermination, which forms the sixth article of faith in the Muslim religion.

It presupposes that the fate (*takdir*) or luck (*kismet*) of every individual, community and nation has already been fixed by God, whose will is unalterable. The notion is widely prevalent in Muslim thought and is reflected in popular proverbs. 'What is not destined cannot be; what is destined cannot but be.' 'You cannot avoid what is fated; nor encounter what is not fated.' 'If you are appointed to eat, your daily bread will find you; if not, you will seek it in vain.'

The doctrine of predestination was given its classical form by the theologian Abul Hasan Ali al-Ashari (d. 935), whose stark fatalism was criticized by many Muslim thinkers. In its extremest form God is not depicted in a benevolent light but is shown to be relentless and forbidding. Thus, among the ninety-nine honorific titles bestowed upon Allah we find the following more ominous ones: al-Muzil, 'the Destroyer'; al-Zar, 'the Afflicter'; al-Mumit, 'the Slayer'; al-Fattah, 'the Decider'; al-Kabid, 'the Withholder'; al-Muntakim, 'the Avenger'; al-Mani, 'the Depriver'; al-Mudhil, 'the Humiliator'; al-Khafid, 'the Degrader'.

A Muslim supplication goes, 'We seek refuge from God for the stratagems of God [*makr Allah*].' In the words of the Koran, 'Man plots, and God plots; and of all plotters God is best' (8:30). The life of this world is only a sport and a pastime (57:19). It is wisest to submit to one's destiny, which is the Muslim's duty, for 'Islam' means 'submission'.

God's decisions are wilful and arbitrary, for, as the Koran says, 'God bestows his grace on whom he will' (5:59), 'God forgives whom he pleases, and punishes whom he pleases' (3:124), and 'He chastises whom he will, and whom he will he forgives' (5:44).

The Almighty may even deceive for his own mysterious ends: 'God misleads whom he will; and whom he will he guides' (14:4). And, since God is in control of all things, 'God will not guide those he chooses to lead astray, and those who are thus misled shall have no helper' (16:39).

Belief and disbelief, faith and infidelity are also determined by divine decree. 'No soul can believe but by the permission of God' (10:100). 'No soul can transgress unless God will it' (76:30). 'He to whom God has not given light has no light at all' (24:40). 'God has locked the heart, sealed the ears, and veiled the eyes of those he causes deliberately to err' (45:22).

The Koran repeatedly makes clear God's final direction of the fate of all things. Nothing can happen to us except what God has already destined for us (9:51). Individuals have their allotted time, and when their 'appointed time' (*ajal*) has come God gives the soul no further time (63:11). No man can die except by God's permission and according to the book that has fixed his term of life (3:139). Likewise with nations, for each of which a period is fixed, and when its hour is come its end cannot be postponed (7:32).

And, after death, our further destiny is also predetermined. It is related in the traditions that when God was creating the human race he took a clod of earth in his hands and divided it into two portions. He threw one into heaven, saying, 'These are for paradise, as I will,' and the other he hurled into everlasting fire, saying, 'These are for hell, and I care not.' This is confirmed by the Koranic distinction between the 'people of the right hand' (56:26), who go to paradise, and the 'people of the left hand' (56:40), who are for ever damned.

14.15 The Last Days

In the Koran, Muslims are advised when asked about the end of the world to reply, 'God alone has knowledge of it. Who can tell?' (33:63). At the same time it is important to remember that the end may be imminent: 'the hour may be close at hand' (33:63) and 'the time of reckoning nigh' (21:1).

Muhammad himself seemed to believe that the hour (*saah*) or day (*yawm*) when the world would draw to a close was not far off. When he once found two men repairing a house, he remarked enigmatically, 'I think the affair will outlast that,' which by some has been interpreted to mean that the Day of Judgement would overtake their endeavour.

According to Muslim tradition, certain signs will presage the doom of creation. As the end of the world draws nearer, Allah will leave the earth's inhabitants to their own devices. There will be a rapid decline in faith and morals, and people will become more and more irreligious.

As the Koran has proceeded from God, so in the end it will return to him. Copies of the holy book and its verses will gradually become blank, and people will find that nothing of it remains. According to one tradition mentioned by Ibn Maja (d. 886), the Koran will be excised from the hearts and minds of all Muslims, and knowledge of the book and its contents will vanish utterly from the earth.

According to a prophecy attributed to Muhammad himself (Sale, 1886, p. 90), the Kaaba will be destroyed by the Ethiopians and will never again be rebuilt. The Arabs will once again pay homage to Allat, Ozza and their other deities and revert to their old pagan ways. In one hadith Muhammad says, 'The world will not pass away until the buttocks of the women of Daus wriggle again around the image of Dhul Khalasa and they worship as they were wont to do before Islam' (Faris, 1952, p. 32).

As the Bible tells of a beast that will come out of the earth at the end of time and speak like a dragon (Rev. 13:11), so the Koran tells of a beast (*Dabba*) which will appear out of the earth during the last days (27:84) and will speak to the people for three days. Then Antichrist will come and create chaos and confusion in the world until Christ returns, defeats Antichrist and brings peace and order to the earth. This second advent of Jesus will be the last great sign before the coming judgement (see Section 10.16).

14.16 Hell

After death, each person will lie in the grave and will be questioned about his or her beliefs by two black angels, called Munkar and Nakir. True believers will give the correct responses to the questions asked, but unbelievers, not knowing what to say, will give the wrong answers and will be beaten. After the interrogation, the person will fall into a deep sleep.

At the end of time there will come a great shout (*sayha*) and a thunderclap (*sakha*), and Israfil, the angel of death, will sound a great blast on his trumpet (27:89). The mountains will turn to dust, the seas will boil up, the sun will darken, the stars will fall, and then the sky will be rolled away.

There will be a resurrection (*kiyama*) of the dead of all the nations of the world, who will proceed in great fear to the hall of judgement. In the life to come, according to some Muslim beliefs, Jesus will preside at this tribunal (Kazi and Flynn, 1984, p. 53) and will decide the fate of all who have lived on earth.

After being judged, each individual will have to pass over a bridge (*sirat*) which is described as being finer than a hair and sharper than a sword. The word '*sirat*' and the concept of the bridge are both of Zoroastrian derivation (Tisdall, 1911, p. 252). The bridge spans the seven fires of hell (*jahannam*), which has seven gates (15:44), and each hell is designed for a special class of sinner. The Koran does not say anything about the seven hells, but the commentators give details. The word for hell comes from the Hebrew *gehinnom*, and the concept of seven hells is derived from the Talmud.

Everyone will go to hell, for, as the Koran says, 'Not one is there of you who shall not go down into it. This is the settled decree with the Lord' (19:72). The good Muslim will pass over most of the bridge, but as he nears the end he will fall a short way into the uppermost of the hells, where he will suffer for a time in the purgatorial fire to be purified of his sins.

Christians, followed by Jews and Zoroastrians, after walking about halfway across the bridge, will fall into the second, third and fourth hells. Being people of the book, they will not burn but will suffer the flames of remorse for all time for not having accepted Islam.

The fifth, sixth and seventh hells are the most terrifying, being reserved for infidels, idolators, hypocrites, apostates and those who opposed and ridiculed the Prophet, along with their families – like the little girl who was condemned to hell because her father, Okba, had opposed Muhammad. All these people, having taken their first few steps across the bridge, will fall into the deepest pits of the blazing infernos, and here they will remain for ever (2:37).

Condemned to these lowest hells were all Muhammad's personal enemies, including Abu Lahab and his wife, and Abu Jahal, and Jews like Zabir. Another Jew, named Kozman, who had fought with incredible valour on Muhammad's side at the Battle of Ohod and lay dying, on being commended for his bravery remarked that he had only fought for his own people and to save his native city. Hearing this, Muhammad burst out that he was 'a child of hell-fire'.

The Prophet consigned to the fires of eternal damnation the ancestors of all Muslims who had lived before Islam, because they had lived and died in idolatry and were therefore infidels. His own mother, Amina, who had died more than thirty years before the birth of Islam, was in hell-fire. His grandfather Abdul Muttalib and his uncle Abu Talib, both of whom had helped him in his youth, were also consigned to eternal torment, because they were not of the faith and had not embraced Islam.

A Koranic verse (9:114) revealed to Muhammad forbids Muslims from praying for the forgiveness of anyone, even their own kindred, who had died an infidel, for infidels were the 'inmates of hell'.

14.17 Paradise

Except for a brief purificatory interval, the true Muslim will pass without danger or mishap across the bridge over hell and will enter paradise (*jannat*, 'garden'). As in hell, there are seven regions in heaven, and the rewards awaiting the faithful there are detailed in more than a dozen passages in the Koran. Muhammad had promised his followers, 'I have brought you the best of this world and the next.'

In their delightful pleasure domes, says the Koran, the men will be attended by young boys (*waldan*) for ever in bloom, beautiful as embedded pearls, 'in whom you will find delights and a great kingdom' (76:19). These youths (also called *ghilman* in the commentaries) will serve the elect with wine in goblets and beautiful ewers. This wine, mixed with the water flowing in the highest pavilions of paradise, will not cause the head to ache or disturb the reason (56:19).

The blessed will lie face to face with dark-eyed damsels (*houris*) of stainless purity (56:22), virgins with swelling breasts (78:33) whom neither man nor jinn has touched, and will be united with them. Like the ghilman, the houris will remain ever young, ever beautiful, and ever ready to serve.

Many more graphic and explicit descriptions of the raptures to come are developed in the commentaries, which go on to say that the intensity of the pleasures experienced in the abode of bliss will be infinitely greater than any known on earth. Faithful wives and true Muslim women, it should be mentioned, will also enter paradise (43:70), but are not promised the reward of youthful male company.

Muslims who fight and slay in a holy war (*jihad*) or in any undertaking for the advancement of Islam (9:112), or who kill an infidel, do not have to await the Day of Judgement but are transported at the instant of their death to the special paradise reserved for them. The enjoyment of wealth and beauty in our world, wrote Gibbon, 'was a feeble type of the joys of paradise prepared for the valiant martyrs of the faith'.

The prospect of being waited on by a bevy of ravishing beauties inspired many an ardent Muslim to kill his kafir or die a martyr's death to speed up the desirable end. The first Islamic martyr was a lad of sixteen named Omayr ibn Hubab. He was eating a handful of dates when he heard the Prophet say during the Battle of Badr that God had promised paradise to those who died fighting in God's cause. He immediately jumped up crying, 'Then only the munching of these dates separates me from paradise.' Flinging aside the dates, he seized his sword, rushed into the fray, and was killed.

It is recorded that at the Battle of Siffin (AD 657) a leading citizen aged eighty years saw a man die in the fight and imagined he beheld the heavens opening up and gazelle-eyed women, scantily attired, clasping the martyr in their embrace. Unable to wait to meet a similar fate, he armed himself and tottered out into the battlefield and was soon cut down.

The picture of paradise presented in the Koran, it has been said, suggests not a divine vision but the salacious dreams of a sensualist. And the idea that paradise would be populated by voluptuaries and assassins aroused the ridicule of Muhammad's contemporaries and the contempt of Jews and Christians.

15

THE DILEMMA OF ISLAM

The early centuries of contact between Islam and the West did not leave the Muslims in any doubt about their own superiority. Their days of conquest culminated in their being overlords of half the known world. They were in the forefront of all achievement, occupied large parts of southern and eastern Europe, and were the teachers of the West.

They could describe their Western pupils – and with some justification they did – as lacking in the civilized virtues, devoid of any understanding of social behaviour, ignorant of the laws of hospitality, and having no deep regard for family or children and little reverence for religious principles, even their own. The Westerners were coarse by nature, uncouth in manners and dull of comprehension. In brief, they were among the most stupid, rude and brutish of the nations of mankind.

But the Europeans were not slow to learn, and, during the centuries in which Islam, surfeited with success, was becalmed in the doldrums, they made enormous strides in crucial areas by military strength, commercial acumen and scientific progress, and then began their slow advance in successive waves across the Islamic world.

15.1 The Europeans

At first the European nations were interested primarily in trade. They had no territorial ambitions and did not, as a rule, seek to make converts to Christianity. Their first close encounter with the Muslims was during the Crusades, which were fought for access to the Holy Land – although it is said that in 1182 one of the Frankish crusading knights, Raynald of Châtillon, led a party of soldiers in an abortive attempt to take Medina, landing at Yenbo, the port of Medina, and starting to march inland towards the city before being repulsed by a nephew of Saladin.

The Muslim states of the Mediterranean prospered as long as they had suzerainty over the trade routes of the East. The corsairs of the Barbary (Berber) coast from Morocco to Tripolitania (Libya) and the sultans of Egypt preyed on foreign shipping in the Mediterranean, levied 'appeasement' tribute, or demanded 'protection' money from the European countries in the form of exorbitant taxes on cargoes that passed their shores or through their territories.

The rise of the great European powers really began with the end of the fifteenth century. In January 1492 the Moors were expelled from Spain. In

October 1492 Christopher Columbus discovered the New World and opened a fresh chapter in the history of the West. In 1498 Vasco da Gama found a way to India via the Cape of Good Hope, thus opening an alternative and cheaper route to India and the Far East, which also outflanked the Muslims.

The Europeans were now desirous of increasing their trade with the East, and started to assert themselves with greater vigour, often aided by corsairs and pirates of their own brand. The Portuguese, like the Spaniards, had built ships to withstand the oceanic gales, and were now better able to fend off the Muslim navies that tried to harass them, and thus in some measure they deprived the Mediterranean pirates of their plunder and avoided the taxes of the Egyptian rulers.

By the sixteenth century they had penetrated into the Persian Gulf, occupied Muscat, and erected several forts along Ormuz (Hormuz) and the Red Sea, to guard their trading settlements. They effectively repulsed all attempts to oust them. In 1515 the viceroy of Portuguese India, Alfonzo d'Albuquerque, planned but did not carry out a raid on Mecca, and in 1517 Lopo Soares de Albergaria threatened but did not attack Jedda.

Some decades later the Turkish flood across the Balkans and western Europe was checked when Don John of Austria destroyed the Turkish fleet of the sultan Selim II (the successor of Suleiman the Magnificent) at the Battle of Lepanto (1571); then John Sobieski defeated the Turkish armies at the gates of Vienna (1683). Skirmishes and major battles continued between the Muslim and European armies sporadically thereafter, with a slow and steady loss of territory by the Muslims.

When Napoleon Bonaparte stormed into the Ottoman Middle East with the invasion of Egypt in 1798, he found that religious obscurantism had brought learning to a pitiably low ebb. There were no suitable Arab-speaking Egyptians to take over positions of authority in the administration, and he was forced to employ Turks, Albanians and other foreigners to fill the posts. He had brought with him scientists, archaeologists, engineers and scholars, and a printing-press with Arabic type – to print news-sheets and proclamations – and these were all put into active use.

With the arrival of the Europeans the trade routes and shipping lanes became safer, especially after the French had finally wiped out piracy on the Barbary coast by about 1830. But it was only with the building of the Suez Canal in 1869, by the French engineer Ferdinand de Lesseps, that some measure of importance returned to the Muslim lands of the Mediterranean.

From then on there was a vast expansion of European interests in the East, and from trading stations and a network of defensive outposts grew the great empires of the West. The moral decay, administrative corruption and military weakness of the Muslim states made conquest easy, especially with the disciplined armies and the new weapons the West possessed.

By the middle of the nineteenth century Britain, France, Spain, Portugal,

Holland and Russia had conquered, colonized, annexed, put under 'protection', or otherwise dominated most of the countries of the Muslim world. Saudi Arabia, Turkey, Iran and Afghanistan were the only Muslim lands to retain some semblance of self-rule – because it served the purpose of the Western nations to have neutral buffer states between their own separate areas of dominance.

When the full flood of the European advance came upon the Islamic world, it appeared to the Europeans that the Muslim nations had passed out of the mainstream of world history and were in a stagnant backwater. In every part of the world where Islam prevailed the nations were in decline.

The German philosopher G. W. F. Hegel (d. 1831) went so far as to write, 'Islam has long vanished from the stage of history and has retreated into oriental ease and repose.' It was as if Islam during its zenith had taken what it could from others, and when it could borrow no more it had closed its mind, retired into a world of its own, and remained in a state of slumber for five or more centuries. Its hour of glory had come and gone, and from the Middle Ages Islam had remained in a state of arrested development, as if fossilized at all levels.

The religion had lost its spiritual power. The Koran describes Islam as a baptism (*sibga*) of God (2:132), using a term which means 'dye', an external colouring. And Islam – by now set in rigid patterns – seemed to have become little more than a routine of external observances – prayer, pilgrimage and fasting – with a taboo on 'wine and swine'.

The greater world around Muslims had become a closed book. What is more, they had no wish to open the book and read. They had long ceased to follow the Prophet's injunction to 'seek knowledge even as far as China'. Islam was afflicted with intellectual rigor mortis. The French religious writer Ernest Renan spoke of an 'iron circle' enclosing the head of the faithful in the Orient and Africa, making them impervious to fresh ideas and incapable of accepting anything new.

But the military, commercial and scientific success of the Europeans could not be ignored, nor the inevitable changes be long resisted. The steamship, railways, the printing-press, the telegraph, radio and other communications media were all being rapidly introduced into the strongholds of Islam, along with municipal amenities like water and electric installations, and in time the motor car.

Western travellers, archaeologists and epigraphists ventured into remote parts of Arabia – often at personal risk to their lives – and were the first to decipher and interpret the rock inscriptions on the ancient Arabian monuments that had been forgotten for nearly two thousand years. With this material, European orientalists and Arabists unravelled the tangled history of the pre-Islamic period and thus put Arabs in touch with their own past.

Arabic books were first printed in Europe, to be circulated in Muslim countries, and these gave an impetus to Islamic studies, revealing in a new light the advances made by the Arabs in bygone days. The half-forgotten Arabic classics reappeared in editions, carefully edited by European scholars, that shed a new light on the early writings.

A growing interest in Islam among Western scholars could not leave the Koran and the Prophet's biographies immune to the radical 'higher criticism' of the kind that had been brought to bear on the Bible at the end of the nineteenth century, revealing disturbing facts and raising uncomfortable questions about the origins and growth of Islam – to the strong objections of the orthodox.

There were also some objections from Muslim divines to the actual printing of the Koran, because it was felt that the word of God should not be subjected to the indignity of being stamped out on a printing-press. Later there were to be similar objections to the mass reproduction of the Koran on 'technical contraptions', and to the muezzin making the call to prayer over a loudspeaker, but all these protests were overcome and such innovations are now universal in Islamic countries.

Muslim scholars flocked to the new schools and universities that were being opened in their cities, using up-to-date Western textbooks either in the original European languages or translated into Arabic. Those who could afford it went to Europe for higher studies in engineering and technology. Arab writers started newspapers and periodicals in which views of all kinds began to be expressed, and ancient beliefs and practices were questioned with great freedom.

The occupying European powers introduced changes in government administration, to bring it into line with systems in the West. They also modernized the judicial framework, and many Muslim states still retain the systems so established. Politically, new ideas were introduced about democracy and constitutional government, based on the representation of the people in elected assemblies. In large measure the present Islamic resurgence is due to these innovations.

During the period of European infiltration and occupation the Muslims made remarkably few complaints about Western imperialism. The Muslims understood imperialism. For centuries they themselves had been arch-imperialists on a grand and global scale. Their fight for freedom seems to have been inspired by the Europeans themselves. Democracy and representative government were part of what the West had brought in, and, starting from India, the independence movements in Muslim countries began to gain momentum.

India saw the end of the Mughal empire after the Indian Mutiny of 1857, when the British took over and ruled India (including what later became Pakistan and Bangladesh) till 1947. Malaysia had been occupied successively by the Portuguese (1511), the Dutch (1641) and the British (1824); it became independent in 1963. Indonesia was Dutch till 1945. Brunei (in Borneo) was a British protectorate till 1983.

In North Africa, the states of Mauretania, Morocco, Algeria, Tunisia and Libya attained their independence from the French between 1952 and 1962; Syria and Lebanon in 1946. Egypt was a British protectorate till 1936; Iraq till 1932; Jordan till 1946; Palestine till 1948.

In central and east Africa, Mali, Chad, Senegal, Gambia, Niger and Guinea were French till the 1960s. Sudan was British till the country's independence in 1956. Aden (South Yemen) was a British Crown Colony till 1967. Somalia by the end of the nineteenth century was divided between the Italians, British and French; it became independent in 1960. All the small states of the Persian Gulf were British protectorates, Kuwait becoming independent in 1961, followed by Bahrain, Qatar and the others.

By 1881 Russia had annexed the whole region of Turkestan in Central Asia, made up of the khanates of Kazakhstan, Kirgizia, Tadzhikistan, Turkmenistan and Uzbekistan, all of which became autonomous by 1990.

15.2 The Fundamentalists

The rapid and widespread influence of the West provoked a strong reaction among the fundamentalists of Islam, led by the Muslim theologians and hierophants such as the imams, ayatollahs, ulema, mullahs and muftis. They resisted the introduction of Western ideas since these opened the door to change and ushered in an alien world they could not understand and were unable to control. The power of the West was disruptive, and threatening to their way of life.

Modernization, secularization and liberal movements were regarded by the orthodox as insidious forms of atheism. They were not only non-religious, they were also anti-religious, and sought to remove certain important features of life beyond the scope of religious jurisdiction. The mullahs regarded some aspects of Western life and morals as particularly satanic because they undermined long-established Islamic institutions. For example, they encouraged women to make demands for freedom not permitted by the law. Again, the West advocated civil liberties, which weaken authority; and espoused democracy, which debases governments. The rule of autocrats is seen as preferable because it retains and strengthens the old and hallowed traditions.

The fundamentalists regard as unacceptable any inquiry into the validity of the basic principles of Islam or the questioning of its truths. The Koran has anticipated all modern contingencies and is sufficient for the guidance of Muslims in all situations. And, as the word of God was revealed literally, it must be interpreted and applied literally and not be construed to suit reformers.

The fundamentalists insist on a revival of all the old-time laws as codified in the sharia, without any dilution of its precepts to accommodate modern sentiments, as well as the establishment of the religious courts where these laws would be enforced and the old-time punishments imposed for their infraction.

They look back nostalgically to the golden age of the ancients (*salaf*), when Islam, under the rule of the Medinan caliphs, was at its purest and most perfect, and to the days of conquest, when the glory of Islam was blazoned throughout the world. Today they can only reflect with bitterness that they who were once the mentors of the West have now fallen so low as to have to turn to the West for assistance.

The tendency of Muslim orthodoxy is inflexible, and because of its suspicion and fear it also tends to be militant. Radical Islamic activists believe in campaigns of intimidation, hostage-taking and assassination as legitimate methods of promoting their cause. Indeed, international terrorism finds many adherents among Islamic fundamentalists (Taheri, 1987; H. M. T. Ahmad, 1989): they believe it is in consonance with the doctrine of 'unending jihad'. Extremists look forward to the day when they will have the 'Islamic nuclear bomb', which will give them instant parity with the West and once more restore to them the power to conquer and convert.

15.3 The Reformers

Proponents of reform point out that the outlook of the fundamentalist has fallen far behind enlightened opinion among many Muslim thinkers today. The success of fundamentalism presupposes a despotic government and a repressive clergy who thrive on the ignorance and backwardness of the people.

There is little point in harking back to the past, which is now lost and beyond recovery. In any event, that bygone Utopia never existed. It is a mirage and a delusion. There never was a golden age. From the outset Islam has been torn with schism. Muslim states have been as full of violence as any others, and Islamic kingdoms have fought with one another throughout history.

Nor is Islam united today, except perhaps in a common and wasteful hatred of Israel, which is regarded as an extension of the West into the bosom of the Islamic world. The jihad against 'Zionism' initiated by the combined forces of Egypt, Jordan, Syria and Iraq to put an end to Israel turned into a humiliating six-day war (5–10 June 1967) in which Israel delivered a devastating blow to their pride and power. The aim of acquiring an 'Islamic nuclear bomb' for the restoration of Islamic glory is an objective too iniquitous to be contemplated by any sane person.

In more practical terms, the rigid adherence to the precepts of the Koran and sharia and to the many interdictions arising from the Prophet's strongly puritanical outlook would mean many awkward changes having to be made in the lifestyle of Muslims and a reversion to a very primitive mode of existence.

It would mean an end to all forms of secular music and the playing of all musical instruments. It would mean a ban on all illustrations in books, magazines and posters and, above all, would proscribe all photography, cinemas and television. The Koranic law strictly enforced would mean the virtual imprisonment of women in their homes, a return to the days of slavery and concubinage, the reintroduction of public flogging, amputation of limbs, beheading, crucifixion, stoning to death and the persecution of infidels. All these and many more prohibitions and obligations are unequivocally and incontestably demanded by Koranic or sharia precepts.

One would have to be a very subtle dialectician to escape from the predicament faced by the fundamentalist who insists on a literalist interpretation of the law. The more one fundamentalizes in this fashion, the more impracticable modern life becomes. Islam offers no scope for change that does not violate some religious precept interpreted literally, and it is not likely that many Muslims, including the fundamentalist, would care to live in a country regulated on rigid fundamentalist principles.

In all fields of life, say the liberals, adaptation and compromise are the prerequisites of survival. Muslims have to accept and most have accepted the changes that occur in a constantly changing world. Much of recent change has come through Western influence – an influence that cannot be avoided. The Islamic world shares common problems with the rest of the human race and should join the West in facing the challenges that will confront the world in the coming century.

The reformers maintain that it is foolish and dishonest to denounce Westernization when at every turn the peoples of the Islamic world today depend on the products, inventions, discoveries and achievements of the West for their livelihood and business, their entertainment and comforts, their defence and security, their transport and communications, their health and welfare.

After contact with the West, Islam is experiencing a renaissance, but a reformation is now also due. To those who object to reform coming from outside, the reformers say that they do not need the guidance of the West in their quest for reform. Throughout the centuries Muslim thinkers have subjected every feature of Islamic life – political, social and religious – to critical scrutiny, and many today continue to do so in the face of fierce orthodox opposition.

To those who object to reform from outside the Koranic framework the reformers argue that the Koran, like all other scriptures, has more than one level of significance – metaphorical, metaphysical, allegorical, symbolic – and Muslims should strive to find a more moderate and liberal meaning along those lines, and not always adhere to the strict letter of the text.

Theocratic and totalitarian regimes are no longer acceptable to thoughtful Muslims. It is essential to separate the state from religion, or Islam will remain under the dead hand of a self-righteous and sanctimonious clique of clerics, and the flower of Muslim life will wither in the desert air.

BIBLIOGRAPHY

Abbott, Nabia. 1939. *The Rise of the North Arabic Script in its Kuranic Development.*, Chicago University Press

Abbott, Nabia. 1985. *Aishah the Beloved of Mohammed*. London: Saqi Books (orig. pub. Chicago University Press, 1942)

Abdel-Jalil, Jean. 1950. *Marie et l'Islam*. Paris: Beauchesne

Addison, J. T. 1942. *The Christian Approach to the Moslem*. New York: Scribners

Ahmad, Hasrat Mirza Tahir. 1989. *Murder in the Name of Allah*. Cambridge: Lutterworth Press

Ahmad, Maqbul. 1969. *Indo-Arab Relations. An Account of India's Relations with the Arab World from Ancient up to Modern Times*. New Delhi: Taj Printers

Ahmed, Leila. 1992. *Women and Gender in Islam*. New Haven: Yale University Press

Ahrens, Karl. 1935. *Muhammad und Religionsstifter*. Leipzig: Griebus

Ajijola, Alhaj A. D. 1975. *The Myth of the Cross*. Lahore: Islamic Publications

Akhtar, Shabbir. 1989. *Be Careful with Muhammad!* London: Bellew

Ali, M. 1921. *Muhammad and Christ*. Lahore: Lahore Printers.

Ameer Ali, Syed. 1965. *The Spirit of Islam*. London: Methuen (orig. pub. London: Christophers, 1922)

Andrae, Tor. 1955. *Les Origines de l'Islam et le Christianisme*. Paris: Adrien-Maisonneuve

Andrae, Tor. 1960. *Mohammed: The Man and His Faith*. New York: Harper

Arberry, A. J. 1956. *Sufism: An Account of the Mystics of Islam*. London: Allen & Unwin

Arberry, A. J. 1964. *Aspects of Islamic Civilization*. London: Allen & Unwin

Archer, John Clark. 1924. *Mystical Elements in Mohammed*. New Haven: Yale University Press

Armstrong, Karen. 1991. *Muhammad: A Western Attempt to Understand Islam*. London: Gollancz

Arnaldez, Roger. 1980. *Jésus, fils de Marie, prophète de l'Islam*. Paris: Desclée

Arnold, J. M. 1874. *Islam and Christianity*. London: Longmans

Arnold, Thomas, and Guillaume, Alfred, eds. 1965. *The Legacy of Islam*. Oxford University Press

Ascher, A. 1979. *The Mutual Effects of the Islamic and Judeo-Christian Worlds*. New York: Brooklyn College Press

Ayoub, Mahmoud. 1989. Roots of Muslim–Christian Conflict. *The Muslim World*, 79, 31

Bakhtiar, Laleh. 1976. *Sufi: Expressions of the Mystic Orient*. London: Thames and Hudson

Baljon, J. M. S. 1961. *Modern Muslim Koran Interpretation, 1880–1960*. Leiden: Brill

Balyuzi, H. M. 1976. *Muhammad and the Course of Islam*. Oxford University Press

Bat Ye'or. 1985. *The Dhimmi: Jews and Christians Under Islam*. Rutherford, NJ: Dickinson University Press

Beck, Edmund. 1946. *Das christliche Mönchtum im Koran*. Helsinki: Oriental Society

Becker, C. H. 1909. *Christianity and Islam*. London: Norwood

Beckingham, C. F. 1984. *Between Islam and Christendom. Travellers, Facts and Legends in the Middle Ages and Renaissance*. London: Variorum Reprints

Bell, Richard. 1937, 1939. *The Qur'an*. 2 vols. Edinburgh University Press

Bell, Richard. 1953. *Introduction to the Qur'an*. Edinburgh University Press

Bell, Richard. 1968. *The Origin of Islam in Its Christian Environment*. 2nd edn. London: Macmillan (orig. pub. 1926)

Bethmann, Erich. 1953. *Bridge to Islam*. London: Allen & Unwin

Birkeland, Harris. 1955. *Old Muslim Opposition Against Interpretation of the Koran*. Oslo: Kommisjon Hos Jacob Dybwad

Birkeland, Harris. 1956. *The Lord Giveth: Studies on Primitive Islam*. Oslo: Aschehoug

Blunt, Wilfrid Scawen, and Blunt, Lady Anne. 1903. *The Seven Golden Odes of Pagan Arabia also Known as the Moallakat*. London: Blunt

Bormans, Maurice. 1981. *Orientations pour un dialogue entre chrétiens et musulmans*. Paris: Cerf

Bouhdiba, Abdelwahab. 1985. *Sexuality in Islam*. London: Routledge & Kegan Paul

Bouquet, A. C. 1951. *Comparative Religion*. Harmondsworth: Penguin

Brandon, S. G. F., ed. 1970. *A Dictionary of Comparative Religion*. London: Weidenfeld & Nicolson

Bravmann, M. M. 1972. *The Spiritual Background of Early Islam: Studies in Ancient Arab Concepts*. Leiden: Brill

Brown, John P. 1968. *The Dervishes, or Oriental Spiritualism*. London: Frank Cass (orig. pub. 1868)

Browne, Edward Granville. 1921. *Arabian Medicine*. Cambridge University Press

Browne, Edward Granville. 1957. *Literary History of Persia*. Cambridge University Press (orig. pub. London: Fisher Unwin, 1909)

Browne, Laurence. 1933. *The Eclipse of Christianity in Asia*. Cambridge University Press

Budge, E. A. W. 1932. *The Queen of Sheba and Her Only Son Menyelek*. Oxford University Press

Buhl, Frants. 1961. *Das Leben Muhammads*. Heidelberg University Press

Bulliet, R. 1979. *Conversion to Islam in the Medieval Period*. Cambridge, Mass.: Harvard University Press

Burckhardt, John Lewis. 1829. *Travels in Arabia*, Cambridge University Press

Burke, O. Michael. 1976. *Among the Dervishes*. London: Octagon Press

Burton, John. 1977. *The Collection of the Qur'an*. Cambridge University Press

Caetani, Leone. 1905. *Annali dell'Islam*. Milan: Hoepli

Cash, W. Wilson. 1937. *Christendom and Islam*. New York: Harper

Chapman, Colin. 1993. *Cross and Crescent*. Leicester: Inter-Varsity Press

Cleveland, William. 1985. *Islam Against the West*. Austin: Texas University Press

Cook, Michael. 1981. *Early Muslim Dogma*. Cambridge University Press

Cook, Michael. 1983. *Muhammad*. Oxford University Press

Corbin, Henry. 1978. *The Man of Light in Iranian Sufism*. Colorado and London: Shambhala

Cragg, Kenneth. 1984. *Muhammad and the Christian*. London: Darton, Longman & Todd

Cragg, Kenneth. 1985. *Jesus and the Muslim: An Exploration*. London: Allen & Unwin

Cresswell, K. A. C. 1969. *Early Muslim Architecture*. 2nd edn. Oxford University Press

Crone, Patricia. 1987. *Meccan Trade and the Rise of Islam*. Oxford: Blackwell. Princeton University Press

Crone, Patricia, and Cook, Michael. 1977. *Hagarism: The Making of the Islamic World*. Cambridge University Press

Crone, Patricia, and Hinds, Martin. 1987. *God's Caliph: Religious Authority and the First Centuries of Islam*. Cambridge University Press

Cutler, Allan Harris, and Cutler, Helen Elmquist. 1976. *The Jew as Ally of the Muslim: Medieval Roots of Anti-Semitism*. Indianapolis: Notre Dame University Press

Daniel, Norman. 1960. *Islam and the West: The Making of an Image*. Edinburgh University Press

Daniel, Norman. 1975. *The Arabs and Medieval Europe*. London: Longmans

Danner, Victor. 1988. *The Islamic Tradition: An Introduction*. Amity, NY: Amity House

Dawood, N. J. (trans). 1990. *The Koran, with a Parallel Arabic Text*. London: Penguin

Dennett, D. 1950. *Conversion and the Poll-Tax in Early Islam*. Cambridge, Mass.: Harvard University Press

Dermenghem, Emile. 1958. *Muhammad and the Islamic Tradition*. New York: Harper. London: Longmans

Diringer, David. 1947. *The Alphabet: A Key to the History of Mankind*. London: Hutchinson

Donner, E. McGraw. 1981. *The Early Islamic Conquests*. Princeton University Press

Doughty, Charles Montagu. 1888. *Travels in Arabia Deserta*. Cambridge University Press (reprinted 1924)

Dover, Cedric. 1937. *Half-Caste*. London: Secker & Warburg

Dunlop, D. M. 1971. *Arab Civilization to AD 1500*. London: Hutchinson

Duri, Abdal Aziz. 1983. *The Rise of Historical Writing Among the Arabs*. Princeton University Press

Esin, Emel. 1963. *Mecca the Blessed, Medina the Radiant*. London: Elek

Faris, Nabih Amin (trans). 1952. *The Book of Idols, being a Translation from the Arabic of the Kitab al-Asnam by Hisham al-Kalbi*. Princeton University Press

Freely, John. 1987. *Istanbul*. New York: Norton

Frieling, Rudolf. 1978. *Christianity and Islam*. Edinburgh: Floris Books

Fyzee, A. A. A. 1949. *Outlines of Muhammadan Art*. Oxford University Press

Gabus, Jean-Paul, Ali Merad, and Youakim Moubarac. 1982. *Islam et Christianisme en dialogue*. Paris: Cerf

Geagea, Nilo. 1984. *Mary of the Koran: A Meeting Point Between Christianity and Islam*. New York: Philosophical Library

Geiger, Rabbi Abraham. 1970. *Judaism and Islam: What did Muhammad take from Judaism?* New York: Ktav (orig. pub. as *Was hat Mohammed aus dem Judenthum aufgenommen?* Bonn, 1833; English trans. Madras, 1898)

Gellner, Ernest. 1981. *Muslim Society*. Cambridge University Press

Gerholm, Tomas, and Lithman, Yngve Georg, eds. 1989. *The New Islamic Presence in Europe*. London: Mansell

Gibb, H. A. R. 1969. *Mohammedanism: A Historical Survey*, 2nd edn. Oxford University Press

Gibb, H. A. R. 1974. *Arabic Literature*, 2nd edn. Oxford University Press

Gibb, H. A. R., and Kramers, J. H. 1974. *Shorter Encyclopedia of Islam*.Leiden: Brill

Gilsenan, Michael. 1973. *Saints and Sufis in Modern Egypt*. Oxford University Press

Glick, Thomas F. 1980. *Islamic and Christian Spain in the Early Middle Ages*. Princeton University Press

Glubb, John Bagot, (Glubb Pasha). 1979. *The Life and Times of Muhammad*. London: Hodder & Stoughton

Glueck, Nelson. 1966. *Deities and Dolphins: The Story of the Nabataeans*. London: Cassell

Goldziher, Ignaz. 1967, 1971. *Muslim Studies*, ed. S. M. Stern. 2 vols. London: Allen & Unwin

Goldziher, Ignaz. 1981. *Introduction to Islamic Theology and Law*. Princeton University Press

Griffiths, Sidney. 1988. The monks of Palestine and the growth of Christian literature in Arabia. *The Muslim World*, 78, 1–28

Grunebaum, Gustav von. 1961. *Medieval Islam*. Chicago University Press

Grunebaum, Gustav von. 1976. *Islam and Medieval Hellenism: Social and Cultural Perspectives*. London: Variorum Reprints

Guillaume, Alfred. 1955. *The Life of Muhammad: A Translation of Ibn Ishaq's Sirat Rasul Allah*. Oxford University Press

Guillaume, Alfred. 1960. *New Light on the Life of Muhammad*. Manchester University Press

Guillaume, Alfred. 1983. *Islam*. Rev. edn. Harmondsworth: Penguin (orig. pub. 1956)

Guthrie, A., and Bishop, E. F. 1951. The Paraclete, Almunhamanna and Ahmad. *The Muslim World*, 41, 251–6

Hamidullah, Muhammad. 1974. *Muhammad Rasulallah: Concise Life and Work of the Founder of Islam*. London: Apex

Hamidullah, Muhammad. 1981. *The Battlefields of the Prophet Muhammad*. London: Apex.

Hammond, Philip. 1970. *The Nabataeans: Their History, Culture and Archaeology*. Gothenburg: Paul Astroms

Hasluck, Frederick. 1929. *Christianity and Islam under the Sultans*. 2 vols. Oxford University Press

Hassan, Ahmad al-, and Hill, Donald R. 1987. *Islamic Technology: An Illustrated History*. Cambridge: UNESCO

Hawting, G. R. 1986. *The First Dynasty of Islam: The Umayyad Caliphate, AD 661–750*. London: Croom Helm

Hayek, Michel. 1959. *Le Christ de l'Islam*. Paris: Giraud

Hiro, Dilip. 1988. *Islamic Fundamentalism*. London: Paladin

Hirschfeld, Hartwig. 1902. *New Researches into the Composition and Exegesis of the Koran*. London: Murray

Hiskett, Mervyn. 1993. *Some to Mecca Turn to Pray*. London: Claridge Press

Hitti, P. K. 1951. *History of the Arabs*.London: Macmillan

Hitti, P. K. 1973. *Capital Cities of Arab Islam*. Minneapolis: Minnesota University Press

Hodgkin, E. C. 1966. *The Arabs*. Oxford University Press

Hoffmann, Helmut. 1961. *The Religions of Tibet*. London: Allen & Unwin

Hoodbhoy, Pervez. 1992. *Islam and Science: Religious Orthodoxy and the Battle for Rationality*. London: Zed Books

Horovitz, Josef. 1925. Jewish proper names and derivations in the Koran. *Hebrew Union College Annual*, ii, Cincinnati

Hourani, Albert. 1947. *Minorities in the Arab World*. Oxford University Press

Hourani, Albert. 1991. *A History of the Arab Peoples*. London: Faber

Hourani, Albert. 1991. *Islam in European Thought*. Cambridge University Press

Hughes, Thomas Patrick. 1977. *A Dictionary of Islam*. New Delhi: Cosmo Publications (orig. pub. London: Allen, 1885)

Ibn Hajar, *see* Sprenger, 1856–88

Ibn Ishaq, *see* Guillaume, 1955

Jeffery, Arthur. 1937. *Materials for the History of the Text of the Qur'an*. Leiden: Brill

Jeffery, Arthur. 1938. *The Foreign Vocabulary of the Qur'an*. Baroda: Oriental Institute

Jeffery, Arthur. 1952. *The Qur'an as Scripture*. New York: Moore

Johnson, Paul. 1979. *Civilizations of the Holy Land*. London: Weidenfeld & Nicolson

Jomier, Jacques. 1969. *Bible and Koran*. New York: Desclier

Jones, L. Bevan. 1920. The Paraclete or Mohammed. *The Muslim World*, 10, 112–25

Joseph, J. 1961. *The Nestorians and their Muslim Neighbours*. Princeton University Press

Jurgi, Edward Jabra. 1938. *Illumination in Islamic Mysticism*. Princeton University Press

Juynboll, G. H. A., ed. 1982. *Papers on Islamic History. Studies on the First Centuries of Islamic Society*. Carbondale: Southern Illinois University Press

Juynboll, G. H. A. 1983. *Muslim Tradition*. Cambridge University Press

Kalbi, Hisham al- *see* Faris, 1952

Kamal, Ahmad-Bey. 1902. *Les idoles arabes et les divinités égyptiennes*. Paris: Giraud

Kateregga, Badru D., and Shenk, David W. 1981. *Islam and Christianity*. Grand Rapids, Mich.: Eerdmans

Katsch, A. I. 1954. *Judaism and Islam: Biblical and Talmudic Backgrounds of the Koran and its Commentaries*. New York: Weiser

Kazi, A. K., and Flynn, J. G., trans. 1984. *Muslim Sects and Divisions*, by Muhammad al- Shahrastani. London: Routledge & Kegan Paul

Kennedy, Hugh. 1986. *The Prophet and the Age of the Caliphates*. London: Longmans

Kepel, Gilles. 1994. *The Revenge of God. The Resurgence of Islam, Christianity and Judaism in the Modern World*. London: Polity Press

Kinross, Lord. 1964. *Atatürk: The Rebirth of a Nation*. London: Weidenfeld & Nicolson

Kister, M. J. 1980. *Studies in Jahiliyya and Early Islam*. London: Variorum Reprints

Kritzeck, James, ed. 1964. *Anthology of Islamic Literature*. Harmondsworth: Penguin

Laffin, John. 1981. *The Dagger of Islam*. London: Sphere

Lalaguna, Juan. 1990. *A Traveller's History of Spain*. Moreton-in-Marsh: Windrush Press

Lammens, Henri. 1914. *The Cradle of Islam (Le berceau de l'Islam)*. Rome and Paris: Colonna

Ledit, Charles J. 1956. *Mahomet, Israel et le Christ*. Paris: La Colombe

Leroy, Jules. 1963. *Monks and Monasteries of the Near East*. London: Harrap

Leslie, E. A. 1936. *Old Testament Religion in the Light of its Canaanite Background*. New York: Scribners

Leszynsky, R. 1910. *Die Juden in Arabien zur Zeit Mohammads*. Berlin: Baradorf

Levonian, L. 1940. *Studies in the Relationship Between Islam and Christianity, Psychological and Historical*. New York: Stechert

Lewis, Bernard. 1966. *The Arabs in History*, 4th edn. London: Hutchinson

Lewis, Bernard. 1971. *Race and Colour in Islam*. Princeton University Press

Lewis, Bernard. 1983. *The Jews of Islam*. Princeton University Press (and London: Routledge & Kegan Paul, 1984)

Lings, Martin. 1971. *A Sufi Saint of the Twentieth Century*. London: Allen & Unwin

Lings, Martin. 1983. *Muhammad: His Life Based on the Earliest Sources*. London: Allen & Unwin

Lyall, Charles James. 1930. *Translations of Ancient Arabic Poetry*. London: Williams & Norgate

McAuliffe, Jane Dammen. 1981. Chosen of all women: Mary and Fatima in Quranic exegesis. *Islamochristiana*, 7, 19–28

McAuliffe, Jane Dammen. 1991. *Quranic Christians: An Analysis of Classical and Modern Exegesis*. Cambridge University Press

McCurry, Don M., ed. 1979. *The Gospel and Islam: A Compendium*. Monrovia, Cal.: Marc

Macdonald, Duncan B. 1909. *The Religious Life and Attitude in Islam*. Chicago University Press

Majumdar, R. C. 1948. *An Advanced History of India*. London: Macmillan

Makdisi, George. 1981. *The Rise of Colleges: Institutions of Learning in Islam and the West*. Edinburgh University Press

Mango, Cyril. 1988. *Byzantium: The Empire of the New Rome*. London: Weidenfeld & Nicolson

Margoliouth, David S. 1924. *The Relations Between Arabs and Israelites Prior to the Rise of Islam*. London: Schweich Lectures

Margoliouth, David S. 1926. *The Early Development of Mohammedanism*. London: Murray

Matt, Daniel Chanan. 1983. *Zohar: The Book of Enlightenment*. London, SPCK

Mernissi, F. 1975. *Beyond the Veil*. Cambridge, Mass.: Harvard University Press

Michaud, Henri. 1960. *Jésus selon le Coran*. Neuchâtel: Delachaux

Miller, J. Innes. 1969. *The Spice Trade of the Roman Empire*. Oxford University Press

Minai, Naila. 1981. *Women in Islam*. New York: Seaview Books

Mingana, A. 1927. Syriac influence on the style of the Kur'an. *Rylands Bulletin*, Manchester

Montgomery, James A. 1934. *Arabia and the Bible*. Oxford University Press. Philadelphia: University of Pennsylvania Press

Moubarac, Father Y. 1958. *Abraham dans le Coran*. Paris: Niclaus

Moucarry, Chawkat Georges. 1988. *Islam and Christianity at the Crossroads*. Tring: Lion

Muir, Sir William. 1878. *The Coran: Its Composition and Teaching, and the Testimony it Bears to the Holy Scriptures*. Edinburgh University Press

Muir, Sir William. 1882. *The Apology of Al Kindy*. Cambridge University Press

Muir, Sir William. 1912. *The Life Of Mohammed, from Original Sources*. Rev. edn. Edinburgh: John Grant (orig. pub. 1858–61)

Muir, Sir William. 1924. *The Caliphate: Its Rise, Decline and Fall*. Edinburgh: John Grant

Musallam, Basim. 1983. *Sex and Society in Islam*. Cambridge University Press

Naipaul, V. S. 1981. *Among the Believers: An Islamic Journey*. London: André Deutsch

Nasr, Seyyed Hossein. 1987. *Science and Civilization in Islam*. 2nd edn. Cambridge: Islamic Texts Society

Nazir Ali, Michael. 1987. *Frontiers in Muslim–Christian Encounter*. Oxford: Regnum Books

Needham, Joseph. 1959. *Science and Civilization in China*. Vol. III. Cambridge University Press

Newby, Gordon. 1988. *A History of the Jews of Arabia*. Columbia: South Carolina University Press

Nicholson, Reynold A. 1923. *The Idea of Personality in Sufism*. Cambridge University Press

Nicholson, Reynold A. 1963. *The Mystics of Islam*. 2nd edn. London: Routledge & Kegan Paul

Nicholson, Reynold A. 1967. *Studies in Islamic Mysticism*. Cambridge University Press

Nicholson, Reynold A. 1969. *A Literary History of the Arabs*. 2nd edn. Cambridge University Press

Nizam, Ashraf F. 1981. *Namaz: the Yoga of Islam*. Bombay: Taraporevala

Nöldeke, Theodor. 1858. Hatte Muhammed christliche Lehrer? *Zeitschrift der deutschen Morgenländischen Gesellschaft*, **xii**

Nöldeke, Theodor. 1860. *History of the Qoran*. Göttingen University Press

O'Leary, De Lacy. 1922. *Arabic Thought and its Place in History*. London: Longmans

O'Leary, De Lacy. 1927. *Arabia Before Muhammad*. New York: Dutton. London: Kegan Paul, Trench, Trubner

Parrinder, Geoffrey. 1976. *Mysticism in the World's Religions*. London: Sheldon Press

Parrinder, Geoffrey. 1979. *Jesus in the Qur'an*. London: Sheldon Press

Parrinder, Geoffrey. 1983. *An Illustrated History of the World's Religions*. London: Newnes

Parshall, Phil. 1990. *The Cross and the Crescent*. Amsterdam: Scripture Press

Patton, Walter, M. 1897. *Ahmad ibn Hanbal and the Mihna*. Leiden: Brill

Peters, F. E. 1968. *Aristotle and the Arabs: The Aristotlian Tradition in Islam*. New York: Harper

Petersen, Erling Ladewig. 1974. *Ali and Muawiya in Early Arabic Tradition*. Copenhagen: Odense

Petrushevsky, I. P. 1988. *Islam and Iran*. London: Athlone Press

Philby, H. St John B. 1947. *The Background of Islam: Being a Sketch of Arabian History in Pre-Islamic Times*. Alexandria: Whitehead Morris

Phillips, Wendell. 1955. *Qataban and Sheba*. New York: Harcourt, Brace

Pinault, David. 1987. Images of Christ in Arabic literature. *Die Welt des Islams*, 17, 103–25

Pipes, Daniel. 1981. *Slave Soldiers and Islam*. New Haven: Yale University Press

Rahman, Fazlur. 1966. *Islam*. London: Weidenfeld & Nicolson

Rahman, Fazlur. 1980. *Major Themes of the Qur'an*. Minneapolis: Bibliotheca Islamica

Rawlinson, H. G. 1954. *India: A Short Cultural History*. London: Cresset Press

Rice, Cyprian. 1964. *The Persian Sufis*. London: Allen & Unwin

Rice, D. Talbot. 1971. *Islamic Painting: A Survey*. Edinburgh University Press

Ringgren, H. 1955. *Studies in Arabian Fatalism*. Uppsala University Press

Rivoira, G. T. 1919. *Moslem Architecture: Its Origin and Development*. Oxford University Press

Robson, J. 1929. *Christ in Islam*. London: Murray

Rodinson, Maxime. 1976. *Mohammed*, trans. Anne Carter. Harmondsworth: Penguin

Rodwell, J. M., trans. 1915. *The Koran*. London: Dent

Ronan, Colin A. 1984. *Cambridge Illustrated History of the World's Science*. Cambridge University Press

Rosenthal, F. 1952. *A History of Muslim Historiography*. Leiden: Brill

Rousseau, Richard W., ed. 1985. *Christianity and Islam: The Struggling Dialogue*. Montrose, Pa.: Ridge Row Press

Rudolph, W. 1922. *Die Abhängigkeit des Qorans vom Judenthum und Christenthum*. Stuttgart: Kahn

Ruthven, Malise. 1984. *Islam in the World*. Harmondsworth: Penguin

Ruthven, Malise. 1990. *A Satanic Affair: Salman Rushdie and the Rage of Islam*. London: Chatto & Windus

Ryckmans, G. 1951. *Les Religions arabes préislamiques*. Louvain: Museum Library

Said, Edward W. 1985. *Orientalism: Western Conceptions of the Orient*. Harmondsworth: Penguin

Sale, George, trans. 1886. *The Koran: With a Preliminary Discourse and Explanatory Notes*. London: Orlando Hodgson

Schacht, Joseph. 1964. *Introduction to Islamic Law*. Oxford University Press

Schacht, Joseph, and Bosworth, C. E., eds. 1974. *The Legacy of Islam*. 2nd ed. Oxford University Press

Schedl, Claus. 1978. *Muhammad und Jesu*, Vienna: Herder

Schimmel, Annemarie. 1975. *Mystical Dimensions of Islam*. Chapel Hill: University of North Carolina Press

Schimmel, Annemarie. 1985. *And Muhammad is His Messenger*. Chapel Hill: University of North Carolina Press

Schimmel, Annemarie, and Falaturi, Abdoljavad, eds. 1979. *We Believe in One God: The Experience of God in Christianity and Islam*. London: Burns & Oates. New York: Seabury

Schoy, C. 1924. *The Geography of the Muslims of the Middle Ages*. New York: American Geographical Society

Schuon, Frithjof. 1976. *Islam and the Perennial Philosophy*. London: Eyre & Spottiswoode

Searle, M. S. 1978. *Quran and Bible*. London: Croom Helm

Séguy, Marie-Rose. 1977. *The Miraculous Journey of Mahomet*. New York: Braziller

SEI. 1974. (*Shorter Encyclopedia of Islam*. ed. H. A. R. Gibb and J. H. Kramers) Leiden: Brill

Shafaat, Ahmad. 1981. *The Gospel According to Islam*. New York: Vantage Press

Shahid, I. 1977. Pre-Islamic Arabia, in *The Cambridge History of Islam*, Vol. 1A. Cambridge University Press

Shahid, I. 1984. *Rome and the Arabs*. Washington DC: American University Press

Shahrastani, al- *see* Kazi and Flynn, 1984

Sharma, S. R. 1947. *The Making of Modern India*. Bombay: Signet Press

Sivan, Emmanuel. 1985. *Radical Islam: Medieval Theory and Modern Politics*. New Haven: Yale University Press

Smart, Ninian. 1977. *Background to the Long Search*. London: BBC

Smith, H. P. 1897. *The Bible and Islam*. New York: Franklin

Smith, Jane I. 1975. *An Historical and Semantic Study of the Term 'Islam' as Seen in a Sequence of the Qur'an Commentaries*. Missoula, Mont.: Scholars Press

Smith, Margaret. 1972. *Readings from the Mystics of Islam*. London: Luzac

Smith, Wilfred Cantwell. 1975. *Islam in Modern History*. Oxford University Press

Smith, W. Robertson. 1966. *Kinship and Marriage in Early Arabia*. Oosterhout: Anthropological Publications. Netherlands (orig. pub. Cambridge University Press, 1907)

Southern, R. W. 1962. *Western Views of Islam in the Middle Ages*. Cambridge, Mass.: Harvard University Press

Spencer, S. 1963. *Mysticism in World Religion*. Harmondsworth: Penguin

Sprenger, Aloys. 1851. *The Life of Muhammad from Original Sources*. Allahabad: Presbyterian Mission Press

Sprenger, Aloys, ed. 1856–88. *A Biographical Dictionary of Persons who knew Mohammed*, by Ibn Hajar al-Asqalani. 4 vols. Calcutta University Press

Strzygowski, J. 1923. *Origin of Christian Church Art*. Oxford University Press

Sugana, G. M. 1968. *The Life and Times of Mohammed*. London: Hamlyn

Suhrawardy, Abdulla, ed. 1905. *The Sayings of Muhammad*. London: Constable

Swartz, Merlin L., ed. 1981. *Studies on Islam*. Oxford University Press

Sweetman, J. Windrew. 1985. *Islam and Christian Theology*. Birmingham: Selly Oak College (abridged edn, ed. J. S. Moon, of 4 vols. pub. London: Lutterworth Press, 1945–67)

Taheri, Amir. 1987. *Holy Terror. The Inside Story of Islamic Terrorism*. London: Hutchinson

Tannahill, Reay. 1980. *Sex in History*. London: Hamish Hamilton

Tarn, W. W., and Griffith, G. T. 1952. *Hellenistic Civilization*. London: Longmans

Thaalibi, Ismail al-. 1968. *Lata'if al-Ma'arif. The Book of Curious and Entertaining Information*, ed. C. E. Bosworth. Edinburgh University Press

Tisdall, William St Clair. 1911. *The Original Sources of the Qur'an*. London: SPCK

Torrey, Charles Cutler. 1892. *The Commercial-Theological Terms in the Koran*. Leiden: Brill

Torrey, Charles Cutler. 1967. *The Jewish Foundations of Islam*. 2nd edn. New York: Ktav

Trimingham, J. Spencer. 1979. *Christianity Among the Arabs in Pre-Islamic Times*. London: Longmans

Tritton, Arthur Stanley. 1930. *The Caliphs and their Non-Muslim Subjects*. London: Murray

Ullendorff, E. 1968. *Ethiopia and the Bible*. London: Dent

Vryonis, Speros. 1971. *The Decline of Medieval Hellenism in Asia Minor and the Process of Islamization from the Eleventh through the Fifteenth Century*. Berkeley: University of California Press

Wagtendonk, K. 1968. *Fasting in the Qur'an*. Leiden: Brill

Walker, Benjamin. 1989. *Gnosticism: Its History and Influence*. London: Crucible

Walker, Benjamin. 1995. *Hindu World*. 3rd edn. New Delhi: HarperCollins (orig. pub. London: Allen & Unwin, 1968)

Walzer, Richard. 1962. *Greek into Arabic: Essays on Islamic Philosophy*. Oxford: Cassirer

Wansbrough, John. 1977. *Quranic Studies*. Oxford University Press

Wansbrough, John. 1978. *The Sectarian Milieu: Content and Composition of Islamic Salvation History*. Oxford University Press

Watt, W. Montgomery. 1953. *Muhammad at Mecca*. Oxford University Press

Watt, W. Montgomery. 1956. *Muhammad at Medina*. Oxford University Press

Watt, W. Montgomery. 1961. *Muhammad: Prophet and Statesman*. Oxford University Press

Watt, W. Montgomery. 1970. *Bell's Introduction to the Qur'an*. Edinburgh University Press

Watt, W. Montgomery. 1990. *The Majesty that was Islam: The Islamic World 600–1100*. London: Sidgwick & Jackson

Weil, Gustav. 1943. *Mohammed der Prophet*. Stuttgart, Heinz

Wellhausen, Julius. 1885. *Muhammad in Medina*, Berlin: Ebering

Wellhausen, Julius. 1927. *Reste arabischen Heidentums*. Berlin: Ebering (orig. pub. 1887)

Wensinck, Arent Jan. 1927. *Handbook of Early Muhammadan Tradition*. Leiden: Brill

Wensinck, Arent Jan. 1982. *Muhammad and the Jews of Medina*. Berlin: Adiyok

West, M. L. 1971. *Early Greek Philosophy and the Orient*. Oxford University Press

Westermarck, Edward. 1933. *Pagan Survivals in Mohammedan Civilization*. London: Macmillan

Widengren, Geo. 1955. *Muhammad the Apostle of God and His Ascension*. Uppsala: Lundequistska

Williams, John Alden. 1961. *Islam*. New York: Braziller

Wiseman, D. J., ed. 1973. *Peoples of Old Testament Times*. Oxford University Press

Wismer, Don. 1977. *The Islamic Jesus: An Annotated Bibliography of Sources in English and French*. New York: Garland Publishing

Wright, T. 1855. *Early Christianity in Arabia*. London: Wright

Yusuf Ali, Abdullah, trans. 1991. *The Holy Qur'an*. New Delhi: Kitab Bhavan

Zaehner, R. C., ed. 1971. *The Concise Encyclopedia of Living Faiths*. London: Hutchinson

Zakaria, Rafiq. 1989. *The Struggle Within Islam*. Harmondsworth: Penguin

Zwemer, Samuel M. 1912. *The Moslem Christ*. Edinburgh: Oliphant

Zwemer, Samuel M. 1925. *The Law of Apostasy in Islam*. London: Longmans

Zwettler, Michael. 1975. *The Oral Tradition of Classical Arabic Poetry*. Columbus: Ohio State University Press

INDEX